A COM

THE CHESAPEAKE BAY BOOK

The Pride of Baltimore II *sails past the Chesapeake Bay Bridge near Annapolis.* Middleton Evans

A COMPLETE GUIDE

6TH EDITION

THE CHESAPEAKE BAY BOOK

Allison Blake

The Countryman Press
Woodstock, Vermont

We welcome your comments and suggestions. Please contact Great Destinations Guide Editor, The Countryman Press, P.O. Box 748, Woodstock, VT 05091, or e-mail countrymanpress@wwnorton.com.

Sixth Edition

ISBN 1-58157-073-2
ISSN 1553-829X

Maps by Mapping Specialists Ltd., © The Countryman Press
Book design by Bodenweber Design
Text composition by Melinda Belter
Cover photograph by Pat Vojtech
Interior photographs by the author unless otherwise indicated

Published by The Countryman Press, P.O. Box 748, Woodstock, VT 05091

Distributed by W. W. Norton & Company, Inc., 500 Fifth Avenue, New York, NY 10110

Printed in the United States of America

10 9 8 7 6 5 4 3 2 1

GREAT DESTINATIONS TRAVEL GUIDEBOOK SERIES

Recommended by *National Geographic Traveler* and *Travel & Leisure* magazines.

[A] CRISP AND CRITICAL APPROACH, FOR TRAVELERS WHO WANT TO LIVE LIKE LOCALS.
— *USA Today*

Great Destinations™ guidebooks are known for their comprehensive, critical coverage of regions of extraordinary cultural interest and natural beauty. The authors in this series are professional travel writers who have lived for many years in the regions they describe. Each title in this series is continuously updated with each printing to ensure accurate and timely information.

Neither the publisher, the authors, the reviewers, nor other contributors accept complimentary lodgings, meals, or any other consideration (such as advertising) while gathering information for any book in this series.

Current titles available:

THE ADIRONDACK BOOK

THE BERKSHIRE BOOK

THE BIG SUR, MONTEREY BAY & GOLD COAST WINE COUNTRY BOOK

THE CHARLESTON, SAVANNAH & COASTAL ISLANDS BOOK

THE CHESAPEAKE BAY BOOK

THE COAST OF MAINE BOOK

THE FINGER LAKES BOOK

THE HAMPTONS BOOK

THE HUDSON VALLEY BOOK

THE NANTUCKET BOOK

THE NAPA & SONOMA BOOK

PALM BEACH, MIAMI & THE FLORIDA KEYS

THE SANTA FE & TAOS BOOK

THE SEATTLE & VANCOUVER BOOK

THE SHENANDOAH VALLEY BOOK

THE TEXAS HILL COUNTRY BOOK

TOURING EAST COAST WINE COUNTRY

If you are traveling to, moving to, residing in, or just interested in any of these enchanting regions, a Great Destinations guidebook is a superior companion. Honest and painstakingly critical, full of information only a local can provide, Great Destinations guidebooks give you all the practical knowledge you need to enjoy the best of each region.

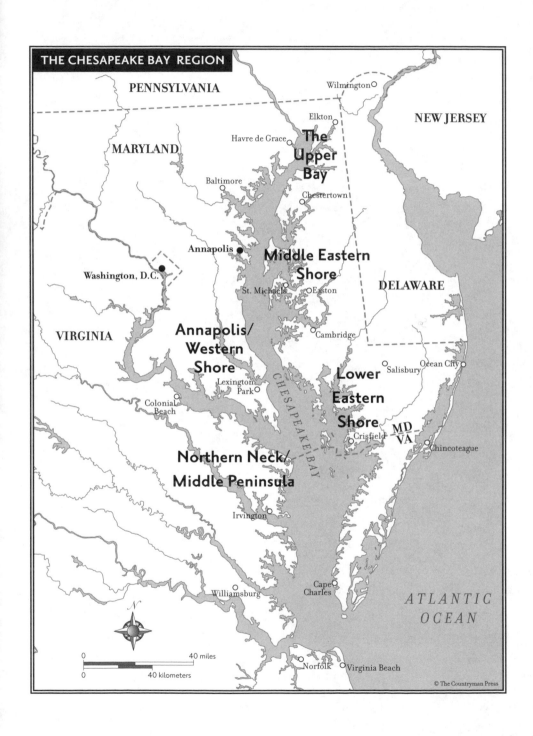

THE CHESAPEAKE BAY REGION

PENNSYLVANIA

Wilmington

Elkton

NEW JERSEY

Havre de Grace

MARYLAND

The Upper Bay

Baltimore

Chestertown

Annapolis

Middle Eastern Shore

Washington, D.C.

DELAWARE

St. Michaels   Easton

VIRGINIA

Annapolis/ Western Shore

Cambridge

CHESAPEAKE BAY

Salisbury   Ocean City

Lexington Park

Lower Eastern Shore

Colonial Beach

MD VA

Crisfield

Chincoteague

Northern Neck/ Middle Peninsula

Irvington

N

Williamsburg

Cape Charles

ATLANTIC OCEAN

0   40 miles

0   40 kilometers

Norfolk   Virginia Beach

© The Countryman Press

Contents

Acknowledgments

This edition of *The Chesapeake Bay Book*, as always, owes a debt of gratitude to many people.

Donna Bozza Packer updated and wrote about the Eastern Shore of Virginia and Hampton Roads; Nancy Drury Duncan provided research on the Information and Transportation chapters; Beth Rubin updated Annapolis and contributed some of its restaurant profiles; Jan Callahan added restaurant profiles on the Upper Eastern Shore; and Dr. Rania Lisas added restaurant profiles from Southern Maryland.

For their professional assistance, thanks to: Mindy Bianca of the Maryland Office of Tourism; Kerry Wargo Clough of the Chesapeake Maritime Museum; Susan Wilkinson of Historic St. Mary's City; Ellen General of the Avalon Theatre; Chris Connors of the Chesapeake Bay Program; and the dozens of others I met during my travels. Also, thanks to Kay Kahler Vose, who has provided insight into the Northern Neck over the years, and Annapolis fisherman John Neely.

My mother-in-law, Easton columnist Anne Stinson, wrote many restaurant profiles from the Middle Eastern Shore and shared with me tales of her Chesapeake reporter days, times not so long ago that are, sadly, passing us by: of muskratting in Dorchester marshes and oystering on skipjacks when Chesapeake's distinctive all-sail fleet, docked at Tilghman's Dogwood Harbor, still was devoted only to work.

Thanks also to Joshua Gillelan II for his usual patience and insight. And thank you to everyone who ever helped out in editions past. Their efforts have always provided a foundation upon which to build.

It's been my privilege to wander the Bay area since 1991, when I first ventured out to chronicle the region on behalf of the first *Chesapeake Bay Book*, published in 1992 under Berkshire House Publishers. Editor Kathryn Flynn gets particular thanks; she's had my back for years. Also thanks to Philip Rich, Jennifer Thompson, and Kermit Hummel. The good folks at The Countryman Press have generously taken up where the Berkshire House folks left off, and their kind assistance is much appreciated.

INTRODUCTION

Crossing the eastbound span of the Chesapeake Bay Bridge is kind of like watching the orange slit of day break up ahead on a transatlantic red-eye. The promise of adventure brings a twinge of excitement.

Mainland suburbia melts away as the bridge arcs toward the Eastern Shore. White wakes and white sails mix on the Bay below. Bright mornings bring a splat of reflected sunlight edged in yellow rippling broadly across the water below, unfolding like the day's promise.

"But you get that same feeling when you pull up to Point Lookout or arrive in Solomons Island," my husband says.

He's got a point. Point Lookout is land's farewell to the Potomac River. At Solomons, the Patuxent River joins the Bay. Here in Chesapeake Country, territory riven by Bay-bound creeks and rivers, it seems the traveler is always crossing from land to water, sometimes via terrain that isn't quite either. The path always leads to something new.

Consider other Chesapeake crossings that bring anticipation, like traversing a tended country drawbridge. On the Eastern Shore, there's one at Knapp's Narrows going to Tilghman Island. Another, a just-passing-through kind of bridge, crosses the Sassafras River above Chestertown on the Upper Eastern Shore. Or you could clank aboard one of the Bay area's small ferries, like the Whitehaven Ferry south of Salisbury, to take the scenic route home. Not far from the mouth of the Rappahannock River, deep in Tidewater Virginia, a long bridge links two peninsulas, passing from the Northern Neck to the Middle Peninsula between White Stone and Urbanna.

There's no mistaking the charm of Bay travel: Possibilities always exist on the other side.

At least, that's my soul-nurturing explanation of the excited feeling I always get crossing the Chesapeake Bay Bridge. My foodie friend Amy says it's all nature, hard-wired with the memory of Chesapeake soft-shell crabs and Eastern Shore tomatoes.

— Allison Blake, Annapolis, Maryland

THE WAY THIS BOOK WORKS

Organization

This book focuses on the Chesapeake's small cities and rural towns, which are covered in geographically arranged chapters that circle the Bay in clockwise fashion starting with Annapolis. Readers will find Annapolis and its adventures south of town to the Potomac River—an area known as both the Western Shore and Southern Maryland—in one chapter. Baltimore, Md., Hampton Roads, Va., and urban Bay attractions come at the end of the book, corralling the region's more populated areas in one chapter.

Lodgings and restaurants within the chapters are all organized geographically.

Every effort was made to ensure the information in this book was correct as of publication time, but, as always, prices and policies change. It's always best to call ahead. In particular, we suggest you talk with your innkeeper about any specific needs or requests you may have—and ask if policies on children or handicapped access have changed.

Prices

Because prices change, we guide readers via a price range system. Our lodging rates reflect a high-season rate for double occupancy, but lodgings often offer different rates for in-season and off-season, then slice the pie further with weekday and weekend rates in either season. High-season weekends are generally the most expensive. Two-night minimum stays may be encountered, and specific rules regarding deposits and their return in the event of cancellation often apply. Always check ahead. In addition, ask ahead if a third person is allowed in the room; this may be frowned upon in B&Bs . . . but not always.

Restaurant prices reflect the cost of a dinner appetizer, entrée, and dessert *sans* drinks, tax, and tip. It's fair to say lunch prices will be less, often considerably so. In cases such as a small breakfast joint or café, general store or sandwich shop, where one simply doesn't eat in formal fashion, price codes reflect the restaurant's norm. Prices may change.

Single price codes for lodging and restaurants govern the entire book in order to ensure consistency, but the Chesapeake region varies widely in terms of price. Travelers will find the rural areas are often priced well below Annapolis and the tourism centers in the Middle Shore and Upper Shore, as well as Baltimore.

Price Codes

	Lodging	*Dining*
Inexpensive	Up to $75	Up to $10
Moderate	$75 to $125	$10 to $20
Expensive	$125 to $175	$30 to $40
Very Expensive	Over $175	Over $40

The Maryland Statehouse dome is one of Annapolis's best-known landmarks.

1

HISTORY
"A Very Goodly Bay"

There is but one entrance by Sea into this Country, and that is at the mouth of a very goodly Bay, 18 or 20 myles broad. The cape on the South is called Cape Henry, in honour of our most notable Prince. The North Edge is called Cape Charles, in honour of the worthy Duke of Yorke. Within is a country that may have the prerogative over the most pleasant places. Heaven and earth never agreed better to frame a place for man's habitation. Here are mountains, hills, plaines, valleyes, rivers, and brookes, all running into a faire Bay, compassed but for the mouth, with fruitful and delightsome land.

Capt. John Smith, 1607

Archaeologists digging in this cradle of U.S. history have unearthed countless remnants of an even deeper past. Layered in sand and clay along Chesapeake Bay shores are oyster shells, some thousands of years old. The largest cache was a 30-acre Indian shell midden spread across Popes Creek, off the Potomac River. Long before Chesapeake watermen took up their tongs, the Bay was feeding her people.

The native inhabitants called her Chesapeake Bay, "the Great Shellfish Bay." In the 16th century, a Jesuit priest sailed through the Virginia capes described by John Smith and bestowed a second name: *La Bahía de la Madre de Dios*—the Bay of the Mother of God.

The Chesapeake has always looked after those who lived here. Just as the Native Americans thrived on Bay oysters, so early European settlers grew crops in rich Bay soil. As the indigenous peoples paddled canoes from encampment to encampment, so ferries linked later settlements.

Today, the waters of this ancient river valley fan out into a complex network of urban bridges and rural lanes. Here endures the heart of the modern Mid-Atlantic megalopolis and the soul of 19th-century fishing villages. U.S. history here is old; geological history is young.

The Chesapeake Bay is bookended by two major metropolitan areas in two states: Baltimore, Maryland's largest city, and Norfolk–Hampton Roads in Virginia's Tidewater. Both are major Atlantic ports. Near John Smith's Virginia capes, now spanned by the 17.6-mile Chesapeake Bay Bridge-Tunnel, Naval Station Norfolk presides over the Navy's strong Tidewater presence.

Much of Maryland's Western Shore life looks to urban centers, as city dwellers willing to endure the hour-plus commute to Washington, D.C., or Baltimore increasingly flood

Annapolis and nearby Kent Island, drawing these former Bay outposts into the region's suburbs. For their highway-bound hours during the week, these government types are repaid with long sails on the Bay or afternoons anchored in secluded "gunkholes," shallow coves where green or great blue herons fly from nearby marshes. On the Eastern Shore, fishing, farming, tourism, and the retirement business spur local economic life.

Up the Bay's major tributaries stand the region's major cities: Washington, D.C., on the Potomac; Richmond, Virginia, on the James; and Baltimore, on the Patapsco. Maryland's capital, Annapolis, stands at the mouth of the Severn River, near where the William Preston Lane Jr. Memorial Bridge—better known simply as the Bay Bridge—links the Eastern and Western Shores.

Even as the Chesapeake is defined by her waters, so she is defined by her history. A stop at the Maryland Statehouse in Annapolis, where George Washington resigned his Continental Army commission, is as integral to a Chesapeake Country visit as a charter boat fishing trip from Tilghman Island. In 1607, America's first permanent colonial English settlement was established at Jamestown, Virginia. The first Catholic settlers landed farther north, on the Potomac River, and established Maryland at St. Marys City in 1634. Washington and his peers used the Bay first to transport their tobacco, the region's first sizable cash crop, and then to their military advantage as they plotted their navigational comings and goings during the Revolutionary War.

For all of the Bay's history and navigability, however, she shares a problem with virtually every other heavily populated estuary. A confluence of pressures has threatened the health of her rich waters since European settlers first chopped down forests to create fields to farm. Soil from the fertile lands lining the Bay's shores has slipped into the water, silting in harbors and obscuring marshy invertebrate nurseries. Damage has been compounded by 20th-century wastes: fertilizers, air pollution, and sewage bring phosphorous and nitrogen, nutrients that damage the Bay.

Many say the magnificent Chesapeake is at the most crucial crossroads of her most recent geological incarnation. A massive assault against pollution has been under way since the late 1970s and is producing some good results. Perhaps, like the estuary's flushing by fresh water from the north and by saltwater tides from the south, the diverse mix of urban and rural can maintain a beneficial balance in La Bahía de la Madre de Dios.

NATURAL HISTORY

Cargo ships journeying the 200-mile length of the Chesapeake Bay travel in a deep channel that more than 10,000 years ago cradled the ancient Susquehanna River. The mighty river flowed south to the ocean, drawing in the waters of many tributaries but for one independent soul: the present-day James River. Then came the great shift in the glaciers of the last Ice Age, when the thick sheets of ice that stopped just north of the Chesapeake region—in what is now northern Pennsylvania and New York State—began to melt under warming temperatures. As the Pleistocene Era ended, torrents of released water filled the oceans. The Susquehanna River valley flooded once, twice, and probably more, settling eventually within the bounds of the present-day Chesapeake Bay.

A 1990s discovery may cast new light on evidence of an even earlier event that helped to shape the Bay. An asteroid or comet hurtling 50,000 miles per hour into the earth is thought to have left the mile-deep, 56-mile-wide Chesapeake Bay Impact Crater near what is now the mouth of the Bay, apparently the largest such crater in the United States.

The Blackwater National Wildlife Refuge in Cambridge, Maryland, is home to the largest nesting population of bald eagles north of Florida. Mark D. Raab

The shifts of the earth and, perhaps, the remnants of space have left behind North America's largest estuary. Estuaries are schizophrenic bodies of water, mixing the fresh waters of inland mountain streams and rivers with salty ocean currents. The undulating brew of fresh and salt stirs a habitat that supports a huge range of creatures. Clams, crabs, oysters, American shad, striped bass (known hereabouts as rockfish), menhaden, and more have always thrived in these waters, living a solitary life in the deep as bottom dwellers, bedding down in the shallows, or navigating to the fresh water to spawn.

The Susquehanna River, supplying 50 percent of the Chesapeake's fresh water, flows into the head of the Bay. The Potomac River adds another 20 percent. Even the glacial-era renegade James River finally joined other Chesapeake tributaries, adding fresh water that helps to nourish the vast mix of species living in the Bay.

Solid evidence of a prehistoric past lies layered along the Western Shore of the Bay, perhaps most famously at Calvert Cliffs, located 53 miles south of Annapolis. In a swath traveling from here south to the Virginia side of the Potomac River, sharks' teeth and other fossils still wash up from time to time. These are 12- to 17-million-year-old forebears to the Bay's crabs, menhaden, and oysters that lived in a Miocene Era sea that stretched to present-day Washington, D.C. Crocodiles, rhinoceroses, and mastodons lived along the cliffs that were once the uplands of the ancient Susquehanna River valley.

Where Land and Water Meet

Consider the Chesapeake's considerable statistics: she has a 4,479-square-mile area that includes dozens of tidal tributaries and all manner of coves, creeks, and tidal rivers. Shoreline length for the Bay and tidal rivers equals 11,684 miles. The total system is filled by 18 *trillion* gallons of water, with the estuary's fresher water in the upper Bay and the saltier farther south.

The Bay's width ranges from 4 miles at Annapolis to 30 miles at Point Lookout, Maryland, where the Potomac River meets the Bay, dividing Maryland and Virginia. Despite the enormity of this expansive body of water, the Chesapeake is surprisingly shallow. Its average depth is 21 feet, although at the so-called Deep Trough off Kent Island, just over the bridge from Annapolis, depths reach 174 feet.

Beyond the waters of the Bay, within her six-state, 64,000-square-mile watershed, is geological diversity: the metamorphic rock of the Appalachian plateau, the weathered, iron-rich soil of the Piedmont, and the low-lying coastal plain.

A shoreline that seems to snake forever along marshes, creeks, and rivers provides ample habitat for thousands of species of resident or migratory wildlife and aquatic

An osprey sits near its distinctive nest on a Bay-area channel marker.

dwellers. Rookeries of great blue herons and colonies of terns nest on isolated islands, and even brown pelicans appear in the southern reaches of the Bay, increasingly traveling north to locations such as Virginia's Tangier Island, near the Maryland border.

Overhead each fall come the migratory waterfowl—tundra swans, Canada geese, brants, and, of course, ducks: mallards, pintails, canvasbacks, and teals—all following the Atlantic flyway. The mighty osprey is common, back from its severely depleted numbers after the insecticide DDT was banned in the early 1970s. Visitors can easily see osprey nests upon navigational markers and buoys throughout the Bay. And don't be surprised if that other distinctive raptor with a white head glimpsed near a marsh turns out to be a bald eagle. Numbers of the formerly endangered birds are so improved that it has been suggested the eagle could lose its scaled-back "threatened" status.

Deep on the Eastern Shore, in the lowlands of Dorchester County, the brackish marshes of the Blackwater National Wildlife Refuge welcome the red-cockaded woodpecker, peregrine falcon, and bald eagle, which breeds here. The great horned owl likewise nests in this marshy blackwater, and the rare Delmarva fox squirrel also makes this area its home. Secretive river otters can occasionally be spotted; more likely, you've seen a muskrat.

Just as it's a surprise to see the pelicans this far north, so it seems surprising that bald cypress exist this far north. Sharp-eyed hikers in the mid-Bay region will spot cypress knees along some wetland trails. In Calvert County, Maryland—not far from the fossils of Calvert Cliffs—stands the Battle Creek Cypress Swamp, where a low boardwalk winds through this mysterious habitat.

But far more common are the Chesapeake's tidal wetlands, crucial creature nurseries once thought to be no more than mosquito breeding grounds. Saltwater grasses adapted to this habitat between land and sea once grew profusely, sheltering critters such as molting crabs and protecting the sea from the land.

Talk to a salty waterman who has worked the Bay and her rivers for a few decades, though, and he'll tell you the once-prolific underwater Bay grasses are nothing compared to what they once were. Bay environmentalists consider this "submerged aquatic vegetation," or SAV, as a sort of clarity gauge of the Bay. Sediment and nutrients from pollution feed algal blooms, which then block the sunlight and prevent growth of the grasses. Efforts to bring back these protectors have been somewhat successful in recent years, helping to return an important nursery to young creatures such as rockfish and crabs.

Officially, 350 species of fish live in Bay waters; only some of these create reliable fisheries. Finfish, including striped bass, bluefish, American shad, croaker, Atlantic menhaden, and alewives, are among those who live here. But most famed among the Bay's aquatic residents are the blue crab and the oyster. Both are the focus of considerable attention in the ongoing effort to restore the ecological health of the Bay.

The numbers go up and down, but as of this writing the blue crab population seems to be stabilizing at low numbers. Oysters, with the native population at a historical low, are the subject of massive restoration efforts that may eventually include introducing a non-native, Asian oyster into the Bay.

Saving the Bay

Time and tide have sent shoreline crumbling into the Bay, and the debris of human development has followed, speeding the Bay's decline. In addition to chemical fertilizers from farms and suburban lawns throughout this vast watershed, waste discharged from even vastly improved, modern sewage treatment plants continues to flow in. Air pollution from cars and coal-fired power plants funnels more nitrogen into the Chesapeake.

Efforts to bring back the Chesapeake's historical health stretch back to 1977, when formal federal and state programs allied to launch a massive Bay research and cleanup program. Interestingly, in 1964 President Lyndon B. Johnson announced the federally supported start to a cleanup of the famed Potomac River, a Bay tributary. The $1 billion project is considered a great success story, inspiration to the many agencies now devoting millions of dollars and countless hours to a Bay-wide cleanup.

Research launched in 1977 culminated in a landmark agreement that established a nuts-and-bolts plan to renew the Bay's deteriorating habitat. This accord, the Chesapeake Bay Agreement of 1983, was signed by Maryland, Virginia, Pennsylvania, the District of Columbia, the federal Environmental Protection Agency, and the Chesapeake Bay Commission, a group of area legislators. When the agreement was launched, the focus was on cleaning up the Bay per se. Two updates have followed. In 1987, additional focus was placed on conserving Bay flora and fauna. Chesapeake 2000 guides the process further, establishing a more interdisciplinary effort aimed at improving water quality and protecting living resources. This brings new attention to local action and "smart growth" efforts to contain sprawl—which has been significant throughout the region. The goal? To see the Bay removed from a federal roster of impaired waters by the year 2010. The results have been mixed, trending slightly up or down from year to year in different areas, but never heralding reason for major optimism.

The blue crab, mainstay of a Chesapeake summer diet, has become a source of concern throughout the Bay region, and both Maryland and Virginia have tightened harvesting regulations in an effort to ensure the continued future availability of this astronomically popular crustacean. Reports of low spawning stocks have emerged recently.

This doesn't mean that blue crabs aren't available—tables fill at crab houses throughout the Chesapeake all summer long—but do *Callinectes sapidus* a favor when dropping your crab net in the water: take only as much as you'll need for dinner, and return the females to

Canada geese and goslings swim through the Chesapeake Bay Environmental Center. Queen Annes County Tourism Office

the water. (And don't be surprised if crabs are imported from North Carolina at Memorial Day—the Chesapeake season doesn't get rolling until midsummer, and the best local crabs are often available in fall, when prices drop.)

Perhaps signaling a brighter future for the crab are the success stories behind the return of the rockfish and the American shad. Commercial fishermen once enjoyed steady rockfish catches of 5 million pounds annually, then watched as stocks dropped to 2 million pounds in the late 1970s. In 1985, Maryland put in place a temporary moratorium on rockfish harvesting. Virginia followed in 1989. Stocks were officially declared restored in 1995, and scientists monitoring the rockfish report continued good news. Habitat restoration and the two fishing moratoria are given credit for bringing back the rockfish, a great success story.

More recently, the historic American shad, source of shad roe, has been the beneficiary of efforts to install fish passages to help this migratory species get upriver to breed. At the Conowingo Dam on the Susquehanna River, where scientists count the annual shad run, more than 200,000 fish passed through in 2001, by far the best year since the 1970s. Slow but steady restoration continues.

Visitors can expect to see increased development around the Chesapeake as subdivisions grow from former farmland. But they also can expect to see enthusiastic local support for the beloved Bay, as its residents participate in everything from organized SAV-planting canoe trips to the annual Bay Bridge Walk near Annapolis in late spring (followed by early summer's annual Chesapeake Bay Swim). In both Maryland and Virginia, cars sport Chesapeake Bay specialty license plates, and in Maryland you can check off a box on your state tax return to give money to clean up the Bay.

In the years since the cleanup began, the Bay's health has slowly improved, but caution remains the watchword. Sailing and boating thrive; recreational fishers still go after striped bass. The central effort for all Bay lovers and residents is to help restore the estuary and nurture it as the Mid-Atlantic region continues to grow. The balance, though tough to strike, is the fulcrum of efforts to bring back the Bay.

SOCIAL HISTORY

The first settlers of the Chesapeake region lived here during the last Ice Age. These Paleo-Indians were hunters, following mammoth and bison on their migrations. The melting of the glaciers marked the beginning of the Archaic period, when these forebears of the

Piscataway and Nanticoke tribes convened in villages and began to eat oysters and other shell- and finfish from the Bay. About 3,000 years ago, they began to farm these shores, raising maize, ancestor to the stacks of corn found at farm stands throughout the region come August, and tobacco, which the English settlers later converted into the region's early economic foundation.

Early Settlers

Dutch and Spanish explorers of the 16th century were reportedly the first Europeans to sail into the Bay, although Vikings may have visited even earlier. The first Europeans to settle permanently, however, were the English. In 1607, Capt. Christopher Newport left England, crossed the Atlantic to the West Indies, then sailed north into the Bay. He navigated up what would come to be called the James River. Those aboard Newport's three-ship fleet, the 49-foot *Discovery*, the 68-foot *Godspeed*, and the 111-foot *Susan Constant*, settled Jamestown.

The new colony, chartered by the Virginia Company, proved to be a near disaster. Hostiles and disease either drove off or killed many of the original settlers. Among the survivors was Captain John Smith, by all accounts an adventurer. It was here that Smith's fabled rescue by the maiden Pocahontas took place—an event recorded in Smith's journal but questioned by scholars. As the story goes, the young captain was captured and taken to a village where the old "powhatan," or chief, was to preside over Smith's execution. Even as the warriors threatened with raised clubs, the chief's young daughter threw herself upon the English captain, thus saving him from a brutal fate.

Smith was also the first Englishman to explore the Bay, and indeed he charted it rather accurately. He set out on his exploration from Jamestown in 1608, accompanied by 14 men on an open barge. They sailed first up the "Easterne Shore," where sources of fresh water proved poor. While still in what came to be called Virginia, Smith wrote, ". . . the first people we saw were 2 grimme and stout Salvages upon Cape-Charles, with long poles like Javelings, headed with bone. They boldly demanded what we were, and what we would, but after many circumstances, they in time seemed very kinde. . . . " Smith learned from them "such descriptions of the Bay, Isles, and rivers, that often did us exceeding pleasure." The party then went on across the Bay to its western shore, sailing as fast as they could ahead of a fearsome storm. "Such an extreame gust of wind, rayne, thunder, and lightening happened, that with great danger we escaped the unmercifull raging of that Ocean-like water," Smith wrote.

Early Jamestown survived as Virginia's colonial capital until the end of the 17th century. Meanwhile, English migration across the Atlantic continued. In 1631, William Claiborne established his trading post on Kent Island, mid-Bay, setting himself up to become arguably the first settler of Maryland. In ensuing years, on behalf of the Virginia Company, he provided ample rivalry for Maryland's "proprietors," or royal grant holders, the Calverts.

George Calvert, the first Lord Baltimore, hoped to settle his own Avalon. He first sought to establish a colony in Newfoundland but soon abandoned the harsh northern land. A second grant for a new colony passed to his son, the second Lord Baltimore, Cecil Calvert. The younger Calvert, a Catholic, knew that Virginia would not welcome the new settlement and feared that enemies in England would try to undermine his colony. He put his younger brother, Leonard, in charge of the settlers who boarded the ships *Ark* and *Dove* and sailed off to found Maryland, named in honor of Charles I's queen, near the mouth of the

The old Bazzell Church deep in Dorchester County on Maryland's Eastern Shore.

Potomac River at St. Clement's Island. Visitors can still take a weekend boat out to the island, now shrunk from 400 acres to about 40.

The 128 hardy souls aboard the two ships landed on March 25, 1634, after taking a route similar to that taken by Christopher Newport. Upon landing, Leonard Calvert, as governor, led a party of men up the river to meet the "tayac," or leader, of the Piscataways. The tayac gave the settlers permission to settle where they would; their village was to become Maryland's first capital, St. Marys City. These Native Americans also taught the English settlers how to farm unfamiliar lands in an unfamiliar climate.

Among the Marylanders' first crops was tobacco, soon to be a staple of the Chesapeake economy and already being harvested farther south along the Virginia Bay coast. In the years that followed, farmers would discover just how damaging tobacco proved to be in costs to both the land and humans. Because the crop sapped the soil's nutrients, without fertilizers a field was used up after a couple of seasons, so more land constantly had to be cleared and planted. This called for labor. While some Englishmen indentured themselves to this life in exchange for transatlantic passage to the colonies, tobacco farming was nevertheless responsible for the beginnings of African slave labor along the Chesapeake. By the late 17th century, wealthy planters had begun to "invest" in slaves as "assets."

Up and down the Chesapeake grew a tobacco coast, fueled by demand from English traders. From its beginnings as a friendly home to new settlers, the Bay grew into a sea-going highway for the burgeoning tobacco trade. Soon came fishing and boatbuilding.

A rural manorial society grew up around St. Marys City, which itself was never very large. Perhaps a dozen families lived within its 5 square miles. Planters raised tobacco, a fort was established, and government business eventually brought inns and stables. In 1650, a settlement named Providence was established about 100 miles to the north, near what is now Annapolis. In 1695, the new governor, Francis Nicholson, moved Maryland's capital to Annapolis, near the mouth of the Severn River. By 1720, St. Marys City was gone. That colony's heyday has been re-created, however, in a living museum complete with wild Ossabaw pigs. Archaeological work continues on the site as well. In the early 1990s, three lead coffins holding the remains of members of the Calvert clan were unearthed and authenticated.

Nicholson's Annapolis, considered America's first Baroque-style city, remains evident to any visitor. Two circles, State Circle and Church Circle, form hubs from which the streets of today's Historic District radiate. Three statehouses have stood inside State Circle, the most recent begun in 1772. This was the building used as the national capitol during the period of the Articles of Confederation, and it is the nation's oldest state capitol in continual use. From the center of Church Circle rises the spire of St. Anne's Church, the third on the site since 1696.

Known also as "the Ancient City," Annapolis grew into a thriving late 17th- and 18th-century town, renowned as the social gathering spot for colonial gentlemen and ladies. Here, the provincial court and the legislature met. Planters "wintered" here amid fashionable society; among social clubs, the most famed included the witty men of the Tuesday Club, whose members, such as colonial painter Charles Willson Peale, gathered at the homes of its members for music and poetry.

Elsewhere along the Chesapeake, other settlements were emerging. Chestertown was established as a seaport and Kent County seat in 1706. Near the head of the Bay, "Baltimore Town" was first carved in 1729 from 60 acres owned by the wealthy Carroll family. Those who couldn't survive the fluctuations of the tobacco market turned to tonging for oysters, fishing for herring, or shipbuilding.

The Chesapeake in Wartime

During the Revolutionary War, Annapolis's central port location drew blockade-runners and Continental colonels alike. Both Americans and British used the Bay to transport troops. War meetings that included George Washington and the Marquis de Lafayette were held beneath the Liberty Tree, a 400- to 600-year-old tulip tree that stood on the campus of St. John's College until dealt a final blow by a hurricane in 1999.

Three Annapolitans—Samuel Chase, William Paca, and Charles Carroll of Carrollton—signed the Declaration of Independence in 1776; their colonial-era homes have been preserved and are open for public tours. The fourth Maryland signer, Thomas Stone, later took up residence here, too, in what is now known as the Peggy Stewart House. The war finally ended in 1781 at Yorktown, Virginia, near Jamestown. Reinforcements traveled south along the Bay to meet up with Washington's gathering troops, and the French Admiral de Grasse barricaded the mouth of the Bay. Lord Cornwallis, the British commander, surrendered.

In 1783, during a meeting of the Continental Congress in the Maryland Statehouse in Annapolis, George Washington resigned his Army commission; visitors can still see the chamber where this occurred. This is also where the Treaty of Paris was ratified in 1784, formally ending the war. Likewise, Annapolis itself saw an end to its glittery social role. The city soon fell quiet, awakened only by the 1845 establishment of the U.S. Naval Academy, which overshadowed much of city life for at least the next century.

Peace with the British after the Revolution was short-lived. Soon came the War of 1812, the final time hostile British troops reached the new nation's shores. The British established their operations center at Tangier Island, and many battles and skirmishes ensued upon the Bay. Visitors to Virginia Island will learn about the Methodist "Parson of the Islands," Joshua Thomas, who predicted defeat when he preached to the British before they sailed up the Bay to Baltimore.

The citizens of the young nation, including those at the shipbuilding center of St. Michaels, were not eager to bow to the British. Blockade-runners routinely left the Eastern Shore port, and hostility ran high. Late on the night of August 9, 1813, amid rumors of an impending British attack, the good citizens of St. Michaels blew out their lanterns. Just before dawn, the British attacked a nearby fort. The wily shorefolk were ready. They hoisted their lanterns into the treetops, the British fired too high, and the town, except for the now-renowned "Cannonball House," was saved. For this, St. Michaels calls itself "the Town That Fooled the British."

A year later came the war's decisive battle. In September 1814, a man watched the fire of cannons and guns as the Americans successfully defended Fort McHenry, which guards the entrance to Baltimore Harbor. The next morning, that man, Francis Scott Key, saw a tattered U.S. flag flying and, inspired, penned the words to "The Star-Spangled Banner," thus creating what would become the U.S. national anthem in 1931.

19th-Century Life

Once this second war ended, the denizens of 19th-century Chesapeake Country turned to building their economy. Tobacco declined; shipbuilding grew. Smaller Chesapeake shore towns such as Chestertown and Annapolis lost commercial prominence to Baltimore, which grew into the Upper Bay region's major trade center. Steamships were launched, and the Baltimore & Ohio Railroad more speedily connected the region to points west. Eastern Shore–grown wheat and the watermen's catch of oysters, menhaden, and more were exported. By all accounts, there was no love lost between the landed gentry, who controlled the region, and the Chesapeake watermen. These scrappy individualists may have been one-time small farmers down on their luck or descendants of released indentured servants who had once served the wealthy class.

During this era, Chesapeake's shoals saw their first aids to navigation erected as lightships were sent out to warn passing ships of the worst sandbars. In 1819, Congress made provisions to set two lightships in Virginia waters. This experiment in safety was popular, and by 1833, 10 lightships stood sentinel at the mouth of the Rappahannock River and elsewhere in the Bay. The mid-19th century saw construction of the Chesapeake's distinctive screw-pile lighthouses, with pilings that could be driven securely into the muddy bottom of the Bay. Today, only three stand—two at maritime museums at Solomons and St. Michaels, Maryland, and one in action in the Bay just southeast of Annapolis, off Thomas Point. The Thomas Point Lighthouse was manned until automation came in 1986.

As the Bay became easier to travel, the people who spent the most time on the water discovered perhaps her greatest wealth. In the 19th century, demand increased for the famous Chesapeake oysters. Watermen went after them in an early ancestor to many Bay-built boat designs, the log canoe. Boats like the fast oceangoing schooners known as

Baltimore clippers already were being built, but oyster dredging and tonging required boats that could skip over shoals, run fast, and allow a man to haul gear over the side. Log canoes have unusually low freeboard; crab pots and oyster tongs can be worked over their sides with relative ease. These successors to dugout canoes were given sails and shallow-draft hulls so that they could navigate shoals. With their top-heavy sails and low sides, these log canoes now present one of a yachtsman's greatest challenges. Shifting their weight just ahead of the wind, sailors race them most summer weekends in St. Michaels on the Eastern Shore.

The Bay's 120-year steamboat era arrived in 1813, seven years after packets first carried passengers on a ship-and-stagecoach journey from Baltimore to Philadelphia. The steam-boat *Chesapeake* paddled out of Baltimore Harbor on June 13, 1813, bound for Frenchtown, Maryland, a now-extinct town at the head of the Bay. Within a week, a trip was offered to Rock Hall, on Maryland's Eastern Shore, for 75 cents. By 1848, the steamship company that came to be called the Old Bay Line ran the 200-mile length of the Bay, from Baltimore to Norfolk. Steamships ran in the Bay into the 1960s.

The Civil War and Slavery

Even as the Chesapeake Bay fueled a growing 19th-century economy, these were the years of growing North-South hostility. The Chesapeake region was largely slaveholding, although the nearby Mason-Dixon Line (the southern boundary of Pennsylvania) to the north beckoned many slaves to freedom. Historical accounts say this tended to moderate the behavior of many Maryland slaveholders, who feared their slaves would run away.

The history of slavery here had started with tobacco farming in the late 1600s; by 1770, tobacco exports reached 100 million pounds in the Western Shore region. When the tobacco trade declined in the 19th century, the services of many slaves were no longer needed. Abolitionist Quakers living in the Bay area campaigned to free many slaves, and free blacks were not uncommon in Annapolis and Baltimore in the first half of the 19th century. Many Eastern Shore watermen were free blacks who mixed with white watermen in mutual contempt for the wealthy.

In 1817, abolitionist and writer Frederick Douglass was born into slavery in Talbot County, Maryland. As a boy, he worked at the Wye Plantation, owned by Edward Lloyd V, the scion of a political dynasty in Maryland. Following alternately civil treatment in Baltimore and brutal treatment as an Eastern Shore field hand, Douglass escaped to Philadelphia at age 21 and became a free man.

Because the upper reaches of the Bay were so close to freedom, the Underground Railroad thrived here. The best-known local conductor was Harriet Tubman, an escaped slave from Dorchester County, Maryland, who became known as "the Moses of Her People," as she led nearly 300 slaves north during her lifetime.

When the Civil War broke out in 1861, the Virginia half of the Chesapeake quickly turned to Richmond, located at the head of navigation of the James River. Maryland struggled over its political loyalties, and many Chesapeake families would be divided by North-South rivalries.

Naval warfare changed forever on the waters of the Civil War Bay, when the ironclads *Monitor* and *Merrimack* met at Hampton Roads. The *Merrimack*, having been salvaged, rebuilt as an ironclad, and renamed *Virginia* by the Confederates, had already rammed and sunk the Union *Cumberland* and disabled the *Congress*, which burned and sank. The next day, the ironclad *Monitor*, with her two guns protected in a swiveling turret, arrived to

The exterior of a surviving slave cabin at Sotterley Plantation in St. Marys County.

engage the *Merrimack*'s fixed guns. Neither ship sank the other and neither side won, but the encounter was the first battle between armored battleships.

Ironically, when the Emancipation Proclamation went into effect in January 1863, slaves laboring on the Virginia shores of the Chesapeake were freed where federal law—via Union occupation—prevailed; slaves in Union Maryland were not. The proclamation freed only those in the states "in rebellion against the United States." It wasn't until September 1864, when Maryland voted for its own new constitution, that those in bondage in the state were freed.

The Oyster Boom

In the years before the war, shrewd Baltimore businessmen had opened oyster-packing plants. With the war over, enterprising Chesapeake business was renewed. The fertile oyster bars of the Bay's famed shoals fueled a much-needed economic burst on the Eastern Shore.

Chesapeake oyster production peaked at 20 million bushels a year in the 1880s, the height of the great oyster boom that started after the Civil War. At the same time, the Eastern Shore Railroad snaked through the flatlands to Dorchester County, where one John Crisfield, former Maryland congressman, set about capitalizing on it. At the head of Tangier Sound, where watermen dredged or tonged millions of oysters from the rich waters, Crisfield built his namesake town, which now calls itself "the Crab Capital of the

World." The town was literally built upon millions of oyster shells. An enormous wharf stretched along Somer's Cove, and the railroad depot stood nearby. Shuckers and packers set to work once the daily catch was landed; the cargo was shipped out on the railroad line, and newly developed refrigeration techniques kept it fresh on its way deep into the nation's interior.

Like Crisfield, Solomons, Maryland, on the Western Shore, sprang from the oyster rush. Isaac Solomon came from Baltimore, taking his patented pasteurizing canning process to the tiny village, where he set up a successful packing plant.

From this gold mine grew greed, and the famed Chesapeake Oyster Wars ensued. Virginia and Maryland oystermen—the tongers and dredgers, known as "drudgers"—battled over rights to oyster beds. Tempers ran high, and shots were fired. Maryland

Both Maryland and Virginia have taken steps to protect the population of the region's famous blue crabs. Maryland Office of Tourism Development

authorities, already funding an "Oyster Navy" to maintain some measure of decorum on the Bay, were angered that Virginia was less than helpful when it came to keeping its watermen within its boundaries, wherever exactly they were.

The Oyster Wars proved to be the catalyst that finally forced Maryland and Virginia to define their disputed Bay border. Three years of negotiations at the federal bargaining table set the boundary in 1877 at about where it is today. The southern shore of the Potomac was always the boundary between the two states, but how far down that shore the river ended and the Bay began, from which point to draw the line east across the Bay, was subject to dispute. The two states agreed to draw the line across Smith Point to Watkins Point on the Eastern Shore's Pocomoke River. Today, the boundary has been further refined: Maryland extends to the low-tide line of the river on the Virginia shore.

Chesapeake Tourism

The late 19th century brought the first tourists to the Bay, lured by clever investors who built the first resorts. Vacationers from Baltimore and Philadelphia turned to the Chesapeake, staying at new hotels built at Betterton and Tolchester on Maryland's Eastern Shore. On the Western Shore, Chesapeake Beach, just south of the Anne Arundel–Calvert County line, was carved from the shore by businessmen from the Pennsylvania Railroad. A new train station built there gave easy access to people from Baltimore and Washington, D.C.

Until about 1920, the Bay and its tributaries were the region's highways. Ferries connected to railroad lines crisscrossed the network of water and land, and steamships traveled everywhere. Farming and fishing supported much of the rural Western and Eastern shores in both Maryland and Virginia. Following World War II, the Chesapeake region mirrored the rest of the country, as industry and shipping propelled Baltimore and Norfolk into a new prosperity.

The automobile, too, fueled change, and by the mid-20th century the time had come to span the Bay by highway. On October 1, 1949, construction of the Chesapeake Bay Bridge began. Less than three years later, on July 30, 1952, the $112 million, 4.3-mile bridge opened. Over the next 30 years, travelers "discovered" the Eastern Shore as never before. As far south as Salisbury, Maryland, towns saw growth; Talbot and Kent Counties in particular became home to many retirees from the cities—and, increasingly, Washington or Baltimore commuters.

In 1964, the other end of the Bay was spanned. The spectacular Chesapeake Bay Bridge-Tunnel was more than three years in the making, at $200 million, and in the late 1990s its multimillion-dollar twin span was opened. Two mile-long tunnels and 12 miles of trestled roadway alternately soar above, then dive beneath, the Chesapeake Bay. Four constructed islands serve as supports between bridge and road, as the bridge-tunnel spans the entryway through which early explorers first found the Chesapeake.

What is the future of the Bay area? Apparently, it depends on the self-control of those who live here—and of those within the watershed that spreads all the way to upstate New York, as the debris of their lives ultimately trickles into the Bay. Annapolis, with ties to Baltimore and Washington, D.C., increasingly is caught in the region's web of urban growth, yet its Historic District maintains its colonial charm. Development clearly is on the march throughout the region, though, with talk of subdivisions in places that were rural not so long ago and waterfront condos beginning to rise in areas where they've heretofore not been seen.

The Bay area still retains its rural places. Along the Northern Neck of Virginia, it's still fairly quiet, although residents were talking when a stoplight went in at Callao not long ago—Northumberland County's first, and perhaps that area's canary in the development coal mine. On the Eastern Shore, the old shipbuilding port of Oxford still is a quiet, colonial-style village, counting among its residents many people who have escaped the city.

The first English settlers, Protestant and Catholic, brought diversity when they came to live among the Native Americans already here. So it is today, as city dwellers and those who fall in love with "the land of pleasant living" move in among the old families whose forebears long ago planted and fished along the Chesapeake Bay.

The Oxford–Bellevue Ferry is one of several ferries that still ply the waterways of the Chesapeake region. It's been in operation since 1683. Tim Tadder

2

TRANSPORTATION

Of Ferries & Freeways

The history of Chesapeake transportation is intimately tied to this vast inland sea, plied in ancient days by dugout canoes, later by indigenous sail craft, and today by massive steel cargo ships and yachts.

For centuries, native inhabitants—the Susquehannock, Wicomico, and Nanticoke—had the Bay to themselves. Then came the Spanish explorers and, in 1607, the Englishmen who settled first at Jamestown, Virginia. Soon after the vessels *Ark* and *Dove* delivered Maryland's first settlers in 1634, commerce drove the development of a ferry system across the Bay's rivers and creeks.

By the late 1600s, ferries crossed the South River south of present-day Annapolis to deposit traders at London Town, where they swapped furs for supplies. In 1683, what is now said to be the oldest privately operated ferry service in the country launched its run between Oxford and Bellevue on Maryland's Eastern Shore—and still makes the crossing today.

Later came the steamship era, ultimately symbolized by the Baltimore Steam Packet Company, known as the Old Bay Line, which launched in 1839 with wooden, then steel, paddle wheelers and steamships that operated into the 1960s. Visitors will increasingly find local museum exhibitions devoted to those days, especially in small towns formerly served by steamships.

Even as boat routes linking small towns spread across the Bay, ambitious plans connected the Chesapeake with the young nation's expanding interior. In 1850, the 184.5-mile Chesapeake and Ohio Canal opened after 20 years of construction. The canal was built alongside the non-navigable section of the Potomac River above Washington, D.C., which in turn is strategically linked to the Bay via the navigable waters of the lower Potomac. Just about the time this marvel of modern engineering opened, the first rails were laid for the Baltimore & Ohio Railroad.

The B&O was the first railroad to connect Chesapeake Country to the "outside," but others soon followed. Working in tandem with packet and steamship lines, railroads dramatically opened up the area. Passenger and freight stations ran deep on the Eastern Shore to places like Crisfield, which boomed as a result of oyster exports in the late 19th century.

A bridge didn't span the Bay until 1952, when the 4.3-mile William Preston Lane Jr. Memorial Bridge (known locally as the Bay Bridge) replaced a ferry, first with a single span, and later with a second. Travel to the Eastern Shore and Atlantic beaches by tourists and city dwellers boomed. In 1991, a new bridge replaced an aging drawbridge at Kent Narrows, just east of the Bay Bridge, greatly easing beach-bound traffic over the busy Narrows.

Soon after the Middle Eastern Shore was opened up to cars, a feat of engineering did the same at the mouth of the Bay. Where Vikings once may have sailed, the Chesapeake Bay Bridge-Tunnel now stands. The massive, 17.6-mile span alternates bridge and tunnel across four constructed islands to Cape Charles from the Virginia mainland, and not long ago a span opened headed in the other direction. For those who haven't crossed the bridge-tunnel since the last millennium, this means traffic moves through four lanes going north and south, except when lanes converge back to a two-lane highway as the road dips beneath the Bay's shipping channels. At that point, traffic funnels through two 1-mile tunnels.

Travelers can reach the gateway cities to the Chesapeake—Washington, D.C.; Baltimore; and Norfolk–Hampton Roads—by air, bus, or train. Mass transportation outside the cities is limited, although some connections can be made. To get the most out of

A sailboat heads up the Patuxent River at the Gov. Thomas Johnson Bridge at Solomons Island.

your visit, rent a car to explore the small towns and back roads of the largely rural, rambling Chesapeake region. For a taste of local adventure, cross tributary creeks and rivers the same way European forebears did as early as the late 1600s: by ferry.

GETTING TO THE CHESAPEAKE BAY

Unless you plan to spend your entire visit in Baltimore or Annapolis, the area's rambling country roads and tidewater lanes are best explored by car. Rent one at the airport, or tool into town in your own.

By Air

Four major airports serve the region—in Baltimore, in Washington, D.C., outside D.C. in nearby northern Virginia, and in the Norfolk–Hampton Roads area. In addition, regional airports in Salisbury, Maryland, and the Newport News–Williamsburg, Virginia, area offer commuter service. Check airport websites for important information subject to change, such as ground transportation schedules.

WASHINGTON, D.C.–BALTIMORE METROPOLITAN AREA

Baltimore-Washington International Airport (1-800-435-9294 or 410-859-7111 in the Baltimore area, 301-261-1000 in the Washington area; www.bwiairport.com; P.O. Box 8766, BWI Airport, MD 21240) BWI lies an easy 25-mile drive north of Annapolis via I-97, and fewer than 15 minutes from Baltimore's Inner Harbor. A massive expansion project is in process; a newly expanded terminal is scheduled to open in 2005.

Ronald Reagan Washington National Airport (703-417-8000; www.metwashairports
.com; Ronald Reagan Washington National Airport, Washington, DC 20001) Located at the
edge of the city, with easy access to highways leading to Annapolis.

Washington Dulles International Airport (703-572-2700; www.metwashairports.com;
Washington Dulles International Airport, Dulles, VA 20101) Thirty miles to the west
of D.C. in northern Virginia; a hike from Annapolis, especially given the area's
tremendous traffic.

The airports' websites provide information on ground transportation and security
questions. Among your options at each of the three airports is the **SuperShuttle**, which
circulates through all airports every 15 minutes between 6 AM and 2 AM. Service is on a
first-come, first-served basis, and fares are determined by zip code. For further information, call 1-800-BLUEVAN, visit www.supershuttle.com, or check with the SuperShuttle
representative stationed at each airport. To contact the service after hours from all three
airports, call 703-416-7873 or 1-800-258-3826.

Travelers trying to get between Dulles and Washington may want to contact the
Washington Flyer at 1-888-WASHFLY or www.washfly.com. The shuttles connect to the
city's Metro subway system (202-637-7000; www.wmata.com) at the West Falls Church
(Virginia) Metro station. From there, ride the Metro to Union Station, which has
connections to Amtrak. In addition, Baltimore-bound travelers can hop aboard the
Maryland Area Rail Commuter (MARC) trains (410-539-5000 or 1-800-325-RAIL) at
Union Station.

Finally, weekday travelers may want to use the commuter bus that runs into Washington
or Baltimore from Kent Island and Annapolis/Anne Arundel County in the morning and
back in the evenings. For information, contact Dillon Bus Service (410-647-2321 or
1-800-827-3490).

NORFOLK–HAMPTON ROADS, VA.
Norfolk International Airport (Norfolk Aviation Administration, 757-857-3351; www
.norfolkairport.com; 2200 Norview Ave., Norfolk, VA 23518) The area's aviation hub, with
numerous airlines, including discount carriers Southwest Airlines and Independence Air.
To catch a ride from the airport, try the **Norfolk Airport Express** (757-857-3991), which
offers transport throughout the Norfolk–Hampton Roads area and up to the Eastern Shore.
Charges are per person, and cost is determined by the zip code of your destination.

Regional Airports

COMMERCIAL SERVICE
Newport News–Williamsburg International Airport (757-877-0221; www.nnwairport
.com; 900 Bland Blvd., Newport News, VA 23602) The military's former Camp Patrick
Henry hosts service via US Airways Express, AirTran Airways, and Delta Connection. For
wide-ranging ground transportation throughout the area, contact **Williamsburg
Limousine Service** (757-877-0279).

Salisbury–Ocean City–Wicomico Regional Airport (410-548-4827; Airport Manager's
Office, 5485 Airport Terminal Rd., Unit A, Salisbury, MD 21804) Deep into Maryland's
Eastern Shore, this airport offers service to Washington and Philadelphia via US Airways
Express.

The 4.3-mile William Preston Lane Jr. Memorial Bridge, also known as the Bay Bridge, connects Maryland's Eastern and Western shores. Maryland Office of Tourism

PRIVATE PLANES

Pilots with their own planes can check out these regional airports:

Accomack County Airport (757-787-4600; 29194 Parkway North, Melfa, VA 23410) Fuel, tie-downs, and charter service.

Bay Bridge Airport (410-643-4364; 202 Airport Rd., Stevensville, MD 21666) Flight school, tie-downs, and repairs. Can arrange shuttles.

Cambridge-Dorchester Airport (410-228-4571; 5223 Bucktown Rd., Cambridge, MD 21613) Tie-downs and other support, including a restaurant.

Easton Municipal Airport (410-770-8055; 29137 Newnam Rd., Easton, MD 21601) Fuel, tie-downs, and charter service.

Freeway Airport (301-390-6424; 3900 Church Rd., Bowie, MD 20721) Fuel available daily 8 AM to dark. Tie-downs and maintenance.

Lee Airport (410-956-1280; www.leeairport.org; Old Solomons Island Rd./P.O. Box 273, Edgewater, MD 21037). Tie-downs. No charter service. Located 2 miles south of Annapolis.

By Rental Car

Having three airports clustered in the Baltimore-Washington, D.C., area means that rental car agencies often let you rent a car at BWI, for example, and return it to National or Dulles without an extra drop-off cost. Call to inquire.

Alamo (1-800-327-9633; www.alamo.com)

Avis (1-800-452-1494; www.avis.com)

Dollar (1-800-800-4000; www.dollar.com)

Hertz (1-800-654-3131; www.hertz.com)

National (1-800-227-7368; www.nationalcar.com)

Thrifty (1-800-847-4389; www.thrifty.com)

CHESAPEAKE BAY AREA ACCESS

Here are approximate distances and approximate driving times from the following major cities to Annapolis, according to AAA.

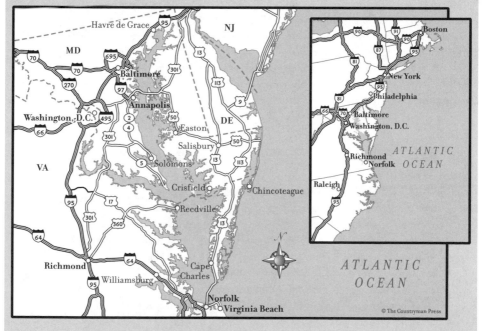

City	Miles	Hours
Atlanta	672	11
Boston	444	7
Chicago	723	11.2
New York	215	3.3
Norfolk	228	3.7
Philadelphia	128	2.1
Raleigh	295	5.2
Richmond	142	2.3

By Bus

Travelers with a sense of adventure may want to reach the Bay area by bus, but service is limited. As always, call ahead. For information, contact **Greyhound** (202-289-5154 or 1-800-231-2222; fare and schedule information: 1-800-229-9424; www.greyhound.com) or **Trailways** (410-752-0868, 202-484-2510, or 1-800-343-9999; www.trailways.com).

By Car

From New York and points north: Take I-95 south to Delaware and cross the head of the Chesapeake at the Susquehanna River at Havre de Grace. Your most straightforward path through Baltimore means staying on I-95 via the Fort McHenry Tunnel. Circling the city to the east via I-695 (the Baltimore Beltway) takes perhaps 20 minutes more, but the route crosses a high span with a spectacular view of the city and its harbor, guarded by Fort McHenry in the fork of the river to your right. From Baltimore, it's a smooth ride to I-97 south to Annapolis. For a scenic alternative, pick up DE 896 south toward Middletown, Del., after crossing the Delaware Memorial Bridge, then take US 301 south through the Delmarva Peninsula. Journey through the Shore on US 50. To reach Annapolis, cross the 4.3-mile-long William Preston Lane Jr. Memorial Bridge.

From Pittsburgh and points west: The Pennsylvania Turnpike connects with I-70 at Breezewood, Pa., your quickest route to the Bay region. (For a scenic route through rolling farmland, take alternate US 40, which reconnects with I-70 just east of Frederick, Md.) Reach Annapolis and the Eastern Shore via I-70 by way of Baltimore or via I-270 by way of Washington, D.C. Then take US 50 into Annapolis.

Travel Tips for Drivers

Circumnavigating Washington, D.C.: Washington's famed **Capital Beltway** is more than a political concept for the pundits. It's the major artery circling the city. The eastern half of the elliptical roadway is known as I-95 north and south—even as it proceeds east and west. The western half is called I-495. Travelers headed clockwise will find the road referred to as west, north, and east. Locals refer to the clockwise lanes as the Beltway's "inner loop," the counterclockwise route is known as the "outer loop." It's often crowded, even when it's not rush hour.

Meanwhile, an anachronism rules the Beltway's southeastern corner: a drawbridge. The **Woodrow Wilson Memorial Bridge** across the Potomac, while offering a spectacular view of the river, opens occasionally, so travelers weary of the highway may want to avoid the possibility. Construction of a multibillion-dollar replacement is under way and slated for completion in stages over the coming years.

Baltimore's Harbor Tunnel can get backed up during rush hour or the weekend rush to the Atlantic beaches. To bypass, take I-695 east to the **Francis Scott Key Bridge.** The trip is a bit longer, but the view is much better.

And as long as we're talking about summer weekends, consider crossing the **William Preston Lane Jr. Memorial Bridge** (aka the **Bay Bridge**) at US 50 near Annapolis sometime other than eastbound at 5 PM on a Friday or westbound at 4 PM on a Sunday. Construction on the Bay Bridge may mean lane closures. For information, call 1-877-229-7726 or visit www.baybridgeinfo.com.

From western Virginia and Dulles Airport: Take I-66 east. The road connects with the Washington Beltway (I-495) 7 miles east of Vienna, Va. Take the Beltway's inner loop north to I-95 to Baltimore; take the outer loop south to reach US 50 and Annapolis.

From points south: To go directly to the tip of Virginia's Eastern Shore, pick up US 13 in North Carolina, take it to the Norfolk area, and follow the signs for the Chesapeake Bay Bridge-Tunnel. Or continue on I-95 to Richmond and take I-64 east down the historic peninsula between the James and York rivers. At the end of the peninsula, the highway tunnels under the mouth of the James River to Norfolk. Pick up the Chesapeake Bay Bridge-Tunnel to the Shore.

If you're headed to Annapolis, take I-95 to I-495, the Washington Beltway, and circumnavigate the eastern side of the city. Go east on US 50. Since the I-95/I-495 intersection south of the city in northern Virginia often is traffic choked, consider turning off I-95 30 miles north of Richmond for a scenic ride that's not all that much longer. Follow VA 207 northeast to Bowling Green and pick up US 301 north to travel across the Rappahannock and Potomac rivers and into Maryland. Expect a 20-mile stretch of stop-and-go traffic around Waldorf, Md. The road merges with US 50 east 12 miles west of Annapolis.

Maps

Virginia and Maryland offer among the best maps, gratis, which highlight scenic routes or historical tidbits. Pick up the Maryland Department of Transportation's highway or scenic routes map by contacting MDOT, State Highway Administration, 410-545-8747; www.marylandroads.com; 707 N. Calvert St., Baltimore, MD 21202. Or contact the Maryland Office of Tourism Development, 410-767-3400 or 1-800-543-1036; 217 E. Redwood St., Baltimore, MD 21201.

Virginia's Department of Transportation also gives away a very detailed highway map. Contact the VDOT Information Center, 804-786-2801; www.virginiadot.org; 1221 E. Broad St., Richmond, VA 23219.

For a few well-spent dollars, you also can buy an excellent map of the Chesapeake Bay region that includes historical markers and eliminates the need to switch maps if you cross state lines. The Alexandria Drafting Co., aka ADC Maps, puts out this gem, which is available at area stores. Or buy directly from the company: ADC Maps, 1-800-232-6277; www.adcmap.com; 6440 General Green Way, Alexandria, VA 22312.

If you want to visit the Northern Neck, take US 301 until it intersects with VA 3. Bear right on US 360 to Reedville, or stay on VA 3 to Kilmarnock.

If you're headed to Southern Maryland, cross into the state on US 301 on the only bridge downriver from Washington, D.C. About 25 miles later, MD 234 connects to MD 5 south, taking you to Leonardtown and St. Marys City, from which you can wend your way up the Bay on MD 235, 4, and 2 past Solomons and Prince Frederick to Annapolis.

By Train

Amtrak's classic train stations operate in fully renovated pre–World War II elegance: in Baltimore, Pennsylvania Station (1500 N. Charles St.), and in Washington, Union Station (Massachusetts and Louisiana Aves.). Amtrak also operates a rail station at BWI Airport, a short ride from the terminal, on the line connecting Washington, D.C., and Baltimore (1-800-USA-RAIL; www.amtrak.com).

Water taxis are one way to navigate Baltimore's Inner Harbor.

GETTING AROUND THE CHESAPEAKE BAY AREA

By Bus

The Washington Greyhound terminal (202-289-5154; for schedules and fares, 1-800-231-2222 or 1-800-229-9424 English, 1-800-531-5332 Spanish; www.greyhound.com) is located at 1005 First St. N.E. To get from Washington, D.C., to Annapolis, board the Washington Metro at Union Station, ride the Red Line to Metro Center, change to the Orange Line, and head for New Carrollton, Md. During the workweek, take the Dillon Bus Service commuter bus into Annapolis (410-647-2321 or 1-800-827-3490). From Baltimore's bus station at 210 W. Fayette St. (410-752-7682), you can find Trailways connections to the Eastern Shore.

MARYLAND
Greyhound offers daily service from Baltimore and Washington, D.C., to Easton (410-822-3333; US 50 at Cordova Rd.), Cambridge (410-228-5825; 2903 Ocean Gateway Dr.), and Salisbury (410-749-4121; 350 Cypress St.). The Baltimore-to-Salisbury run operates four times a day. For fare and schedule information on public bus service around Annapolis, contact the city's Department of Public Transportation at 410-263-7964.

VIRGINIA
Trailways (757-625-7500; 701 Monticello Ave., Norfolk, VA 23501) makes four trips daily from Norfolk to Exmore, on Virginia's Eastern Shore, and back again. For municipal service around Virginia's Norfolk–Hampton Roads area call Hampton Roads Transit at 757-222-6100.

By Car

To ease confusion for road trippers: US 301 runs north–south from the Potomac River to US 50 at Bowie, Md., where it turns east with US 50. The northbound road becomes MD 3 to Baltimore. South of the Potomac toll bridge, US 301 traverses Virginia's northern Tidewater area to Richmond. From that route, you can drive southeast along intersecting VA 3 or VA 17.

US 50, meanwhile, is the eastbound thoroughfare from Washington, D.C., toward Annapolis, and it picks up a US 50/301 designation at Bowie. Soon after crossing onto the Eastern Shore, the road splits. US 50 heads south, providing the Shore's major north–south artery, then turns east after crossing the Choptank River at Cambridge. North of the split, US 301 goes solo again past the far Upper Eastern Shore. US 13 is the other major north–south highway on the Shore, running all the way up Virginia's Eastern Shore from the Chesapeake Bay Bridge-Tunnel at Kiptopeke, through the middle of Maryland's Lower Shore, and up the Delmarva Peninsula through Delaware.

By Rental Car

If you failed to pick up a car at the airport and need one once you arrive in Chesapeake Country, here are some local offices.

ANNAPOLIS/WESTERN SHORE

Budget (410-266-5030; 2002 West St., Annapolis)

Enterprise (in Annapolis: 410-268-7751, 1023 Spa Rd.; 410-224-2940, 913-A Commerce Rd.; or 410-897-0420, 1900 West St.)

Hertz (301-863-0033; 22711 Three Notch Rd., Lexington Park)

LOWER EASTERN SHORE

Avis (Salisbury–Ocean City, Md.: 410-742-8566; Salisbury–Ocean City–Wicomico Regional Airport)

Hertz (Salisbury–Ocean City, Md.: 410-749-2235; Salisbury–Ocean City–Wicomico Regional Airport)

U-Save (410-957-1421; 1727 Market St., Pocomoke City, Md.)

By Ferry

The 300-year-old ferryboat tradition remains in this region of snaking rivers, creeks, and can't-get-there-from-here roadways. For assistance, check your maps or ask around for exact locations of these low-load ferries suited to the moseying motorist.

NORTHERN NECK/MIDDLE PENINSULA

Merry Point Ferry (804-333-3696) The Merry Point, in Lancaster County, offers trips across the Corrotoman River. Free. Except for extreme high tides/bad weather, open year-round, 7–7 Mon. through Sat.

Sunnybank Ferry (804-333-3696) Near Smith Point at the mouth of the Potomac River in Northumberland County, this small ferry crosses the Little Wicomico River at Ophelia. Free. Except for extreme high tides/bad weather, open year-round, 7–7 Mon. through Sat.

MIDDLE EASTERN SHORE
Oxford–Bellevue Ferry (410-745-9023; www.oxford–bellevueferry.com) The oldest continuously operating private ferry in the country was launched on November 20, 1683, allowing easy access between Oxford and St. Michaels in Talbot County. Runs Apr. through Nov., 7 AM–sunset Mon. through Fri., 9 AM–sunset Sat. and Sun. Closed Dec. through Mar. Car and driver are $7 one-way, $12 round-trip. Passengers, whether in a vehicle or walk-on, are $2 one-way. Bicycles are $3 one-way, $5 round-trip. Motorcycles are $4 one-way, $7 round-trip.

LOWER EASTERN SHORE
Whitehaven Ferry (410-548-4873) This tiny ferry crosses the scenic Wicomico River about 18 miles southwest of Salisbury on MD 352. Free. Open year-round, 6 AM–7:30 PM in summer, 7 AM–6 PM in winter. The **Upper Ferry** (410-334-2798) also crosses the Wicomico near Salisbury. Free. Open year-round, same hours as the Whitehaven.

Several ferries also operate out of Crisfield to Smith and Tangier islands; one runs from Onancock, Va., to Tangier, and another runs from Reedville, Va., to Smith Island. For information on all of these, check full listings in the Smith and Tangier Islands section of chapter 6, "Lower Eastern Shore." If you're visiting Smith Island, be sure to arrange accommodations in advance if you intend to stay overnight.

The Whitehaven Ferry crosses the scenic Wicomico River.

As part of a visit to the Calvert Marine Museum in Solomons, the William B. Tennyson discharges her passengers at the Drum Point Lighthouse, one of only three remaining screw-pile lights.

3

ANNAPOLIS & SOUTHERN MARYLAND

A Capital Destination

On a clear day in early September, station yourself near City Dock and look out to the harbor, where white sails catch the wind on a gentle breeze. Or go out to Sandy Point State Park to watch sailboats, powerboats, or huge container ships pushing through the Bay's main channel. For all the historic charm of this 300-year-old capital city, its downtown clustered with good restaurants, fun shops, and, no doubt, the house you wish you owned, it's these sparkly days that make folks fall in love with Annapolis.

Clean, waterfront light shines crisply from the top of Church Circle, only steps from where the first colonial capitol building was constructed. That came in 1699, soon after royal governor Francis Nicholson moved the seat of government north from St. Marys City on the Potomac to this town along the Severn River and built the Baroque-style streets that colonists would still recognize.

From these early beginnings spring tales of patriots passing through Annapolis, where Maryland's four signers of the Declaration of Independence owned homes that still stand. For a brief time—November 1783 to August 1784—Annapolis served as the new nation's capital city. In the current Statehouse, George Washington resigned his commission from the Continental Army and patriots signed the Treaty of Paris, which ended the Revolutionary War.

Evidence of the city's colonial and post-colonial Golden Age remains. St. John's College, the intellectual home of the "Great Books" program, descends from King William's School, founded in 1696. This makes St. John's the nation's third-oldest school, after the College of William and Mary and Harvard University. Benjamin Franklin sent cousin Jonas Green from Philadelphia to become the city's printer in 1738; visitors seeking true colonial accommodations can stay in his house, now a B&B operated by direct descendants. It's considered one of the two oldest houses in this city of old houses, where Colonial Georgian, Federal, and even Greek Revival structures line the streets. By 1845, the U.S. Naval Academy was established, renewed by stunning Beaux Arts buildings after the Civil War, during which the academy and St. John's College were taken over as hospitals.

Recent times have brought sailors and city refugees who commute to their offices in Baltimore or Washington, D.C., about an hour away, depending on increasingly heavy rush hours. Downtown, state legislators continue to bring present-day politicking to this Chesapeake city, which still serves as Maryland's capital.

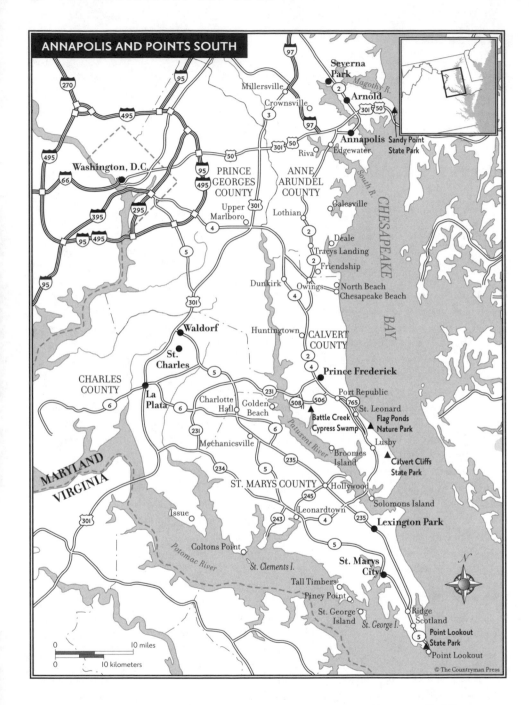

ANNAPOLIS AND POINTS SOUTH

Across the Spa Creek Bridge from Annapolis sits the maritime district called Eastport, giving working credence to the city's claim of being "America's Sailing Capital." The city annexed this former workingman's neighborhood decades back, and from yacht brokers and other boating industry businesses has sprung a fine group of restaurants—perhaps the city's reliably best. Take a walking tour of Eastport or the Historic District to learn more about the city, though neither takes in all of Annapolis, which has grown outward from its colonial Severn River nexus.

Parking in the city is notoriously difficult. Feed the parking meters, don't exceed the nonresident time limit in the neighborhoods, and if the parking garages in town are full, park at the Navy–Marine Corps Memorial Stadium on Rowe Boulevard for $5. Two shuttles run downtown: State is direct during the workweek and Navy Blue makes several stops and runs every day. The "State" shuttle operates continuously from 6:30 AM–8 PM during the week, and until 10:30 PM during the legislative session from Jan. through mid-Apr. The "Navy Blue" shuttle operates on the hour and half hour, 9–6 Mon. through Fri. and 10–6 on weekends. For information, call 410-263-7964 or visit www.annapolis.gov.

Also look for the City Dock–based Jiffy Water Taxi (410-263-0033) for a quick ride across Spa or Back Creek, the former being the small creek separating the Historic District and Eastport. Visitors to

Visitors to Annapolis may want to watch a dress parade at the United States Naval Academy.
Middleton Evans

Annapolis also should check chapter 5, "Middle Eastern Shore," for ideas for nearby explorations, including Kent Island. Although it's officially part of the Eastern Shore, the island has essentially become a suburb of Annapolis. It's just a quick hop across the Chesapeake Bay Bridge. For additional info on Annapolis, visit www.visit-annapolis.org.

LODGING

Members of the Annapolis Bed and Breakfast Association (http://annapolisbandb.com) have worked out a half-price discount deal for parking in city garages. You can't come and go during the period without repaying, but it's easier to walk the Historic District and Eastport anyway. Many good B&Bs are not association members, but those that are can make referrals to member establishments if needed.

Lodging prices may vary according to day of the week and time of the year. In general, prices peak during high season and are higher on weekends than during the week. In Annapolis, high season runs well into October, when the city hosts popular boat shows and U.S. Naval Academy home football games.

Lodgings with more than two rooms are taxed at 12 percent, 7 percent of that being a lodging tax for Anne Arundel County, where Annapolis is located.

Other considerations when booking a room: Check to see whether lodgings have two-night minimums or cancellation policies. Their websites may provide information about these and changing specials or packages.

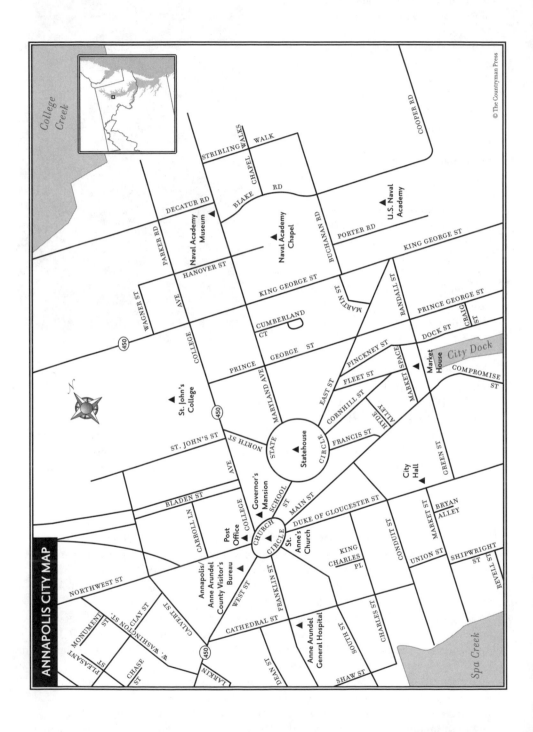

© The Countryman Press

College Creek

ANNAPOLIS CITY MAP

COOPER RD

STRIBLING WALKS
WALK
CHAPEL WALK
BLAKE RD
DECATUR RD

▲ Naval Academy Museum

▲ Naval Academy Chapel

▲ U.S. Naval Academy

PORTER RD

KING GEORGE ST

BUCHANAN RD

PARKER RD

HANOVER ST

WAGNER ST

AVE

COLLEGE

KING GEORGE ST

CUMBERLAND CT

MARTIN ST

RANDALL ST

PRINCE GEORGE ST

CRAIG ST

DOCK ST

City Dock

Market House

COMPROMISE ST

PRINCE GEORGE ST

PINCKNEY ST

MARKET SPACE

▲ St. John's College

EAST ST

FLEET ST

CORNHILL ST

HYDE ALLEY

ST. JOHN'S ST

NORTH ST

MARYLAND AVE

STATE

Statehouse

CIRCLE

FRANCIS ST

GREEN ST

City Hall ▲

BLADEN ST

CARROLL LN

Post Office

COLLEGE

Governor's Mansion ▲

SCHOOL ST

MAIN ST

CHURCH

St. Anne's Church ▲

DUKE OF GLOUCESTER ST

MARKET ST

BRYAN ALLEY

CONDUIT ST

UNION ST

SHIPWRIGHT ST

REVELL ST

NORTHWEST ST

CLAY ST

CALVERT ST

Annapolis/ Anne Arundel County Visitor's Bureau ▲

WEST ST

FRANKLIN ST

CIRCLE

KING CHARLES PL

CHARLES ST

W. WASHINGTON ST.

MONUMENT ST

CATHEDRAL ST

Anne Arundel General Hospital ▲

SOUTH ST

PLEASANT ST

CHASE ST

LARKIN

DEAN ST

SHAW ST

Spa Creek

Lodging rates, based on high-season prices, fall within this scale:

Inexpensive:	Up to $75
Moderate:	$75 to $120
Expensive:	$120 to $175
Very expensive:	$175 and up

Credit card abbreviations are:
AE—American Express
CB—Carte Blanche
DC—Diners Club
D—Discover
MC—MasterCard
V—Visa

ANNAPOLIS INN

Innkeepers: Joe Lespier and Alex De Vivo.
410-295-5200.
www.annapolisinn.com.
144 Prince George St., Annapolis, MD 21401.
Price: Very expensive.
Credit Cards: AE, MC, V.
Handicapped Access: No.
Restrictions: No guests under 18.

It's hard to overstate the upscale level of Cupid-and-Psyche romance at this renovated 1770s home. Gilded rosette moldings crown the downstairs salons, and etched-glass doors separate bedroom from sitting room in an upstairs suite. King-size beds are dressed up in the finest cotton linens; tapestries hang from walls; and French and English reproductions or antiques furnish the house. The three accommodations include the Murray Suite, which has a heated marble bathroom floor, and the Rutland Suite on the third floor, with its bath of three kinds of marble, a remote-controlled whirlpool tub, and easy access to the roof deck. This onetime home to a doctor to Thomas Jefferson fills a top-tier niche in this luxe city's diverse selection of B&Bs and lodgings. Plan to tuck in to a pampered good time. Breakfast starts at 8 AM.

ANNAPOLIS MARRIOTT WATERFRONT

410-268-7555; reservations 1-800-336-0072.
www.annapolismarriott.com.
80 Compromise St., Annapolis, MD 21401.
Price: Very expensive.
Credit Cards: AE, DC, D, MC, V.
Handicapped Access: Yes.
Special Features: Smoking rooms available.

This hotel offers an Annapolis commodity: the Historic District's only waterfront rooms, with views over mast-filled Spa Creek and out to the Severn River. The 150 rooms include water and city views, with irons, high-speed Internet access, hair dryers, and coffee makers. Room rates are based on whether there's a water view. Suites, king-size beds, a small on-site fitness room, and concierge service are available. Valet parking costs $15 per night. Visitors also will find a fine location for a cold one at the hotel's Pusser's Landing, a pub right on the waters of Ego Alley, so named for the parade of boaters showing off their crafts.

THE BARN ON HOWARD'S COVE

Innkeepers: Graham and Mary Gutsche.
410-571-9511.
www.bnbweb.com/howards-cove.html.
500 Wilson Rd., Annapolis, MD 21401.
Price: Expensive.
Credit Cards: No; personal checks OK.
Handicapped Access: No.

Ordinarily, we skip lodgings that offer only two rooms—even if one is a suite. However, the Barn on Howard's Cove is a particular find for many reasons. You can bring the kids (even infants!), park easily just 2 miles outside the Historic District, and, best of all, put a canoe or kayak in a Chesapeake tributary on the property. Plus, the place is a good value. Your hosts have renovated this waterside 1850s barn to ensure a lovely year-round view of Howard's Cove, and the rooms, with quilts and floral wallpaper, are very comfortable. One large room, one suite with sitting room, and amenities such as VCRs and ceiling fans await. An excellent choice for families. Full breakfast; bicycles.

CHEZ AMIS

Owners: Don and Mickie Deline.
410-263-6631 or 1-888-224-6455.
www.chezamis.com.
85 East St., Annapolis, MD 21401.
Price: Expensive.
Credit Cards: AE, MC, V.
Handicapped Access: No.
Restrictions: No children under 10.

This cute and cozy former corner store comes with a pressed-tin ceiling downstairs and breakfast at the Stammtisch, named for the German table where family and friends gather. Four rooms in all start with a downstairs suite (king-size bed and trundle bed) suitable for a family. Upstairs, the Capital Room salutes both the Maryland Statehouse, visible out the window, and the nation's capital, where Mickie was once a tour guide (husband Don was a longtime Army lawyer). Photos of politicians line the walls, just as judges' photos hold forth in the Judge's Chambers, where guests can sleep in a queen-size sleigh bed. The smaller, nautical-themed Captain's Quarters is the only room whose private bath requires a brief trip down the hall; the others are attached to the guest rooms. A kind of nook-and-cranny quality marks the two-toned, rose-colored house, with handmade quilts hanging from the walls and a collection of bunnies and bears throughout.

EASTPORT HOUSE BED AND BREAKFAST

Hostess: Susan Denis.
410-295-9710.
www.eastporthouse.com.
101 Severn Ave., Annapolis, MD 21403.
Price: Expensive.

Credit Cards: MC, V.
Handicapped Access: No.
Restrictions: No children under 8.

Looking to Orvis or maybe L. L. Bean for inspiration, this renovated 1860 house one block from the water in the Eastport maritime neighborhood creates a clean Chesapeake theme with rooms to match: the Fish Room, the Duck Room, the Captain's Quarters, the Sailboat Room, and the Maryland Blue Crab Room. The Captain's Quarters may be the most muted, with white and blue accenting original floors. The Duck Room comes in green and white, replete with a half-canoe shelf, while wooden Costa Rican fish mark their namesake room. There are televisions in all rooms, a guest refrigerator, Wi-Fi, and phones. There's also a nice backyard porch, where breakfast is served in-season. All rooms have attached baths except for the two on the uppermost floor (with a sink in each), which makes this a good choice for traveling companions. Street parking.

55 EAST

Innkeepers: Tricia and Mat Herban.
410-295-0202.
www.55east.com.
55 East St., Annapolis, MD 21401.
Price: Expensive; very expensive during special events.
Credit Cards: AE, D, MC, V.
Handicapped Access: No.
Restrictions: No children under 12.

"Handsome" leaps to mind to describe this tucked-away B&B, which manages to marry worldly aplomb with enough tradition so you'll still know that you're in the cradle of the nation's colonial history. Guests can relax and listen to music or watch television in two classic downstairs parlor areas, including one painted the most enviously adventuresome color of blue-green you ever saw. Out French doors stands a treat: a New Orleans–inspired courtyard with a

handmade brick fountain and roses blooming in pots. A second-floor balcony overlooks the scene, accessible from two guest
rooms. In all, three rooms come with either
queen beds or a king that converts to twins.
Each has an attached bath, two with full-
body spray showers. The rooms are uncluttered, with original drawings or Vermont
Casting stoves. Breakfast is served on china
and crystal. Cable hookups and phone
lines; sophisticated, upscale taste.

FLAG HOUSE INN
Owners: Charlotte and Bill Schmickle.
410-280-2721 or 1-800-437-4825.
www.flaghouseinn.com.
26 Randall St., Annapolis, MD 21401.
Price: Expensive to very expensive.
Credit Cards: MC, V.
Handicapped Access: No.
Restrictions: No children under 10.

Located less than a block from the U.S.
Naval Academy's main gate, the Flag House
offers a central location and sociable
innkeepers who have sent a son through the
academy. The Schmickles have been re-
doing this five-guest-room gem, where
guests will find the rooms quite comfortable, with king-size beds, televisions, and
European-style split bathrooms in some.
Ask for the room wallpapered in gorgeous
purple toile or the room done up in red
toile. A two-room suite can accommodate
up to three people. A friendly industrious-
ness seems to be at work here; the last time
we pulled out of the driveway, Bill was
adjusting the clever irrigation system he'd
created for the plants that hang from the
wide front porch, where the state or
national flag of each guest in residence
flies. Full breakfast is served in the dining
room downstairs. Off-street parking; the
quietest rooms are in the back of the house.

HARBOR VIEW INN
Innkeepers: Andrea and Chuck
Manfredonia.
410-626-9802.
www.harborviewinnofannapolis.com.
1 St. Mary's St., Annapolis, MD 21401.
Price: Expensive to very expensive.
Credit Cards: No; personal checks OK.
Handicapped Access: No.
Restrictions: No children under 14.

A wide-open contemporary home hides
behind the gray siding and bright green
shutters of this downtown B&B. The architectural detail here is terrific. An oval
opening cuts through the tiled foyer leading
to a second-floor guest room, allowing even
more light to filter downstairs. Three
rooms are in residence here, two with
patios. A room highlighted in cobalt blue is
a favorite, with a built-in wainscoted
"headboard" and a deck looking toward the
water, and guests need only step briefly
into the hall to reach the accompanying
bath. The gardens out back change with the
seasons, and you can hide from life in a
hammock tucked into a far, shaded corner.
A change from much of what you'll find in
the Historic District, the Harbor View harbors nary an Oriental rug. Full breakfast.

HISTORIC INNS OF ANNAPOLIS
Owner: Remington Hotels.
410-263-2641 or 1-800-847-8882.
www.historicinnsofannapolis.com.
58 State Circle, Annapolis, MD 21401.
Price: Very expensive.
Credit Cards: AE, D, MC, V.
Handicapped Access: Yes.
Special Features: Smoking rooms available;
valet parking; includes the Maryland Inn,
Governor Calvert House, and Robert
Johnson House.

With three inns set on two circles, the
Historic Inns has a unique setup. No matter
where you're staying, you'll check in at the
Governor Calvert House on State Circle,

directly across from the Maryland State-house. Management does its best to efficiently shepherd guests through the process, down to a valet in a minivan to take you to your room. Guests may request a favorite inn, although it's possible the inns may not be able to comply. In all, 124 rooms are available, and each is different. The most modern of the three, fully renovated in 1983, is the Governor Calvert House, part of which dates to the 18th century. During construction, archaeologists discovered a 1730 hypocaust, a central heating system originally engineered by the Romans that is now preserved in a Plexiglas-covered floor. The 1773 Robert Johnson House is probably the quietest inn. The Maryland Inn, part of which dates to the Revolutionary era, started life as an inn early on and remained so until a post–World War I hiatus as an office/apartment complex. The Maryland Inn is a sentimental favorite among many Annapolitans and visitors, with its intimate brick-walled Treaty of Paris restaurant and two pubs, the King of France Tavern and the Drummer's Lot. Renovations are on tap for the Maryland Inn.

JONAS GREEN HOUSE

Owners: Randy and Dede Brown.
410-263-5892 or 1-877-892-4845.
www.jonasgreenhouse.com.
124 Charles St., Annapolis, MD 21401.
Price: Moderate.
Credit Cards: AE, D, MC, V.
Handicapped Access: No.
Special Features: Children and pets allowed with prior notice.

Stand in the 18th-century dining room and look through the 19th-century hallway that connects to the 17th-century kitchen: this

Waterside B&Bs offer tranquil spots to relax along the Bay.

house is the genuine article for visitors seeking colonial accommodations. Widely considered one of the two oldest homes in Annapolis, the Jonas Green House is operated by its namesake's great-great-great-great-great-grandson and wife. Green himself was the colony's printer, taught the trade by cousin Ben Franklin. The current owners renovated the old house in the early 1990s and can offer complete tours to architecture buffs. The home's decor is carefully reproduced, with white walls and colonial wainscoting. Three guest rooms offer antique beds with modern, custom-made mattresses and spare, period accents, like a spinning wheel in one room. Pine floors and fireplaces in each room; full breakfasts in the morning. Two rooms share a bath. Easygoing, uncluttered atmosphere; off-street parking and a short walk to the thick of the Historic District's offerings.

LOEWS ANNAPOLIS HOTEL

General Manager: Larry Beiderman.
410-263-7777 or 1-800-526-2593.
www.loewshotels.com.
126 West St., Annapolis, MD 21401.
Price: Very expensive.
Credit Cards: AE, DC, D, MC, V.
Handicapped Access: Yes.
Special Features: Smoking and pet rooms available.

Considered perhaps the city's finest hotel, Loews provides all of the amenities in a brick courtyard-style hotel located just blocks from the Historic District. The 217 guest rooms and suites were under full renovation at deadline, to be completed in a regatta theme of blues and reds with amenities ranging from hypoallergenic pillows to high-speed Internet. The hotel restaurant also has been recently updated; it is now named Breeze and serves regional cuisine. Hotel services include child care, and kids under 18 stay in their parents'

room for free. Valet parking costs $13 per night; self-parking is $10 per night. Lovely meeting and party spaces include those in the complex's brick Powerhouse Conference Center. Ideal for visitors seeking well-located lodgings with all the amenities.

1908 WILLIAM PAGE INN

Owner: Robert Zuchelli.
410-626-1506 or 1-800-364-4160.
www.williampageinn.com.
8 Martin St., Annapolis, MD 21401.
Price: Expensive to very expensive.
Credit Cards: MC, V.
Handicapped Access: No.
Restrictions: No children under 12.

Well located on a quiet street just around the corner from the Historic District's hustle and bustle, this 1908 house offers five rooms. They include the Marilyn Suite on the top floor, with a big sitting area and television. Two rooms share a bath and two others have their own, including one with a whirlpool. While antiques and family collectibles add flavor to the turn-of-the-century, cedar-shingled home, they don't clutter. For a treat, ask for the private Fern Room, which opens onto the wraparound porch. Zuchelli, long active in the local B&B industry, opened the inn in the mid-1980s and knows how to run a classy operation, providing luxury and privacy without a fuss. Off-street parking; full breakfast.

SCHOONER WOODWIND

Innkeepers: Ken and Ellen Kaye.
410-263-7837.
www.schoonerwoodwind.com.
P.O. Box 3254, Annapolis, MD 21403.
Price: Very expensive.
Credit Cards: AE, D, MC, V.
Handicapped Access: No.
Restrictions: No children under 16; available Sat. only, early May through late Sept.

Sleep aboard the schooner *Woodwind* and see what it's like to wake up with the sun peeking through the porthole. The boat stays docked at its berth alongside the Annapolis Waterfront Marriott through the night, and a captain stays on board. Guests will share heads (aka bathrooms), and those in the two forward-most cabins can even open the hatch. Double berths; breakfast on deck. A two-hour sunset sail goes along with your stay.

TWO-O-ONE BED AND BREAKFAST

Innkeepers: Graham Gardner and Robert A. Bryant.
410-268-8053.
www.201bb.com.
201 Prince George St., Annapolis, MD 21401.
Price: Expensive to very expensive.
Credit Cards: AE, D, MC, V.
Handicapped Access: No.
Restrictions: No children.

This elegant Georgian home, furnished with English and American period antiques, also comes with a surprisingly large yard for the Historic District. Your hosts have beautifully landscaped this back area, creating garden rooms large enough to offer a measure of privacy to their guests. Expect this same sensibility to extend to the guest rooms, which are spacious and comfortable and come with enough towels to last the weekend. The four suites include two with whirlpool tubs. All have refrigerators. Fun antique finds include a Beau Brummel, which is, essentially, a vanity for gentlemen of a certain era; this one came from Pickfair. This well-located B&B offers a full breakfast and on-site parking. A dog and a parrot live here as well.

Additional Hotels and Motels

Radisson Hotel Annapolis (410-224-3150; www.radisson.com; 210 Holiday Ct.) Located on the west side of the city, about 10 minutes from the Historic District, with 219 rooms, a swimming pool, a restaurant, a fitness center, and a free shuttle into town. Handicapped access. Moderate to very expensive.

Country Inn & Suites (410-571-6700; www.countryinns.com/annapolismd_west; 2600 Housley Rd.) Budget option located on the west side of the city not far from the Westfield Shoppingtown Annapolis (which locals still call the Annapolis Mall). Of the 100 rooms, 60 are suites. Indoor pool, fitness center, high-speed Internet access. A shuttle operates within a 5-mile radius of the hotel, and that includes the Historic District. Handicapped access. Moderate to very expensive.

O'Callaghan Hotel Annapolis (410-263-7700 or 1-866-782-9624; www.ocallaghan-hotels.com/annapolis; 174 West St.) The Annapolis outpost of this small Irish hotel chain is well located within walking distance of the city's hubbub. The John Barry Restaurant and Bar sits off the European-style lobby, 120 rooms are available, and there's a fitness center, DSL, 24-hour room service, and a shuttle that operates within a 5-mile radius. Expensive to very expensive.

RESTAURANTS

From the colonial taverns ringing City Dock to more adventurous Pacific Rim cuisine in well-appointed eateries, diversity reigns among Annapolis restaurants. An Irish invasion has left three Irish pubs in town, and steak lovers hungering for a New York strip in a clubby atmosphere won't be disappointed. While crab cakes aplenty, crab imperial, and crab dip (best served on French bread) show up on local menus, those with a hankerin' for hard-shell crabs spilled across brown-paper-lined tables will find their best bets are just outside of town.

Price ranges, which include dinner entrée, appetizer, and dessert, are as follows:

Inexpensive:	Up to $20
Moderate:	$20 to $30
Expensive:	$30 to $40
Very expensive:	$40 or more

Credit card abbreviations are:
AE—American Express
CB—Carte Blanche
DC—Diners Club
D—Discover
MC—MasterCard
V—Visa

The following abbreviations are used to denote meals served:
B = Breakfast; L = Lunch; D = Dinner;
SB = Sunday Brunch

ANNAPOLIS
AQUA TERRA
410-263-1985.
164 Main St.
Open: Tues. through Sun.
Price: Expensive to very expensive.
Cuisine: Asian fusion, contemporary American.
Serving: D.
Credit Cards: AE, MC, V.
Reservations: Strongly recommended Thurs. through Sun.
Handicapped Access: Yes.
Special Features: Valet parking on Fri. and Sat.

Ask the downtown locals where they recommend, and you're likely to hear about Aqua Terra. Focused on fashionable Pan-Asian food and looks, the restaurant nevertheless makes sensible use of its storefront quarters. The old-fashioned pressed-tin ceiling matches the grayish slate-blue walls, creating stylish uniformity. A recent expansion into the next-door space continues the theme, with cobalt accents against the muted colors. Cobalt blue projections even light the walls. This is one of a handful of highly non-Chesapeake restaurants that have moved into the city in recent years, and one glance at the menu tells more. A crab cake appetizer may be tempura'd and served with tamarind teriyaki and spicy mustard. Peking duck breast may come pan-roasted and served over white chocolate and rosemary mashed potatoes, finished with a port wine and air-dried cherry sauce. Candles flicker between the mirrors lining one wall, while the chefs sear tunas and blow-torch crème brûlées behind a counter in the open kitchen across the room.

BACK PORCH CAFE
410-280-0380.
Annapolis Landing Marina, 980 Awald Dr. (off Bembe Beach Rd.).
Open: Wed. through Sun.
Price: Inexpensive to moderate.
Cuisine: American, light fare.
Serving: B, L.
Credit Cards: AE, MC, V.
Reservations: No.
Handicapped Access: Yes.

Thank the creator of Ken's Creative Kitchen, a highly successful Annapolis catering business, for this gem on Back Creek. As its name implies, the dozen or so tables set with pastel cloths and fresh flowers sit on a back porch overlooking marinas and boats for as far as the eye can see. Of the dozen or so times we've been there, a steady breeze has blown through, making it extremely comfortable even on the warmest of days. But enough about weather. Come here for breakfast (crème brûlée French toast, vegetable frittata, crab and ham omelet, and the like) or lunch (smoked-salmon club sandwich that's to die for, lump crab and corn chowder, Gulf shrimp Louis, curried breast of chicken salad, etc.). The generous lump-crab-cake sandwich (no filler!) with a humongous side of potato salad or coleslaw is as fine as any we've had on the Bay. Do try to squeeze in one of the exceptional desserts (mousse, key lime pie, pecan pie, and whatever else the chef is in the mood for), or box it for later on. No alcohol served. The fresh-squeezed lemon-ade and iced tea are delicious, and servers will refill your glass until you beg for mercy. Don't go if you're in a rush, as service can be a mite slow. But we think the setting is so pleasant and the food so good, it would be a shame to hurry.

CAFÉ NORMANDIE
410-263-3382.
185 Main St.
Open: Daily.
Price: Moderate to expensive.
Cuisine: French.
Serving: B (Sat. and Sun.), L, D.
Credit Cards: AE, DC, D, MC, V.
Reservations: Recommended on weekends, during special events, and for the Jan. through mid-Apr. legislative session.
Handicapped Access: Yes.

Long before the word "Provence" started appearing in many best-seller titles, Café Normandie was delivering country-French style on upper Main Street. Wood-backed booths downstairs look to a fireplace, and a row of tables upstairs peers out over the street. The menu caters to different tastes, offering higher-priced entrées (filet mignon, veal) for serious appetites and a good selection of moderately priced meals for those who want less. Portions are plenti-ful. The Caesar salad here is one of the city's best, and the crepe selection is legendary, delivered in regular or buckwheat batter and served with a good-size side salad. Like so many restaurants in town, Café Normandie names one of its signature dishes for its locale (even though none of the seafood ingredients is local to the Bay): the Annapolis crepe—$10.95 at lunch, $12.95 at dinner—rolls shrimp, scallops, mushrooms, and dill into a tasty lobster sauce.

CANTLER'S RIVERSIDE INN
410-757-1311.
458 Forest Beach Rd.
Open: Daily.
Price: Inexpensive to very expensive.
Cuisine: Seafood.
Serving: L, D.
Credit Cards: AE, DC, D, MC, V.
Reservations: No.
Handicapped Access: Limited; not to bathrooms.

Family owned and operated, Cantler's, reached via a twisting ride out of town, is the area's premier crab-picking spot. Located on scenic Mill Creek, it rakes in awards year after year. Have it your way: hot from the pot and laden with spices, as a soft-shell sandwich, mixed with seasoning and filler in a crab cake (sandwich or plat-ter), or stuffed in your favorite fish. Despite scanty harvests and escalating prices (up to $50 for a dozen large in 2004), visitors from all over the world hun-ker down with mallet and knife at these famed paper-covered tables, both indoors and out. Which explains the backup waiting to get into the parking lot. You'd think this place was a religious shrine. For many, it is. And, for the few who don't eat crabmeat, there's fresh fish, fried shrimp and chicken, light fare, even hamburgers and hot dogs. If you have kids in tow, walk down to the dock to see the peeler crabs and the diamondback terrapin and tortoise nurs-ery. Try to come on a weekday or at off times on weekends and holidays. For direc-tions, visit www.cantlers.com.

CARROL'S CREEK CAFÉ
410-263-8102.
410 Severn Ave., Annapolis City Marina.
Open: Daily.
Price: Moderate to very expensive.
Cuisine: Contemporary American.
Serving: L, D, SB.
Credit Cards: AE, DC, D, MC, V.

Reservations: Accepted Fri. night, Sat., and Sun.; Wed. in summer.
Handicapped Access: Yes.
Special Features: Waterside deck and view.

The blue-ribbon view of Spa Creek from Carrol's Creek just got better. As part of a recent renovation, the bar area shifted to a back dining room, opening up the dining-room views and expanding window tables from four to 15. We recommend you reserve one, then sit back and enjoy the treats this kitchen has been creating for years. While the main menu changes about every six months, the cream of crab soup remains legendary, and we can't fawn enough over a sea scallop starter. The scallops are rolled in shredded phyllo, fried, and served with wilted spinach, lump crab, and prosciutto—and are enough for a light meal. Fancy sandwiches join entrées on the lunch menu, while dinner features contemporary American takes on seafood, beef, and poultry. The lengthy wine list offers something for every budget, the outdoor deck offers primo sunset watching, and there's even parking for those who aren't strolling to Eastport across the Spa Creek Bridge from the Historic District. (You also can take the water taxi.)

CHICK & RUTH'S DELLY
410-269-6737.
165 Main St.
Open: Daily, except Thanksgiving and Dec. 25–31.
Price: Inexpensive.
Cuisine: American, kosher.
Serving: B, L, D.
Credit Cards: No.
Reservations: No.
Handicapped Access: Limited.

Check out the Formica decor and dip into the kosher pickles at this centrally located Annapolis institution where state politicians, locals, and out-of-towners all come to sample the diner food, reasonable prices, and ambience that hasn't changed a whit since Chick & Ruth's opened in 1965. "Comfort" is the operative word here, as in *comfort* food served in *comfort*able surroundings, replete with celebrity photos blanketing the walls. Fall into the delly for the breakfast platters, served all day, with delly fries. The peppery, onion-laden potatoes (actually home fries) are among the best we've ever tasted. Come here also for the homemade soups, hamburgers, and generous sandwiches named for state lawmakers. When in doubt, go for the No. 1, the Main Street—corned beef, coleslaw, and Russian dressing on rye. You'll need a bath when you finish, or at least a moist towelette. The soda fountain drinks are treats, the waitstaff is pleasant, and kid-size portions with appropriately adjusted prices are available for rugrats. You should be able to eat for less than $10. Expect a line on weekends, especially for breakfast, when locals join owner Ted Levitt in the Pledge of Allegiance at 9:30 AM; weekdays, make that 8:30.

DAVIS'S PUB
410-268-7432.
400 Chester Ave. (at Fourth St.), Eastport.
Open: Daily.
Price: Inexpensive to moderate.
Cuisine: Seafood, pub fare.
Serving: L, D.
Credit Cards: AE, MC, V.
Reservations: No.
Handicapped Access: Yes.

Davis's Pub is a quintessential neighborhood spot that feels welcoming even if you're not from the 'hood (in this case, Eastport). Those who live here and/or work in one of the many local maritime businesses keep the friendly waitstaff and bartenders hopping. We think the burgers are tops, and the crispy seasoned fries are positively habit forming. The crab cakes are zesty and reasonably priced, if a tad overseasoned for some tastes. You can't go wrong with a crab cake sandwich or a platter of two with fries and coleslaw. Order a steak for less than half what you'd shell out at pricey steak houses elsewhere. Really hungry? Have the steak and (crab) cake combo platter. Fall into the old reliable Davis's anytime you're in Eastport and want a quick, tasty, reasonably priced meal served up in a no-frills setting. Sidewalk tables are available, weather permitting.

GALWAY BAY IRISH RESTAURANT AND PUB
410-263-8333.
61-63 Maryland Ave.
Open: Daily.
Price: Moderate to expensive.
Cuisine: Authentic Irish.
Serving: L, D, SB.
Credit Cards: AE, DC, D, MC, V.
Reservations: Recommended on weekends.
Handicapped Access: Yes.

This is no prefabricated, faux-Irish eatery concocted to capitalize on Celtic chic. Owner-manager Michael Galway is an émigré from Erin's lovely shore, and his restaurant has garnered both regional awards and a devoted following. Its popularity can be attributed both to atmosphere and to cuisine. The feeling is inviting and evocative: exposed brick walls, a high ceiling, vintage Irish art, and soft strains of Irish music. The menu sports a handsome array of Hibernian fare, both no-frills and fancy. Starters include Oysters O'Reilly (a flavorful way to enjoy a regional favorite), cockles and mussels, and charbroiled lamb tenderloin marinated in Guinness Stout. The potato and leek soup is therapeutic, and the soda bread is homemade from coarse whole-meal flour imported from Ireland. Entrées feature Irish favorites—corned beef and cabbage, shepherd's pie, Irish stew, fish and chips—that are prepared here in expert fashion. Higher-end

offerings include Chicken Breast Cashel Blue, Pork Tenderloin Armagh, Jerpoint Oatmeal Trout, and Steak Tullach Mor. For lighter appetites, the salads are lovely. And in September, look for a huge discounted portion of corned beef and cabbage because, after all, it's halfway to St. Patrick's Day.

HARRY BROWNE'S
410-263-4332.
66 State Circle.
Open: Daily.
Price: Expensive to very expensive.
Cuisine: New American.
Serving: L, D, SB.
Credit Cards: AE, DC, D, MC, V.
Reservations: Recommended.
Handicapped Access: Yes.
Special Features: View of Statehouse; outdoor dining (at sidewalk tables).

For a fine-dining experience, it doesn't get much better than Harry Browne's. The ambience is intimate and sophisticated, the service attentive and unobtrusive. When making a reservation, request a window table for a picture-postcard view of the Maryland Statehouse. Bathed in moonlight, it's something to write home about. The clubby Grill Room is open Thurs. through Sun. evenings and features Tuscan cuisine. The main menu changes seasonally, and the kitchen seldom, if ever, takes shortcuts. We like to start with the baked oysters Annapolitan (topped with, what else, crabmeat), Caesar or mixed green salad, or cream of crab soup. Fresh fish and seafood shine here, as do the beef, duck, and lamb. Entrées are between $23 and $29. If you have room, try the rum raisin bread pudding, bananas Foster, crème brûlée, or homemade ice cream. Lunch is memorable, with a host of reasonably priced soups, salads, sandwiches, and hot entrées. Sunday, line up for the brunch buffet ($14.95) or choose from the à la carte menu ($8–$14).

Annapolis's City Dock area is busy with boats, visitors, restaurants, and shops. Patrick Soran

Both include a glass of champagne or wine or a mimosa.

JOSS CAFÉ & SUSHI BAR
410-263-4688.
195 Main St.
Open: Daily.
Price: Inexpensive to very expensive.
Cuisine: Japanese.
Serving: L, D.
Credit Cards: AE, MC, V.
Reservations: No.
Handicapped Access: Yes.

This is the granddaddy of Annapolis sushi restaurants and never disappoints. Two intimate dining rooms add to a social atmosphere that starts upon entering, when the sushi chefs behind the bar shout out "Iras-shai," Japanese for "welcome." Tuck into a corner table and start with a terrific sesame-tinged seaweed salad. Follow with any type of sushi you can imagine; our household favorite is the rainbow roll with salmon, tuna, and flounder topping avocado, all rolled in roe. Japanese-food lovers also will find tempuras, teriyakis, sukiyaki, and other traditional favorites on the menu. A tip for the dinner crowd: get there at 5:30, because a line is likely to spill from the tiny waiting vestibule onto the street as the evening progresses.

LES FOLIES BRASSERIE
410-573-0970.
2552 Riva Rd.
Open: Daily.
Price: Expensive to very expensive.
Cuisine: Regional French.
Serving: L, D (Sat. and Sun. D only).
Credit Cards: AE, D, MC, V.
Reservations: Strongly recommended, especially on weekends.
Handicapped Access: Yes.

Don't let the institutional exterior put you off. Inside Les Folies, a 10-minute drive from City Dock, you'll find earth-tone stucco walls and slate floors, fresh flowers, and Muccha's French posters. The setting and staff encourage leisurely dining, thank heavens, since the food here is well worth savoring. At a recent dinner, our table encountered both authentic kir royale and marvelous escargot. The extensive menu includes French iterations of such entrées as ahi tuna, crab cakes, seafood, poultry, and beef. Dessert soufflés are well worth a try, the raw bar is extensive, and the level of service is high. Co-owners Alain Matrat and Jean-Claude Galan both have years in the business. Matrat once ran the front of the house at fabled Michel Richard's Citronelle in Washington, D.C., and Galan formerly was chef at the notable Mansion on Turtle Creek in Dallas.

LEWNES' STEAKHOUSE
410-263-1617.
401 Fourth St.
Open: Daily.
Price: Expensive to very expensive.
Cuisine: Steak house.
Serving: D.
Credit Cards: AE, DC, MC, V.
Reservations: Strongly recommended.
Handicapped Access: Yes.

Lewnes' has the look of a New York or Chicago steak house: spare and clubby. We go for the fork-tender prime-aged steaks and generous sides of salad, potatoes, and vegetables. Arrive with an appetite and full wallet. Entrées are $16.95 (grilled double breast of chicken) to $32.95 (porterhouse steak). Leave your caloric cheat sheet and cholesterol counter at home. The beef is cooked to perfection and served with a bit of melted butter. At your request, the kitchen will forgo the butter or add more. Trust us, it adds to the flavor. The salads serve two unless your appetite equals Henry VIII's. We favor the mashed or hash brown potatoes and sautéed mushrooms with a New York strip, leaving with half the meat

for a midnight snack or lunch the next day. Nearby on-street parking is usually scarce, so if you're up to it, park in the Historic District and enjoy the 10- to 15-minute walk. Go over the Spa Creek Bridge, turn left at Severn Avenue, and continue two blocks to Fourth Street. The after-dinner walk aids digestion—so maybe you'll have room for ice cream.

MCGARVEY'S SALOON & OYSTER BAR
410-263-5700.
8 Market Space.
Open: Daily except Thanksgiving day (open that night) and Christmas.
Price: Inexpensive to expensive.
Cuisine: American, seafood, pub fare.
Serving: L, D, SB.
Credit Cards: AE, MC, V.
Reservations: Not accepted on weekends or holidays.
Handicapped Access: No.

Longtime Annapolis favorite McGarvey's offers polished wood, brass, and Tiffany-style lamps that create a welcoming atmosphere in the usually packed and noisy bar area. We prefer the less frenetic, natural-light-filled back room. Start with half a dozen oysters, steamed clams, or spiced shrimp from the raw bar. Pub fare shines here; it includes smoked bluefish appetizer served with horseradish cream sauce, bread, and crackers; a smoked turkey Reuben; open-faced filet with béarnaise sauce; soft-shell crab sandwich with coleslaw and fries; good hamburgers; and Caesar salad topped with Nova Scotia salmon. Kick back with an Aviator, the house lager, or Old Hydraulic root beer. (Owner Mike Ashford's passion for biplanes creates the connection between airplanes and beverages.) At dinner, we usually find the beef and fish entrées reasonably priced. Comfort food—meat loaf, turkey, and the like—star on the nightly dinner specials. Service is friendly and reliable. Eat at off times on weekends or plan to wait.

MIDDLETON TAVERN

410-263-3323.
2 Market Space.
Open: Daily.
Price: Inexpensive to very expensive.
Cuisine: Seafood, American, tavern fare.
Serving: L, D, weekend B.
Credit Cards: AE, D, MC, V.
Reservations: No, but offers "priority seating" for those who call ahead.
Handicapped Access: No.

Located at City Dock, barn-red Middleton Tavern lays authentic claim to tavernhood dating to 1740. Ye olde place houses cozy wallpapered dining rooms suitable for ladies' luncheons in front and a back bar known for its 99-cent "oyster shooters," in which you drown an oyster in cocktail sauce and chase it with beer. In tone, the menu ranges as widely as the dining areas. Order Thai- and Szechuan-touched side veggies, Italian pastas, soups (Cuban black bean—big thumbs-up), or steaks and smoked bluefish. Pay $10–$11 for a hefty sandwich with chips or fries, or $32.95 for a crab-stuffed rockfish (by special order only). Try the pan-seared rockfish with crabmeat and mushrooms on top served on a bed of mixed greens for $27.95. Over the years, we've tended to come here for lunch or late-night meals, or on Sunday, when they serve the breakfast menu until 2 PM. The wide front porch, a great people-watching spot, is almost as much a city landmark as the Naval Academy chapel dome.

NORTHWOODS

410-268-2609.
609 Melvin Ave.
Open: Daily.
Price: Expensive to very expensive.
Cuisine: Continental.
Serving: D.
Credit Cards: AE, D, MC, V.
Reservations: Recommended.
Handicapped Access: No.

Well past age 20, Northwoods continues to reap culinary kudos and a loyal local following, serving fine food via wonderful service in a subdued dining room. You can't do better than the prix fixe, four-course dinner, available any night but Saturday. Choose appetizer, salad, entrée, and dessert from the entire menu, all for a mere $32.95. Appetizers recall trips to Europe and include gambas ajillo (shrimp sautéed in garlic, red pepper, olive oil, and lemon). For an entrée, bite into a rare tuna steak with its lemony relish of hearts of palm, artichoke hearts, and shrimp or a king salmon grill topped with tarragon-orange beurre blanc. The wine list is well considered; the dessert cart will make your eyes pop. Owners Leslie and Russell Brown (he is the executive chef) have their restaurant details down delightfully pat—duly noted with an award of excellence from DiRoNA, the Distinguished Restaurants of North America. If you need one more excuse to visit, we'll give you two: lot parking is easy, and the restaurant has easy access to US 50's Rowe Blvd. exit.

O'LEARYS

410-263-0884.
310 Third St.
Open: Daily.
Price: Expensive to very expensive.
Cuisine: Seafood, nouveau.
Serving: D.
Credit Cards: AE, DC, MC, V.
Reservations: Yes.
Handicapped Access: Yes.

One of the best restaurants in town, O'Learys is unbeatable for its seafood. The spare dining room lets the food take center stage, although it's always fun to gaze at the black-and-white Annapolis maritime photos lining the mustard yellow walls. The restaurant's signature is six types of fish done in your choice of one of six different ways. That means your red snapper or tuna could be grilled with capers, olive oil, and lemon and served with warm orzo salad and broccolini, or it could be lightly blackened and served with Creole crème, black beans, and rice alongside broccolini. The lengthy menu also promises creative executions of shrimp, crab, filet mignon, or herb-encrusted lamb chops. Look for seasonal changes, such as the addition of Muscovy duck come fall. All you need now is a nice glass of wine, chosen from the long and well-considered list. Located in the Eastport maritime district, the restaurant resides in the former home of a waterman who ran a fish market on the property. Seafood-loving visitors to Annapolis would be remiss if they didn't finagle a reservation at this popular establishment, noticed by regional reviewers from the *Washington Post* to *Baltimore* magazine.

PICCOLA ROMA

410-268-7898.
200 Main St.
Open: Daily.
Price: Moderate to very expensive.
Cuisine: Italian regional.
Serving: L (Mon. through Fri.), D daily.
Credit Cards: AE, CB, DC, D, MC, V.
Reservations: Highly recommended on weekends.
Handicapped Access: No.

This upper Main Street institution, owned and operated since the late 1990s by Silvana Recine and husband Arturo Silvestrini, has been drawing devotees for years. Silvana brought with her many years in the business, including work at notable restaurants in Washington, D.C., and nearby Tyson's Corner, Va. She handles the menu, showing the kitchen the way around regional Italian dishes. A variety of pastas and insaladas (excellent for lunch) are featured, as well as seconds such as fancy scampi and scaloppini. The former, for instance, features jumbo black tiger shrimp

sautéed in an almond-flour crust, served with yellow and red peppers sautéed with onions, basil, and olive oil infused with red pepper. The sautéed veal scaloppini is done with roasted lemons, capers, butter, and lemon sauce and served with roasted potatoes with garlic and rosemary and peas sautéed with pancetta. The food takes center stage in a white-tablecloth dining room with wide windows onto Main Street, complete with a local corner power table that fills up at lunch.

RAMS HEAD TAVERN (AND FORDHAM BREWERY)

410-268-4545.
33 West St.
Open: Daily; closed Christmas Day and early on Christmas Eve.
Price: Inexpensive to expensive.
Cuisine: American, pub fare.
Serving: L, D, SB.
Credit Cards: AE, D, MC, V.
Reservations: Recommended.
Handicapped Access: Yes.
Special Features: Outdoor dining, on-site performance space.

Locals remember back when the Rams Head was a basement hole-in-the-wall where Naval Academy midshipmen and locals packed the closet-size brickskeller to munch burgers and drink their way through 300-plus brands of beer. My, how times have changed. After several expansions, the Rams Head couldn't be more happening. Depending on their mood and the weather, diners can opt for the cozy, paneled Tea Room, the dining room (with mostly booths), the bustling bar area, or, weather permitting, the New Orleans–style patio. The food is hearty and eclectic. Hamburgers, sandwiches, soups, salads (try the Greek or Caesar topped with chicken), and seafood dishes anchor the menu. The award-winning chili is just what the doctor ordered on a nippy day or night. With close

Whether at a restaurant on the water or an event outside town, crab feasts are Chesapeake rites of summer.
Middleton Evans

to a dozen entrées priced around $10, Sunday brunch is a steal, especially when enjoyed in the brick courtyard. Under the same roof, the Fordham Brewery turns out better-than-average microbrews. See the "Nightlife" section later in this chapter for details about performances in the adjacent performance space. The staff is generally attentive, enthusiastic, and personable. No wonder repeat patrons pack the Rams Head.

RIORDAN'S
410-263-5449.
26 Market Space.
Open: Daily.
Price: Inexpensive to expensive.
Cuisine: Seafood, American, pub fare.
Serving: L, D, SB.
Credit Cards: AE, D, MC, V.
Reservations: Fri. and Sat. for upstairs dining room only.
Handicapped Access: Limited.

Belly up to the bar at this popular saloon along City Dock. If you're waiting for a table, enjoy a frosty mug; the pub purveys more than 30 beers. The wood bar, brass accents, and Naval Academy and sports memorabilia create a casual ambience that nurtures the spirit as well as the stomach. Start with the loaded potato skins, hot crab dip (a meal in itself), or a raw bar offering. Burgers and oversize sandwiches with steak-cut fries are available at lunch and dinner. Heartier appetites applaud the baby-back ribs, grilled fish, and pasta entrées. Sunday brunch is an Annapolis tradition. Arrive early or plan on a wait. Most entrées are $8–$11 and include a mimosa or glass of champagne. The child's brunch is $6.95. Service is consistent and efficient at Annapolis's answer to Cheers.

TSUNAMI
410-990-9868.
51 West St.
Open: Daily.

Price: Moderate to very expensive.
Cuisine: Asian fusion.
Serving: L, D.
Credit Cards: AE, MC, V.
Reservations: Recommended.
Handicapped Access: Yes.
Special Features: Sushi bar open until 1 AM; lounge open until 2 AM.

Looking for fast-forward fare? Try Tsunami, which brought the Asian-fusion trend to Annapolis. It remains more or less the most visibly hip place in town, with spare decor anchored by royal blue walls, top-notch food, and affable service. Fusion fare includes a nod to the Chesapeake in the form of crab cakes served with citrus-wasabi aioli. More likely, however, are generally Asian touches added to crispy whole fish or a pepper tenderloin. The sushi menu covers the nigiri-hosomaki-sashimi universe. This is also a late-night gathering spot; think martinis, and don't be surprised if a crowd has gathered well into a weekend night.

WILD ORCHID CAFÉ
410-268-8009.
909 Bay Ridge Ave.
Open: Tues. through Sun.
Price: Expensive to very expensive.
Cuisine: American.
Serving: L, D, SB.
Credit Cards: AE, DC, D, MC, V.
Reservations: Recommended, especially for dinner.
Handicapped Access: Limited.
Special Features: Garden patio; Sunday tea.

With its squash yellow walls, polished wood floors, and green tabletops, the Wild Orchid is an inviting, country-inn-style bungalow located less than 2 miles from City Dock. At lunch, locals, business types, and out-of-towners fill the dining rooms (one large, one small) and patio. Pique your appetite with the butternut squash–crab soup, a delectable variation on standard cream of crab. Half a dozen salads—all with eye and taste appeal—several sandwiches, and a handful of hot entrées are priced between $4 (cup of soup) and $12 (backfin crab-cake sandwich). The $37 fixed-price dinner includes bread with spinach/mushroom/leek spread, soup, salad, any entrée on the menu (seafood, beef, fowl, fish, or vegetarian), and any dessert. Speaking of desserts, try Chocolate Decadence, a flourless chocolate cake more like fudge. Sunday brunch is served from 9 to 3, followed by tea from 3 to 5 (reservations required). Service is prompt and friendly yet courteous. A side note: We appreciate the Wild Orchid's staff addressing us as Ma'am and Sir, not "you guys." We hope other restaurants take note.

Deale
HAPPY HARBOR INN
410-867-0949 or 301-261-5297.
533 Deale Rd.
Open: Daily.
Price: Inexpensive to expensive.
Cuisine: Seafood.
Serving: B, L, D.
Credit Cards: D, MC, V.
Reservations: No.
Handicapped Access: Yes.

Watching the charter boats come in to their slips on Rockhold Creek just outside the wide glass patio of Happy Harbor is half the fun of eating here. The catch of the day is held high, and witnesses from the dining room can respond by digging in to their own seafood bacchanal: the oysters, crabs, or fish that reliably arrive here in-season. On Tuesday nights from April through October, enjoy the seafood buffet's steamed shrimp or crab legs. Open year-round, Happy Harbor is one of those places that makes for a good escape. (Note: The restaurant doesn't serve hard-shell crabs.)

SKIPPER'S PIER

410-867-7110.
6158 Drum Point Rd.
Open: Tues. through Sun.
Price: Moderate.
Cuisine: Seafood, crab deck.
Serving: L, D.
Credit Cards: AE, DC, D, MC, V.
Reservations: For parties of 10 or more.
Handicapped Access: Yes.

Skipper's is one of the best waterside crab-pickin' spots around. A recent renovation has given the outdoor deck a more permanent covered patio area, but it's still open to the water. The hard-shell crabs here are regularly excellent, but the menu also includes other seafood, steak, chicken, burgers, and fries. Get here in the late afternoon and you should have no trouble getting a small picnic table right along the water. If rain threatens, grab a table in the covered porch area. The dock bar, Barnacles, can get loud some weekends, but it provides a great rooftop deck for stargazing. One July Fourth we even found ourselves witnessing one of the small-town fireworks displays up the river. For directions, visit www.skipperspier.com.

RIVA

MIKE'S RESTAURANT & CRAB HOUSE

410-956-2784.
3030 Old Riva Rd.
Open: Daily.

Price: Moderate to very expensive.
Cuisine: Seafood.
Serving: L, D.
Credit Cards: AE, MC, V.
Reservations: For large parties only.
Handicapped Access: Yes.
Special Features: Outdoor waterside deck and tiki bar; dockage.

We like Mike's and have for years. Located on the outskirts of town, it's an easy place to meet friends coming from out of town without having to explain how to navigate Annapolis's sometimes confusing Historic District. It also comes with parking, overlooks the South River, and serves great hard-shell crabs and big seafood platters. It's a lively scene on the outdoor deck in midsummer. Even into Oct., the deck stays open if the weather is good. Boats dock alongside, mallards paddle in, and, with everybody cracking crabs, it's the consummate Chesapeake scene in full glory. The cavernous indoor dining room is as full as the parking lot during summer crab season, but if you come early, during the week, or in the off-season, you should have no problems. The menu's steak and rib entrées should make the beef eaters happy, and a fresh but utilitarian salad bar is offered alongside the bar, where bands gather and folks boogie on the small dance floor. A popular place.

FOOD PURVEYORS

Sitting down for a fine meal is no problem in Annapolis and environs, but sometimes you're on the run. Here are some local food purveyors who'll do right by you. Stop in for ice cream or pick through the world's best sweet corn before heading to the seafood market for hard-shell crabs.

Coffee Bars, Cafés, and Delis

Café Guru's (410-295-0601, 601 Second St., Eastport) Ready for a long walk and a break from the tourist life? Ensconced in a far corner of the down-home but yachty Eastport district, Guru's offers good coffees, sandwiches, and fruity, nutritious elixirs. Opens at 7 AM for breakfast. The kids' menu has four items, $2.25–$3.25. Sunday morning performances by local musicians.

City Dock Café (410-269-0969; 18 Market Space) Bright, clean, and often packed. A variety of coffees, sandwiches, fat cookies, and pastries. Front windows and sidewalk tables offer a fine view of City Dock. Open Sun. through Thurs. 6:30 AM–10 PM, Fri. and Sat. 6:30 AM–midnight. A second location at 71 Maryland Ave., 410-263-9747, is open Mon. through Sat. 6:30–6:30 and Sun. 8 AM–6:30 PM.

Giolliti Delicatessen (410-266-8600; 2068 Somerville Rd.) A bit outside of the usual tourist loop, but well worth knowing about. Excellent Italian food available for takeout or lunchtime eat-in; good selection of wines, cheeses, desserts, and other tasty Italian delights.

Farmer's Markets
Anne Arundel County Farmer's Market (Harry S. Truman Pkwy., Riva) This popular market operates on weekends with a wide variety of produce and goods. For information, contact the Annapolis and Anne Arundel County Conference and Visitors Bureau at 410-280-0445.

Pennsylvania Dutch Farmer's Market (410-573-0770; 2472 Solomons Island Rd., Annapolis Harbour Center) Stalls filled with everything from subs to fresh produce and meat and top-quality baked goods. Amish quilts, furniture, and on-site restaurant. Open Thurs. through Sat.

Ice Cream
Annapolis Ice Cream Company (410-482-3895; 196 Main St.) New in the neighborhood, serving delectable ice cream.

Ben & Jerry's (410-268-6700; 139 Main St.) Within sight of City Dock.

Storm Brothers Ice Cream Factory (410-263-3376; 130 Dock St.) Longtime resident of the City Dock area; serves 45 flavors of ice cream, also shakes, sundaes, and four types of sherbet. Very limited seating. Open 10:30 AM–11 PM in summer (midnight on weekends); closes one hour earlier in winter.

Natural/Whole Foods
Sun and Earth Natural Foods (410-266-6862; 1933 West St.) Beloved old health and whole foods shop stocks all of the necessities, including Green Goddess sandwiches. Open Mon. through Sat. 9:30–6:30, Sun. noon–4.

Whole Foods (410-573-1800; 2504 Solomons Island Rd., Annapolis Harbour Center) Not that this whole foods giant needs a plug from us, but the locals fill the aisles here. Favorites: focaccia topped pizza-style with artichokes; Coleman's antibiotic-free beef; Arctic char; great buffalo mozzarella. Good takeout if you're off for a day on the Bay or too tired to cook. Open Mon. through Sat. 8–10, Sun. 8–9 (year-round).

Seafood Markets
Annapolis Seafood Market (410-269-5380; Forest Dr. and Tyler Ave.) Longtime popular seafood market, beautifully organized from in-season sweet corn to the line at the crab and spiced-shrimp counter to the excellent takeout sandwiches for folks on the go (the shrimp salad takes only a minute). All kinds of good and fresh seafood. Other locations include the

Park Plaza shopping center on Ritchie Highway (MD 2) in Severna Park, 3105 Solomons Island Rd. (MD 2) in Edgewater, and Route 301 in Waldorf.

CULTURE

Cinema

Crown Theaters operates Annapolis's two commercial movie houses: **Crown Harbour 9 & Art House** (410-224-1145; 2474 Solomons Island Rd.), which devotes two screens to foreign/art house films, and **Crown Annapolis Mall 11** (410-224-1145; Westfield Shoppingtown Annapolis), showing first-run fare.

Galleries

The visual arts scene in Annapolis revolves around the Historic District's commercial galleries. Watercolors of local scenes and marine prints are more likely to hang than cutting-edge abstracts, although interesting work can be found at these galleries.

ELIZABETH MYERS MITCHELL ART

410-626-2556.
Mellon Hall (attached to the Francis Scott Key auditorium lobby), St. John's College, 60 College Ave.
Open: Tues. through Sun. noon–5, Fri. 7–8 during school year; hours may vary in summer.

Your best chance in Annapolis to see major works by major artists. Visiting shows often are curated elsewhere by groups like the Smithsonian Institution's Traveling Exhibition Service or the American Federation of Art in New York. Recent shows have spotlighted Milton Avery and Louise Nevelson. Lectures, gallery talks, and group tours are held in conjunction with exhibitions. Check www.sjca.edu ("Campus Resources") for schedules.

MARYLAND FEDERATION OF ART CIRCLE GALLERY

410-268-4566.
www.mdfedart.org.
18 State Circle.
Open: Tues. through Sun. 11–5.

Originally built in the mid-1800s as a storage loft for the Jones and Franklin General Store, the building's exposed brick walls serve as backdrop for changing shows, which include paintings, sculpture, wearable art, and photographs by the nearly 400-member roster. Two rooms host monthly exhibitions, which often feature small group shows. A good place to look for a well-priced piece from an unknown. If you're in Baltimore, stop by the MFA's City Gallery (410-685-0300; 330 N. Charles St.).

Historic Buildings, Memorials, and Sites

Visitors interested in the city's history will want to check in with the **Historic Annapolis Foundation** (410-267-7619 or 1-800-603-4020; www.annapolis.org; 18 Pinkney St.), which for more than 50 years has worked to preserve and restore the city's architectural and historic treasures. The foundation operates historic sites, including its flagship William Paca House and Garden described below, as well as the Barracks, the Shiplap

House, the Waterfront Warehouse, and the old Customs House, which now serves as the museum store. The foundation also operates the Archaeology in Annapolis program, in conjunction with the University of Maryland's Department of Anthropology, unearthing numerous treasures and offering the public a chance to participate. As you walk the city's streets, you'll notice historic markers indicating the age of the houses, from green for "17th-century vernacular" (1681–1708) to ochre for "20th-century distinctive" (1901–1938). The eight designations include solid bronze for Georgian Buildings of National Importance.

ANNAPOLIS

CHARLES CARROLL HOUSE OF ANNAPOLIS
For tours, 410-268-0735.
107 Duke of Gloucester St.
Open: Tours by appt. on Sat. 10–2 and Sun. noon–2 from May–Oct.
Handicapped Access: Yes.

Four Marylanders signed the Declaration of Independence; all of them, at least for a time, owned homes in Annapolis. This was the birthplace and boyhood home of Charles Carroll of Carrollton, the only Roman Catholic to sign the Declaration. Located on the grounds of St. Mary's Church, his home housed a chapel in which Catholics worshiped during the mid-18th century, when the religion was forced underground. Archaeological digs in the formal gardens have turned up artifacts, likely from a tavern that once operated on the property. Construction of the original family house began in 1721; later additions included another story, an A-frame room, and a three-story wing in 1770.

CHASE-LLOYD HOUSE
410-263-2723.
22 Maryland Ave.
Open: Mar. through Dec., Tues. through Sat. 2–4.
Admission: $2; children 8 and under free.

Samuel Chase, yet another Annapolitan to sign the Declaration of Independence, started this house in 1769, before he became one of the new nation's first Supreme Court justices. Later, he sold the home, unfinished, to Edward Lloyd IV, member of a prominent Maryland political dynasty. The brick mansion is most noted for the spectacular "flying" stairway, which has no visible means of support.

GOVERNMENT HOUSE
410-974-3531.
State and Church Circles.
Open: By appt. only.

The official residence of Maryland's governors is an 1870 Georgian-style mansion, filled with Maryland arts and antiques.

HAMMOND-HARWOOD HOUSE
410-263-4683.
19 Maryland Ave.

Open: Apr. through Oct., Tues. through Sun. 10–5, last tour at 4; Nov. through Mar., closed except for group tours.
Admission: Adults $6, children $3.

Widely considered one of the nation's finest remaining examples of Georgian architecture, this 1770s center-block house, preserved as a museum since 1926, boasts two wings connected by two hyphens, a style known as a five-point Maryland house (a Palladian varietal that turned up only in colonial Maryland). The symmetry is meticulous: false doors balance actual entrances. Inside hang portraits by onetime Annapolitan Charles Willson Peale and furniture by noted Annapolis coffin- and cabinetmaker John Shaw. Intricately carved ribbons and roses mark the front entrance. Gift shop and exhibitions.

MARYLAND STATEHOUSE
410-974-3400.
www.mdarchives.state.md.us.
State Circle.
Open: Mon. through Fri. 9–5, Sat. and Sun. 10–4; tours at 11 and 3, except on Thanksgiving, Christmas, and New Year's.
Handicapped access: Yes.

The first statehouse was built on this hill in 1699; the current building is the third. Fire, the scourge of so many colonial-era buildings, destroyed the first building, which was replaced in 1705. The second lasted until 1766, when the government decided to build a more architecturally distinguished capitol building. Marylanders now boast that theirs is the country's oldest state capitol building in continuous use. From Nov. 26, 1783, to Aug. 13, 1784, the building served as the capitol to a new nation. The Old Senate Chamber where George Washington resigned his commission in the Continental Army in 1783 remains. And the Treaty of Paris, which officially ended the Revolutionary War, was ratified here in 1784. You can also see here Charles Willson Peale's portrait of Washington with Marylander Tench Tilghman and the Marquis de Lafayette at Yorktown. The General Assembly convenes here for the annual 90-day legislative session from winter into spring, and a visitor's center in the first-floor lobby offers abundant state travel information. Security measures mean you'll need a photo ID to enter and will have to pass through a metal detector.

ST. ANNE'S EPISCOPAL CHURCH
410-267-9333.
www.stannes-annapolis.org.
Church Circle (Parish House, 199 Duke of Gloucester St.).
Open: Tours by appt.

This is the third church built on this hallowed Annapolis site. Fire destroyed much of the second (1792–1858), but parts of the old building were incorporated when the new church went up in 1859. Many graves in the old churchyard were moved when Church Circle was widened years ago, but the graves of Annapolis's first mayor, Amos Garret, and Maryland's last colonial governor, Sir Robert Eden, remain. Inside is a silver communion service given by King William III and dating from the 1690s. A concert series presented by the church and the Annapolis Chorale is held here during the winter, with performances by the chorale as well as regional notables such as the Kennedy Center Chamber Players.

WILLIAM PACA HOUSE AND GARDEN
410-263-5553.
www.annapolis.org.
186 Prince George St.
Open: Late Mar. through early Jan., Mon. through Sat. 10–5 (tours begin at 10:30 AM and every half hour thereafter) and Sun. noon–5; early Jan. through late Mar., Fri. and Sat. 10–5 and Sun. noon–5.
Admission: Adults $5 house/$5 gardens, $8 combo; seniors $4 each, $7 combo; children 6–17 $3 each, $5 combo; children 5 and under free.

William Paca, three-time colonial governor of Maryland and signer of the Declaration of Independence, built his magnificent Georgian mansion between 1763 and 1765. Here he entertained during the era known as Annapolis's golden age. During meticulous renovations in the 1960s and 1970s, X-rays revealed that two architectural styles found in the main staircase dated to the same era, a mixing and matching apparently chosen by Mr. Paca himself. First-floor antiques date to Paca's residency; the second floor is decorated to reflect the Paca era. In 1965, high-rise apartments were slated to replace the building, which was a hotel at the time. The Historic Annapolis Foundation bought the house and, in six weeks' time, convinced the Maryland General Assembly to buy the 2-acre garden site in back. Archaeologists set about reconstructing the gardens and knew that they had hit pay dirt when they uncovered an original pond—it promptly refilled from a spring beneath. A must-see for any gardener, the formal, terraced Paca Gardens boast a reconstructed pavilion and Chinese-style bridge and create a favorite respite in the middle of town. Watch for a variety of special events, from music to special plant sales. Recorded tours available. The Historic Annapolis Foundation, which owns the Paca House, also operates other historic buildings around town; call 410-267-7619 for information. Coupons for other local attractions are available with the purchase of a ticket here.

WORLD WAR II MEMORIAL
MD 450, north side of U.S. Naval Academy Bridge.
Open: Dawn to dusk.

Come here for a spectacular view of the U.S. Naval Academy, downtown Annapolis, and the juncture of Spa Creek and the Bay, and to pay your respects to the veterans of World War II.

EDGEWATER
LONDON TOWN AND GARDENS
410-222-1919.
www.historiclondontown.com.
839 Londontown Rd.(Take MD 2 south from Annapolis; 1 mile past the South River Bridge, turn left onto Mayo Rd. (MD 253); after 1 mile, turn left onto Londontown Rd.)
Open: Tues. through Sat. 10–3, Sun. noon–3; the William Brown House is closed for tours in Jan. and Feb. Gardens open Tues. through Sat. 10–3, weather permitting.
Tours: House and garden tours available on the hour; see website for details.
Admission: Guided house and garden tour $7 for adults, $5 for seniors; $4 for house or garden tour only; $3 for kids 7–12; free for kids under 7.

Cross the South River Bridge to visit this 18th-century Georgian tavern on the riverbank, site of a once-booming town. In addition to 8 acres of marvelous gardens and an ongoing archaeological dig, visitors will find the house-turned-tavern built by William Brown in 1764. Traveling colonial-era men of limited means once shared beds upstairs; traveling gentleman professionals—an itinerant dentist, for example —had their own rooms while they stayed in town to do business.

Historic Schools
ST. JOHN'S COLLEGE
410-263-2371; for events, 410-626-2539.
www.sjca.edu.
60 College Ave.

"Johnnies," as students at St. John's College are called, study only the Great Books during their years here, where intellect is greatly valued and humor tends toward plays on Greek or Latin phrases. The college, descended from King William's School in 1696, claims to be the nation's third oldest. The oldest building on campus, McDowell Hall, houses the venerable Great Hall, where a banquet was tossed for the aging General Lafayette in 1824 and a hospital was set up during the Civil War. The 1934 Maryland Archives building now houses the college library. Visitors interested in the school's history should join a tour by an organized tour group (see the "Tours" section later in this chapter).

UNITED STATES NAVAL ACADEMY
Armel-Leftwich Visitor Center.
410-263-6933; for athletic event ticket information, 1-800-US4-NAVY or www.navy-sports.com; for community relations/general public inquiries, 410-293-2293 or www.usna.edu.
www.navyonline.com.
52 King George St. (Enter the academy grounds at Gate 1, at the foot of King George St., then head to the Armel-Leftwich Visitor Center, next to Halsey Field House.)
Visitor Center Hours: Mar. through Dec. 9–5, Jan. and Feb. 9–4.
Tour Fees: Adults $7.50, seniors $6.50, students in first through 12th grade $5.50. Schedules change seasonally. Guided walking tours several times daily, except on Thanksgiving, Christmas, and New Year's Day. Security requires that everyone 16 and older must have a photo ID to enter the grounds; there is no visitor parking. See the website for details.

For many people around the world, "Annapolis" and "U.S. Naval Academy" are synonymous. Locals who know their city's rich heritage might beg to differ, but none would disagree that the U.S. Naval Academy has been—and remains—a great influence on the city. Founded in 1845 at old Fort Severn, the Academy's long history includes its notable move from Annapolis to Newport, R.I., during the Civil War, prompted by the Maryland city's overwhelming Southern sympathies. During the war, both the Academy and nearby St. John's College became military hospitals. Upon their return, naval officers found the campus in great need of military spit-shine. So commenced plans for a "new Academy," the collection of Beaux Arts buildings designed by architect Ernest Flagg that visitors now see, constructed between 1899 and 1908.

Beneath the Academy chapel, begun in 1904, is the final resting place of the "Father of the U.S. Navy," John Paul Jones, finally entombed in 1913 after a fantastic journey. He was buried in Paris in 1792, but his grave was lost in the turmoil of the French Revolution as the cemetery, owned by the House of Bourbon, was seized, sold by the Revolutionary government, and later developed. After a concerted search, Jones's tomb was rediscovered 100 years later. Following much politicking, it was determined that the admiral should be laid to rest in the Academy chapel—then still under construction. The casket arrived at the Academy in 1906 but spent seven somewhat ignominious years beneath the grand staircase leading to Memorial Hall from the giant dormitory Bancroft Hall. To see the spectacular marble sarcophagus, enter from the outside, beneath the chapel. The names of the seven ships that Jones commanded are inscribed in the floor encircling the tomb.

Lovers of ships and naval history should visit the **U.S. Naval Academy Museum** (410-293-2108; www.usna.edu; open Mon. through Sat. 9–5, Sun. 11–5; closed Thanksgiving, Christmas, New Year's Day). Collection highlights, which range from paintings to naval gear to ship's instruments, include the Beverley R. Robinson Collection of prints depicting naval battles and ships dating back to the 1600s, located in Halligan Hall. The Class of 1951 Gallery of Ships at the museum displays a wide range of fabulous ship models. Notable is the spectacular Henry H. Rogers Collection of more than 100 models, including some that are well over 300 years old. In addition, the museum shows "dockyard" models of ships built by order of the British Royal Navy and exquisite ships' cases dating to the Jacobean, William and Mary, and Queen Anne periods. And don't miss the world's largest collection of bone models, carved from leftovers of beef rations given French prisoners of war, generally from 1756 to 1815.

Exhibitions are also held at the Armel-Leftwich Visitor Center. Recent displays included historical naval flags and uniform traditions at the Academy.

Noon meal formations by the Brigade of Midshipmen at full military attention occur at Tecumseh Court most weekdays during the school year, weather permitting. There's plenty more, too. Call the visitor center or check www.navyonline.com for current information.

Libraries

Interested in learning more about the Chesapeake, or maybe your family's genealogical past? Visit the **Maryland State Archives** (410-260-6400; www.mdarchives.state.md.us; 350 Rowe Blvd.) to peruse thousands of different series of records, from vital statistics to church registers, including many from the Roman Catholic Archdiocese of Baltimore. Here author Alex Haley of *Roots* fame found his African ancestor, the slave Kunta Kinte, after the late historian and longtime archivist Phebe Jacobsen figured out how to use manumissions and other documents of slaveholders to help African Americans trace their pasts. Call or check the website for hours and registration information.

Museums
ANNAPOLIS MARITIME MUSEUM
410-295-0104.
www.annapolismaritimemuseum.org. Check for programs and events.

Plans are in the works to reconstruct the docks and the former McNasby Oyster Packing building that houses the museum, all damaged after Tropical Storm Isabel wreaked havoc on the site in 2003. Also in the works are plans to take visitors to Thomas Point Lighthouse.

BANNEKER-DOUGLASS MUSEUM
410-216-6180.
www.mdhousing.org.

The U.S. Naval Academy in Annapolis is known for its stunning Beaux Arts buildings. Patrick Soran

84 Franklin St.
Open: Tues. through Fri. 10–3, Sat. noon–4.
Admission: Donations welcome.

Victorian Mount Moriah African Methodist Episcopal Church, built in 1874, stands amid what was the Historic District's black neighborhood dating to the mid-19th century. Named for two prominent black Marylanders—Frederick Douglass, born in the Eastern Shore's Talbot County, and Benjamin Banneker, who helped survey Federal City, now Washington, D.C., in the 1790s—the museum celebrates Maryland's African American life. A significant expansion is slated for completion in 2005, doubling the gallery and office space and creating room for performance space. "Deep Roots, Rising Waters: A Celebration of African Americans in Maryland" will trace the history of African Americans—mostly from Annapolis and the Chesapeake region—from the 1630s through the Civil Rights era. In addition, an improved research center will result.

Nightlife

Nighttime around 'Naptown offers variety. Folks head for City Dock, where places that are quaint colonial taverns at lunchtime open their doors to the music and tourist scene at night. Summer weekends can be mobbed, but even locals try to slip in one night downtown to soak up the warm breezes off the water. **West Street**, up the hill from City Dock, is home to the area's best live music. And over the Spa Creek Bridge lies Eastport, a hotbed of sailors and some good places to grab a drink.

The hottest live music ticket is **Rams Head On Stage** (410-268-4545; 33 West St.), host to the biggest name bands coming through town, like Suzanne Vega, Roy Clark, and The Iguanas, and also part of the Rams Head Tavern, home to the Fordham Brewing Co. microbrewery. A couple of doors up stands **49 West Coffeehouse, Wine Bar and Gallery** (410-626-9796; 49 West St.), a European-style café with regular art openings and jazz or classical guitar music, as well as being a good place for a leisurely bite at lunch. Martinis? Try **Tsunami** (410-990-9868; 51 West St.).

A favorite cozy brick pub located downstairs at the Maryland Inn at the top of Main Street, the tiny **Drummer's Lot** (410-263-2641) is a terrific spot for a quiet drink. It's situated next to the **King of France Tavern** (410-216-6340), which features weekend jazz. For drinks on the water try the **Chart House** (410-268-7166; 300 Second St., Eastport). Big windows onto the water give a great view of Annapolis Harbor, and a recent renovation has the place looking spiffy. Also in Eastport are the indoor bar and waterside deck (spring through fall, weather permitting) at **Carrol's Creek Café** (410-263-8102; 410 Severn Ave.), with lots of local camaraderie. Back on the Historic District side of Spa Creek, try **Pusser's Landing** at the Annapolis Marriott Waterfront Hotel (410-268-7555; 80 Compromise St.), with its outdoor deck and terrific black-and-white lobby photos of old Annapolis by acclaimed local photographer Marion Warren.

Irish bars have their adherents and, often, music. They include **Sean Donlon's Irish Pub and Restaurant** (410-263-1993; 37 West St.), **Castlebay Irish Pub** (410-626-0165; 193 Main St.), and **Galway Bay** (410-263-8333; 61-63 Maryland Ave.).

Pubs ring City Dock, and many offer live music. **Armadillo's** (410-280-0228; 132 Dock St.) hosts bands and DJs. Just up the street, **Acme Bar and Grill** (410-280-6486; 163 Main St.) has live music Mon., Tues., and during Fri. happy hour and a DJ Wed. through Sat. **McGarvey's Saloon** (410-263-5700; 8 Market Space) brings an uptown saloon flavor, with mirror-backed, heavily polished, dark wood bars that are often crowded on weekends; it serves late. Nearby **Riordan's Saloon** (410-263-5449; 26 Market Space) is still claimed by the locals, who love the burgers, and it serves late, too. Also at City Dock are **Griffin's** (410-268-2576; 22-24 Market Space) and **O'Brien's Oyster Bar & Restaurant** (410-268-6288; 115 Main St.).

Performing Arts

ANNAPOLIS CHORALE
410-263-1906.
www.annapolischorale.org.
Maryland Hall for the Creative Arts, 801 Chase St.
Tickets: Adults $28, students $12; $35 for Christmas concert.

This ambitious 150-voice chorale, which has performed at Carnegie Hall, includes the smaller Chamber Chorus and the Annapolis Chamber Orchestra. Up to 10 performances each season at Maryland Hall and St. Anne's Church may range from Verdi's *Requiem* to Rogers and Hammerstein's *Carousel.* Sellouts are the ever popular annual "*Messiah* by Candlelight" at St. Anne's and a rousing Christmas concert.

ANNAPOLIS OPERA
410-267-8135.
www.annapolisopera.org.
Maryland Hall for the Creative Arts, 801 Chase St.
Tickets: $32.50–$60; $165 for subscription series (four events).

In addition to a major annual production such as *La Boheme* or *Madama Butterfly*, the opera company offers such delights as "Mozart by Candlelight" (dessert buffet follows) and "Pasta and Puccini." The opera also sponsors an annual vocal competition, and the finals are open to the public.

ANNAPOLIS SUMMER GARDEN THEATRE
410-268-9212.
www.summergarden.com.
143 Compromise St.
Season: Memorial Day through Labor Day.
Tickets: Adults $12, students, senior citizens, and large groups $10; no credit cards.

This blacksmith shop near City Dock dates from 1696 and may even have housed George Washington's horses out back—right where the audience sits today. Established in 1966, the theater offers musicals and comedies under the stars, with three productions per season from late May through July. Recent productions have included Shakespeare's *The Taming of the Shrew* and the award-winning musical *Gypsy*.

ANNAPOLIS SYMPHONY ORCHESTRA
For tickets, 410-263-0907; for administration, 410-269-1132.
www.annapolissymphony.org.
Maryland Hall for the Creative Arts, 801 Chase St.
Season: Sept. through May.

The Kunta Kinte Festival, held each August, celebrates Maryland's African-American heritage. Claude Brooks

Tickets: $25–$35; full-time students 21 and younger $10; family concerts (recommended for children 4 and older) $10 all seats.

Ambitious, multiconcert fall-spring seasons have included such performances as Brahms's *Symphony No. 2* and a Mozart clarinet concerto. Call early for tickets; the best go to subscribers. A holiday pops concert is held each December. Summer concerts are held outdoors; typical venues include Anne Arundel Community College in Arnold and Quiet Waters Park in Annapolis.

BALLET THEATRE OF MARYLAND
For tickets, 410-263-2909; for information, 410-263-8289.
www.balletmaryland.org.
Maryland Hall for the Creative Arts, 801 Chase St.
Season: Fall through spring.
Tickets: Adults $24, children $12; $1 handling fee.

Regional company with its own school and principal dancers. Four major performances each year at Maryland Hall generally include a modern production and updated classics. The annual *Nutcracker* is a holiday sellout (matinee tickets go first).

COLONIAL PLAYERS
410-268-7373.
www.cplayers.com.
108 East St.
Season: Fall through spring; shows are Thurs. through Sun., with some Sun. matinees.
Tickets: $15; $10 for seniors 65 and older and full-time students with ID.
Handicapped Access: Yes.

More than 50 years old and known for its breadth, theater-in-the-round, and well-priced tickets, Colonial Players does everything from comedies to modern classics, like *A Funny Thing Happened on the Way to the Forum*, A. R. Gurney's *Sylvia*, a recent *Proof* (winner of the 2001 Pulitzer and Tony), and an annual *Christmas Carol* that sells out early.

MARYLAND HALL FOR THE CREATIVE ARTS
410-263-5544.
www.mdhallarts.org.
801 Chase St.
Open: Check website for schedule.

The artistic and cultural hub of the city, Maryland Hall attracts a wide and diverse audience to performances by the Annapolis Chorale, Opera, and Symphony, as well as the Ballet Theatre of Maryland. All are housed in this former high school building that bustles with creative activity daily. Classes in the performing and visual arts for babies to seniors run the gamut, from creative movement to rumba lessons to photography and painting. Galleries with changing exhibitions by students, teachers, and professional artists (some of whom have studios here) and a café featuring author talks and poetry readings have helped put this Annapolis gem on the map.

NAVAL ACADEMY MUSICAL PERFORMANCES
For tickets, 410-293-TIXS; for information, 410-293-2439.
U.S. Naval Academy Music Department, Alumni Hall.
Prices: Range broadly; call ticket office for information.

From Glee Club concerts to world-class symphonies, the Naval Academy offers a broad variety of musical performances. Don't pass up a chance to hear an organ concert in the exquisite Academy Chapel, such as the Halloween concert by Juilliard-trained academy organist Monte Maxwell, replete with a laser light show. The annual *Messiah*, performed with the Hood College Choir and noted soloists, is a holiday favorite. In addition, the Women's Glee Club offers an annual Christmas concert. The Distinguished Artists Series brings in five productions a year by traveling groups such as the Russian State Symphony and the London City Opera, plus a choral concert by the academy's Glee Club and the Annapolis Symphony Orchestra. These are held in the Bob Hope Performing Arts Center in Alumni Hall. Also, the Glee Club is known for an annual winter musical such as *HMS Pinafore*. Call early; tickets are heavily subscribed with priority for the Brigade of Midshipmen. Also keep an eye out for concerts by the Academy's Gospel Choir. Check www.usna.edu/Music for schedules and information.

Summer Concerts
The **Annapolis Maritime Museum** presents a Summertime Lunchtime Maritime Concert Series at City Dock at noon Wed. from late June through mid-Sept. The series features artists with Chesapeake ties. For the schedule, check www.annapolismaritimemuseum.org or call 410-295-0104.

Quiet Waters Park, located out on the Annapolis peninsula about 3 miles from City Dock, at the entrance to the Hillsmere community, offers Sat. concerts from mid-June to early Sept., often featuring jazz, blues, and rock or groups such as the Annapolis Symphony Orchestra and the Annapolis Opera. Call 410-222-1777 for the schedule.

The **Summer Serenade Concert Series,** held at 7:30 PM most Tues. from the second week in July through the third week in Aug., features the U.S. Naval Academy Band and guest performers at City Dock. Bring a chair. Call 410-293-0263 or check www.usna.edu/USNABand for the schedule.

Seasonal Events and Festivals

A couple of easy rules: oysters in the "R" months and crabs all summer long. Keep an eye peeled for the many festivals, church suppers, and volunteer firemen's association events that include a chance to chow down on these Chesapeake delicacies. For current information about happenings, pick up a copy of *Maryland Celebrates,* an annual calendar of festivals and events, at area visitor's centers. Or contact the **Maryland Office of Tourism Development** (1-800-MDISFUN; www.mdisfun.org) or the **Annapolis and Anne Arundel County Conference and Visitors Bureau** (www.visit-annapolis.org).

If the thought of a gut-busting, all-you-can-eat seafood session leaves you salivating, move the **Annapolis Rotary Club Crabfeast** to the top of your summer must-do list. *National Geographic* has even covered this event. It's generally held the first Fri. of Aug. at the Navy–Marine Corps Memorial Stadium. For more information, check the website, www.annapolisrotary.com.

Thousands show up for the annual **Chesapeake Bay Bridge Walk,** held the first Sunday in May after the early morning **Governor's Bay Bridge Run,** which fills up far in advance. Shuttles take bridge walkers from the Navy–Marine Corps Memorial Stadium and other locations. For information, call 1-877-BAYSPAN. Whatever you do, don't plan a drive across the Bay that day. One span of the bridge is open, but you don't want to deal with the bottleneck.

Celebrate Maryland's African American history at the **Kunta Kinte Heritage Festival,** named for *Roots* author Alex Haley's African forebear who stepped off a slave ship at Annapolis City Dock. Regional entertainment includes dance troupes, steel drum bands, crafts, food, and more. The festival is held the second weekend in Aug. at the Anne Arundel County Fairgrounds west of Annapolis in Crownsville. For information, call 410-349-0338 or visit www.kuntakinte.org.

Held since 1975 at the private Roedown Farm southwest of Annapolis in Davidsonville, the early April **Marlborough Hunt Races** draw hundreds to watch the thoroughbred point-to-point timber race. For information, contact the Annapolis and Anne Arundel County Conference and Visitors Bureau (410-280-0445).

From its start on the weekend before Labor Day, 16th-century England is the order of nine consecutive weekends at the **Maryland Renaissance Festival,** held just west of Annapolis in Crownsville. You'll find bearded men wrestling in the mud, lovely ladies working the crowd and a roving band of jesters, crafters, jugglers, magicians, and minstrels may be seen. Admission fee. For information, call 410-266-7304 or visit www.rennfest.com.

The **Maryland Seafood Festival** (410-268-7682; www.mdseafoodfestival.com) features lots of different music and lots of seafood. Generally held the weekend after Labor Day at Sandy Point State Park near Annapolis. Kids' activities.

Every mariner for miles around attends Columbus Day weekend's **U.S. Sailboat Show** at Annapolis's City Dock. The very latest in sailboat designs, from racing to cruising vessels, is found in the water along with every imaginable service or sailing gimcrack. In-town parking will be a nightmare (try the shuttle from the Navy–Marine Corps Memorial

Stadium), but expect bargains, deals, and celebrations among the restaurants and bars. Admission fee. The following weekend, check out the **U.S. Powerboat Show** at the same location. Here's your chance to see the newest boats for work or play in the water, from yachts to inflatables. Admission fee. For information, call 410-268-8828 or visit www.usboat.com.

Tours

The **Historic Annapolis Foundation** (410-268-5576) offers two "Acoustiguide" recorded tours of this 300-year-old city's history: one of its colonial past (narrated by Chesapeake sailor Walter Cronkite) and the other of its African American heritage. Reserve an hour for the African-American heritage tour and 90 minutes for the colonial history tour. Tapes rented at the foundation's Museum Store at City Dock. Available daily; $5 per person.

Annapolis Tours (410-263-5401; www.annapolis-tours.com) formerly Three Centuries Tours, sends out guides in colonial dress to lead groups through city streets and the U.S. Naval Academy, point out the highlights, and disclose tales that you'd

otherwise miss. Group tours, garden tours, tavern suppers, candlelight tours, haunted tours, and excursions to the Eastern Shore are also offered year-round. Daily walk-up tours leave Apr. 1 through Oct. 31 at 10:30 AM from the city's visitor's center at 26 West St. and at 1:30 PM from the City Dock information booth. No reservations required; fee.

The interiors of buildings at the U.S. Naval Academy are as beautiful as the exteriors. Tim Tadder

Discover Annapolis (410-626-6000; www.discover-annapolis.com) takes visitors for one-hour minibus rides through the city's sights, departing the city's visitor's center at 26 West St. Fee; no credit cards. Make reservations at the visitor's center.

Ghosts of Annapolis Tours (410-263-9686; www.ghostsofannapolis.com; 92 Maryland Ave.) Imparts to visitors the spirited secrets of the city's Historic District during this walking tour of less than a mile. Up to 25 per tour group; $15 for adults, $8 for kids under 12 (although we might advise thinking twice before taking little ones). Available year-round. The 21-and-older crowd also can take a two-hour haunted pub crawl for $20, complete with 25-minute fueling stops.

Pleasure boats can be rented by those who want to be on the water, not just near it.

RECREATION

Bicycling

A friendly heads-up to cyclists: You can't cross the William Preston Lane Jr. Memorial Bridge—aka the Bay Bridge—on a bike. Officially, you're on your own to arrange transportation, like a taxi. Check chapter 9, "Information," for state cycling information.

To reach the 13.3-mile **Baltimore & Annapolis Trail** from town: Cross the Severn River via the U.S. Naval Academy Bridge (MD 450). Continue on MD 450 to a left turn at Boulters Way. The trail, on your left, is built along the old railroad bed and travels north to Glen Burnie. You'll share it with in-line skaters and walkers. For information, call 410-222-6244.

Another favored local spot for family cycling is **Quiet Waters Park** on the south side of town off Hillsmere Drive. Paved trails of just under 6 miles wind through woods and open parkland and end overlooking the South River. For information, call 410-222-1777; closed Tues.

Local Cycling Shops

Bike Doctor (410-266-7383; 160-C Jennifer Rd.).

Capital Bicycle Center (410-626-2197; 300 Chinquapin Round Rd.).

Pedal Pushers (410-544-2323; 546 Baltimore Annapolis Blvd., Severna Park) Located right at the Baltimore & Annapolis Trail.

Bird-Watching

Situated along the Atlantic flyway, Bayside **Sandy Point State Park** offers good year-round birding—but offers particular treats in winter and spring. Northern waterfowl (loons, grebes, and gannets) and all owl species have been spotted in winter. Breeding birds, many of them songbirds, have been spotted in the restricted back acreage of the park, which is a bird sanctuary, in spring. Check at the park office (410-974-2149; 1100 E. College Pkwy., Annapolis, MD 21401) to see whether you can get access, or find out about walks hosted by local bird clubs.

Boating

Deck shoes are de rigueur, and masts fill Spa Creek in the middle of America's Sailing Capital, where everybody can talk a little boat talk. On Wed. evenings in summer, the Annapolis Yacht Club hosts races on Spa Creek—the starting gun goes off at approximately 6 PM. To watch, stake out a spot at the Eastport bridge, or visit a creekside restaurant to see the start or finish.

Charters, Cruises, and Boat Rentals

ANNAPOLIS

Annapolis Bay Charters (1-800-991-1776; www.annapolisbaycharters.net; Port Annapolis Marina, Bembe Beach Rd., Annapolis, MD 21403) A top chartering company in the area. Boats in the fleet range from 28 to 55 feet, but they can arrange for smaller or larger vessels.

Pirate Adventures (443-398-6270; www.chesapeakepirates.com) Shiver me timbers! Kids pull on their eye patches as they dress up and sail out under the Jolly Roger during this creative cruise that operates from mid-May through Oct., six times daily during the summer, weekends only after Labor Day. Park at the Annapolis City Marina and check in at the parking lot there. $16 per person, $8 under age 3. Check the website for additional information. Reservations required.

Schooner Woodwind (410-263-7837; www.schoonerwoodwind.com; Annapolis Marriott Waterfront dock, 80 Compromise St., Annapolis, MD 21401) Twin 74-foot wooden *Woodwind I* and *II* ply Annapolis Harbor. On Thurs. sunset sails, catch the popular Songs of the Bay concert series featuring original Chesapeake music and musicians. Other tours are available on other evenings of the week, such as a history tour on Mon. and Maryland microbrew tastings on Tues. Sails are available daily; call or check the website for the schedule. Adults $32, kids under 12 $18. Discounts during the week; destination cruises, too.

Watermark Cruises (410-268-7600; www.watermarkcruises.com; Annapolis City Dock, P.O. Box 3350, Annapolis, MD 21403) This longtime city business offers 40- and 90-minute tours of Annapolis Harbor and the Severn River, or trips across the Bay to St. Michaels and Rock Hall. Its vessels includes the 297-passenger *Harbor Queen*. Specialty cruises range from moonlit wine cruises to music cruises offered in conjunction with local radio station WRNR, as well as pirate cruises.

EDGEWATER

South River Boat Rentals (410-956-9729; www.southriverboatrentals.com; Pier 7 Marina, 48 South River Rd., Edgewater, MD 21037) Open daily, mid-Mar. through Nov. Half- or full-day rentals; multiday charters, captained or bareboat. Fleet from 17 to 33 feet.

Suntime Rentals of Annapolis (410-266-6020; 2820 Solomons Island Rd., Edgewater, MD 21037) Powerboats (19-footers), Jet Skis, waterskiing equipment, and wakeboards just south of Annapolis on the South River at the foot of the South River Bridge. Two-hour minimum; daily rates available. May 1 through Oct. 1.

GALESVILLE

Hartge Chesapeake Charters & Yacht Sales (410-867-7240; www.hartge.com; 4880 Church Lane, Galesville, MD 20765) Charter fleet includes sailboats from 28 to 36 feet. Located south of Annapolis. All bareboat. Also, fishing charter available aboard the 37-foot *Dancer*.

Landings and Boat Ramps

See chapter 9, "Information," for information on free maps of Chesapeake landings.

Marinas

In Annapolis, try the following: **Annapolis City Marina** (410-268-0660; 410 Severn Ave.), right in the midst of the city bustle. Groceries, laundry, showers, fuel, and pump-out station. The **Annapolis Landing Marina** (410-263-0090; 980 Awald Rd.) on the city's Back Creek has fuel, showers, laundry, café (see Back Porch Café in the "Restaurants" section), pump-out station, and swimming pool. **Annapolis Yacht Basin** (410-263-3544; www.yachtbasin.com; 2 Compromise St.) offers fuel, showers, and laundry. **Bert Jabin's Yacht Yard** (410-268-9667; www.bjyy.com; 7310 Edgewood Rd.) is one of the biggest marinas in the area, with about 400 slips and a huge yard with all services. A small grocery store provides essentials such as snacks and sandwiches. **Chesapeake Harbour Marina** (410-268-1969; www.chesapeakeharbourmarina.com; 2030 Chesapeake Harbour Dr. E.) has a bathhouse, a good restaurant, and two pools. Water taxi to City Dock area. **Mears Marina** (410-268-8282 or 301-261-1234; www.mearsmarinas.com; 519 Chester Ave.) is the Annapolis branch of this marina, which you'll find elsewhere around the Bay. Transient slips fluctuate among the 236 slips, including a few that accommodate boats up to 80 feet. Call in advance. Pool, tennis courts, headquarters of Severn River Yacht Club. **Port Annapolis** (410-269-1990; www.portannapolis.com; 7074 Bembe Beach Rd.) has bikes, a pool, a café, and pump-out. No fuel.

North of Annapolis on the Magothy River in Severna Park is **Magothy Marina** (410-647-2356; www.magothymarina.com; 360 Magothy Rd.), with a swimming pool, marina services, and deep-draft slips, including some off the 17-foot channel. Just north of the Bay Bridge.

South of Annapolis, at Friendship and Tracey's Landing, is **Herrington Harbour** (www.herringtonharbour.com). The yacht yard (1-800-297-1930; 389 Deale Rd., Tracey's Landing) is to the north, and the resort (1-800-213-9438; MD 261, Friendship) to the south. Dining available at each. The resort offers everything from nature trails to a beach-front motel. Hundreds of slips.

Sailing and Powerboat Schools

Annapolis Sailing School (410-267-7205 or 1-800-638-9192; www.annapolissailing .com; 601 Sixth St., Annapolis, MD 21403) Classes offered by a venerable, reputable school. Experienced instructors teach courses ranging from "Become a Sailor in One Weekend" to "Coastal Navigation." Rentals of 24-foot Rainbow daysailers are available. Also home to KidShip, where sailors as young as 5 learn to tack. Bytes are 12 feet; Americans and Barnetts are 14 feet. Also, the companion Annapolis Powerboat School offers two- and five-day courses.

Chesapeake Sailing School (410-269-1594 or 1-800-966-0032; www.sailingclasses.com; 7080 Bembe Beach Rd., Annapolis, MD 21403) Well-established school offers a wide range of sailing courses on vessels ranging from 8-foot Optis for children to Tanzer 22s for older folks. Also offers the "Kids on Boats" program for families. Rentals are available in summer.

J World (410-280-2040; www.sailjworld.com; 213 Eastern Ave., Annapolis, MD 21403) Begun in Annapolis in the early 1990s, this J-boat-oriented sailing school offers weekend programs for folks who want to learn to sail or improve their skills, as well as five-day classes that can mix and match skills. Courses available for those interested in racing, cruising, or simply getting started.

Womanship (1-800-342-9295; www.womanship.com; 137 Conduit St., Annapolis, MD 21401) This reputable school was started by women for women and now has spread to numerous locations. Classes of varying duration and topic, including daytime classes for beginners.

Canoeing and Kayaking

Wild rice grows with midsummer abandon along Jug Bay, a suburban outpost along the Patuxent River west of Annapolis. Three centuries ago, this was a deep-water harbor, but time, siltation, and an old railroad bed have conspired to create a quiet paddler's paradise, studded by marshmallows and home to kingbirds, territorial red-wing blackbirds, and largemouth bass and perch. Access to this tidal river includes the **Jug Bay Wetlands Sanctuary** (410-741-9330; 1361 Wrighton Rd., Lothian, MD 20711; open Wed., Sat., and Sun. 9–5; closed Sun. Dec. through Feb.; call in advance for reservations for access) on the east bank in Anne Arundel County, offering guided canoe trips from time to time and nature programs on weekends. **The Patuxent River Park Jug Bay Natural Area** (301-627-6074; 16000 Croom Airport Rd., Upper Marlboro, MD 20772), across the river in Prince Georges County, has two landings. Buy a nominally priced permit to paddle and a fishing license to cast. Check for canoe trips, even pontoon boat trips. Canoe and kayak rentals. Call for prices.

Other Rentals

Amphibious Horizons (410-267-8742 or 1-888-I-LUV-SUN; www.amphibioushorizons .com; 600 Quiet Waters Park Rd., Annapolis, MD 21403) Operates out of Quiet Waters Park from Apr. through Oct. Singles, doubles, and sit-on-top kayak rentals, plus canoes and paddleboats for folks who venture to the park. All but the most experienced kayakers stay in Harness Creek. Kayak classes and trips are available to explore different streams and rivers around the Bay.

The Springriver Corp. (410-263-2303 or 301-888-1377; www.springriver.com; 311 Third St., Annapolis, MD 21403) Reasonably priced half- or full-day rentals. Call by Thurs. for weekend reservations. Located on Spa Creek in Eastport. Open daily.

Fishing
Boat Ramps

In Annapolis, **Sandy Point State Park** (410-974-2149; www.dnr.state.md.us; 1100 E. College Pkwy.; nominal entry fee) gets you right onto the Bay. Twenty-two ramps launch boaters into Mezick Pond, a little inlet on the Chesapeake. Very popular and reasonable. Sandy Point also has piers for day use and a marina store.

Spa Creek access is at **Truxtun Park** (410-263-7958; Hilltop Lane; nominal fee to launch; no park entry fee) in the middle of town outside the Historic District.

Charter Fishing Boats

EDGEWATER

Sportfishing on the Chesapeake Bay (301-261-4207 or 1-800-638-7871; www.belinda gail.com; P.O. Box 53, Edgewater, MD 21037) Capt. Jerry Lastfogel, former officer for the Maryland Charterboat Association, has been running charter boat fishing expeditions for years. Fish aboard the 42-foot *Belinda Gail III*. Half- and full-day trips out of Collins Marine Railway on Rockhold Creek in Deale.

DEALE

Deale Captains Association (www.dealecaptains.com) An association of about 40 captains operating out of Rockhold Creek and other areas around Deale, which is in southern Anne Arundel County and easily reached from Washington, D.C. Fish from the Bay Bridge south to Cove Point at the mouth of the Patuxent River.

Golf

Annapolis Golf Club (410-263-6771; 2638 Carrollton Rd., Annapolis) 9 holes. Nice, local course; semiprivate. Located in the Annapolis Roads community.

Atlantic Golf at South River (410-798-5865 or 1-800-SO-RIVER; www.mdgolf.com; 3451 Solomons Island Rd., Edgewater) 18 holes. Challenging public course. Driving range, putting green. Earned 3 1/2 stars in *Golf Digest's* 2000–2001 "Places to Play."

Bay Hills Golf Club (410-974-0669; www.bayhillsgolf.com; 545 Bay Hills Dr., Arnold) 18 holes; semiprivate. Located north of Annapolis.

Dwight D. Eisenhower Golf Course (410-571-0973; www.eisenhowergolf.com; 1576 Generals Hwy., Crownsville) 18 holes. Popular public course located just outside Annapolis; book online up to eight days in advance.

Natural Places: State, National, and Private Refuges and Parks

Jug Bay Wetlands Sanctuary (410-741-9330; 1361 Wrighton Rd., Lothian, MD 20711) Located on the Patuxent River. Seven miles of uncrowded trails; limited hours. If you're lucky, you might—and we mean might—catch a glimpse of the elusive river otter. Open Wed., Sat., and Sun. March through Nov.; small entrance fee. Call for reservations and winter hours.

Sandy Point State Park (410-974-2149; www.dnr.state.md.us/publiclands/southern/sandypoint.html; 1100 E. College Pkwy., Annapolis, MD 21401) More than 780 acres located on US 50 near the last exit before the Bay Bridge. It's fun to hang out here and watch what goes on in the Bay—from passing scows and barges to the crisp white sails of the yachting set in summer. Plus, there's an up-close-and-personal view of the Bay Bridge. Beach for swimming, fishing, bird-watching, crabbing; marina for boating (rowboats and motorboats for rent), windsurfing; 22 boat ramps; bait, tackle, fuel, and fishing licenses. Costs vary depending on date and season.

Sporting Goods and Camping Supply Stores

Angler's Sport Center (410-757-3442; 1456 Whitehall Rd., Annapolis) The dean of local sporting goods. Hunting and fishing licenses, fishing gear, decoys, outdoor clothing, supplies for archery and hunting. Located between Annapolis and the Bay Bridge. Exit 30 off US 50, east of Cape St. Claire.

Marty's Sporting Goods (410-956-2238; 95 Mayo Rd., Edgewater) Everything for fishing.

Swimming

Arundel Olympic Swim Center (410-222-7933 or 301-970-2216; www.aacounty.org/RecParks; 2690 Riva Rd., Annapolis) Olympic-size pool operated by the Anne Arundel County Recreation and Parks Department. Nominal entrance fees. Open Mon. through Thurs. 6 AM–10 PM, Fri. 6 AM–9 PM, Sat. 8 AM–6 PM, Sun. 10 AM–6 PM.

Sandy Point State Park (410-974-2149; www.dnr.state.md.us/publiclands/southern/sandypoint.html; 1100 E. College Pkwy., Annapolis) One of the few sandy beaches on the Bay. Costs vary according to season. Take the last exit off US 50 before the Bay Bridge.

Tennis

In Anne Arundel County, 45 county parks have tennis courts; eight have lights for nighttime play. Visitors to Annapolis, where court time is harder to find, may want to use courts in nearby towns in less-congested central or rural south county. For information, contact the Anne Arundel County Department of Recreation and Parks at 410-222-7300.

SHOPPING

In addition to its shopping malls and shopping centers, the city has retail districts that break down into four general areas: In the Historic District, City Dock and Main Street host clothing, jewelry, and specialty shops amid the tourist draws. At the top of the Historic District, Maryland Avenue has undergone a bit of a renaissance, with a new mix of boutiques that has arrived of late. Nearby, West Street has seen quite the renaissance, with a few shops tucked in among the many businesses and restaurants. For an off-the-beaten-path shopping opportunity, consider West Annapolis, home to specialty shops on Annapolis Street.

Antiques

Annapolis Antique Gallery (410-266-0635; 2009 West St.) An emporium of 40 dealers offering glass, china, and furniture; items ranging from country to empire. Take the Parole exit off US 50 and you're practically there. Closed Mon.

Bon Vivant Antiques (410-263-9651; 104 Annapolis St., West Annapolis) A welcome addition to the West Annapolis shopping corridor; a wonderful antiques shop full of china, silver, and jewelry treasures. Well worth a stop.

Evergreen Antiques, Art & Accessories (410-216-9067; 69 Maryland Ave.) A mix that includes antiques and vintage items. Lots of silver and jewelry. Six dealers.

Hobson's Choice Antiques (410-280-2206; 58 Maryland Ave.) Chinese export porcelain, Oriental rugs, and more. One of the last of the old-line Maryland Avenue antiques shops.

Ron Snyder Antiques (410-266-5452; 2011 West St.) Furniture from the 18th and 19th centuries, and a devotee of the 100-year rule. Marilyn Snyder once told us they like to start at 1830 and work back. Right next to the Annapolis Antique Gallery; longtime local dealer.

West Annapolis Antiques (410-295-1200; 103 Annapolis St., West Annapolis) The women tee-heeing over the fabulous hats they found in this browsable shop were worth the stop here one day.

Art and Craft Galleries

American Craftworks Collection (410-626-1583; 189B Main St.) Excellent selection of fine contemporary crafts. Always fun to browse.

Annapolis Pottery (410-268-6153; 40 State Cir.) A well-loved local institution offering a wide array of stoneware and porcelain pieces, from handy pitchers to art platters to bird feeders. Potters work in back.

ARTFX (410-990-4540; 45 West St.) Mix of styles and media; located in the first block of West Street off Church Circle.

Aurora Gallery (410-263-9150; 67 Maryland Ave.) Paintings and fine crafts in various media. Great jewelry, too.

Chesapeake Photo Gallery (410-268-0050; 92 Maryland Ave.) Devoted to the Bay's photographers, this is a terrific gallery with a range of work. Located right at Church Circle.

Dawson Gallery (410-269-1299; 44 Maryland Ave.) Old-fashioned gallery with worn wooden floors showcasing 19th- and early 20th-century American and European paintings.

Easy Street (410-263-5556; 8 Francis St.) Among the best and most enduring of the city's upscale craft and gift galleries. Specializes in terrific blown glass or art glass pieces.

La Petite Galerie (410-268-2425; 39 Maryland Ave.) Paintings from the 19th and 20th centuries; generally traditional, representational works.

League of Maryland Craftsmen (410-626-1277; 216 Main St.) Upper Main Street gallery focused on Maryland-based craftspeople. Nice turned-wood pieces and crabs done up in any and all media. Glass, sculpture, paintings.

Main Street Gallery (410-270-2787; 109 Main St.) Nice space; a mix of work by local, regional, and national artists. Openings monthly from Mar. through Nov.

A South-of-Town Outing

Crystal, humid-free days have a way of blowing through sultry Chesapeake just as midsummer wanders past, hinting at the coming fall. Now's the time to hit the roads south of Annapolis for **Galesville**, a gentle West River port town about an hour's drive east of Washington, D.C., and only 15 miles south of Annapolis. Annapolitans widely consider this boaters' haven to be an off-the-beaten-path gem. With its couple of restaurants, its couple of shops, and the view across the mast-laden river from its tiny waterfront park, Galesville offers a glimpse of life in old "south county," as this area south of Annapolis is known.

To get there, head down MD 2 south, and feel free to stop at the occasional antiques shop or farm stand you'll find along the way. Turn left onto Muddy Creek Road after 4.4 miles, and stay on this winding road through old farmland for another 5 miles. When you reach Galesville Road, turn left and stay on it into town. You'll pass a few antiques shops here as well.

Closer to the water stands the **West River Market & Deli** (410-867-4844; 1000 Main St.), which has been here more than 100 years, replete with horehound candy in a barrel in the back. You'll also find pies ranging from apple to chocolate cream, breakfast sandwiches, and dinner specials like crab cakes and barbecue. If it's breakfast or lunch, walk a few hundred feet down Main Street to eat at the waterside park, with benches and a collection of boat propellers serving as public art. If it's the weekend, stop next door at the market's granary-turned-art-gallery. The **River Gallery** (410-867-0954; 1000 Main St.) is owned by three artists who show the original artwork of up to 20 consignors. Open Fri. through Sun. 11–5.

If you're more inclined to tuck into a full meal, two delightful spots fill the bill. The **Topside Inn** (410-867-1321; 1004 Galesville Rd.) has a second-floor balcony across the street from the river; try to snare a table there. The Topside also has a loyal local following that includes devotees of its cream of crab soup. Sunday brunch, salmon cakes, and peach cobbler are among the treats here. Prices are moderate to expensive. Call for hours, which change seasonally, although the restaurant is open year-round.

Across the street stands the **Inn at Pirate's Cove** (410-867-2300; 1817 Riverside Dr.), with its seafood-heavy menu and lunch dishes that include eggs and crab benedicts. Ask for a table on the far side of the deck from Big Mary's Dock Bar in summer for quieter dining. This is also home to a small, inexpensive to moderately priced inn and a marina with transient slips. Serving L, D, SB. Prices are moderate to expensive.

Maria's Picture Place (410-263-8282; 45 Maryland Ave.) Small gallery with good frame shop showcases local and regional pieces, including those by famed Annapolis-based Chesapeake photographer Marion Warren.

McBride Gallery (410-267-7077; www.mcbridegallery.com; 215 Main St.) Longtime local gallery hosts a variety of artists, many from Virginia and Maryland, and many with a maritime or shoreside appeal. For the exhibit schedule, check the website.

West Annapolis Gallery (410-295-6880; 108 Annapolis St., West Annapolis) Limited-edition prints and watercolors by Liz Lind, plus a frame shop.

Books

Barnes & Noble (410-573-1115; Annapolis Harbour Center, MD 2 and Aris T. Allen Blvd.) Huge and popular, as one might expect. But it also has a knowledgeable selection of regional and local books ranging from Bay histories and watermen's tales to literature penned by local writers.

Borders (410-571-0923; Westfield Shoppingtown Annapolis, Jennifer and Bestgate Rds., off US 50) The popular chain is located in a huge two-story emporium in Annapolis's main mall. Books and much more.

Children
Be Beep-A-Toy Shop (410-224-4066; Festival at Riva Shopping Center, 2327C Forest Dr.) Quality toys.

Fancy Frocks (410-626-9711; 216B Main St.) Wide variety of clothing for little kids; cute and different.

The Giant Peach (410-268-8776; 110 Annapolis St., West Annapolis) Probably the most venerable children's clothing shop in town.

Clothing
Hats in the Belfry (410-268-6333; 103 Main St.) Something of an impromptu perform-ance space, because everybody tries on hats: felt hats, straw hats (including genuine Panamas), funky hats, sporty hats, Easter bonnets, gardening hats, and more.

Hyde Park Annapolis Haberdashery (410-263-0074; 110 Dock St., Harbour Square) Classic men's clothing.

Johnson's on the Avenue (410-263-6390; 79 Maryland Ave.) In the window hang tradi-tional houndstooth wools and other fine classic menswear for civilians; inside, the Italian sweaters are folded on the counter. This Annapolis institution made uniforms for Navy officers for seven decades and shipped them all over the world. Their trademark military "covers," or hats, are worn by the actors in the TV series *JAG.* Noted for fine service. Some women's items are available as well.

Design Shops
Details (410-269-1965; 918 Bay Ridge Ave.) A bit outside the usual tourist loop, this shop offers a nice array of furniture and home accessories.

Fine Gift Shops
Linens of London (410-990-4655; 62 Maryland Ave.) As the name indicates, this sizable shop carries beautiful linens, but it offers much more, including some vintage clothing. Worth a stop.

Plat du Jour (410-269-1499; 220 Main St.) Filled with tempting French and Italian ceramics and fine linens. Among the most unique shops in the Historic District.

Vie Necessary Luxuries (410-269-6100; 86 Maryland Ave.) As the store itself says— "necessary luxuries." We once purchased a tea towel with a sorcerer on it for a gift that did, indeed, seem necessary. Reproductions, home items.

Jewelry
La Belle Cezanne (410-263-1996; 117 Main St.) One of the best windows to shop in Annapolis. Some unique items.

Tilghman Co. (410-268-7855; 44 State Cir.) The fine old Maryland name of this business tells you that this is a traditional jewelry store featuring classic gold and silver pieces and pearls, plus Lenox, Waterford, and fine sterling. In business since 1928; on State Circle since 1948.

W. R. Chance Jewelers (410-263-2404; 110 Main St.) From traditional to contemporary work; fine service. In business more than 50 years.

Malls and Outlets

Annapolis Harbour Center (410-266-5857; MD 2 and Aris T. Allen Blvd.) This place has been packed since the day it opened in the early 1990s. Tower Records, Office Depot, Whole Foods, Starbucks, Barnes & Noble, Old Navy, and many specialty clothing and home-furnishing stores.

Westfield Shoppingtown Annapolis (410-266-5432; Jennifer and Bestgate Rds., off US 50) More than 180 stores, with Nordstrom, Lord & Taylor, The Hecht Co., and clothing, book, record, shoe, and specialty stores.

Marine Shops

The chain marine stores are well represented in and around Annapolis. In addition to these, the city's spawned a couple of local institutions.

Bacon & Assoc. (410-263-4880; 116 Legion Ave.) Nifty place for used equipment; noted for a broad array of secondhand sails. In business since 1959. Open during the week only, except Sat. 9:30 AM–12:30 PM Apr. through Aug.

Fawcett Boat Supplies (410-267-8681; 110 Compromise St.) Right at City Dock, a local institution for 50 years and a good source of local boating information. Good selection of nautical books.

Specialty Shops and General Stores

A. L. Goodies General Store (410-269-0071; 112 Main St.) The resident, multistory five-and-dime in the trendy City Dock area. Racks and racks of greeting cards, brass weather vanes, even peanut butter cookies. Good for souvenirs.

Annapolis Country Store (410-269-6773; 53 Maryland Ave.) Upscale general store featuring Winnie-the-Pooh, Raggedy Ann, Crabtree & Evelyn, and more.

Art Things (410-268-3520; 2 Annapolis St., West Annapolis) Great art supply shop, where the employees are perennially helpful and cheerful. Paints, brushes, papers, and more.

Avoca Handweavers (410-263-1485; 141-143 Main St.) Avoca has been doing business in Ireland since 1723 and continues to make a splash in the Annapolis Historic District. Exquisite handiwork. Wools, linens, and clothing, as well as Irish glass and pottery.

Chadwick's, the British Shoppe (410-280-BRIT; 10 Annapolis St., West Annapolis) Filled with all kinds of imported British things, including many foods. Books, china, and tea cozies, too.

Chesapeake Trading Company (410-216-9797; 149 Main St.) Books, great jewelry, and outdoor clothing. Also has a location in St. Michaels.

Historic Annapolis Foundation Museum Store (410-268-5576; 77 Main St.) Classic museum-quality gifts as well as a good selection of Chesapeake books in a restored 18th-century warehouse.

Pepper's (410-267-8722; 133 Main St.) Navy T-shirt and sweatshirt central.

Calvert County

New residents discovered this Western Shore county to the tune of a 45 percent population boost in the 1990s, but not to fret. Fishing and exploring are fine hereabouts, with a touch of prehistoric glamour added by the 30-mile, Bay-front Calvert Cliffs. Public access points are few, but you can still find sharks' teeth and other fossils. At the county's southern tip, the Patuxent River meets the Bay at Solomons Island, a boating center and tourist village.

Golfers will be happy to tee off at **Twin Shields Golf Club** (410-257-7800 or 301-855-8228; 2425 Roarty Rd, Dunkirk), an 18-hole, semiprivate course on MD 260 off MD 4 in **Dunkirk**. It's located near the county's northern boundary, west of side-by-side North Beach and Chesapeake Beach, two once-overlooked towns—each with small Bay beaches and boardwalks—that have been rediscovered. Go antiquing in **North Beach** at **Nice & Fleazy Antique Center** (410-257-3044; Seventh St. and Bay Ave.), a large space that even has a section for slot machines, remnants of Southern Maryland's gamblin' past. Quartered in the same space, **Willetta's Antiques** (301-855-3412; open Thurs. through Sun.) routinely carries good-looking furniture and china pieces that most definitely are not the usual suspects. **Coffee, Tea & Whimsey** (410-286-0000; 4109 Seventh St.) has whimsical gifts, especially those with a nautical bent, and a coffee bar in back.

The decades-old **Rod 'N Reel** complex, founded in 1946 and a longtime hub for sport-fishermen, is a key attraction in **Chesapeake Beach,** a town first envisioned as a getaway at the turn of the 19th century. It seems those aspirations continue to make a comeback in the current century, most recently with the addition of the **Chesapeake Beach Hotel and Spa** (1-866-312-5596; www.chesapeakebeachhotelspa.com; 4165 Mears Ave.). The 72-room hotel includes six suites and nine deluxe waterfront rooms with panoramic views and a range of amenities. The full-service spa also offers packages.

Even with the hotel and spa's arrival, however, the Rod 'N Reel hasn't forgotten its roots. Sportfishers can hunt for rockfish, bluefish, and whatever else is biting on fishing charters scheduled by the marina here (301-855-8450; MD 261 and Mears Ave.). Boats go out from Apr. through mid-Dec.

The complex's **Rod 'N Reel Restaurant** (410-257-2735; L, D daily; B, L, D Sat. and Sun.; moderate to expensive), with wide windows onto the marina and an expansive stretch of the Bay, likely provides the area's best dining option. A seafood-heavy dinner menu doesn't forget the beef eaters (New York strip, filet mignon, and veal chops). Moderate to very expensive. Out front in good weather, the **Boardwalk Café** (410-257-2735) offers a tiny taste of Ocean City along the Western Shore, while **Smokey Joe's** (410-257-2427) cooks up ribs and barbecue—and breakfast—year-round.

Across the street stands the **Chesapeake Beach Water Park** (410-257-1404; 4079 Creekside Dr.), with eight slides, a "dreamland river" where you can tube or swim, and more, including a separate "diaper" pool. Fee. Open Memorial Day through Labor Day.

Five miles south stands the **Breezy Point Beach & Campground** (410-535-0259 from May through Oct., otherwise 301-855-1243; office: 175 Main St., Prince Frederick, MD

20678), where nets off the beach help protect swimmers from sea nettles. You also can fish, crab, or camp here. Open May through Oct., 6 AM–dusk. Fee.

Farther south, on MD 4 at **Huntingtown**, pull into the **Southern Maryland Antique Center** (410-257-1677; 3176 Solomons Island Rd.; open Thurs. through Sat. 10–5, Sun. 11–5) when you see the red, white, and blue "antiques" flag flying. Good furniture finds are possible at this large and worthwhile multidealer center.

A mix of habitat throughout the county means good bird-watching (herons, kingfishers, American woodcocks, and bald eagles can be seen), hiking, and even beach time. Visit the 100-acre **Battle Creek Cypress Swamp** in **Prince Frederick** (410-535-5327; Gray's Rd. off MD 506; open Apr. through Sept., Tues. through Sat. 10–5, Sun. 1–5; Oct. through Mar. closes at 4:30) to stroll the boardwalk running through the nation's largest stand of bald cypress this far north, an intriguing and unique Bay-area habitat.

Seven miles south at **St. Leonard** is 500-acre **Jefferson Patterson Park and Museum** (410-586-8500; www.jefpat.org; 10515 Mackall Rd.; open mid-Apr. through mid-Oct., Wed. through Sun. 10–5), headquarters for much of the state's archaeological work. It features a visitor's center highlighting the Chesapeake's past, along with easy trails through fields and along the Patuxent River. Check the website for special events such as "Children's Day on the Farm" or War of 1812 encampments. The old barn has been transformed into a broad picnic pavilion.

Just a tad south, perhaps a mile, look to the left of MD 2/4 for the sign to **Flag Ponds Nature Park** (410-586-1477; open 9–8 daily Memorial Day through Labor Day, 9–5 weekends the rest of the year; Calvert County residents $4, others $6). Here's one of the larger Bay beaches you're likely to see, along with a fishing pier, fossil hunting, a visitor's center, and a friendly nod to the property's life as a pound-net fishing station from the early 1900s to 1955. Remainders such as the restored Buoy Hotel tell of the fishermen who once stayed here for weeks at a time.

If it's time to eat, **Stoney's**—with locations in **Prince Frederick, Broomes Island,** and **Solomons**—can't be beat. Given a choice, we go to the Stoney's on Broomes Island (410-586-1888; 3938 Oyster House Rd.; serving L, D daily; closed Nov. through early Feb.; moderate), an isle notable because it's where former state senator Bernie Fowler undertakes his "sneaker index" every June to see whether the Bay's clarity has improved. Getting there, down a long and winding tidewater road, is half the adventure, and the broad deck on the water, one of the biggest around, features a floating dock.

But sometimes you're on MD 2/4 through town and you don't have time to wander down a back road, or worse, it's the dead of winter and the Broomes Island Stoney's is closed. This is when we go to the Fox Run Shopping Center Stoney's in Prince Frederick (410-535-1888; 545 N. Solomons Island Rd.; serving L, D daily; moderate), with its clubby Chesapeake waterfowl decor and spacious dining room, as well as a full dinner menu, which you won't find on Broomes Island. Either way, the food's great, particularly the peppery crab soup and the baseball-size "baby" crab cake, which, at 4 ounces, allows substantive crab gluttony—and it comes in an even larger size. On a hot day, the dining room can be sparse. Everybody must be down at the Broomes Island Stoney's, cracking crabs on its waterfront. If it's raining, ask for an upstairs table, order the smoked bluefish appetizer to go along with your crabs (or crab cakes), and settle in for a fine time peering out over the water. More recent years have seen the addition of Stoney's Kingfisher in Solomons; see the following section on that area for details.

If it's the last Sat. in August, consider a stop at the island's 1672 Christ Episcopal Church (3100 Broomes Island Rd.) to celebrate Maryland's official state sport at the **Calvert County Jousting Tournament,** well into its second century. Knights engage in mock battle and a bazaar is set up before the sporting jousts begin. End the day with a country supper at the church. For information, call 410-586-0565.

Just north of Solomons, in **Lusby**, sits a famous throwback, where paper umbrellas stud drinks and the keyboardist has been known to play "Don't Cry for Me, Argentina"—twice. Surely the food's not the only draw at **Vera's White Sands** (410-586-1182; www.veraswhite sands.com; 1200 White Sands Dr., off MD 4; open Apr. through Dec., closed Mon.; serving L [Sat. and Sun.] and D; moderate to expensive). The menu ranges from stuffed shrimp to a seven-boy chicken curry with baked saffron rice to Southern Maryland crab cakes. Perhaps the famed Vera will even appear at dinnertime. Clad in a wildcat-print caftanlike affair (a print more exotic than the leopardskin vinyl that's dressed her bar stools for decades), she once walked us through her restaurant in her gold slings. Appliquéd cloth umbrellas hanging above a table came from India, and the wooden sculptures along the walls from places like Singapore and Bali, she said. Back in the glass-enclosed Palm-Palm Room, husky metal nautical items came from engine rooms—hardworking relics of the seagoing life. Boaters can still tie up here at reasonable rates, and the rest of you should get here while you can.

Solomons Island

The 19th-century oystering village of Solomons Island led a quiet life for decades. It's discovered now and easily is the tourism center of the Maryland Bay's Western Shore region south of Annapolis, with B&Bs, restaurants, shops, and terrific fishing nearby.

Anchoring Solomons is the **Calvert Marine Museum** (410-326-2042; www.calvert marinemuseum.com; 14150 Solomons Island Rd.; open daily 10–5; adults $7, senior citizens $6, children 5–12 $2), right near the town's entrance. Here, the tale of the Patuxent River and Chesapeake marine life is told in all its chapters, from the recently historic to the prehistoric—down to crocodile jaws and the teeth of mastodons dug from nearby Calvert Cliffs. Kids love the aquariums full of Chesapeake critters, including blue crabs sidling through their tanks and, believe it or not, sea horses. River otters play in a tank on the back deck. Take a spin through the post-war recreational boating scene and view leisure craft built by Solomons's M. M. Davis & Sons Shipyard, or inspect more historic craft.

Out back stands the Drum Point Lighthouse, one of only three remaining screw-pile lights. Forty-three of these distinctly Chesapeake sentinels once stood in the Bay's soft bottom, warning mariners off dangerous shoals. This is one of two screw-pile lights stationed at a Bay-area museum (the other is at the Chesapeake Bay Maritime Museum in St. Michaels), and kids like them in part because it feels fairly safe to climb their ladderlike steps to the first floor. They're also a bit like dollhouses. Clamber up a short ladder-style entry into the cozily re-created lighthouse keeper's home—in this case put together with help from the memory of a former keeper's granddaughter, Anna Weems Ewald.

New to the museum in 2005 is "Secrets of the Mermaid's Purse," a huge tank featuring skates and rays. Visitors can touch these creatures that live in the Bay and learn all about them. ("Mermaid's purse," by the way, refers to the four-cornered skate egg case you've likely seen along Atlantic beaches.)

Down the street, the 1934 **J. C. Lore Oyster House** shows how oysters moved from tongers' boats to gourmets' plates. While you're enjoying the museum's offerings, take a one-hour ride around Solomons's Back Creek and into the Patuxent River aboard the *William B. Tennison*, a turn-of-the-19th century "bugeye," one of the indigenous oystering craft. Her sail rig was removed in the early 1900s and an engine installed so she could do duty as a "buyboat," motoring among the oyster dredgers to purchase their catch. Museum staff members tell about the passing shoreline. Cruises are held May through Oct., Wed. through Sun. at 2 PM; these are additional cruises at 12:30 and 3 PM on weekends in July and Aug. Adults $7, children 5–12 $4.

Shops along the town's main street include several good gift shops. Check out **Sea Gull Cove Gifts** (410-326-7182; 14488 Solomons Island Rd.) for souvenirs or **Carmen's Gallery** (410-326-2549; 14550 Solomons Island Rd.) for watercolors, serigraphs, and Chesapeake scenes, primarily by regional artists.

Fishermen will love Solomons, here at its wide, mid-Bay point where the Patuxent River empties into the Bay. Contact the **Solomons Charter Captains Association** (1-800-450-1775; www.fishsolomons.com; P.O. Box 831, Solomons, MD 20688) for year-round charter boat fishing offered aboard more than 40 vessels, all operated by U.S. Coast Guard–licensed captains. **Bunky's Charter Boats** (410-326-3241; 14448 Solomons Island Rd. S.) has long been the center for Solomons's sportfishing, with charter boats available for half- and full-day trips; head boats for groups. You also can rent a 16-foot fiberglass skiff. Fishing Apr. through Dec.; bait and tackle shop open year-round. Or rent a 15- to 20-foot powerboat or Wave Runner from

Solomons Boat Rental (410-326-4060 or 1-800-535-BOAT; www.boat-rent.net; MD 2 and A St.). For a treat just north of town, drive up Dowell Road and keep an eye out for colorful ceramic gates topped by the sculpted echo of waves to your left. This is the entrance to a 30-acre sculpture garden on St. John Creek called **Annmarie Garden** (410 326-4640; www.annmariegarden.org; 13480 Dowell Rd.; open daily 10–5 year-round). A bronze oyster tonger (an oysterman using tongs, a cross between scissors and a pair of long-handled rakes) greets visitors. Amid the well-landscaped woods, find pieces like *The Council Ring* by B. Amore and Woody Dorsey, quietly inviting reflection, or *The Surveyor's Map* by Jann Rosen-Queralt and Roma Campanile, an aluminum "boardwalk" into (and even over) the woods. Enjoy the **ArtsFest** here in mid- to late Sept., and check the website for other events.

LODGINGS, MARINAS, AND RESTAURANTS

Lodging prices are likely to drop midweek or in the off-season. Also be sure to check cancellation policies, and assume you can't bring your pet or smoke inside unless told otherwise.

Lodging rates, based on high-season prices, fall within this scale:

Inexpensive:	Up to $75
Moderate:	$75 to $120
Expensive:	$120 to $175
Very expensive:	$175 and up

Credit card abbreviations are:

AE—American Express
CB—Carte Blanche
DC—Diners Club
D—Discover
MC—MasterCard
V—Visa

BACK CREEK INN B&B

Innkeepers: Carol Pennock and Lin
Cochran.
410-326-2022.
www.bbonline.com/md/backcreek.
210 Alexander Lane/P.O. Box 520,
Solomons, MD 20688.
Price: Moderate to very expensive.
Credit Cards: MC, V.
Handicapped Access: Yes.
Special Features: Deep-water dock (draws
8 feet).

You may spend the day in the gardens at
this waterside inn, perhaps lounging
beside the softly gurgling fountain. Among
the perennials and bulbs are irises trans-
planted from one of the owners' great-
grandmother's garden, blooming happily
in May alongside peonies and foxglove. For
a break in the action, wander down to the
dock and dangle your feet over Back Creek.
Laid-back and comfortable, this B&B is
quartered in an 1880s waterman's house
and has been in business so long that you'll
no doubt reap the benefits of the innkeepers' experience. A cottage in the garden's
corner draws its steady stream of return
guests; if you can't book it, then any one of
six rooms and two suites in the house and
annex, named for herbs, will prove comfy
for the night. The rooms, all with king- or
queen-size beds, are all different, from
the large Thyme Room, with a fireplace
and television, to smaller upstairs rooms
at the back of the house, with garden
views. Downstairs, a glassed-in common
room with stereo and television looks out
to the water, where a yachtsperson in
need of a shower and a bed can tie up at
the deep-water dock. Full breakfast is
served at individual tables in the breakfast room, where tea is served Thurs. in
good china cups.

SOLOMONS VICTORIAN INN

Owners: Helen and Richard Bauer.
410-326-4811.
www.solomonsvictorianinn.com.
125 Charles St./P.O. Box 759, Solomons,
MD 20688.
Price: Moderate to very expensive.
Credit Cards: AE, MC, V.
Handicapped Access: Yes.
Restrictions: Only children over age 13.

From a sailor's peaked and varnished top-
floor suite to a simple bedroom with a
bathroom, this B&B covers the accommodations waterfront. Five rooms, all with
attached baths and furnished in antiques or
reproductions, are quartered in the 1906
Victorian home, formerly owned by the
locally notable boatbuilding Davis family.
Upstairs is the yachty top-floor suite,
replete with a blue in-room whirlpool
under a skylight and a built-in seating area
with matching blue cushions and a small
galley. The view of the harbor is enough to
make you buy a boat. The 1998 carriage
house offers two big rooms, including a
classy hideaway upstairs with a king-size
bed across from an in-room whirlpool. Full
breakfast (shrimp soufflé most Sun.
mornings); if the coffeepot's not on by 7 AM
you can fix your own hot drink on the
breakfast porch.

*The gardens are a treat at the Back Creek Inn B&B
on the water in Solomons.*

Hotels and Marinas

Comfort Inn/Beacon Marina (410-326-6303 or 1-800-228-5150; 255 Lore Rd./P.O. Box 869, Solomons, MD 20688) Sixty rooms include 10 whirlpool suites. Restaurant, outdoor pool, 186-slip marina. Moderate to expensive.

Holiday Inn Select (410-326-6311 or 1-800-356-2009; 155 Holiday Dr., Solomons, MD 20688) More than 300 rooms include 50 suites, some with views or whirlpools. Gift shop, waterfront dining. Moderate to very expensive.

Hospitality Harbor Marina (410-326-1052; 205 Holiday Dr./P.O. Box 382, Solomons, MD 20688) Pool, tennis courts, weight room—all of the amenities from the Holiday Inn next door. About 80 slips, with roughly 25 slips available for transients.

Spring Cove Marina (410-326-2161; www.springcovemarina.com; 455 Lore Rd., Solomons, MD 20688) Fuel, laundry, Naughty Gull restaurant. Approximately 250 slips, with 40 for transients. Swimming pool is heated and has underwater music. Open year-round.

Zahniser's Yachting Center (410-326-2166; www.zahnisers.com; 245 C St./P.O. Box 760, Solomons, MD 20688) Pump-out station, pool, bar and grill, sail loft, yacht brokerage. More than 300 slips; transient slips available (reservations recommended). Courtesy bikes, ice, laundry, full-service ship store, marine surveyor on-site, repair yard, dinghy dock. Also home to the fine Dry Dock restaurant (see below).

Restaurants

Restaurant price ranges, which include dinner entrée, appetizer, and dessert, are as follows:

Inexpensive: Up to $20
Moderate: $20 to $30
Expensive: $30 to $40
Very expensive: $40 or more

The following abbreviations are used to denote meals served:
B = Breakfast; L = Lunch; D = Dinner; SB = Sunday Brunch

THE C. D. CAFÉ

410-326-3877.
14350 Solomons Island Rd.
Open: Daily.
Price: Moderate
Cuisine: Creative regional
Serving: L, D, SB.
Credit Cards: MC, V.
Reservations: No.
Handicapped Access: Yes.

Grillades: Now there's a breakfast meal you won't find at the local IHOP. But you'll find the Louisiana beef dish at the Sunday brunch served at this small and comfortable café. The creative menu isn't devoted only to Cajun and Creole-style dishes, but those that you'll find tend to be authentic, not depressingly faux like so many this far north. In addition, the C. D. Café offers an array of creative salads, sandwiches, and entrées that use fresh ingredients and ingenuity. The Popeye burger comes with wilted fresh spinach and Boursin cheese, and the roasted veggie sandwiches can't be beat. From its handful of tables, the café's customers have views across the road to the Patuxent River and the arcing Gov. Thomas Johnson Bridge. The café's Next Door Lounge offers lighter fare and is a comfy place for a good glass of wine, after-dinner drinks, or dessert. Like the café, it's small but stylish.

THE DRY DOCK

410-326-4817.
C Street.
Open: Daily.
Price: Expensive to very expensive.
Cuisine: Traditional and innovative

American.
Serving: D, SB.
Credit Cards: AE, CB, DC, MC, V.
Reservations: Strongly suggested.
Handicapped Access: No.
Special Features: Call ahead for boat tie-up.

Located in Zahniser's Yachting Center, overlooking Back Creek and a forest of sailboat masts, is the Dry Dock, a small upstairs restaurant. Inside, the long, fully stocked bar is decorated with decoys, and a rowboat rests on the rafters above diners. Both inside and outside dining on the balcony afford great views of the marina. Inventive food combinations and some great basics grace the menu, which changes daily. A definite highlight is the butterflied New York strip steak with tarragon-bacon butter and seasoned brown rice. If you love garlic and butter, don't miss the large escargot appetizer with grilled bread that will satisfy the entire table. Chicken, pork, seafood, and vegetarian entrées are presented with creative sauces and sides, including jumbo shrimp with an apple-maple barbecue sauce and seared tuna with sweet soy-wasabi aioli, cucumber salsa, and lemon-sherry couscous. Save room for the homemade desserts, especially the strawberry-rhubarb pie served warm with real vanilla bean ice cream. All this good food and creativity comes with a big price tag, so make it a special evening out with friends and share the different tastes, the great view, and good company.

LIGHTHOUSE INN

410-326-2444.
14,636 Solomons Island Rd. S.
Open: Daily.
Price: Moderate to very expensive.
Cuisine: Seafood, American.
Serving: L (Sat. and Sun. only Apr. through Oct. on the deck), D.
Credit Cards: AE, DC, D, MC, V.
Reservations: Recommended for inside dining.

Handicapped Access: Yes.
Special Features: Waterfront dining; free dockage available.

With its expansive deck and dining room offering views of Solomons's harbor, the Lighthouse Inn is one of the small island's prettiest places to eat. Its cathedral ceilings and skipjack bar (complete with sails), designed and built by local master carver "Pepper" Langley, add to the festive atmosphere. Depending on when you go, you have a number of choices in seating. If you prefer casual, ask for a table on the deck outside, where you can choose from the usual assortment of appetizers (mozzarella sticks and steamed shrimp), as well as crab cake sandwiches and the like. In the double-tiered dining room inside, the menu features somewhat more refined dining, including such selections as the inn's hand-cut, grilled filet mignon paired with a crab cake or a daily fish selection. Stuffed shrimp is a popular offering.

STONEY'S KINGFISHER

410-394-0236.
14442 Main St.
Open: Daily.
Price: Moderate to expensive.
Cuisine: Seafood.
Serving: L, D.
Credit Cards: MC, V.
Reservations: Recommended on weekends.
Handicapped Access: Yes.

The Solomons location in the middle of town is the third for this Southern Maryland institution, where excellent seafood reigns and fine crab cakes are the size of softballs. Comfortably casual, this restaurant offers outdoor seating along Back Creek, murals of nautical scenes, wood carvings of Bay creatures, and windows on the water. The menu is pretty much the same as at the Prince Frederick location, featuring seafood in all its iterations. You can even order deviled crab.

St. Marys County

Maryland's first colonists stepped ashore in rural St. Marys County, at St. Clement's Island in the Potomac River. Now preserved as a state park, the peaceable island sits out in the river upstream from St. Marys City, site of the colony's first capital and location of a village that re-creates the original, which is being excavated.

An easy daytrip from Annapolis, Washington, D.C., or Baltimore, the county mixes history alongside rural Chesapeake, with good mid-Bay fishing and even beach parkland in places like **Point Lookout State Park** at the county's southernmost tip, where more than 50,000 Confederate troops were imprisoned during the Civil War.

Reach St. Marys County via MD 235, 5, or 2/4. Off MD 235 on the Patuxent River side of the county, in Hollywood, stands a colonial grande dame. From its bluff overlooking the Patuxent River, **Sotterley Plantation** (301-373-2280 or 1-800-681-0850; www.sotterley .com; MD 245, Hollywood) is an architectural treasures that weathered the passing generations in relative obscurity. That, despite an intriguing group of owners that includes early Maryland governor George Plater III, who corresponded with his friend George Washington from here. U.S. troops mustered here during the War of 1812, and Confederate sympathizers were here during the Civil War.

Among the remaining relics of the plantation is a rare, small slave cabin—where 19 to 24 people slept—dating to the 1830s. An extensive renovation is under way at the manor house, and more than 6 miles of trails and 23 outbuildings are also located here. Special events are held throughout the year; check the website for details. The plantation is located 9 miles east of Leonardtown on MD 245. The grounds are open year-round, Tues. through Sun. 10–4; the manor house is open May through Oct., Tues. through Sun. 10–4. Admission: adults $7, children 6–16 $5; ground fee $2; group tour rates available.

In quaint **Leonardtown**, the **Maryland Antiques Center** (301-475-1960; MD 5 south of MD 243) features furniture and nauticals, as well as two galleries and a tea room serving lunch and high tea from 11 AM to 4 PM. Also in town is an artists' co-op called the **North End Gallery** (301-475-3130; 41625 Fenwick St.; open Tues. through Sun.), offering exhibitions and a range of talent. Bibliophiles should stop by **Fenwick Street Used Books & Music** (301-475-2859; 41655A Fenwick St.) for a worthwhile browse. Consider a visit to town on the third weekend in Oct. to enjoy the famed **St. Marys County Oyster Festival**, held at the county fairgrounds on MD 5 and home to the National Oyster Shucking Championship. For information, call 1-800-327-9023.

To reach St. Clement's Island and the **St. Clement's Island/Potomac River Museum** (301-769-2222; 38370 Point Breeze Rd., Colton's Point; open late Mar. through late Oct., Mon. through Fri. 9–5, Sat. and Sun. noon–5; winter, Wed. through Sun. noon–4; $1 for ages 12 and up) at **Colton's Point** on the Potomac River side of the county, follow brown history-marker signs on back roads from MD 5. The small but well-considered museum offers a fine review of early Maryland history, saluting its English settlers, who arrived just across the channel at St. Clement's Island in 1634. Among the museum's exhibits is a room that details the beginnings of the Church of England's separation from the Catholic Church. The Calverts, successive Lords Baltimore and Maryland's founders, were Catholics with political clout with the Stuart kings of England in the first half of the 17th century. (Maryland was the first New World colony to actively promote religious tolerance.)

Also detailed here are the colonists' journey aboard the *Ark* and *Dove*, their fortunate first meeting with the Piscataway tribe members, and Potomac River life.

Trails, outbuildings, and special events tell the fascinating story of Sotterley Plantation in St. Marys County.

It's a great destination—even for folks who aren't Maryland history buffs—with riverfront picnic tables, a fishing pier (licenses required), and, best of all, a summer weekend water taxi shuttling to the 40-acre island, which features mown paths, narrow beaches, picnic tables, and multitudinous osprey. Stay for about an hour, or catch the second boat back midafternoon. The boat runs Memorial Day through Oct., Sat. and Sun. 12:30–4, weather permitting, and costs $5 for adults and $3 for children. The ride takes about 15 minutes.

Near the tip of the county stands **St. Marys City**, home to **Historic St. Marys City**, the re-created 1634 colonial capital, and the small liberal arts **St. Marys College**, one of only two public honors colleges in the country (240-895-4380 for event information; www.smcm.edu; St. Marys City, MD 20686).

The original capital city was abandoned when the capital moved to Annapolis, and it was dismantled by 1720, but it's still the subject of extensive archaeological work. Among tantalizing discoveries: three lead coffins found in the early 1990s. After NASA finished testing the air to see whether it dated to the 17th century, researchers concluded that the remains inside likely belonged to members of the Calvert family.

Visitors walking the trails at this riverside site will see framed houses marking a particular dig. In addition, costumed interpreters explain the re-created elements of the city, from a Yaocomaco Indian village with sleeping furs inside the grass witchotts, or dwellings, to Godiah Spray's tobacco plantation populated with cows, chickens, and Ossabaw pigs, a species that first roamed here 300 years ago. The square-rigger *Maryland Dove* (a big hit with kids), a typical period representation of the two vessels that brought early settlers, docks in the St. Marys River and is fun to check out. Also on the grounds is a 1934 reproduction of the statehouse. Currently, a brick chapel is being re-created on an original 1667 foundation.

Stop at the visitor's center for an overview, picnic at the riverside tables, and find snacks at the Shop at Farthing's Ordinary. To contact St. Marys City: 1-800-762-1634; 240-895-4960 (administration); 240-895-4990 (visitor's center); www.stmaryscity.org; 18559 Hogaboom Lane. Open mid-Mar. through Nov. In spring and fall, open Tues. through Sat. (call for hours); summer, Wed. through Sun 10–5. Adults $7.50, seniors and students $6, ages 6–12 $3.50; prices lower on off-season weekends.

Outdoor-lovers visiting St. Marys County will find plenty to do. Cyclists drawn to flat tidewater back roads should stop by area tourism departments or visitor's centers to pick up a copy of the Southern Maryland bicycling map, with its routes plotted through the region and details about traffic. (Note: No crossing major bridges.) Or go bass fishing on the 250-acre lake at **St. Marys River State Park** (301-872-5688; Camp Cosoma Rd.), a two-site park where the lake, encircled by an 11.5-mile trail, can be reached by taking

MD 5 to Camp Cosoma Road between Leonardtown and Great Mills. Or duck down to **Ridge,** home of **Scheible's Fishing Center** (301-872-5185; www.scheibles.homestead.com; 48342 Wynne Rd.), where the longtime charter fleet takes fishers in search of striped bass or bluefish. Half- or full-day charters. Restaurant, lodge.

Farther south, at the end of MD 5, where the Potomac River meets the Chesapeake Bay, stands **Point Lookout State Park** (301-872-5688; 11175 Point Lookout Rd., Scotland, MD 20687), once a Revolution-era lookout and later a Civil War–era Confederate prison camp. Sun yourself on the beach or surf cast. Swim in designated areas. Hike back along the beach to the reconstruction of the Civil War's **Fort Lincoln** and, at the park's tip, check out its lighthouse. Grills, picnic area, and camping. The Civil War Museum/Marshland Nature Center, located in the campground, is open seasonally. In all, 1,046 acres. Also, you can cruise to **Smith Island,** one of the Bay's last two inhabited islands, from the park (see chapter 6, "Lower Eastern Shore," for more about the island). **Smith Island Cruises** (410-425-2771) departs Point Lookout during the season. Call for prices and schedules.

LODGING, MARINAS, AND RESTAURANTS

Lodging rates, based on high-season prices, fall within this scale:

Inexpensive: Up to $75
Moderate: $75 to $120
Expensive: $120 to $175
Very expensive: $175 and up

Restaurant price ranges, which include dinner entrée, appetizer, and dessert, are as follows.

Inexpensive:	Up to $20
Moderate:	$20 to $30
Expensive:	$30 to $40
Very expensive:	$40 or more

Credit card abbreviations are:
AE—American Express
CB—Carte Blanche
DC—Diners Club
D—Discover
MC—MasterCard
V—Visa

The following abbreviations are used to denote meals served:

B = Breakfast; L = Lunch; D = Dinner; SB = Sunday Brunch

THE BROME-HOWARD INN

Innkeepers: Lisa and Michael Kelley.
301-866-0656.
www.bromehowardinn.com.
18281 Rosecroft Rd./P.O. Box 476, St. Marys City, MD 20686.
Room Prices: Expensive to very expensive.
Restaurant Hours: Thurs. 5:30–9, Fri. and Sat. 5:30–10, SB 11–2, Sun. D 5–9.
Restaurant Prices: Expensive to very expensive.
Cuisine: Seafood, continental.
Serving: D, SB.
Credit Cards: AE, D, MC, V.
Reservations: Yes, on warm weather weekends.
Handicapped Access: For restaurant only.

Situated on 30 acres of farmland overlooking St. Marys River near Historic St. Marys City, the 19th-century Brome-Howard Inn offers top-notch cuisine, bed and breakfast services, catering, and 5 miles of hiking trails along the riverbank. Though dining is a bit pricey and formal (classical opera may fill the parlors, and the tables are set with hand-painted china and fresh roses from the inn's working gardens), the management and waitstaff welcome the more casually dressed diner and are highly

Interpreters alongside the re-created statehouse at Historic St. Mary's City. Susan Wilkinson, Historic St. Mary's City

attentive and accommodating. Inside, the decor is comfortable. If the weather invites, request outdoor dining and enjoy the river view. The menu changes and ranges through beef, seafood, and poultry selections prepared in a New American style. For instance, grilled halibut with shrimp and shiitake compote may be served in a reduction of chardonnay and garlic butter sauce.

Overnight guests will find feather beds on pencil-post bed frames, as well as bright

A visit to St. Marys County wouldn't be complete without a history lesson aboard the square-rigger Maryland Dove. Susan Wilkinson, Historic St. Mary's City

baths. Four rooms have fireplaces, but ask for a room with view out onto the river. Enjoy full breakfasts, bicycles, and a fabulous back porch and garden overlooking the river. Check the website for special events, such as mystery or wine dinners.

Motels in Lexington Park, deep in the county near the Patuxent Naval Air Station, include a **Days Inn** (301-863-6666; 21847 Three Notch Rd., Lexington Park, MD 20653; inexpensive to moderate) with 165 rooms, and a **Hampton Inn** (301-863-3200 or 1-800-HAMPTON; 22211 Three Notch Rd., Lexington Park, MD 20653;

moderate with 111 rooms.

Transient dockage is available at **Point Lookout Marina** (301-872-5000 or 1-877-384-9716; www.pointlookoutmarina.com; 16244 Miller's Wharf Rd., Ridge, MD 20680) off the Potomac River on Jutlan and Smith creeks.

CAPTAIN LEONARD'S SEAFOOD HOUSE

301-884-3701.
MD 235, Mechanicsville.
Open: Wed. through Sun.
Price: Moderate.

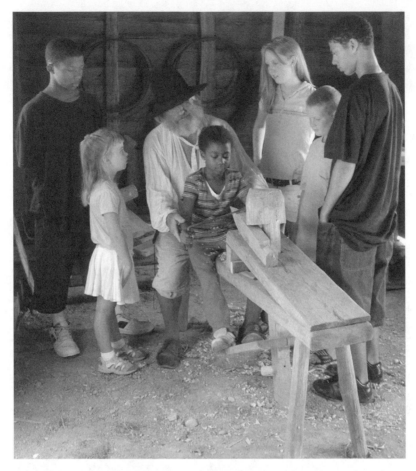

An interpreter at Historic St. Mary's City shows a group of children how he works with an adze, a cutting tool used for shaping wood. Susan Wilkinson, Historic St. Mary's City

Cuisine: Seafood.
Serving: L, D.
Credit Cards: MC, V.
Reservations: No.
Handicapped Access: Yes.

For folks en route to St. Marys County or returning home, *the* place to stop is Captain Leonard's. Right on MD 235 at the southern junction of MD 6, this gem is easy to dismiss if judged by the exterior. Locals know better. Once inside, if you can find a space in the packed parking lot, piles of pickin' crabs and mugs of beer sit in front of folks who make the restaurant ring with laughter and conversation. The service is welcoming and it matches the relaxed atmosphere. The crabs are the best, but also consider oysters, scallops, cherrystone clams, snow crab legs, catfish, trout, flounder, and spiced or delicately breaded fried shrimp and oysters—far better than the usual overbreaded Maryland fare. Even frog legs. Those who prefer turf to surf can find chicken, hamburgers, and New York strip steak. From the appetizer list, the crab balls are prime with lump crab and heartily seasoned, and seasonal raw oysters on the half shell are a fresh favorite. Soups include oyster stew and Maryland red and cream of crab. A definite Southern Maryland treasure you'll want to share with your friends.

Family Fun: Fossil Hunting

Eons ago, the Bay was a Miocene Era sea. Remnants of that past turn up along Calvert Cliffs, as fossils dating 15 to 20 million years back wash ashore. The cliffs run from the north of Calvert County south, and ancient sharks' teeth are the prize. You also can find age-old sand dollars, scallops, and other shells. Public access points are few. Common wisdom says get there at low tide, but great finds depend on the weather, luck, whether the beach has been picked over during a run of calm days, or whether you arrive just after a storm's kicked things up. Author Allison Blake once took her niece, Shannon, then age 10, to Calvert Cliffs State Park to look for fossils early one June morning. Here's Shannon's report:

"Calvert Cliffs State Park is a nice place to spend the day, but I didn't really find many fossils there. The cliffs are 30 feet long and sort of like a straight walk up. Luckily, when we were at the park, we saw a geologist and he showed us fossilized sand dollars. There's a beach a little north from there called Flag Pond Nature Center where you can find sharks' teeth, but we had no luck there. Flag Pond is more like a beach, I thought.

"My aunt went to Brownie's Beach [author's note: now called Bay Front Park] after I left and found seven sharks' teeth. It is at the north end of the 30-mile range of the cliffs, and the other two locations we went to were on the south. But if you do go to Calvert Cliffs State Park, you should keep in mind that it is a 1.8-mile walk, and if you're going to play at the beach, then you should be ready to walk 1.8 miles back. Also, the bugs are bad so bring bug spray. Also, DO NOT CLIMB ON THE CLIFFS!!! Lastly, you should get there at low tide to look for shells and low tide is according to the position of the moon."

NATURAL PLACES

Well, there you have it. The geology buff we encountered at the state park put us on to **Flag Ponds Nature Center** (410-586-1477; 10 mi. south of Prince Frederick on MD 2/4, look for the sign on your left). We also found locals identifying their finds in a section of the **Calvert Marine Museum** (see the "Solomons Island" section for details) that has lots of fossils and information about them. Digging in Calvert Cliffs is prohibited.

Additional fossil-hunting haunts: **Bay Front Park** (410-257-2230; about half a mile south of Chesapeake Beach) A thin beach widens noticeably at low tide; we found seven sharks' teeth in an hour one afternoon!

Calvert Cliffs State Park (301-743-7613; 14 mi. south of Prince Frederick off MD 2/4 in Lusby) Thirteen miles of hiking trails include a nice 1.8-mile walk to the beach that starts out next to a babbling brook, passes a haunting wetland (you can walk out on a boardwalk), then takes you to the narrow beach. No lifeguards. Open sunrise to sunset. Take only what you find on the beach; the cliffs are off-limits.

This statue in Rock Hall honors the work of the area's watermen. Tim Tadder

4

The Upper Bay

Decoys, Docks & Lazy Days

Havre de Grace Around the Head of the Bay to Chestertown and Rock Hall

Fields of corn and soybeans go on forever as the countryside starts to roll north of the Chesapeake Bay Bridge on the Eastern Shore, toward the stately brick buildings of Chestertown, a major 18th-century port, and on to crossroads towns beloved by antiquers and marinas alongside rivers named Chester, Sassafras, and Bohemia. Rounding the head of the Bay, the traveler salutes the Chesapcake & Delaware Canal at Chesapeake City, a recovered Victorian gem where plaques on the front of each colorful home announce the name of its 19th-century founder. Past Elkton and North East (and the top-of-the-Bay Elk and North East rivers), one finally crosses high above the mighty Susquehanna River. Here is the prehistoric forebear to the Bay, a wide river whose nearby towns include churches and mansions built of granite from its shores at nearby Port Deposit. Tougher stuff than you'll find in the southern Bay.

Look to the river as you cross to see the Susquehanna Flats, which once drew U.S. presidents and merchants of industry to partake in the sportsman's "gunning" life. Here, the Northeast is coming on; travelers headed north on I-95 will find themselves on the New Jersey Turnpike in less than an hour. They'd do well to stop where the river meets the Bay: in Havre de Grace, "Decoy Capital of the World" and a growing tourist town. From many points in town, you can see the water.

This part of Bay Country tends to look more to Philadelphia or Baltimore than, say, Washington, D.C., but nowhere in Chesapeake does one escape colonial U.S. history. George Washington passed through the Upper Shore as he went about his Revolution-era duties.

Chestertown, with its abundant restored 18th-century buildings, sits snug alongside the Chester River. Cross the bridge into this prosperous town, where shops and restaurants line the streets. The Imperial Hotel and White Swan Tavern, famed restorations, hold court across High Street from one another. Washington College dates to 1782 and provides a cultural center for the town. With its wealth of terrific lodgings, restaurants, and other amenities, Chestertown makes a central headquarters for exploring the Upper Eastern Shore area.

From here, you can head straight for the Bay, down MD 20 to **Rock Hall.** This little watermen's town increasingly is claimed by boaters who dock their craft at multitudinous

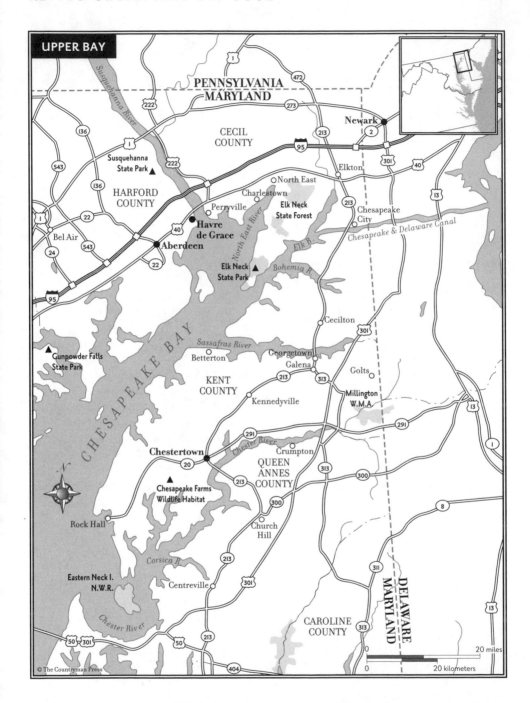

marinas or stay in its pretty B&Bs. A ferry here transported Revolution-era travelers to and from Annapolis, including the fabled Marylander Tench Tilghman, who carried news of the colonial troops' victory at Yorktown as he passed through en route to Philadelphia, where the Continental Congress was meeting. The handful of gallery-style shops here offer original work by regional artists and crafters. And don't forget to visit Eastern Neck National

Wildlife Refuge, an island hugging the Eastern Shore's left bank past Rock Hall. Walk out on a boardwalk and look over the water for shorebirds in summer, or for the famed tundra swans that arrive as cooler days signal the coming of winter.

Antique lovers won't want to miss the crossroads town of **Galena,** 15 miles from Chestertown up MD 213, the most scenic primary route through this part of the shore. Antiques shops here make for some good browsing, and you may find treats like pie safes and pine sinks, sturdy furniture from an earlier era. This little town isn't far from **Crumpton,** home of Dixon's Furniture and the notable Wednesday auction that spans 30 acres.

The War of 1812 saw combat here in Kent County with the Battle of Caulk's Field in 1814. The house where the British commander purportedly died is now a B&B, the Inn at Mitchell House. In addition, just up MD 213 from Chestertown, the famed Kitty Knight stood up to the marauding British troops at Georgetown. The Kitty Knight House—saved from fire—also is now an inn.

Farther on up MD 213 stands **Chesapeake City,** famous for the 14-mile long Chesapeake & Delaware Canal that links the Bay with the Delaware River, as well as the Bayard House, a fine dining establishment whose physical rebirth may be as significant as its food. It was restored in the mid-1980s as this Victorian town's renaissance was under way. Bring your binoculars when you visit, since watching the major ships pass through the canal is a prime Chesapeake City activity. Just outside of town, the C&D Canal Museum even has a TV screen set up so you can watch the maritime parade.

Havre de Grace, less than an hour west of here across the tip of the Bay, qualifies as one of the more industrious Bay towns when it comes to tourism. Over recent years, the city has built—and, since Tropical Storm Isabel in September 2003, has rebuilt—a lovely boardwalk along its Susquehanna River waterfront and welcomed a variety of cruising craft to town. It is thought that the town's name derives from the Marquis de Lafayette, who compared this with Le Havre in his own France. Dating to 1658, Havre de Grace still feels like a hometown despite the arrival of newcomers and changes along the waterfront. Along Washington Street, for instance, antiques shops have moved into old department stores. Visitors of a certain age will recognize the feel of old downtowns from childhood.

Travelers along these rolling tidewater roads can't help but notice how many long lanes stretch back from farms or historic homes with names like "Tranquility." It's true that new homes are popping up, but the indelible impression of cornfields and working farms (including horse farms) remains. Marinas cluster along the edge of the rivers, where boaters enjoy the charms of gentle rivers that flow to the Bay.

LODGING

The villages and crossroads towns of the Upper Bay region offer B&Bs and small inns that may be reproduction Georgians or old Victorians. Have tea on a brick patio during summer afternoons, or relax in a hot tub alongside the Chesapeake & Delaware Canal. Prices are highest during high-season weekends and tend to go down midweek and again in the off-season. Of course, they are subject to change. Check cancellation policies, and don't be surprised if your inn has a two-night minimum, especially in high season. Assume smoking and pets are prohibited unless otherwise noted, and check lodging websites for other policies that can change or for specials.

Rates

Lodging rates, based on high-season prices, fall within this scale:

Inexpensive:	Up to $75
Moderate:	$75 to $120
Expensive:	$120 to $175
Very expensive:	$175 and up

Credit card abbreviations are:

AE—American Express
CB—Carte Blanche
DC—Diners Club
D—Discover
MC—MasterCard
V—Visa

HAVRE DE GRACE

LA CLE D'OR GUESTHOUSE

Proprietor: Ron Browning.
410-939-6562 or 1-888-HUG-GUEST.
www.lacledorguesthouse.com.
226 N. Union Ave., Havre de Grace, MD
21078.
Price: Moderate to expensive.
Credit Cards: MC, V.
Handicapped Access: No.
Restrictions: Call to make arrangements for children under 12.

La Cle D'or looks sturdily prosperous from the outside, but check out the crystal chandeliers and shiny gold wallpaper in the parlor! The 1868 brick house, once owned by members of the Johns Hopkins family, is surprisingly luxurious, and host Ron Browning knows a thing or two about antiques. Guest rooms retain a French flair —this is, after all, Havre de Grace, the "Harbor of Grace" named by Lafayette— right down to the Napoleonic wallpaper. The Rochambeaux Room comes with an antique double bed and a bath around the corner. Next door find the pleasant DeGrace Suite, rented only with the Rochambeaux, making a nice accommodation for traveling couples willing to share a hall bath. Then there's the Lafayette Suite, with a queen-size bed and a window-lined sitting room overlooking the home's secluded walled garden. Each room comes with a television and VCR. Full breakfast.

SPENCER-SILVER MANSION

Innkeeper: Carol Nemeth.
410-939-1097 or 1-800-780-1485.
www.spencersilvermansion.com.
200 S. Union Ave., Havre de Grace, MD
21078.
Price: Moderate to expensive.
Credit Cards: AE, DC, D, MC, V.
Handicapped Access: In the carriage house.
Special Features: Kids OK; pets allowed in the carriage house.

"J. N. Spencer, 1896" reads the marble plate surrounding the doorbell at this Victorian, authentic from the turret atop the house to the intricate woodwork in the hallway. A bronze Art Deco figure even presents itself on the newel post. Original stained glass atop many windows is worth the price of your night's stay, and innkeeper Carol Nemeth has been at it for so many years it's hard to imagine a detail she hasn't foreseen. Not only that, but this is a good bargain. Four rooms, each with amenities such as ironing boards and televisions, are located inside the house and include marble-topped tables or corner cabinets with inset glass. Two enormous front rooms share a bath; two have private baths. Enter one of the private baths, with its two-person whirlpool tub, through stained-glass doors. The stone carriage house out back is cozy enough to spend the winter, with a queen-size bed and window seat in the wood-stained bedroom at the top of the iron spiral staircase. Downstairs expect a daybed, whirlpool, TV/DVD player, and kitchenette. In a relative rarity, breakfast at the Spencer-Silver is served until 10:30 AM.

VANDIVER INN

Innkeepers: Susan and John Muldoon.
410-939-5200 or 1-800-245-1655.
www.vandiverinn.com.

301 S. Union Ave., Havre de Grace, MD
21078.
Price: Moderate to expensive.
Credit Cards: AE, D, MC, V.
Handicapped Access: Limited; call to
discuss.

The venerable Vandiver, onetime home to
the local mayor and Maryland politician of
the same name, nearly doubled its longtime
accommodations recently when it expanded
into two houses next door. Now visitors can
stay in the landmark 1886 Victorian, nine
rooms in all, with elaborate tiled fireplaces
or twin flues, claw-foot tubs, and antique
full-size beds, or head next door for the
eight rooms located in the Kent and
Murphy Houses. Either way, your old-
fashioned-flavored stay comes with modern touches like hair dryers and televisions
in all rooms and a range of amenities. Beds
range from twin to king-size, and whirlpool
suites are available. A jazz dinner is held
once a month.

*The Victorian Vandiver Inn offers lovely accommo-
dations in Havre de Grace.*

*Victorian accents decorate the Inn at the Canal in
Chesapeake City.*

CHESAPEAKE CITY
INN AT THE CANAL
Innkeepers: Mary and Al Ioppolo.
410-885 5995.
www.innatthecanal.com.
104 Bohemia Ave./P.O. Box 187,
Chesapeake City, MD 21915.
Price: Moderate to very expensive.
Credit Cards: AE, DC, D, MC, V.
Handicapped Access: No.
Restrictions: Call about children under 10.

Replete with elaborate hand-painted ceiling
murals in both the parlor and the dining
room, this Victorian is still known locally as
the Brady-Rees House, after the Bradys who
owned and operated tugboats on the nearby
canal. Six rooms and a suite reflect the owners' longtime experience in the B&B biz.
Each is uncluttered, with easily accessible
luggage racks so there's no mystery about
where your suitcase is supposed to go. Nice
touches include bureaus converted to sinks
in the bathrooms and four-poster rice beds.
Individual climate control, televisions, and

telephones with data ports are in the rooms, which are good-looking without a lot of fuss. Upstairs find a third-floor suite with a balcony overlooking the marina and water. Breakfast is served at individual tables, and guests will want to visit Inntiques, located in the former milking room.

OLD WHARF COTTAGE B&B

Operator: The Bayard House.
410-885-5040 or 1-877-582-4049.
www.bayardhouse.com.
10 Bohemia Ave., Chesapeake City, MD 21915.
Price: Expensive to very expensive.
Credit Cards: AE, D, MC, V.
Handicapped Access: No.
Special Features: Children OK.

This little building along the C&D Canal has had several lives, including an early one as an icehouse, and later as a gift shop. Now it's a small cottage-style inn settled across the street from the Bayard House Restaurant, with lots of privacy. On the first floor find a sitting room, kitchen, and bath, and upstairs a bedroom with its own balcony. Ceilings are low. These unique accommodations should not be missed if you're looking for a true getaway. Continental breakfast.

SHIP WATCH INN

Owners: Gilda and Gianmarco Martuscelli.
410-885-5300.
www.shipwatchinn.com.
401 First St., Chesapeake City, MD 21915.
Price: Moderate to very expensive.
Credit Cards: AE, MC, V.
Handicapped Access: Yes.
Restriction: No children under 12.

Porches or balconies span each of the three waterside floors here, allowing comfortable and ample opportunity to watch the maritime parade along the C&D Canal. A mid-1990s renovation to this 1920s building left pine floors covered with Oriental-style

Guest rooms at the Ship Watch Inn have views of the C&D Canal.

runners, while a 2004 addition added two handsome new suites with Hemingway-esque British colonial decor. All of the inn's suites and rooms vary along a comfortably elegant design scale, detailed nicely with lovely furnishings. All have glass doors that open onto the inn's canal-side balconies. Small televisions are in the rooms, and there's an outdoor hot tub. Full breakfast is served on the first-floor porch in good weather. The Martuscellis also operate the popular Chesapeake Inn nearby.

A view of the C&D Canal from the guest room porches at the Ship Watch Inn.

CHESTERTOWN
THE BRAMPTON INN
Owners: Michael and Danielle Hanscom.
410-778-1860 or 1-866-305-1860.
www.bramptoninn.com.
25227 Chestertown Rd., Chestertown, MD
21620.
Price: Expensive to very expensive.
Credit Cards: D, MC, V.
Handicapped Access: Yes.
Restrictions: No children under 12; call
about small pets.

You'll feel yourself start to relax as you pull
up to this 1860 plantation house, fronted
with century-old trees and boxwoods set on
35 acres between the Chester River and the
Chesapeake Bay. Inside, the ceilings are
high, the furnishings mix antiques and
reproductions, and old wood dominates,
from Georgia pine floors to a three-and-a-
half-story walnut and ash central staircase.
Nine smartly decorated guest rooms have
private baths and AC, eight have working
fireplaces, and five have whirlpool tubs.
The second-floor Blue Room, with windows in the trees, is lovely in the fall and
has a double-jet shower, while the two-
story Fairy Hill Suite, once a kitchen
topped by slave quarters, is charming. The
wraparound porch has been rebuilt at this
Select Registry, Distinguished Inns of
North America member inn, where full
breakfast and afternoon tea are served,
classic videos are available for viewing, and
the warm hosts have been in the business
since 1987.

GREAT OAK MANOR B&B
Innkeepers: Cassandra and John Fedas.
410-778-5943 or 1-800-504-3098.
www.greatoak.com.
10568 Cliff Rd., Chestertown, MD 21620.
Price: Expensive to very expensive.
Credit Cards: MC, V.
Handicapped Access: Yes.
Restrictions: No children.

A stunning Bay-side inn, Great Oak Manor
is unusual among the many Eastern Shore
mansions built in the 1930s because this
faithful Georgian reproduction used old
brick, probably shipped as ballast in Grace
Line ships. Detail and carvings are meticulous, guest rooms are handsomely furnished—some with antiques—and the
public rooms are varied and interesting. A
recently added conservatory departs from
the colonial theme but adds an elegant
touch of contemporary warmth. All 12
guest rooms are attractively decorated and
spacious, many with Bay views and/or fireplaces. The old third-floor gambling room

*Great Oak Manor near Chestertown features 12
handsomely decorated guest rooms.*

is spacious and clubby, with a high ceiling,
king-size bed, and knotty pine paneling on
some of its walls. Set on 12 acres, Great
Oak offers an expansive waterside backyard where the Adirondack chairs beckon.
Room amenities range from hair dryers to
irons to safes, and guests have access to
complimentary bikes as well as nearby
Great Oak Landing, which has a 9-hole golf
course, tennis, and a swimming pool. Full
breakfast. Member of Select Registry,
Distinguished Inns of North America.

IMPERIAL HOTEL
Innkeepers: Jan MacDonald and Richard O'Neill.
410-778-5000.
www.imperialchestertown.com.
208 High St., Chestertown, MD 21620.
Price: Moderate to very expensive.
Credit Cards: AE, MC, V.
Handicapped Access: No.

This 1903 hotel, fully renovated in 1985 and improved upon ever since, creates intimacy and privacy in its 11 rooms, suite, and courtyard carriage house, all beautifully appointed with period furnishings. Upscale amenities such as towel warmers ensure that guests feel pampered, while a clubby double veranda overlooking the Historic District is a prime spot for watching downtown Chestertown pass by. A lovely courtyard in back is available for private parties during the summer. In the colder months, the cozy Chester River Lounge in the lobby area is an ideal place for a fireside cocktail. For a cozy escape, you can't do better than the Imperial, a comfortable Victorian-style hotel.

THE INN AT MITCHELL HOUSE
Owners: Jim and Tracy Stone.
410-778-6500.
www.innatmitchellhouse.com.
8796 Maryland Pkwy., Chestertown, MD 21620.
Price: Moderate to expensive.
Credit Cards: MC, V.
Handicapped Access: No.
Restrictions: Children accepted by prior arrangement only.

This longtime B&B, an 18th-century manor house, boasts a much older history of welcoming guests. British commander Sir Peter Parker allegedly was brought here after the nearby Battle of Caulk's Field in 1814, fought during the War of 1812. When surgery upon the kitchen table failed to save his life, they pickled Peter Parker in a keg of rum and sent him back to England. You'll find your stay here far more pleasant. Located in the country close to Chestertown, Rock Hall, and the once-bustling resort town of Tolchester, this 1743 manor house sits on 10 acres at the end of a long, tree-lined drive by a pond. Inside are five full rooms with private baths (a sixth room is rented only as part of a suite), four with fireplaces, fire logs provided. Four more fireplaces stand in the house's public areas, which have an outdoor motif of mounted waterfowl, marsh grass, and riding hats. It all makes for a suitable introduction to rural Kent County. A full country breakfast is served in a dining room decorated with china plates.

THE PARKER HOUSE
Owners: Marcy and John Parker.
410-778-9041.
www.chestertown.com/parker.
108 Spring Ave., Chestertown, MD 21620.
Price: Expensive.
Credit Cards: No.
Handicapped Access: Yes.
Special Features: Children welcome.

When regulars said the stairs gave them trouble, the Parkers turned their inn's family room into a spacious first-floor guest room with king-size bed and private bath. That gives you an idea of the warm welcome that awaits in this circa-1876 Victorian in the heart of Chestertown. Large common areas are lavishly furnished with antiques. There's only one bathroom upstairs, so the two upstairs rooms—one with a queen bed, one with two twins—either are rented together to traveling companions, or only one room is rented. Marcy's popovers and Amish sticky buns delight guests at the continental breakfast served in the formal dining room. There's an interesting history here, too. This former home to Kent County's first millionaire had the county's

The White Swan Tavern in Chestertown is a well-known colonial restoration.

first indoor bathroom and electricity. By the mid-1960s, it was vacant, in disrepair, and called a ghost house by local kids. Now the Parker House is a post-restoration showcase.

THE WHITE SWAN TAVERN

Manager: Mary Susan Maisel.
410-778-2300.
www.whiteswantavern.com.
231 High St., Chestertown, MD 21620.
Price: Expensive to very expensive.
Credit Cards: MC, V.
Handicapped Access: Yes.
Special Features: Children welcome.

Perhaps the most authentic, meticulous colonial restoration on the Eastern Shore, the 1733 White Swan is a time capsule, handsome, dignified, and located on the Historic District's main street. A collection of people in waistcoats and breeches gathered in its public rooms would create a per-

fect time warp. Guest rooms, however, have modern comforts, with private baths, non-working fireplaces (although fires blaze in the common areas), and refrigerators. Accommodations range from the John Lovegrove Kitchen room, with its massive fireplace and exposed beams dating to 1705, to the winding T. W. Eliason Victorian Suite, complete with parlor. Even if you can't stay here, stop by for afternoon tea between 3 and 5 daily. Guests also get a continental breakfast brought to their room on request, a complimentary fruit basket, and a bottle of wine. Check the display cabinet to see artifacts found during the 1978 archaeological dig.

GEORGETOWN
KITTY KNIGHT HOUSE

Owners: Joe and Joann Thompson.
410-648-5200.
www.kittyknight.com.
14028 Augustine Herman Hwy., Georgetown, MD 21930
Price: Moderate to expensive.
Credit Cards: AE, DC, D, MC, V.
Handicapped Access: Only in the restaurant.

The fabled Kitty Knight House, its 1750 working kitchen now the tavern for the restaurant downstairs, offers 10 rooms to guests here along the Sassafras River. Comfortable and traditionally decorated, the rooms—one is a two-room suite—offer four-poster beds, coffeemakers, and televisions. In addition, there's a valet cottage here, another local historic building that guests can rent. The restaurant serves a seafood buffet on Fri. nights, and the main dining room overlooks the river. This historic house stands thanks to Kitty Knight, a lass who stood up to the British as they marauded through the area during the War of 1812. She convinced them not to burn the house, which was then home to an elderly local lady.

ROCK HALL

THE INN AT OSPREY POINT

Manager: Christine Will.

410-639-2194.

www.ospreypoint.com.

20786 Rock Hall Ave., Rock Hall, MD 21661.

Price: Moderate to very expensive.

Credit Cards: D, MC, V.

Handicapped Access: No.

Special Features: Children welcome.

Newly built in 1993, this white brick Colonial is modeled after the Coke-Garrett House in Williamsburg, Va. Seven pretty rooms with colonial-style furnishings and decor also have private baths, air-conditioning, cable television, and other pleasantries of the early 21st century. Family- friendly rooms are large enough to accommodate a pullout couch or a cot. Located on 30 lush Swan Creek acres overlooking a marina, with a swimming pool, volleyball, horseshoes, nature trails, and complimentary bicycles, this is more like a small resort than an inn. Management can arrange sailing, fishing, or horseback riding. The restaurant serves dinner Thurs. through Mon.; regulars know to order the cream of crab soup, served with the traditional sherry. Continental breakfast.

MOONLIGHT BAY INN

Owners: Dotty and Bob Santangelo.

410-639-2660.

www.moonlightbayinn.com.

6002 Lawton Ave., Rock Hall, MD 21661.

Price: Expensive.

Credit Cards: D, MC, V.

Handicapped Access: Yes.

Special Features: Two rooms suitable for very young children.

Settle in to your Queen Anne—style room in this romantic Victorian along the water, with lush wallpaper and afternoon high tea to boot. Five rooms in the newer "west wing" have balconies and single whirlpools; four of the five rooms in the main house have water views. Sailors ready to get off the boat for a night can dock at one of the marina's 50 transient boat slips. Two comfy parlors. Full breakfast.

SWAN HAVEN

Innkeepers: Diane Oliver and Harry Newman.

410-639-2527.

www.swanhaven.com.

20950 Rock Hall Ave., Rock Hall, MD 21661.

Price: Moderate to expensive.

Credit Cards: AE, MC, V.

Handicapped Access: No.

Restrictions: No children under 10.

At various times a temporary hospital and a waterman's home, the century-old Swan Haven, a Victorian mansion, is a handy resting place for people in town for sailing, biking, kayaking, or bird-watching. Ten modern rooms, all with private baths and cable television, are pretty and comfortable without being overly fancy. Beds are mostly king- and queen-size. The second-floor Cignet Room features a whirlpool tub for two, a king-size bed, and a grand view of Swan Creek and the marina through double doors that open onto a screened-in porch. After a self-serve continental breakfast, take advantage of the free bikes (also rented to nonguests, along with kayaks, canoes, small boats, and fishing rods), the sprawling deck, and the pier, a perfect place to watch the boats and waterfowl come and go or to take in the sunset. Walk to local restaurants.

Hotels/Motels

Comfort Suites (410-810-0555; 160 Scheeler Rd., Chestertown, MD 21620) Located off MD 213 just outside of town. Fifty-three rooms, indoor pool. Moderate to expensive.

Mears Great Oak Landing and Lodge
(410-778-2100, ext. 171; www.mears
greatoaklanding.com; Great Oak Landing
Rd., Chestertown, MD 21620) Dock at the
accompanying marina and take a night off
from the boat in one of 28 rooms. There's
also a 9-hole golf course, a restaurant, and
renovations on the drawing board. Open
daily in-season and long weekends in winter. Moderate to expensive.

RESTAURANTS

As always around the Bay, dining options
are varied and the seafood can't be beat.

Price ranges, which include dinner
entrée, appetizer, and dessert, are as follows:

Inexpensive:	Up to $20
Moderate:	$20 to $30
Expensive:	$30 to $40
Very expensive:	$40 or more

Credit card abbreviations are:
AE—American Express
CB—Carte Blanche
DC—Diners Club
D—Discover
MC—MasterCard
V—Visa

The following abbreviations are used to
denote meals served:
B = Breakfast; L = Lunch; D = Dinner;
SB = Sunday Brunch

HAVRE DE GRACE
TIDEWATER GRILLE
410-939-3313.
300 Foot of Franklin St.
Open: Daily.
Price: Moderate.
Cuisine: Authentic regional American.
Serving: L, D.
Credit Cards: AE, DC, MC, V.
Reservations: Not accepted.
Handicapped Access: Yes.

This longtime staple along the upper
Susquehanna River reaches of the
Chesapeake Bay has maintained its food
and service at a high if casual level for
years. Long windows open the modern dining room onto the Susquehanna and its
passing railroad bridge, while an ample
deck outside accommodates the al fresco
crowd. Chesapeake-inspired stained-glass
panels of leaping fish and ducks top the
windows, a lovely but unobtrusive touch—
just like the food and service. We've always
been impressed by the crab cakes. The rest
of the well-considered menu includes a
number of salads, seafood dishes, pastas,
and beef.

ST. JOHN GOURMET
410-939-FOOD.
209 N. Washington St./210 St. John St.
Open: Daily.
Price: Inexpensive to moderate.
Cuisine: Northern California meets
Chesapeake Bay.
Serving: L, D, SB.
Credit Cards: AE, MC, V.
Reservations: Yes.
Handicapped Access: No.

Two chefs who've done time in Baltimore's
culinary circles bring their flair to Havre de
Grace, where the front door to their stylish
restaurant is located down a narrow side
alley. Two dining rooms textured with rich
fabrics and fired-up walls greet visitors,
and you can even glimpse the Susquehanna
from a couple of tables in the front. Cholula
hot sauce sits alongside the salt and pepper
shakers on each table, and aioli arrives on
the crab cake sandwiches instead of tartar
sauce. New Englanders would be proud of
the well-made chowder in the chicken corn
chowder we enjoyed at a recent lunch. The
rest of the menu runs from fancy sandwiches at lunch to a Cajun-crusted tenderloin wrapped in phyllo with Havarti and

caramelized onions at dinner. Takeout is available downstairs. As deadline arrived, a new menu was to debut at a newly named section of this popular restaurant, called Laurrapin Grille, the first word being Appalachian for "tasty."

CHESAPEAKE CITY
BAYARD HOUSE RESTAURANT
410-885-5040 or 1-877-582-4049.
11 Bohemia Ave.
Open: Daily.
Price: Expensive to very expensive.
Cuisine: Seafood, continental.
Serving: L, D.
Credit Cards: AE, DC, D, MC, V.
Reservations: Recommended.
Handicapped Access: Yes.

In an earlier life, this 1829 brick establishment served the builders of the C&D Canal. In more recent years, the green Victorian painted lady has welcomed diners in cozy dining rooms or a long, glassed-in canal-side patio with candy-striped fabric draping the inside wall. Local seafood has its luxurious touches, such as the Anaheim peppers stuffed with lump crabmeat, Maine lobster, and shrimp. A noted specialty is the Tournedos Baltimore, one medium rare filet topped with a crab cake, another with a lobster cake, finished with a Madeira cream and a seafood champagne sauce for $28. Chef Brandon Gentry brings country-club kitchen experience and a degree from the Culinary Institute of America to the kitchen. Downstairs you'll find the historic Hole in the Wall pub. Located at the end of Bohemia Avenue, the Bayard House is popular with diners in Chesapeake City.

KENNEDYVILLE
KENNEDYVILLE INN
410-348-2400.
11986 Augustine Herman Hwy. (MD 213).
Open: Wed. through Sun.
Price: Moderate to expensive.
Cuisine: Regional American.
Serving: D.
Credit Cards: D, MC, V.
Reservations: For parties of six or more only.
Handicapped Access: Yes.

Recently taken over by sous chef Jason Hopwood and his partner, Glenn May, the Kennedyville Inn's fabled ribs, smoked in-house, aren't going anywhere. The new owners, who have worked together in the past in Baltimore kitchens, have painted the walls a soft yellow and added some textured fabrics. They expect to focus on fresh seasonal ingredients and continue the popular inn's spirit of casual fine dining. Desserts are made in-house, and a recent fall menu featured lamb shank; salmon with bacon, leeks, walnuts, and apples; and, of course, a seasonal Chesapeake rockfish.

CHESTERTOWN
BLUE HERON CAFÉ
410-778-0188.
236 Cannon St.
Open: Mon. through Sat.
Price: Moderate to very expensive.
Cuisine: Traditional and innovative American.
Serving: L, D.
Credit Cards: AE, D, MC, V.
Reservations: Strongly advised.
Handicapped Access: Yes.

Soft music and high ceilings affixed with quietly spinning fans are part of the casual dining atmosphere at this popular restaurant. The menu focuses on fresh local ingredients, with strong emphasis on creative but classic preparation. There's a nice selection of seafood, including Maryland crab cakes and gently sautéed soft-shell crabs in-season. For those wanting heartier fare, consider entrées such as the roasted rack of lamb rubbed with rosemary and dijon accompanied by a shiitake mushroom sauce, or the grilled filet mignon. For starters, the oyster fritters in a lemon butter sauce are a favorite requested by the loyal patrons—famous enough to get a mention in *Time* magazine a few years back. Outdoor tables in the courtyard out back provide an ideal spot to enjoy your culinary options, a sip or two of wine, and the friendly, easy pace of historic Chestertown.

IMPERIAL HOTEL RESTAURANT
410-778-5000.
208 High St.
Open: Wed. through Sun.
Price: Expensive to very expensive.
Cuisine: Regional American.
Serving: L (Sun. only), D (Wed. through Sat.).
Credit Cards: AE, MC, V.
Reservations: Suggested.
Handicapped Access: Yes.

Formality reigns in the Imperial Hotel's two intimate dining rooms, where diners tread a lush green rug and sit down to tables topped with crisp white linens and flickering votives. Alongside one dining room wall stands a dark wood antique sideboard. Very Victorian; dig out your manners. The menu features updated versions of seafood, beef, and poultry; a recent menu offered a pan-seared duck breast done with roasted polenta, a sweet rhubarb sauce, and crème fraîche. Fresh, seasonal ingredients are the goal, and the kitchen also tries to buy from organic farms when possible. Courtyard dining is available, weather permitting.

KETTLEDRUM TEA ROOM
410-810-1497.
117 Cross St.
Open: Mon. and Thurs. through Sun.
Price: Expensive.
Cuisine: English and American.
Serving: L, D (no D on Mon.).
Credit Cards: MC, V.
Reservations: Suggested.
Handicapped Access: No.
Special Features: BYO wine with $3 corkage fee.

If you have an interest in the art and sensory pleasures of high tea, the KettleDrum Tea Room is a must-visit in Chestertown. In traditional English style, proper tea is served with a multicourse "tea meal" presented on antique dishes and silver plates. Truly an afternoon delight. Both elegant and inviting, the Kettledrum features deep green and cranberry walls and white linen tablecloths atop a cranberry brocade fabric. Tastefully placed crystal chandeliers provide soft lighting from the late afternoon into evening. Although the establishment started as just a tearoom, locals and visitors alike encouraged the owners to offer more of their talents to this quiet community. Now, the Kettledrum offers both lunch and dinner. Lunch, or "tiffin," described as an afternoon meal, consists of homemade soups, salads, wraps, and the "almost famous crab pie," a signature dish that is also offered for dinner. Fresh fish is always on the menu, along with other seasonally available items that utilize the freshest local ingredients.

ROCK HALL
BAY LEAF GOURMET
410-639-2700.
5757 Main St.
Open: Tues. through Sun.
Price: Inexpensive.
Cuisine: Light fare and desserts.
Serving: B, L, takeout D.
Credit Cards: AE, MC, V.
Reservations: No.
Handicapped Access: Yes.

Increasingly, outsiders are discovering Rock Hall, a long-ensconced watermen's town with a bustling harbor at its edge. But let's keep it in perspective. As we gazed out the window over a blue cheese and apple quiche lunch here one summer Tuesday, a man drove his riding lawn mower down the middle of this cute but not entirely remade Main Street and had nary a vehicular competitor in sight. For its part, the Bay Leaf creates a welcome development along Main Street. Open throughout the week year-round, the gourmet café offers homemade soups, design-your-own sandwiches, desserts, and quiches, such as the aforementioned blue cheese and apple—eggy and wonderful and a tough choice over the wild mushroom and leek option. Morning coffee carafes sit out late alongside muffins and pastries. Owner Christine Burgess has cooked in kitchens around the area, and she's created an airy, clean dining room with a menu to match. Closes at 5 PM every day but Sun., when it closes at 3.

P. E. PRUITT'S WATERSIDE RESTAURANT & RAW BAR

410-639-7454.
20895 Bayside Ave.
Open: Daily.
Price: Moderate to expensive.
Cuisine: Seafood.
Serving: L, D, SB.
Credit Cards: AE, D, MC, V.
Reservations: Not taken; priority seating.
Handicapped Access: Yes.

Waterside P. E. Pruitt's offers dining inside and out. Pictures of every manner of sailing vessel adorn the main dining room's ocean-blue walls, and tables are covered in white linen, but the atmosphere is quite casual and comfortable. Outside, you'll find picnic-style tables, the raw clam and oyster bar, and very generous drinks served from the dockside bar. Owner Bob Harris cut his teeth in the Annapolis-area restaurant business and is justifiably proud of the freshness of the fish he serves. The chef is very accommodating, and you can have rockfish, salmon, shrimp, scallops, or the "fresh fish of the day" broiled, baked, blackened, or with crab imperial. Although Pruitt's boasts New Orlean—style food, those acquainted with the real thing, such as jambalaya, might be disappointed. Stick to the fresh fish, simply prepared. Call in advance if you're arriving by boat; they can help you secure a slip or use their dinghy dock.

WATERMAN'S CRAB HOUSE

410-639-2261.
21055 Sharp St.
Open: Daily.
Price: Moderate to expensive.
Cuisine: Eastern Shore.
Serving: L, D.
Credit Cards: AE, D, MC, V.
Reservations: Suggested but not required.
Handicapped Access: Yes.

Located in one of the few remaining waterman enclaves on the Bay, casual Waterman's Crab House offers a front seat on a working harbor. Recently remodeled, Waterman's provides windows on the water inside and a spacious deck outside. If you arrive by boat, tie up free while you eat. The great view is augmented by cold beer, live entertainment most summer nights, and the kind of hard-shell crabs you don't find inland. All-you-can-eat crab feasts are held on Tues. and Thurs. in summer. A traditional menu of Bay seafood dishes (crab cakes, steamed shrimp, crabs, oysters, and fish) is also available.

FOOD PURVEYORS

Coffee Houses

Java by the Bay (410-939-0227; 118 N. Washington St., Havre de Grace) Café-style coffeehouse sells teas and morning Danish, biscotti, and pastries. Easy to find in tourist shopping district. Open Mon. through Sat. 7:30–6 (closes Sat. at 5), Sun. 8:30–4.

Play It Again Sam (410-778-2688; 108 S. Cross St., Chestertown) Coffee bar with sandwiches and desserts inside an old store with a wood floor and pressed-tin ceiling. Open Mon. through Sat. 7–5:30, Sun. 9–4.

Crab Houses and Seafood Markets

E&E Seafood (410-778-6333; Kent Plaza, Chestertown) Open daily. Fish, crabs, sand-wiches, smoked fish.

J&J Seafood (410-639-2325; 21459 Rock Hall Ave., Rock Hall) Hard-shells, soft-shells, whole fish, and fillets. A wide variety of seafood, plus you can dine in or carry out seafood sandwiches and platters. Open daily year-round. Also sells bait and ice.

Price's Seafood Restaurant (410-939-2782; 654 Water St., Havre de Grace) Established in 1944, this is where Havre de Grace cracks crabs. Open Apr. through Nov. Closed Mon.

Woody's Crab House (410-287-3541; 29 S. Main St., North East) The local crab house at the tip of the bay in North East; other seafood available. Open daily for L, D.

Ice Cream and Candy

Bomboy's Home Made Candy & Ice Cream (410-939-2924; 322 & 329 Market St., Havre de Grace) Family-owned since 1978, the candy store smells deliciously of chocolate and resides on one side of the street. Ice cream is on the other side, at the original location. Both closed Mon.

Durding's Store (410-778-7957; 5742 Main St., Rock Hall) Folks still come for ice cream at the soda fountain installed in this 1872 pharmacy in 1923. Rotating favorites include Moose Track (vanilla with fudge and Reese's peanut butter cups) and Muddy Sneakers (vanilla with chocolate caramel). Also cards and some gift items.

Natural Foods

Chestertown Natural Foods (410-778-1677; 214 Cannon St., Chestertown) Natural foods, organic produce, vitamins and supplements, bath products, and snacks.

Sandwich Shops

The Feast of Reason (410-778-3828; 203 High St., Chestertown) A changing daily menu of creative sandwiches made on fresh-baked bread as well as soups, quiches, and salads. PB&J and other nods to kids' appetites also available. No credit cards. Open Mon. through Sat. 10–4.

CULTURE

The thriving Chestertown arts scene is showcased during First Fridays, when galleries, studios, and shops (including many antiques shops) stay open from 5–8 PM on the first Friday of each month. Sip wine, nibble cheese, and listen to classical music. For details on First Fridays or any other Kent County happenings, check the informative monthly arts and entertainment listing at www.kentcounty.com. Another excellent source of arts infor-mation for the area is the Kent County Arts Council website, www.kentcountyarts council.org. The council, an umbrella organization for all of the county's arts activities, operates a gallery at its office, 101 Spring St. Also, to find out about special events at Washington College in Chestertown, call 410-778-7888.

Cinema

Chester 5 Theatres (410-778-2227) at Washington Square on MD 213 in Chestertown offers first-run fare. Also in town, Washington College offers a free weekly film series of first-rate films in the **Norman James Theatre** (410-778-7888) at 7:30 PM on Fri., Sun., and Mon. during the school year.

Galleries

ARTWORKS

410-778-6300.
306 Park Row, Chestertown.
Mon. through Thurs. 11–1; Fri. 11–3; Sat. 9–3; Sun. noon–3.

Formerly called the Chester River Artworks, this arts center focuses on pottery, graphics, and other fine arts and crafts. It also offers classes (recent offerings: "Gold Leaf Frames" and "Plein Air Pastels"), a gift shop, and a gallery featuring a new exhibit each month.

CHESTERTOWN ARTS LEAGUE

410-778-5789.
312 Cannon St., P.O. Box 656, Chestertown.

Established in 1949, the arts league offers classes, exhibits, and workshops in various media. The annual juried show is held at nearby Washington College, and the gallery, which showcases the work of a selection of the 150 members, is open Thurs. through Sat. 10–4.

GIBSON FINE ARTS CENTER GALLERY

410-778-7888.
Washington College, 300 Washington Ave., Chestertown.

The college's primary exhibition space offers an eclectic range of viewing. Recent exhibits have ranged from George Washington–related memorabilia on the anniversary of his death to paintings by noted Baltimore artist Herman Maril. The Constance Stuart Larrabee Arts Center, named for a local resident who was one of World War II's first women photo-journalists, is home to the college's fine arts department and shows student artwork.

Historic Buildings & Sites

CHESTERTOWN
GEDDES-PIPER HOUSE

410-778-3499.
101 Church Alley.
Open: Wed. through Fri. 9:30–4:30; also open Sat. and Sun. 1–4 May through Oct.
Admission: $3 donation requested.

Designed in the "Philadelphia style," this three-and-a-half-story brick town house was built in 1784. Now the museum headquarters of the Historical Society of Kent County, the home and property had been owned by a series of merchants. The first was customs collector for the Port of Chestertown, William Geddes, who owned the lot and holds an infamous place in local history. His was the brigantine ravaged during the 1774 Chestertown Tea Party, still celebrated at a local festival. He sold his property to merchant James Piper,

The Concord Point Lighthouse is located where the Susquehanna meets the Bay.

who built the house. It now features 18th- and 19th-century furnishings, maps, china, and a library. The Chestertown Fall Walking Tour, formerly the Candlelight Walking Tour, is held in Sept.

HAVRE DE GRACE
CONCORD POINT LIGHTHOUSE
410-939-9040; 410-939-0768 to schedule tours, weddings, or special events.
Lafayette and Concord Sts.
Open: Apr. through Oct., Sat. and Sun. 1–5.

The Susquehanna River, the Chesapeake's prehistoric precursor, flows into the Bay at

Havre de Grace. Perhaps the best view—though hours are limited—is from here. Visitors to the 1827 lighthouse will notice the boardwalk that ends out front. The half-mile-long promenade rounds the point along the Susquehanna, affording an exhilarating view.

Historic School

Our country's father gave express permission for use of his name, contributed 50 guineas to its 1782 founding, and served six years on the Board of Visitors and Governors of **Washington College** (410-778-2800; www.washcoll.edu; 300 Washington Ave., Chestertown, MD 21620). Now it's known for its creative writing program and the notable undergraduate literary award, the Sophie Kerr Prize (always a healthy sum; more than $50,000 of late). The school, with its beautiful grounds, is a significant presence in Chestertown. From student concerts to highly thoughtful lectures, the campus is full of activities during the school year. Hear the Jazz Band or the Early Music Consort. Or catch a speech by figures such as Howard Dean or Robert Novak, or a lecture on a notable such as Charles Willson Peale, courtesy of one of the college's lecture series. For a monthly listing of activities, contact the Special Events Office (410-778-7849) or check the schedule on the college's website.

Museums

CHESAPEAKE CITY
C&D CANAL MUSEUM
410-885-5621.
815 Bethel Rd.
Open: Year-round, Mon. through Fri. 8:15–4:15.
Admission: Free.

The 14-mile-long Chesapeake & Delaware Canal severs the top of the Delmarva Peninsula from the mainland, linking the Upper Chesapeake Bay with the Delaware River. In so doing, the grand old C&D shaves 300 miles off an otherwise roundabout journey from Philadelphia to Baltimore by way of Norfolk and the Virginia capes. Discussed for 150 years before it was finally dug by 2,600 men in the 1820s, the canal cost a whopping $2.5 million to build and opened in 1829. Photos, models, maps, and a 38-foot, 19th-century waterwheel, at the time considered a marvel of engineering, are on display at the tiny museum—the former pump house for the old locks. Interactive exhibits and a TV monitor track the ships headed through the canal. It's awe inspiring. Run by the U.S. Army Corps of Engineers, which operates the canal.

HAVRE DE GRACE
HAVRE DE GRACE DECOY MUSEUM
410-939-3739.
www.decoymuseum.com.
215 Giles St.
Open: Daily 11–4; closed major holidays.
Admission: Adults $6, seniors $5, youth 9–18 $2.
Handicapped Access: Yes.

So you want to know about decoy carving? This is the place, a proud piece of the past in this growing tourist/sailing town that calls itself "Decoy Capital of the World." The museum is

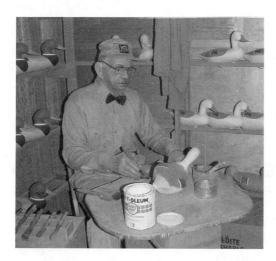

Fabled Bay decoy carver Madison Mitchell's workshop and the master himself are re-created at the Havre de Grace Decoy Museum.

dedicated to preserving the Bay's old "gunning" tradition, the art of hunting with decoys. Works by noted carvers R. Madison Mitchell, Bob McGaw, Paul Gibson, Charlie Joiner, and Charlie Bryan are shown, as well as tools of the trade and displays recalling the early 20th-century days when carvers gathered around the stove. Perhaps most intriguing is a peek into why conservation measures have become so important: the sinkbox. This clever contraption was outlawed in the mid 1930s "because it was too effective," chuckled a longtime Chesapeake outdoor enthusiast. Shaped like a bathtub with square wings and weighted down with flat-bottomed decoys, the sinkbox held a hunter who took to the duck hunt at the nearby Susquehanna Flats, which drew rich and famous hunters from Baltimore, Washington, D.C., and Philadelphia. Out back stands the workshop of local decoy carver Mitchell.

HAVRE DE GRACE MARITIME MUSEUM

100 Lafayette St.
www.hdgmaritimemuseum.com.
410-939-4800.
Open: Sept. through May, Mon., Wed., and Fri. 11–5; Jun. through Aug., daily 11–5. Admission: Adults $2, seniors and students $1, free for children under 6. Guided tours available by appt. for $3.

First incorporated in 1988, this maritime museum opened its doors early in the new millennium. The casual visitor finds small exhibits of maritime Bay lore, and anyone interested in working Bay craft will be delighted by the historic wooden canoes under reconstruction—rib by rib—and the other small craft at the Chesapeake Wooden Boat Builder's School here. Special events are held throughout the year, and expansion plans are in the works.

Canoes in the process of being rebuilt at the Havre de Grace Maritime Museum's Chesapeake Wooden Boat Builders' School.

ROCK HALL
ROCK HALL WATERMAN'S MUSEUM
410-778-6697.
Haven Harbour Marina, 20880 Rock Hall Ave.

Open: Daily 8–5; pick up key at the marina's Ditty Bag store.
Admission: Free.

Rock Hall, a sailing and boating center to many, has roots as a watermen's community, celebrated at this charming museum in an old waterman's shanty. Inside find tools of the trade for oystering, crabbing, and fishing, along with photographs, local carvings, and boats.

TOLCHESTER BEACH REVISITED
410-778-5347.
Behind the Shoppes at Oyster Court near Sharp and Main Sts.
Open: Sat. and Sun. 11–3.

Homage to the old resorts of the steamship era is paid here by Pennsylvania native William Betts, who used to visit the old Tolchester Beach amusement park as a child. His collection of Tolchester memorabilia grew until he opened this small museum.

Nightlife
Chesapeake City takes advantage of its C&D Canal-side seat when it comes to live entertainment, which you can find at the dockside terrace of the **New Schaefer's Canal House** (410-885-2200; www.newschaeferscanalhouse.com; off MD 213 on the north side of the canal) Fri. through Sun. in-season, and in its lounge Thurs. through Sat. in-season and Fri. and Sat. in the off-season. Bands also play at the popular **Chesapeake Inn** (410-885-2040; www.chesapeakeinn.com; 605 Second St.) on the other side of the canal, with packed summer schedules and specials. Around **Chestertown,** visit **Andy's** (410-778-6779; 337 High St.), a small, friendly, popular club that regularly hosts live jazz, bluegrass, rock, and blues.

The Prince Theater and the Imperial Hotel are among the highlights on High Street in Chestertown.

Performing Arts

PRINCE THEATRE
410-810-2060.
www.princetheatre.org.
210 High St., Chestertown, MD 21620.

Come hear musicians from far and near (like in Hometones, a new monthly showcase for acoustic locals), see theater, and enjoy all the performances held at this restored 1926 vaudeville theater and movie house. Located on High Street in the center of town.

WASHINGTON COLLEGE CONCERT SERIES
410-778-7839.
Season: Sept. through early May
Tickets: Call for ticket prices and schedule.

The popular five-concert series, held for more than 50 years, draws notable pianists, choral groups, string quartets, and more. Held in the Tawes Theater of the Gibson Performing Arts Center.

CHURCH HILL THEATRE
410-758-1331.
www.churchhilltheatre.org.
103 Walnut St. (MD 19), off MD 213 between Centreville and Chestertown.
Tickets: Prices vary.

This 1929 building has gone full circle, from town hall to movie theater to decline and, finally, to rescue. With its restored Art Deco interior, the Church Hill Players' home has for nearly 20 years maintained a lively performance schedule of productions such as *Bus Stop* and *The Search for Signs of Intelligent Life in the Universe*. Workshops and classes, too.

The Mainstay
410-639-9133.
5753 Main St.

This storefront performance space is home to numerous concerts, including those given by regionally noted musicians. Call for schedules and information.

Seasonal Events
For information on any of these happenings, see the calendar at www.kentcounty.com or call 410-778-0416.

Chestertown commemorates its pre–Revolutionary War tea party on the Sat. of Memorial Day weekend at the **Chestertown Tea Party Festival.** The townwide celebration features such festivities as a colonial parade, music, crafts, a 10-mile race, boat rides for children, food, and a historical reenactment of the 1774 Chestertown Tea Party, where the townspeople rose up against port collector William Geddes and plundered his brigantine *Geddes*,

Boston style. (Maybe it's apocryphal, but some say that they saved the shipment's rum.) Free admission; handicapped access; www.chestertownteaparty.com.

Each Sept. the Historical Society of Kent County hosts its annual **Chestertown Fall Walking Tour**, formerly the Candlelight Walking Tour, in which gorgeous architectural gems are open to the public. For information, call 410-778-3499.

ROCK HALL

Blues, bluegrass, and Irish folk music are featured at the **Rock Hall FallFest**, a celebration of music and mariners. Artists, crafts, children's activities, food, and regional favorites like oysters shucked before your eyes. Evening concerts at the Mainstay on Main St.

Tours

CHESAPEAKE CITY

Chesapeake Horse Country Tours offers a narrated walking tour of this canal town's Historic District, featuring multicolored 19th-century homes that prospered with the C&D Canal. In addition, the company takes people on a variety of other tours around the area, including van tours of the nearby horse country. For fees and information, contact **Hill Travel** (410-287-2290; 130 S. Main Street, North East, MD 21901).

CHESTERTOWN

Learn about the Georgian, Federal, Italianate, and Queen Anne–style buildings that mark the chapters in the life of pretty Chestertown. The *Walking Tour of Historic Chestertown* brochure includes architectural and other highlights and is easy to follow, with stops at the courthouse and the famed White Swan Tavern, where George Washington supposedly supped. Also, check out the driving tour brochure for Kent County, which points out such unexpected relics as the fact that Galena was once the site of a nearby silver mine, closed during the War of 1812 in case the British captured it. For information, contact the **Kent County Tourism Office** (410-778-0416; www.kentcounty.com; 400 High St., Chestertown, MD 21620). Also at the tourism office is the *Driving Tour of the Kent County Peninsula* brochure, which guides drivers through rural and historic highlights.

Historic Chestertown and Kent County Tours takes folks on walking tours of the lower Historic District of Chestertown. Tours take 1 1/2 to 2 hours and prices vary according to the size of the group. For information, call 410-778-2829 or e-mail cliokent@yahoo.com.

Ripken Stadium in Aberdeen is home to the Aberdeen IronBirds, a Baltimore Orioles Class-A team. Photo courtesy of Aberdeen IronBirds

RECREATION

Baseball
Aberdeen IronBirds and Ripken Stadium (IronBirds: 410-297-9292; ironbirdsbase ball.com; 873 Long Dr., Aberdeen, MD 21001) Baseball hero Cal Ripken Jr. hasn't forgotten his hometown. The retired Baltimore Orioles slugger and his brother Bill, also a former major leaguer, head a baseball program that includes the Aberdeen IronBirds, a Baltimore Orioles Class-A team that plays in the New York–Penn League. The IronBirds play in a major stadium complex, visible from I-95, that also houses other baseball programs such as youth camps and clinics. If you're interested in these programs, contact the corporate office of **Ripken Baseball** (410-823-0808; www.ripkenbaseball.com; 1427 Clarkview Rd., Baltimore, MD 21209).

Bicycling
The Eastern Shore's user-friendly topography moves from pleasantly rolling hills at its upper extreme to sprawling flatland farther south, giving cyclists a mix of riding conditions on lightly traveled roads through great coastal scenery. In **Kent County**, the tourism office offers a booklet detailing bike-tour options. Distance and difficulty levels range from the 11-mile Pomona Warm-Up to the 81-mile Pump House Primer, which takes in Chesapeake City and Cecil County's rolling horse country. The Baltimore Bicycling Club developed the routes. For a copy of *The Kent County Bicycle Tour*, contact the **Kent County Tourism Office** (410-778-0416; www.kentcounty.com).

Local Cycling Shops and Rentals
Bikework (410-778-6940; 208 S. Cross St., Chestertown) Bike rentals, including touring bikes, for $6 an hour or $30 a day. Call in advance of busy holiday weekends. Closed Thurs.

Swan Haven Rentals (410-639-2527; 20950 Rock Hall Ave., Rock Hall) Bicycles, boats, and fishing gear. Kayaks and canoes, too.

Bird-Watching
Eastern Neck Wildlife Refuge (410-639-7056; http://easternneck.fws.gov; 1730 Eastern Neck Rd., Rock Hall, MD 21661) The refuge lies at the end of the peninsula that includes Chestertown and Rock Hall. It's a favored birding ground, with 230 species of bird recorded here, including a bountiful collection of migratory birds like pintails, old-squaws, and other sea ducks. Tundra swans can be seen from Nov. through Mar., since there are both migratory swans and a population that overwinters here. Other times of the year, look for bald eagles, ospreys, terns, gulls, woodcocks, woodpeckers, and other migrants.

Boating
Charters, Cruises, and Boat Rentals

CHESAPEAKE CITY
Miss Clare (410-885-5088; baytour@yahoo.com) This classic Chesapeake deadrise—a crab boat design—started life in Cambridge and did duty as a charter fishing boat in the charming Atlantic Ocean town of Lewes, Del., before Capt. Ralph H. Hazel brought her back to the family hometown to do history tours of the C&D Canal. Departs from the city dock in South Chesapeake City, cruising daily in summer and weekends in spring and fall (weekdays by request). Call for details.

Chestertown

Schooner Sultana Projects (410-778-5954; www.schoonersultana.com; P.O. Box 524, Chestertown, MD 21620) The 97-foot floating classroom *Sultana*, launched in 2001, re-creates a 1767 Boston-built vessel that spent time as a British Royal Navy dispatch boat and revenue cruiser. The original patrolled the Chesapeake Bay from 1769–1771. Now, her namesake teaches schoolchildren about history and aquatic science. Although *Sultana*'s homeport is Chestertown, she sails the Chesapeake, so you may catch her in another port, or maybe at home for a public cruise. Check the *Sultana* website for schedules.

Southern Cross Charters (410-778-4460; www.kentcounty.com/southerncross; Great Oak Landing Marina Resort, P.O. Box 426, Chestertown, MD 21620) Day, sunset, and overnight cruises on the Chesapeake Bay in a 41-foot Morgan Out Island ketch-rigged sail yacht. Food service. Overnight cruises to ports such as Baltimore's Inner Harbor, Rock Hall, Annapolis, and Georgetown.

Havre de Grace

Applegarth Cruises (Capt. Paul Thomas, 410-879-6941; 2524 Ady Rd., Forest Hill, MD 21050) Charter this miniature skipjack from a professional captain who can drop you off at one of four nearby islands to explore, picnic, or hang out at the beach. Or go for a sail. Hourly costs drop with each additional hour.

Lantern Queen (410-287-7217 or 1-888-937-3740; www.lanternqueen.com; foot of Congress Ave., Havre de Grace, MD 21078) Take a sunset dinner cruise aboard a Mississippi-style riverboat. Call or check the website for prices and times.

Martha Lewis (410-939-4078; www.skipjackmarthalewis.org; Chesapeake Heritage Conservancy, 121 N. Union Ave., Havre de Grace, MD 21078) This skipjack, restored in 1994, offers public cruises in the summer and fall, as well as specialty cruises like an afternoon tea or sunset cruise.

Rock Hall

Gratitude Yachting Center (410-639-7111; www.gratitudeyachting.com; 5990 Lawton Ave., Rock Hall, MD 21661) Bareboat charters of Island Packets available.

Haven Charters (410-639-7140; www.havencharters.com; 20846 Rock Hall Ave., Rock Hall, MD 21661) Offers 28- to 42-foot sailboats and lessons. Also has an affiliate up the Bay in North East; call 410-287-5948.

Marinas

On the **Susquehanna River**, try **Tidewater Marina** (410-939-0950; www.tidewatermarina .com) in Havre de Grace, with 160 slips, fuel, haul-outs, repairs, a discount marine store, showers, laundry, and a courtesy car.

If you're cruising near **Chesapeake City**, the **Bohemia Bay Yacht Harbor** (410-885-2736; www.bbyh.com) on the eponymous river is a full-service marina with transient slips. A tad south, along the **Sassafras River**, try **Georgetown Yacht Basin** (410-648-5112; www.georgetownyachtbasin.com), with about 300 slips, including 100 that are covered. It also has a swimming pool and complete marine store, and the Granary restaurant and marina are nearby. Or try **Skipjack Cove Yachting Resort** (410-275-2122), which has transient slips, tennis courts, an Olympic-size pool, and boat lifts.

The boardwalk promenade at Havre de Grace.

In **Rock Hall**, a popular Bay boating destination, consider the following: **Osprey Point Marina** (410-639-2663; www.ospreypoint.com) is located on Swan Creek and has floating docks, a bathhouse, a pool, a full-service restaurant, and an inn. Also, try **Rock Hall Landing** (410-639-2224; www.rockhallmd.com/rhlanding), the closest marina to town, in Rock Hall Harbor. They have a pool and are open mid-Apr. through mid-Nov. The **Sailing Emporium** (410-778-1342; www.sailingemporium.com) on the Chesapeake Bay offers laundry, a library with a liberal lending policy, 150 slips, a pool, a pump-out station, fuel, barbecue grills, and picnic tables.

On the **Chester River**, the **Chestertown Marina** (410-778-3616; 211 S. Front St.) has a mechanic on the premises, plus you can walk to everything in the Historic District.

Sailing and Powerboat Schools

BaySail School and Yacht Charters (410-939-2869; www.baysail.net; Tidewater Marina, 100 Bourbon St., Havre de Grace, MD 21078) American Sailing Association-certified courses, beginner to advanced, aboard boats including Capris, Hunters, Beneteaus, and Catalinas of various sizes. Some can be rented upon certification. Beginner sailing classes are also available, as well as captained or bareboat chartering. Call for costs.

Canoeing & Kayaking

The Upper Bay region provides many protected, quiet rivers and creeks. View ospreys, blue and green herons, kingfishers, and terns, and catch a few perch or rockfish in summer. See "Landings & Boat Ramps" in chapter 9, "Information," to find out how to order a free map of Bay access points.

Some good paddles: In **Queen Anne's County**, put in at the **Corsica River** at **Centreville** and poke around upstream or downstream on a pretty stretch of water with homes along the bank. Turner's Creek, which flows northwest into the **Sassafras River** in **Kent County**, affords some scenic canoeing past stunning 60- to 70-foot-high bluffs.

Chester River Kayak Adventures (410-639-2001 or 410-639-2061; www.crkayak adventures.com; 5758 Main St., Rock Hall, MD 21661) Kayak rentals as well as half- and full-day tours available. Ask about other options, and consider staying in one of two inns operated by the owner: the Bay Breeze Inn and Spring Cove Inn. Maps and packages available.

Fishing
Boat Ramps
In **Cecil County**, try the Fredericktown boat launch on the Sassafras River; for informa- tion, call **Cecil County Parks and Recreation** (410-392-4537 or 410-658-3000) or **Elk Neck State Park** (410-287-5333) on the Elk River. Fee.

Easy-to-find ramps in downtown **Havre de Grace** include those at **Jean Roberts Memorial Park** (410-939-0015; $5 fee on weekends and holidays) on the Susquehanna River and at **Tydings Park** at the city yacht basin. Fees for both.

Fishing Charters
Twilight Zone Charters (410-939-2948; 113 N. Union Ave., Havre de Grace, MD 21078) Lifelong resident offers guided fishing charters, but also takes folks out bird-watching and sightseeing and has some kayaks available. Spring is the best time to catch big rockfish in this part of the Bay, when they're spawning. Shad fishing, too.

Golf
Brantwood Golf Club (410-398-8848; 1190 Augustine Herman Hwy., Elkton) 18 holes; semiprivate. Located on MD 213.

Bulle Rock (1-888-285-5375; www.bullerock.com; 320 Blenheim Ln., Havre de Grace) Named one of 16 five-star courses in North America by *Golf Digest* in 2004. Open to the public, with a locker-room attendant, fine-dining restaurant, Bay views. LPGA champi- onship tournament starting in 2005.

Mears Great Oak Landing Resort and Conference Center (410-778-5007 or 1-800- LANDING; Great Oak Landing Rd., Chestertown) 9 holes; executive course. Open to the public.

Horseback Riding
Fair Hill Stables (contact Tailwinds Farm, 410-620-3883; www.fairwindsstables.com; 41 Tailwinds Ln., North East, MD 21901) Hour-long rides through fields or on trails avail- able daily in summer. Located in the Fair Hill Natural Resource Management Area. $30 for ages 8 and older.

Hunting
Hopkins Game Farm (410-348-5287; MD 298/P.O. Box 218, Kennedyville, MD 21645) Game, quail, and pheasant, as well as sporting clays and five stands. Lodging is available.

Natural Areas: State, Private, and Federal Parks

Chesapeake Farms Wildlife Habitat (410-778-8400; 7319 Remington Dr., Chestertown, MD 21620) Features a free driving tour through its 3,300 acres of wildlife and agricultural management demonstration area. The drive is open Apr. through Oct. 10. Privately owned; located between Chestertown and Rock Hall.

Eastern Neck National Wildlife Refuge (410-639-7056; 1730 Eastern Neck Rd., Rock Hall, MD 21661) Nearly 2,300 acres of island with walking trails up to 1.2 miles long. Located at the mouth of the Chester River past Rock Hall in Kent County, this is the Bay's only undeveloped island with Bay access. Four trails, a boat ramp, a boardwalk to an observation deck overlooking the Bay, and a new swan lookout ramp, the better to view the multitudinous migratory tundra swans that come through in Nov. or over winter here.

Elk Neck State Park (410-287-5333; 4395 Turkey Point Rd., North East, MD 21901) Located on MD 272, 9 miles south of North East, where the North East and Elk rivers meet. Swim, hike five different trails, launch a boat or canoe, or stay in one of nine small cabins or campgrounds. Walk the trail to see Turkey Point Lighthouse, where the Elk River meets the Bay. Diverse terrain at this 2,000-plus-acre park includes steep bluffs, forests, marshland, and beaches. Nominal fees.

Millington Wildlife Management Area (410-928-3650; 33626 Maryland Line Rd., Massey, MD 21650) Located off US 301 along the Delaware border. Nature trails, ponds, woods; 3,800 acres. Hunting in-season; fishing for bass, bluegill, crappie.

Susquehanna State Park (410-557-7994; 3318 Rocks Chrome Hill Rd., Jarrettsville, MD 21084) Five miles north of Havre de Grace; 2,639 acres. Good for hiking, with 15 miles of trails; boating, fishing. Check out the Susquehanna River, source of the fresh water in the Bay estuary.

Sporting Goods & Camping Supply Stores

Vonnie's Sporting Goods (410-778-5655; MD 213, Kennedyville) A complete hunting and fishing center with licenses and clothing.

Swimming

Betterton Beach (contact Kent County Parks and Recreation, 410-778-1957; MD 292, Betterton) Deep in the Upper Bay, where freshwater dominates. Noted for reliable swimming conditions devoid of stinging nettles. Picnicking, fishing jetty, bathhouse, beach. Free. Lifeguard only on Sat. and Sun., Memorial Day through Labor Day. Picnic pavilion available for group rental.

North East Beach (410-287-5333; MD 272, North East) Picnicking, bathhouse. Open Apr. through mid-Oct. Along the North East River. Nominal fees.

Rock Hall Public Beach (410-639-7611; Beach Rd., Rock Hall) From this tiny beach you can watch the giant container ships make their way from the Bay Bridge up to Baltimore. No lifeguard at this no-frills beach.

Shopping

Antiques

Folks with a penchant for antiques (or collectibles) find themselves in fine browsing terri-tory on the Upper Bay, with its wealth of antiques shops and unique auctions. Don't miss small Galena, not far from Chestertown.

Residing on the Upper Shore for decades now is a marvel known alternatively as the **Crumpton Auction** or the **Dixon Auction** (Dixon's Furniture, 410-928-3006; MD 290 and MD 544, Crumpton, MD 21628). Reputed to be 30 acres, the auction starts at 9 AM sharp each Wed. You can check out everything in the "$5 field" on Tuesday, but that doesn't include furniture auctions. Finally, check out the big auction at **American Corner** (410-754-8826; 6 miles north of Federalsburg on Auction Rd.). Every Thurs. at 5 PM, buildings full of stuff go on the block. You can find everything from outboard motors to furniture.

CHESTERTOWN

J. R.'s Antiques & Collectibles (410-810-1006; 114 S. Cross St.) Attractive antique shop well worth a stop. Closed Tues.

Village Inn Antiques (410-778-3752; 200 High St.) Nice selection—especially of furni-ture—on the town's main street.

CHESAPEAKE CITY

Black Swan Antiques (410-885-5888; 219 Bohemia Ave.) Particularly good stop for those inclined toward Bay-related items. Nauticals include binnacles, prints, and oyster cans, from Maryland Beauties to the McReady Brothers of Chincoteague.

HAVRE DE GRACE

Bank of Memories (410-939-4343; 319 St. John St.) A range of goodies housed in the town's former First National Bank.

Bayside Antiques (410-939-9397; 232 N. Washington St.) Multiple dealers and great browsing. Decoys to period antiques. Open daily.

Franklin Street Antiques (410-939-4220; 464 Franklin St.) Cookie jar central, for sure, but glass drinking straw dispensers also line one shelf at this chockablock shop. Keep an eye out for decoys, the local pride and joy. Lunch boxes, too.

Gary E. Dennis Antiques Collectibles Gifts (410-942-0100; 205 N. Washington St.) Full and eclectic selection.

Seneca Cannery Antiques (410-942-0701; 201 St. John St.) The enormous space, with stone and brick walls, is almost as interesting as the numerous wares offered by its more than 35 dealers.

Thorofare Antiques (410-939-5455; 220 N. Washington St.) About 20 dealers stationed in a former downtown department store; includes antiques and old hand-painted furniture. Open daily year-round.

Washington Street Books & Antiques (410-939-6215; 131 N. Washington St.) Wonderful used bookshop well worth the stop. Includes 100,000 comic books.

Antiques shops are legendary in Havre de Grace.

GALENA

The Cross Street Station (410-648-5776; 105 Cross St.) On your right just before you hit Main Street coming from Chestertown, this large emporium brings nice furniture (blanket chests, an ancient pie safe) and a fun attitude.

Firehouse Antiques Center (410-648-5639; 102 N. Main St.) Multidealer shop focuses on high quality period furniture and accessories.

Galena Antiques Center (410-648-5781; 108 N. Main St.) The granddaddy of Galena antiques shops, a large multidealer stop, and home to a custom "barnwood" furniture workshop, where turned porch balustrades become custom table legs at great prices. Open daily 10–5.

Books

The Compleat Bookseller (410-778-1480; 301 High St., Chestertown) This fine store has a range of titles that you won't find in the big discount places.

Courtyard Book Shop (410-939-5150; 313 St. John St., Havre de Grace) Terrific, browsable shop.

Seneca Cannery Antiques, one of Havre de Grace's many antique emporiums.

Clothing

Chester River Knitting Co. (410-778-0374; 306 Cannon St., Chestertown) Handmade sweaters, from turtlenecks to crewnecks, from alpaca to cashmere.

Pride & Joy (410-778-2233; 321 High St., Chestertown) Children's apparel and gifts, for new arrivals through older children.

Galleries

Capt. Bob Jobes' Decoys (410-939-1843; www.jobesdecoys.com; 721 Otsego St., Havre de Grace) A paint-stained shed with its ceiling papered in decoy posters might not seem like a gallery, but a similar shed, where famed Upper Bay carver Madison Mitchell once held forth, is now tucked behind the nearby Havre de Grace Decoy Museum. Decoys are America's waterfront folk art, and Jobes, the eldest son of carver Capt. Harry Jobes, once earned $1 an hour working for Mitchell. In his workshop: swans, mallards, canvasbacks, blue herons, and miniatures, plus the requisite friendly black and yellow labs wandering through in search of a pat. Jobes also sells and appraises his forebears' old decoys. Open daily; just stop by.

Carla Massoni Gallery (410-778-7330; www.massoniart.com; 203 High St., Chestertown) Fine art, from realism to abstract. Original paintings, prints, photography, and sculpture.

L'Atelier IV: The Artists' Gallery (410-778-2425; 239 High St., Chestertown) Owned by five artists helped by five associates and a roster of exhibitors, this delightful gallery shows a range of work at a range of prices—including many that won't bust the budget.

Rock Hall Gallery (410-639-2494; 5761 Main St., Rock Hall) Also called the Reuben Rodney Gallery, this is a co-op of regional artists offering a range of photography, watercolors, pottery, woodwork, and textiles.

Vincenti Decoys (410-734-7709; 353 Pennington Ave., Havre de Grace) You'll find not only gorgeous waterfowl carvings here, from pieces by Patrick Vincenti to historic collectibles, but decoy-carving materials, too. Where else are you going to find little plastic packets of glass eyes and pewter duck feet?

Gift Shops and Craft Galleries

Ehrman Tapestry (410-810-3032; 112 S. Cross St., Chestertown) Show-stopping needlepoint kits and tapestry works. Occasional talks and workshops by textile artists. Open daily.

The Finishing Touch (410-778-5292 or 1-800-292-0457; 311 High St., Chestertown) Fine framing, gifts, cards, candles, photo frames, and some truly nice handiwork from local painters and potters.

Kerns Collection (410-778-4044; 210 High St., Chestertown) Whimsical crafts and pottery, unique clothing and jewelry.

Maren's (410-885 2475; 200 Bohemia Ave., Chesapeake City) Christmas shop, collectibles, and floral gifts.

Marine Supply

Chester River Marine Services (410-778-2240; 7501 Church Hill Rd., Chestertown) Full-service marine store.

Tidewater Marina Store (410-939-0950; Bourbon St., Havre de Grace) Full-service marine store.

Outlets

Prime Outlets at Perryville (410-378-9399; 68 Heather Lane, Perryville) Smallish outlet center with 33 shops, including OshKosh, Mikasa, L. L. Bean, and Nike.

Specialty Shops and General Stores

Back Creek General Store (410-885-5377; 100 Bohemia Ave., Chesapeake City) Circa-1861 general store with Cat's Meow items, Bennington & Lang Pottery, and others.

Chesapeake Optics (410-939-9412; 300 St. John St., Havre de Grace) Cool shop featuring telescopes, binoculars, and other optics for birding or stargazing.

Shoppes at Oyster Court (Oyster Court behind Main St., Rock Hall) A cluster of relocated watermen's buildings is home to artists and crafters and some small boutiques. It's open year-round Thurs. through Sun., more days from spring to fall. Telephone numbers of the artist-shopkeepers are on the doors, so if you come when a store is closed, call.

Twigs & Teacups (410-778-1708; 111 S. Cross St., Chestertown) Specialty bath products, dishes, tea things, children's books and toys, clothing, and textiles make this a difficult gift shop to leave.

Talbot Street in St. Michaels is home to many quaint shops. Cindy Tunstall

5

MIDDLE EASTERN SHORE
Time & Tides

There's a genteel, livin'-is-easy mix on the Middle Eastern Shore, where updated trends make careful inroads in a place where old ways stay strong. Traditional oysters, for instance, a declining Bay staple, nonetheless can always be had during their cold weather season. At old, pine-paneled restaurants, they arrive in thick, milky stews. In fancier dining rooms, with buffed-glass halogen lighting and exposed ductwork, champagne and puff pastries infuse the ol' bivalve.

With its hundreds of miles of snaking shoreline, the Mid-Shore area is less marshy than the Lower Eastern Shore, yet flatter than the upland you'll find farther north. We define the area broadly, to include the Shore's gateway, Kent Island. The Mid-Shore extends east to the Delaware line and south to the Choptank River, promising crossroads towns as well as more established tourist draws.

Kent Island ends at the waterway known as Kent Narrows, which is technically on the Eastern Shore, although Kent Island and the Kent Narrows area have become de facto Annapolis suburbs as well as a gateway to the Shore. On the island, the historic enclave of **Stevensville** has seen a few artists and artisans set up shop. The powerboat crowd gathers at the Kent Narrows marinas (August's big race: "Thunder on the Narrows"), and along the area's south side a cluster of venerable waterside seafood restaurants hold court.

Heading east along US 50, on the "mainland" Eastern Shore, the village of **Wye Mills** promises peeks at the past via nature and commerce. Schoolchildren gather 'round to hear ground grain clatter through wooden chutes en route to the millstone during flour-making demonstrations at the mid-18th-century mill, which replaced a 1671 forebear. George Washington's troops at Valley Forge even obtained their ground flour from the mill. This is a good day (or half-day) stop, with picnic tables behind the mill settled, of course, alongside a lovely stream.

Farther south come the better-known towns of Talbot County, to which travelers increasingly flock: busy Easton, the county seat; low-key Oxford, with its Tred Avon–side beach known as "The Strand"; St. Michaels, the county's biggest tourist town; and Tilghman Island, where inroads by visitors seem unlikely to fully dislodge the sturdy breed of watermen who live there.

Centered around its 18th-century courthouse, **Easton** is the business center powering this part of Bay Country. The town's roots go back to the late 17th century and construction of the Third Haven Meeting House, an early Quaker structure visited by William Penn that still can be toured by appointment. Highlights here include the renovated Art Deco Avalon

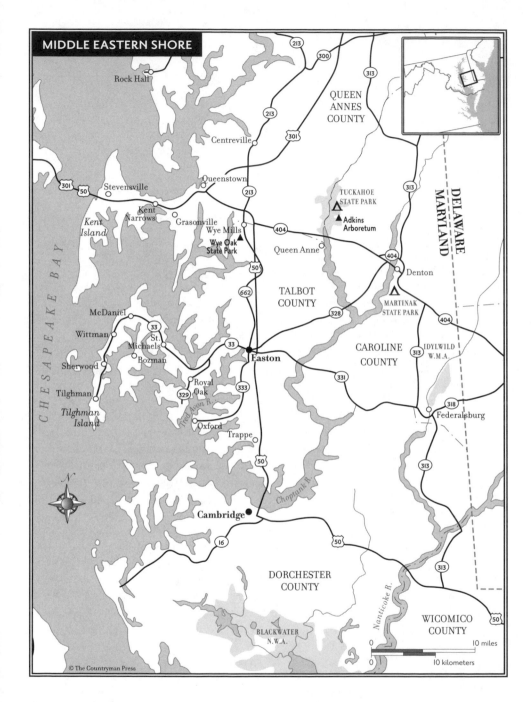

Theatre, with its continuous performing fare that includes notable touring musicians, the Academy Art Museum's high-quality exhibitions, antiques shops, and the contemporary dining establishments in town. This is a central location with a Federal- and Victorian-filled Historic District—though, it must be said, one without a waterfront. A finger of the Tred Avon River pokes into the southwest corner of town.

Watermen work hard on their workboat at Tilghman Island. Tim Tadder

South of Easton, via the "Oxford Road," as the locals call MD 333, sits the hamlet of **Oxford.** A prettier waterside village you won't find. White picket fences, clapboard and grand old manses alternate along Morris Street, the main road into town. This was a colonial deep-water seaport, designated the Eastern Shore's official port of entry in 1694, and an international trade in tobacco and grain bustled here for a time. The so-called financier of the Revolution, Robert Morris, lived in Oxford, his former home a long-standing landmark restaurant and inn that still bears his name.

Yet another remnant of that era, the Oxford–Bellevue Ferry, trundles across the Tred Avon River from March through November, providing a considerable shortcut to St. Michaels. Begun in 1683, it is believed to be the nation's oldest privately operated ferry, and it is a favorite of cyclists looping the county's flat roads. The frontage stretching along the waterfront, known as "the Strand," includes a beach, a good place for visitors of all ages to dip their toes in the water. Afterward, walk up to the Oxford Market & Deli on Morris Street for a hand-dipped ice-cream cone. In Oxford come the sweet pleasures of small moments unencumbered by much too much.

Cross on the ferry and wind through back roads on the way to St. Michaels. In **Bellevue** sits the kind of surprise explorers often find in the Bay's scratch-in-the-sand-size towns: a weaver's studio and gallery with occasional openings. Farther on up the road, through **Royal Oak**, an Italian café has moved into the old general store, and a rambling country inn has held forth for years. Businesses increase on the road into **St. Michaels**; indeed, Talbot Street is the main drag through this tourist town, lined by shops selling aromatic candles or Chesapeake T-shirts, fine-crafted gold pins or women's jackets made of hand-woven fabric. Fine restaurants and plentiful B&Bs are tucked along town streets.

St. Michaels was first developed in 1778, created from auctioned-off land grants, and its historic claim to fame is the incident during the War of 1812 that led to its reputation as "The Town That Fooled the British." One August night in 1813, as rumor circulated of an impending British attack, the people of St. Michaels darkened their homes, hoisted lit lanterns into the treetops, and tricked the enemy into firing too high.

Perhaps now its greatest claim to fame emerges from the town's shipbuilding heritage. The extensive Chesapeake Bay Maritime Museum, a multibuilding complex at Navy Point, offers a seemingly endless collection of Bay boats, from the skipjack *Rosie Parks* to the *Thor* pilothouse on the museum grounds—a magnet for curious kids. The museum's small-boat collection also shows the evolution of the log canoe, from Native American conveyance to oyster tonger's sailboat to the craft with enormous sails now raced in a popular series involving yacht clubs from many Eastern Shore towns. Given the boat's slender shape—and the springboards that hold crewmembers balancing them aboard—this can be exciting racing. On a weekend you might get lucky and see the log canoes along the Miles River in St. Michaels. For information, check www.logcanoes.com. And to get around St. Michaels from the water, consider using the St. Michaels Harbor Shuttle (410-924-2198), a water taxi located at the foot of Mulberry Street.

For a peek at the working version of Chesapeake's most famed workboats, continue down MD 33 to **Tilghman Island** and the town of **Tilghman**. This is home to a skipjack fleet, the nation's last all-sail workboats used for oystering. You'll see them at Knapp's Narrows before crossing onto the island, and again at Dogwood Harbor, not far down the island to your left. Although the skipjacks carry the blue-ribbon reputation, keep an eye out for the distinctive low sides—"lowboard"—of Bay-built workboats used by crabbers and dredgers, with their pretty lines and sturdy, flat wheelhouse roofs. These are the tools of the working watermen who live on Tilghman and around the Bay. But don't be fooled: There's upscale cuisine to be had and fine lodgings available here.

Tilghman mixes old and new Chesapeake as well as any town.

LODGING

From in-town suites with duvets and whirlpool tubs to rooms just off the golf course, Mid-Shore visitors will find a range of accommodations. Off long lanes are former farms—and maybe a manse—that have been turned into B&Bs or inns. These offer best-of-both-worlds lodgings, often on the water. Sail in and tie up at the pier, or perhaps launch a kayak.

Prices for the same lodging can vary widely. Expect two-night minimums on weekends during the high season, when prices are highest. Off-season and midweek rates tend to be lower. Ask about other limitations, including policies regarding the return of deposit checks if you cancel. Assume smoking and pets are not allowed inside unless noted.

Rates

Lodging rates, based on high-season prices, fall within this scale:

Inexpensive:	Up to $75
Moderate:	$75 to $120
Expensive:	$120 to $175
Very expensive:	$175 and up

Credit card abbreviations are:

AE—American Express
CB—Carte Blanche
DC—Diners Club
D—Discover
MC—MasterCard
V—Visa

KENT ISLAND
KENT MANOR INN
Owners: David Meloy and Alan Michaels. 410-643-5757 or 1-800-820-4511. www.kentmanor.com.
500 Kent Manor Dr., Stevensville, MD 21666 (on Kent Island, US 50 to MD 8 S.).
Price: Expensive to very expensive.

Credit Cards: AE, D, MC, V.
Handicapped Access: No.
Special Features: Children welcome.

Kent Manor Inn is a faithful restoration of a
large plantation house. There's a lovely garden house, a pier on the shallow headwaters
of Thompson's Creek, paddleboats, bicycles, and a 1.5-mile trail winding through
the extensive property. All 24 rooms are
tastefully furnished in period style, some
with porches and French marble fireplaces.
A tennis court and pool are available, as
well as a noted restaurant serving fine cuisine. A quiet, dignified getaway.

QUEENSTOWN
PINTAIL POINT MANOR
Innkeeper: Karen Rees.
410-827-6130 or 1-877-897-6130.
www.pintailpoint.com.
511 Pintail Point Ln., Queenstown, MD
21658.
Price: Very expensive.
Credit Cards: D, MC, V.
Handicapped Access: No.
Special Features: Kennel on-site; children
welcome.

Pintail Point comprises 1,000 acres on a
working farm that smartly uses its riverside
fields and buildings as a country retreat,
making available a nationally ranked sporting clay range, fishing charters, and golf.
The farm also features two B&Bs: the
English Tudor–style Manor House along the
Wye River, and a typical Maryland farmhouse done up in "art ducko." The latter,
called the Irishtown Bed & Breakfast, rents
as a whole. The Manor House, built in 1936,
provides finer accommodations, with a
patio open onto the Wye River (one of the
lovelier Bay tributaries) and clubby common rooms. Hunting trophies decorate the
game room, with its pool table, air hockey,
and shuffleboard games. Guest rooms run
from a cottage with floral-covered queen
beds and kitchenette to large, traditional

suites in the house with sitting rooms,
including one that opens onto a balcony.
Bikes and golf carts for rent; gourmet
breakfasts. Kids staying at the complex can
even peek at the Holsteins and their calves
in the farm's working portions.

*A friendly welcome at Easton's Promise, a B&B in
Easton.*

EASTON
THE BISHOP'S HOUSE
Innkeepers: Diane Laird-Ippolito and John
B. Ippolito.
410-820-7290 or 1-800-223-7290.
www.bishopshouse.com.
214 Goldsborough St./P.O. Box 2217,
Easton, MD 21601.
Price: Moderate to expensive; two-night
minimum.
Credit Cards: AE, DC, D, MC, V.
Handicapped Access: No.
Restrictions: No children under 12.

Home to the bishop of the Episcopal Diocese
of Easton for much of the 20th century, this
1880 home serves up Victorian style of the
highest order, from the plaster ceiling
medallions to the claw-foot tubs. The longtime B&B offers antique furnishings, vintage
hats on the walls, and a wraparound porch.
The five guest rooms all have private baths,
although you'll run up the stairs to reach
one. Whirlpool baths and fireplaces are

available, and all beds are either king- or queen-size. Along with the downstairs parlors, guests will find an upstairs sitting room with fridge and microwave. Guests can watch television in their rooms while planning to rent one of the inn's bikes or walk into downtown Easton after a full hot breakfast.

EASTON'S PROMISE
Innkeeper: Carla Cronin.
410-820-9159.
www.eastonspromise.com.
107 Goldsborough St., Easton, MD 21601.
Price: Expensive to very expensive.
Credit Cards: MC, V.
Handicapped Access: No.
Restrictions: No children under 18.

This smart addition to Easton's downtown is located near good restaurants and shops. A welcoming pale yellow parlor with an Oriental rug and attractive seating includes a discreet "real world" touch, should that become necessary: a television tucked into built-in shelves flanking the fireplace. The recently expanded 1890 house has five rooms on two floors. Styles range from spacious and romantic hideaways with queen-size four-poster beds upstairs in the old part of the house to a room with a theme of old-fashioned balloons. The latter is downstairs and has twin beds that will accommodate traveling companions or convert to a king. Look for walk-in showers—including one suitable for two—and amenities such as mini-fridges and hair dryers. Breakfast even includes dessert. Innkeeper Carla Cronin sees to details such as serving champagne at 6 PM or making dinner recommendations.

THE INN AT EASTON
Owners: Andrew and Liz Evans.
410-822-4910 or 1-888-800-8091.
www.theinnateaston.com.
28 S. Harrison St., Easton, MD 21601.
Price: Very expensive.

Credit Cards: AE, MC, V.
Handicapped Access: Restaurant only.
Restrictions: No pets or children under 9.

With bright yellow and aubergine walls and a Balinesque bust on the mantel, this inn's front sitting room instantly signals that this is not your typical Eastern Shore B&B. Located atop the inn's much-heralded restaurant, with its nouveau-Australian cuisine (see "Restaurants"), the inn boasts seven stylish guest rooms featuring Aboriginal art; four are suites with either king- or queen-size beds. Consider the Garden Suite's cozy dormer sitting room just through the bath; or the Holiday Suite, with bright red, yellow, and maroon drapery acting as a headboard. Luxe details prevail throughout, ranging from dimmer lights to featherbeds, Aveda bath products to clock radio/CD players. Handsome white rockers sit on a second-floor veranda overlooking the street, easily accessed by two accommodations in the front of the house. Packages available.

OXFORD
COMBSBERRY
Innkeeper: Cathy Magrogan.
410-226-5353.
www.combsberry.net.
4837 Evergreen Rd., Oxford, MD 21654.
Price: Very expensive.
Credit Cards: AE, MC, V.
Handicapped Access: Yes.
Special Features: Pets OK in the Oxford Cottage; children 12 and older OK.

A long colonial lane leads to stately Combsberry, circa 1730 and centerpiece to this 9-acre waterside estate, joined by the brick Carriage House and cute Oxford Cottage. All are done up in updated English country style, with the seven guest rooms inclined toward floral chintz-covered furniture and floral wallpaper, with whirlpool tubs and water views. The manor house's downstairs features wood-paneled sitting rooms with fireplaces where guests relax in leather chairs. Guest rooms feature such luxury as the Magnolia Suite, with its huge second-floor patio and windows onto the water from the bath, which has a whirlpool tub. The Carriage House, often leased as a whole, offers two guest rooms (cathedral ceilings, whirlpool tubs, luxe bedding, fireplaces) on either end of a broad living/kitchen area that features TV/VCR, a gas fireplace, and windows that open onto Bringman's Cove. Oxford Cottage has a galley kitchen and fainting couch upstairs near the queen bed. Full breakfast is served in the main house in a contemporary sunroom with views of the water. Outdoors, brick patios settle in under magnolias. Two canoes are available, and guests arriving via water can tie up at the dock. All in all, this is as luxurious as you'll find in the area, and it's comfortably situated just outside Oxford.

1876 HOUSE

Owners: Eleanor and Jerry Clark.
410-226-5496.
www.oxfordmd.com/1876house.
110 N. Morris St./P.O. Box 658, Oxford, MD 21654.
Price: Expensive.
Credit Cards: No.
Handicapped Access: No.

Fans of old houses will like this one on Oxford's main street, built in 1876 by a pharmacist as a wedding gift for his daughter and son-in-law. The unique stairway makes a sharp turn around four wedge-shaped steps as you make your way upstairs. That's in no way a criticism of the interesting and well-restored house, with three rooms (one of them a two-room suite) neatly decorated in Queen Anne style. All have private baths, though one is across the hall. A continental-plus breakfast is served in the formal dining room.

ROBERT MORRIS INN

Owners: Wendy and Ken Gibson.
410-226-5111 or 1-888-823-4012.
www.robertmorrisinn.com.
314 N. Morris St./P.O. Box 70, Oxford, MD 21654.
Price: Expensive to very expensive.
Credit Cards: AE, MC, V.
Handicapped Access: Yes.
Restrictions: No children under 10.

George Washington may or may not have slept here, but his pal owned the place. Robert Morris Jr. helped finance the Revolution, and, besides signing checks, he put his signature on the Declaration of Independence, the Articles of Confederation, and the Constitution. The inn's 34 rooms, all with private baths, are split between the mustard-colored clapboard building by the Oxford–Bellevue Ferry landing and the secluded Sandaway Lodge nearby, where rooms provide spectacular views of the Tred Avon River. At the historic inn, rooms ooze historical atmosphere, only fitting given that the inn has stood here since 1710. Visitors will find newer accommodations—including suites and a small cottage—at the Sandaway. One of its suites, the most expensive here, offers amenities down to private use of a boathouse as a sitting room.

ROYAL OAK
THE OAKS

Innkeepers: Shawn and Heather Maloney.
410-745-5053.
www.the-oaks.com.
MD 329 at Acorn Ln.; P.O. Box 187, Royal Oak, MD 21662.
Price: Moderate to very expensive.
Credit Cards: MC, V.
Handicapped Access: No.
Special Features: Kids OK.

Located on the grounds of an original land grant deeded by Lord Baltimore about 1680, this is a former farm with a long history as a country inn. A swimming pool, shuffleboard, and a couple of canoes to put in at Oak Creek set the stage for an easy-going respite off this country road winding south from St. Michaels. The inn hosts 15 rooms with queen- or king-size beds, the former sometimes accompanied by an antique full-bed headboard. Three rooms have decks, and some come with gas fireplaces and whirlpool tubs. Settle in on white wicker furniture on a side screened porch or at a deckside table along Oak Creek.

St. Michaels
BAY COTTAGE
Innkeepers: Jackie and Bob Fletcher.
410-745-9369 or 1-888-558-8008.
www.baycottage.com.
24640 Yacht Club Rd., St. Michaels, MD 21663.
Price: Expensive to very expensive.
Credit Cards: AE, MC, V.
Handicapped Access: No.
Restrictions: No children, no pets.

A swimming pool sits alongside Long Haul Creek not far from the deep-water dock where guests arriving by boat tie up. Set right in the slipstream of a long lane leading to the house, the pool makes a perfect spot to catch a breeze on a sultry Eastern Shore day, or to watch the sun set over the water. Lawn chairs, Adirondack or teak, are easy to come by here at Bay Cottage, a well-located hideaway just beyond St. Michaels. The main house is a former hunting lodge and gathering spot for a previous era's Eastern Shore sportsmen and offers plentiful water views. A tasteful mix of all-American Ralph Lauren or Drexel furnish- ings mixed with Asian antiques such as a Ching Dynasty wardrobe decorate the guest rooms. One room with a single bed connects to another, making them a good option for traveling companions. Breakfast is served out on the porch with yet another view of the water.

DR. DODSON HOUSE BED AND BREAKFAST
Innkeepers: Janet Buck and Gary Nylander.
410-745-3691.
www.drdodsonhouse.com.
200 Cherry St., St. Michaels, MD 21663.
Price: Expensive to very expensive.
Credit Cards: Not accepted; cash or checks OK.
Handicapped Access: No.
Restrictions: Not recommended for chil-, dren under 10.

Victorian decor dominates the fuchsia-tinged dining and guest parlors in this his-toric home, where the owners bring morning coffee to the rooms and guests get to choose breakfast from a menu. Service is a focal point here. The two-bedroom inn sits close to St. Michaels Harbor and offers spacious, traditionally decorated rooms, including one with an extra daybed. With portions built in 1799 and 1872, the house's signature feature may be the two-story porch lining the facade. But the house also comes with a fascinating past. At one time this was the residence of Louisa Bruff, whose father, Thomas Auld, once owned the slave Frederick Douglass. After the Civil War, Douglass visited the home, where the aging Auld then lived with his daughter and son-in-law, to make amends.

FIVE GABLES SPA AND INN
Innkeeper: Marianne Lesher.
410-745-0100 or 1-877-466-0100.
www.fivegables.com.
209 N. Talbot St., St. Michaels, MD 21663.
Price: Expensive to very expensive; spa packages available.
Credit Cards: AE, MC, V.
Handicapped Access: No.
Restrictions: Children discouraged.

Yellow toile and whimsically painted furni-ture are among the touches guests will find in the smart, well-appointed rooms here on the main street of St. Michaels. In all, 14 rooms are located in two buildings, each with a gas fireplace, whirlpool tub, and CD/clock radio—not to mention a porch. Cobalt blue tiles line the indoor courtyard-style pool. Visitors who want the spa treatment can partake of facials, herbal baths, massage therapy, steam, and sauna. Continental breakfast is served, as well as afternoon refreshments. This is a good-looking inn that takes a contemporary approach to Eastern Shore style. Spa packages are detailed on the website, and spa treatments are not included in room rates.

HARBOURTOWNE GOLF RESORT & CONFERENCE CENTER

410-745-9066 or 1-800-446-9066.
www.harbourtowne.com.
Martingham Dr. (just west of St. Michaels, off MD 33); P.O. Box 126, St. Michaels, MD 21663.
Price: Very expensive.
Credit Cards: AE, DC, D, MC, V.
Handicapped Access: Yes.

Drive through a community surrounding an 18-hole Pete Dye–designed golf course to reach Harbourtowne, with its manicured public areas and 111 rooms, all with water views. Each also comes with a terrace or covered porch. Twenty-four rooms have wood-burning fireplaces. It's a true resort, so there are lawn games, tennis, swimming, trails for walking and jogging, biking, volleyball, badminton, horseshoes, massage services, and a fitness center. Harbourtowne also has two restaurants, two bars, and a lounge with a pool table and television. The water view from much of the resort is spectacular.

THE INN AT PERRY CABIN

General Manager: John Volponi.
410-745-2200 or 1-800-722-2949 (reservations).
www.perrycabin.com.
308 Watkins Ln., St. Michaels, MD 21663.
Price: Very expensive.
Credit Cards: AE, DC, MC, V.

The renowned Inn at Perry Cabin has luxurious rooms and a notable restaurant. Photo courtesy of Inn at Perry Cabin

Handicapped Access: Yes.
Special Features: Children and pets welcome; please notify in advance if bringing a pet.

Long a showpiece in Talbot County, this luxury 1820 inn's newest incarnation comes under the direction of Orient Express Hotels. The 40-room historic section has been updated and parts of it renovated, including the notable restaurant, which retains Chef Mark Salter and is now called Sherwood's Landing. Guests can still settle into chintz furniture in the sitting rooms or discover the secret doorway to the "morning room" behind a bookshelf in the salon next door. A new building has recently doubled the number of guest rooms to 80. These rooms have a nautical/British colonial decor that may include an ostrich headboards and a television that rises from a leather "trunk" at the end of the bed. All rooms look out over water and wetlands, and half are suites. Amenities are endless at Perry Cabin: There's a fitness room, a horizon-edge pool, secluded courtyards and porches, attractive gardens, and concierge service that can arrange guest activities such as boat charters. Plans for a spa are on the drawing board. A nautical bar and lounge area also have been added in recent years. All in all, it's quite lovely.

KEMP HOUSE INN

Innkeepers/owners: Steve and Diane Cooper.
410-745-2243.
www.kemphouseinn.com.
412 S. Talbot St./P.O. Box 638, St. Michaels, MD 21663.
Price: Moderate to expensive.
Credit Cards: D, MC, V.
Handicapped Access: No.
Special Features: Children OK.

For historical surroundings at a reasonable price, the 1807 Kemp House offers a best bet. There's no television and no public sitting room, and you'll have to pick up your continental breakfast at the front desk (or the patio in warm weather). But working fireplaces, carved mantelpieces, original pine floors on two floors (brick ones on the first), and reproduction rope beds that may include a trundle for a child offer comfortable authenticity. There are seven rooms in all, plus a cottage out back. One of the rooms has a private balcony. Sleeping here puts you in good company: a young Robert E. Lee stayed two nights here as builder Col. Joseph Kemp's guest. You can even stay in the room that he used, identified with his name.

THE OLD BRICK INN

Innkeepers: Joe and Lynda Sharp.
410-745-3323 or 1-800-434-2143.
www.oldbrickinn.com.
401 S. Talbot St., St. Michaels, MD 21663.
Price: Moderate to very expensive.
Credit Cards: AE, MC, V.
Handicapped Access: No.
Restrictions: Children 12 and older only.

And now for something completely different: the Guinevere Suite, featuring exposed brick walls and a suit of armor in the corner. It's one of this 14-room inn's themed rooms, ranging from the Rainforest Room to the spacious Chesapeake Suite with its handsome white furniture. Guests stay in the middle of town in the historic house or a 1985 carriage house. A small pool is located outside in a brick courtyard. Queen- and king-size beds; full breakfast.

BETWEEN ST. MICHAELS AND TILGHMAN ISLAND
WADE'S POINT INN ON THE BAY

Owner: Betsy Feiler.
410-745-2500 or 1-888-923-3466.
www.wadespoint.com.
Five miles south of St. Michaels on Wade's Point Rd., McDaniel; P.O. Box 7, St. Michaels, MD 21663.

Price: Expensive to very expensive.
Credit Cards: V, MC.
Handicapped Access: Yes.
Special Features: Children welcome, but
no facilities for infants.

A longtime sentimental favorite, this old
inn sprawls along Eastern Bay 5 miles past
St. Michaels. Guests stay in one of several
buildings housing a total of 26 rooms.
These include the Main House, circa
1819, and the eight-room Victorian
Summer Wing, which was renovated
recently. Although the charming, old-
fashioned screen doors here remain, air-
conditioning has been added and the
rooms have private baths and water views.
The former attic of this section has been
renovated and converted into four rooms
with terrific water views. In addition,
there's the Kemp Guest House built in 1990
and a farmhouse you can rent as a whole.
This is Eastern Shore lodging at its best.
Full breakfast during the weekend; expanded continental during the week.
Closed during cold-weather months.

WATERMARK BED & BREAKFAST

Owners: Mac and Carla Buttrill.
410-745-2892 or 1-800-314-7734.
www.watermarkinn.com.
8956 Tilghman Island Rd./P.O. Box 27,
Wittman, MD 21676.
Price: Expensive to very expensive.
Credit Cards: MC, V.
Handicapped Access: No.
Special Features: Kids and pets OK.

Yes, that's blue water issuing from the eye-
popping fountain/sign announcing the
Watermark's long lane. Take it as a fun signal of what's ahead. When last we visited
this creative spread, a goat—one of eight—
was perched atop a shed not far from Mac's
workshop. A fountain sprouts here and
there throughout the Bay-side grounds, but
wait 'til you see the spectacular mosaic
fountain at the edge of the pool. It lights up

At the edge of the pool at the Watermark B&B.

at night. This secluded log lodging set on 7
acres offers a welcoming front room with a
woodstove to keep things warm in winter
and a telescope so nature lovers can peer
out at the Bay. Three guest rooms provide a
whopping 500 square feet of space, two-
person whirlpool tubs set in mosaics,
woodstoves, televisions, king-size beds,
mini-fridges, and Bay views. The downstairs Turtle Cove room is particularly
unique, with stained-glass panels inset into
logs opening onto the whirlpool tub from
the bedroom, and a wet bar area opening
onto the porch. Kennel runs are available in
the backyard for large dogs, while smaller
pets can stay indoors in kennels of their
own. If you can subsist on the full breakfast
served on weekends (continental during
the week) and whatever sustenance you
stash in your mini-fridge, you'll be hard-
pressed to leave.

TILGHMAN ISLAND

BLACK WALNUT POINT INN

Innkeepers: Tom and Brenda Ward.
410-886-2452.
www.blackwalnutpoint.com.
P.O. Box 308, Tilghman Island, MD 21671.
Price: Moderate to expensive.
Credit Cards: D, MC, V.

Relaxing at Black Walnut Point Inn at the tip of Tilghman Island.

Handicapped Access: Yes, in the cottages.
Restrictions: No children under 12.

On a clear day, you can see Cambridge to the east and Chesapeake Beach and North Beach to the west from the spread on this spectacular mid-Bay point. There's nothing overly fancy about the rooms in the 1840s house, what with quilts on the beds and basic baths, but that's the point. If you can watch sunset from across the Chesapeake Bay and sunrise from across the Choptank River, swim in the pool, and settle into the hot tub, what more could you want? Maybe just outstanding fishing, especially for migrating rockfish in the fall. This former farmhouse/hunt club complex includes a sitting room with a television and VCR and a series of stuffed sea ducks bagged by Brenda's grandfather on Hoopers Island, deep in Dorchester's wilds. Three comfy new "cottages" (little premade houses) smell of cedar and offer a

great getaway, with private screened porches and bedrooms with views of the Bay literally feet away. Continental breakfast is served until 10 AM.

CHESAPEAKE WOOD DUCK INN

Innkeepers: Kimberly and Jeffrey Bushey.
410-886-2070 or 1-800-956-2070.
www.woodduckinn.com.
P.O. Box 202, Gibsontown Rd., Tilghman Island, MD 21671.
Price: Expensive to very expensive.
Credit Cards: MC, V.
Handicapped Access: No.
Restrictions: No children under 14.

This Dogwood Harbor–side B&B has taken a turn for the culinary, with Chef Jeffrey Bushey in residence. The six-room Victorian is comfortably furnished in low-key but upscale Eastern Shore fashion, with queen- or king-size beds, and there's a great sitting room looking out on the water. Out back stands a contemporary cottage with a CD player and a fun collection of antique doorknobs. And check out breakfast: a pie made from jumbo lump crab, sweet corn, and spinach is just one specialty of the house. Equally inventive dinners are available as well; call for details.

LAZYJACK INN

Innkeepers: Mike and Carol Richards.
410-886-2215 or 1-800-690-5080.
www.lazyjackinn.com.
5907 Tilghman Island Rd./P.O. Box 248,
Tilghman Island, MD 21671.
Price: Very expensive.
Credit Cards: AE, MC, V.
Handicapped Access: No.
Restrictions: Children over 12 only.

The receding floodwaters of Tropical Storm Isabel prompted a complete and pretty darned hurricane-resistant renovation to this longtime B&B. The Richardses raised their inn 5 full feet, rebuilt first-floor walls, and installed windows that resist winds up to 180 mph (as do the walls). The biggest changes guests will notice to this former waterman's home are the new light flooding in through new windows and the handsome new butler's kitchen for their use. A screened-in porch has been replaced with a lovely sitting room in the Garden Suite downstairs, complete with painted furniture and a headboard created from an old piano. The upstairs rooms remain much the same, including the Nellie Byrd Suite, named for a skipjack, with its cool bathroom with a black whirlpool tub and an open entryway to the bedroom. Well, there is a change in this suite. With the inn's new height, you can now see the bridge spanning the Choptank River to Cambridge. The B&B is located alongside Dogwood Harbor, home to many of Maryland's dwindling skipjacks. The Richards family also operates cruises aboard the 40-foot Bay-built ketch *Lady Patty* and lighthouse tours aboard *M/V Sharps Island* (see "Recreation").

TILGHMAN ISLAND INN

Owners: Jack Redmon and David McCallum.
410-886-2141 or 1-800-866-2141.
www.tilghmanislandinn.com.
21384 Coopertown Rd., Tilghman Island, MD 21671.
Price: Expensive to very expensive.
Credit Cards: AE, DC, D, MC, V.
Handicapped Access: Yes.
Special Features: Pets allowed for additional fee; advance arrangements required.

With 20 attractive rooms, a terrific restaurant, and Knapp's Narrows flowing alongside, you may decide to settle in for the long run here. The rooms are contemporary, many of them recently renovated and featuring lots of pillows, fluffy duvets, contemporary armchairs, and whirlpool tubs. Many also look out on the water. If you aren't in a waterside room, wander around to the back of the inn and settle into one of the Adirondack chairs lining the Narrows. A pool sits at one end of the inn, and an outdoor deck bar is open in summer (see "Restaurants").

Hotels/Motels

Best Western (410-745-3333; for reservations, 1-800-528-1234; 1228 S. Talbot St., St. Michaels, MD 21663) Located before you get to the thick of the town's offerings. Ninety-three rooms, continental breakfast, in-room coffee, pool. Moderate to expensive.

Comfort Inn Kent Narrows (410-827-6767; for reservations 1-800-828-3361; 3101 Main St., Grasonville, MD 21638) Water-view location next to the Kent Narrows. Indoor pool, hot tub, sauna, exercise room, continental breakfast. In all, 92 rooms and two suites. Moderate to very expensive.

Days Inn (410-822-4600; 7018 Ocean Gateway Dr., Easton, MD 21601) Swimming pool, continental breakfast, 239 rooms. Inexpensive to moderate.

Harrison's Chesapeake Country Inn (410-886-2121; www.chesapeakehouse.com; 21551 Chesapeake House Dr., Tilghman, MD 21671) Venerable waterside lodgings, renowned among fishers who can eat breakfast early at the inn's fabled restaurant before heading out on a charter boat from the Harrison's fleet. In all, 70 rooms are available, 50 as guest rooms and the rest as rental houses. Twenty-five rooms have recently been remodeled. Moderate to expensive (inexpensive during the off-season). Packages available. See "Restaurants" and "Recreation" in this chapter for dining and fishing details.

The Tidewater Inn (410-822-1300; www.tidewaterinn.com; 101 E. Dover St., Easton, MD 21601) This venerable Georgian-style 1949 hotel in Easton's town center has new owners and 100 guest rooms, and renovations were under way at deadline. The seats at the sidewalk café are often occupied in good weather, additional dining space is available, and there's an outdoor pool. Moderate to very expensive.

RESTAURANTS

A culinary awakening has been under way in Talbot County in recent years. Easton's Goldsborough Street reached a critical mass of interesting restaurants in the early 2000s and hasn't slowed down. Consider the Inn at Easton, serving contemporary Australian cuisine and quickly scaling the heights of culinary stardom. In St. Michaels, 208 Talbot has held court for eons, and news arrived as we reached deadline that the wine director for New York's hot Pastis and Balthazar would be redesigning the wine list at the popular Bistro St. Michaels. Off the beaten path, Talbot crossroads villages such as Bellevue, best known over the past three centuries for its ferry landing, have awakened to find bistros that stock artisan cheeses moving into town. But don't think for a moment that Chesapeake staples—crabs, oysters, rockfish, sweet corn, and tomatoes—have been forgotten. They may be tempura'd and sautéed with all kinds of exotic herbs and spices these days, but visitors will have no problem finding plenty of old-style restaurants serving much-loved Eastern Shore cuisine such as crab cakes, crab imperial, and oysters on the half shell. Crab decks for pounding hard-shells are easy to come by, too. You can even find fried chicken, done up right in a black iron skillet.

Price ranges, which include dinner entrée, appetizer, and dessert, are as follows:

Inexpensive:	Up to $20
Moderate:	$20 to $30
Expensive:	$30 to $40
Very Expensive:	$40 or more

Credit card abbreviations are:
AE—American Express
CB—Carte Blanche
DC—Diners Club
D—Discover
MC—MasterCard
V—Visa

The following abbreviations are used to denote meals served:
B = Breakfast; L = Lunch; D = Dinner;
SB = Sunday Brunch

KENT ISLAND/GRASONVILLE/KENT NARROWS

FISHERMAN'S INN & CRAB DECK

410-827-8807 (410-827-6666 for the Crab Deck).
3116 Main St./3032 Kent Narrows Way S., Grasonville.
Open: Daily.
Price: Moderate to expensive.
Cuisine: Seafood/Eastern Shore.

Serving: L, D.
Credit Cards: AE, DC, D, MC, V.
Reservations: Not accepted.
Handicapped Access: Yes.

Tried and true, this longtime Narrows establishment has been operated by the same family since 1930. Count on it for reliable Eastern Shore cuisine like stuffed flounder and crab cakes. A miniature train circles the top of the big dining rooms, and a notable collection of oyster plates can be found amid the inn's decor. The menu ranges from oyster stew ($5.50 for a bowl) to broiled or fried fishermen's seafood dinners loaded with everything a hungry seafood lover could want. Beef and nonseafood dishes are also available. Next door is the Crab Deck, a separate restaurant owned by the same family and a good place to pound hard-shells by the water. You'll find an expansive menu that includes a selection of sandwiches and frozen drinks, too. As evening draws nigh, it's also a popular nightspot. In summertime, the parking lot definitely fills up.

HARRIS CRAB HOUSE

410-827-9500.
433 N. Kent Narrows Way, Grasonville.
Open: Daily.
Price: Moderate to expensive.
Cuisine: Seafood.
Serving: L, D.
Credit Cards: MC, V.
Reservations: No.
Handicapped Access: Yes.
Special Features: Public docking;
shops in-season.

Join the crowd to knock open a dozen or so hard crabs at long picnic tables downstairs, at smaller individual tables inside on the "upper deck," or on the outside deck. Both decks overlook the northern end of the Kent Narrows. Fresh steamed crabs, soft-shell crabs, and all other seafood can be had here, including in land-and-sea com

bos such as the one that offers T-bone steak with your choice of fried oysters, shrimp, or scallops or, for an additional $2.50, a crab cake or crab imperial. Landlubbers also will find barbecued chicken and ribs, and there's a kids' menu. This place is so popular we once, no kidding, stood in line behind a man who said he'd driven all the way from New Jersey to eat crabs here.

HOLLY'S RESTAURANT

410-827-8711.
108 Jackson Creek Rd., Grasonville.
Open: Daily.
Price: Inexpensive to moderate.
Cuisine: Eastern Shore.
Serving: B, L, D.
Credit Cards: MC, V.
Reservations: No.
Handicapped Access: Yes.

It's déjà vu every time we settle into a knotty pine booth at Holly's. My husband tells me about his dad bringing him here when he was a boy for a real chocolate milkshake. Or he waxes over bringing his own daughter when she was young, and how they filled time waiting for real chocolate milkshakes by filling out the placemat quiz, "Can you name the states and their capitals?" However, more than nostalgia has kept Holly's thriving for 50 years at its prime Eastern Shore entry locale on US 50. The prices couldn't be more reasonable, and the homemade food means carrots in a spicy Maryland crab soup were likely chopped right in the kitchen. Alert customers passing through the dining room will note the abundance of fried chicken being consumed by their fellow diners, folks clued in to a Holly's signature dish. Pastas, beef (liver and onions, $12.50), poultry, and, of course, seafood are also available. The children's menu is well priced and highly sensible (hot dogs, for example), which must tempt even organic moms after the long and fussy drive back from the beach. The real chocolate milkshakes, by the way, cost $3—and are worth every dime.

KENTMORR RESTAURANT

410-643-2263.
910 Kentmorr Rd., 6 miles down MD 8 S.
Open: Daily.
Price: Moderate to expensive.
Cuisine: Eastern Shore seafood.
Serving: L, D.
Credit Cards: D, MC, V.
Reservations: Accepted.
Handicapped Access: Yes.

When writing about great finds, the temptation to save personal favorites so they won't become overly discovered exists. But that wouldn't be fair to one's readers—plus, Kentmorr has been here for years and lots of folks know about it. Among the Bay's many great crab-picking spots, this is an especially good one, hugging Kent Island's left bank with westerly views toward sunset. A recent renovation has glassed in the deck; it's still open, but not completely open-air. A pool operated by the next-door marina costs $2 a day, plus there's a small sand beach. Sandwiches, burgers, fancier entrées with crab imperial, as well as beef, chicken, and rib dishes are available. The kids' menu is $4.99, plus kids eat free on Thurs. with their parents.

THE NARROWS

410-827-8113.
3023 Kent Narrows Way S., Grasonville.
Open: Daily.
Price: Moderate to very expensive.
Cuisine: Upscale seafood.
Serving: L, D.
Credit Cards: DC, D, MC, V.
Reservations: Encouraged, especially on weekends.
Handicapped Access: Yes.

In an area where restaurants cater to the informal crab-picking crowd, the Narrows stands out as a touch of elegance. The restaurant's crab cakes are legendary, but Chesapeake's signature crustacean is served here in many different dishes with flavorful sauces. Besides the Chesapeake staples of crabs, oysters, clams, and rockfish, you'll also find other seafood dishes and beef and pork entrées. A light supper menu—well priced and less filling for those watching their figures—is offered as well. The Narrows overlooks the busy Kent Narrows, and if you're lucky, on a breezy evening you can dine on the porch and watch the passing boats.

EASTON
ALICE'S CAFE

410-819-8590.
22 N. Harrison St.
Open: Mon. through Sat.
Price: Inexpensive to moderate.
Cuisine: Creative regional.
Serving: B, L.
Credit Cards: None; cash only.
Reservations: Not required.
Handicapped Access: Yes.

In the few short years since it opened, this charming eatery has won hordes of regulars for its homemade soups, salads, and sandwiches. (The BLTs and two kinds of chicken salad are top choices.) A case of gorgeous desserts, all made in-house, are guaranteed to throw calorie counters into a tizzy. Pale yellow walls and black and white toile curtains above black and white checkerboard floor tiles give the place the feel of a sophisticated kitchen. Pleasant, prompt service and food better than your mother made account for the popularity of this gathering spot. In addition to inside tables, you'll find outdoor seating in a tiny garden beneath the trees.

GENERAL TANUKI'S

410-819-0707.
25 Goldsborough St.
Open: Daily.
Price: Moderate to expensive.
Cuisine: Pacific Rim and American.
Serving: D.
Credit Cards: DC, MC, V.
Reservations: Requested on weekends.
Handicapped Access: Yes.

An agreeable mixture of casual and fine dining can be found in this popular spot with exposed ductwork and dark gray walls. On the casual side, burgers, pizzas, and ribs are popular, while serious appetites can opt for steaks, tuna, surf and turf, or a curried chicken entrée with the grandiose name "Evil Devil Prince." Diners also can make a meal of sushi, halemaki, maki, or sashimi teased with wasabi and pickled ginger. Libations from saki to brewskis cool the palate and up the fun.

THE INN AT EASTON

410-822-4910.
28 S. Harrison St.
Open: Wed. through Sun.
Price: Very expensive.
Cuisine: Contemporary Australian.
Serving: D.
Credit Cards: MC, V.
Reservations: Recommended.
Handicapped Access: Yes.

Through the royal blue front door in its Federal facade, the Inn at Easton offers diners contemporary comfort and creative cuisine in a gallery-esque dining room. Under the direction of chef/owner Andrew Evans, the inn's menu changes every two to three weeks, relies on the freshest local ingredients, and takes them Down Under, where Evans got his culinary training. Lamb and sticky fig is a signature dish. As Evans sees it, contemporary Australian food blends Mediterranean with Asian influences and has a "brightness" to it. A tempura of soft-shell crabs, for instance, is served with a Vietnamese touch: warm pork vermicelli and caramelized coconut juice. The wine list draws from the inn's selection of boutique Australian wines. Order à la carte Wed., Thurs., and Sun. On Fri. and Sat., there is no à la carte, simply a $65 prix fixe menu for five courses. Notables have been noticing, including the *Washington Post* and *Food and Wine*.

KENDALL'S STEAK AND SEAFOOD

410-822-9898.
106 N. West St.
Open: Mon. through Sat.
Price: Moderate to expensive.
Cuisine: Regional American with some classic French and Italian.
Serving: L, D.
Credit Cards: AE, D, MC, V.
Reservations: No.
Handicapped Access: Yes.

Crab cakes made with a Smith Island recipe are the big draw at this friendly, two-tiered dining spot. Chef Don Kendall brings his expertise from the Culinary Institute of America and training under Paul Prudhomme at Commander's Palace in New Orleans, Walter Scheib at the White House, and Robert Greaualt at the Bagatelle in D.C. The early bird menu (4–6 PM) and the nightly bar dinners are $9.95 each and offer a choice of three menus. Nonseafood eaters will be delighted to see the menu's aged Black Angus. Airy and bright, tables not too close, and Muzak-free.

MASON'S RESTAURANT

410-822-3204.
22-24 S. Harrison St.
Open: Mon. through Sat.
Price: Expensive to very expensive (D).
Cuisine: Continental and American, seafood.
Serving: L (Mon. through Sat.), D (Tues. through Sat.).

Credit Cards: AE, MC, V.
Reservations: Suggested for lunch and dinner.
Handicapped Access: Yes.

Located on one of downtown Easton's most handsome historic streets, Mason's is a very popular local restaurant, even at lunchtime. The bar's jumbo martinis and the kitchen's upscale sandwiches may explain why. The seasonal dinner menu is far fancier, offering starters such as The Black Tie (scallop, foie gras, and seasonal black truffle wrapped in puff pastry with a port wine sauce), pretty pastas, and well-done fish, lamb, and beef dishes. The recent Duo of Colorado Lamb included a double lamb chop and braised osso bucco with barley gratin, sautéed spinach, and minted lamb jus. Executive Chef Michael Forrester hails from the Culinary Institute of America and has cooked in such New York legends as Le Cirque; his wife Laurie is the sommelier.

OUT OF THE FIRE

410-770-4777.
22 Goldsborough St.
Open: Mon. through Sat.
Price: Moderate to expensive.
Cuisine: Mediterranean.
Serving: L Mon. through Fri., D Sat.
Credit Cards: AE, DC, MC, V.
Reservations: Recommended, particularly on weekends.
Handicapped Access: Yes.

Warm and inviting yet polished as a slick New York City bistro, Out of the Fire is the perfect place to settle in for an evening of good food and great wine. From the sofas just off the wine bar to the open kitchen complete with a wood-burning hearth oven, this restaurant makes every attempt to put you at ease. The menu changes every few weeks, and the oven-fired pizzas (pear and gorgonzola, for example) are a staple. Tapas are available at the wine bar.

RESTAURANT COLUMBIA

410-770-5172.
28 S. Washington St.
Open: Tues. through Sat.
Price: Very expensive.
Cuisine: Contemporary American.
Serving: D.
Credit Cards: AE, MC, V.
Reservations: Recommended, especially on weekends.
Handicapped Access: Partial; call for details.

Each evening, Restaurant Columbia's chef/owner Stephen Mangasarian offers a discreet number of diners—26 during the week, up to 32 on weekends—the opportunity to sample his daily creations. The reason for this is simple: he works alone, and everything is made fresh on the premises, from the cloudlike yeast rolls with whipped butter to the chocolate chip/coconut ice cream for dessert. The menu changes about every three weeks and places great emphasis on fresh ingredients from area growers. And while certain entrées come and go, the pistachio-crusted rack of lamb with a raspberry sauce remains the house's signature dish. When it comes to wine, Columbia doesn't disappoint. *Wine Spectator* gives the 130-plus-bottle cellar of American wines its Award of Excellence, and wines by the glass change with the menu. The classically trained Mangasarian has been at it for years and opened this Easton mainstay after moving south from Vermont in 1998.

Oxford

LATITUDE 38

410-226-5303.
26342 Oxford Rd.
Open: Tues. through Sun.
Price: Moderate to expensive.
Cuisine: Creative regional.
Serving: D, SB.
Credit Cards: AE, D, MC, V.

Fishing boats at Dogwood Harbor on Tilghman Island bring in the fresh seafood served by local restaurants.

Reservations: Recommended on weekends.
Handicapped Access: Yes.

Latitude 38 can well be described as the Cheers of Oxford. If they don't know your name when you enter, you can be darn sure they will by the time you leave. A haven for locals and those just sailing through on the weekends, Latitude 38 offers the best of both worlds: multicourse meals for the sit-down crowd and inexpensive bar dinners for those who just can't face their own kitchens. For the price and the cama-raderie, you can't beat the latter. Your only obstacle will be finding a place at this incredibly popular bar, recently expanded to accommodate its growing following. Bar dinners change every night, while the regu-lar menu varies biweekly.

THE MASTHEAD AT PIER STREET RESTAURANT AND MARINA

410-226-5171.
W. Pier St.
Open: Mid-Mar. through Dec.
Price: Moderate to very expensive.
Cuisine: Eastern Shore seafood.
Serving: L, D.
Credit Cards: DC, MC, V.
Reservations: Only required for parties of 20 or more.
Handicapped Access: Yes.

Tropical Storm Isabel dealt this venerable crab house a near-fatal blow, but new man-agement has rebuilt to create a fresh new look for inside seating and the same famil-iar broad deck for covered dining on the Tred Avon River. Casual dress is the order of the day here, where paper tablecloths can be rolled up to discard the mess from feasting on steamed crabs, clams, mussels, and shrimp. Nonseafood lovers can avert their eyes from the mounds of crab shells and settle for burgers, prime rib sandwiches, or curried chicken salad. Tops among the desserts are key lime pie and the original Masthead Derby Pie, a rich concoction of pecans and chocolate chips. Both are made in-house.

MILL ST. GRILL
410-226-0400.
101 Mill St.
Open: Noon–9; closed Tues.
Price: Moderate to very expensive.
Cuisine: Seafood and prime rib.
Serving: L, D.
Credit Cards: AE, DC, V, MC.
Reservations: No.
Handicapped Access: Yes.

This neighborhood bar and restaurant is informal, with bar seating, a dining room, and porch seating in warm weather. Daily specials offer two seafood or prime rib choices from a menu that changes seasonally. Quick lunches to accommodate workers from nearby boatyards include a $5 Boatyard Special with varied sandwiches, subs, and chips. Low-key and inviting; a good place for a burger.

ROBERT MORRIS INN
410-226-5111.
314 N. Morris St.
Open: Daily Apr. through Nov.; weekends only Mar.; closed Dec. through Feb.
Price: Moderate to expensive.
Cuisine: Regional seafood, continental.
Serving: B, L, D.
Credit Cards: AE, MC, V.
Reservations: Only for parties of eight or more.
Handicapped Access: Yes.

Dating to 1710, the Robert Morris Inn is one of the country's oldest historic inns. Situated along the Tred Avon River in the colonial village of Oxford, it is a favorite destination for residents and tourists who appreciate traditional Maryland fare served in a historic atmosphere. Whether seated in the rustic Tap Room, the Colonial Tavern, or the main dining room, select from the same menu they've been serving for 30 years. Black Angus beef, seafood au gratin cakes (a combination of crab, shrimp, and Monterey Jack and cheddar cheeses), and Chesapeake fries sprinkled with the owner's secret seasoning are just a few of the choices. But the real reason you go to the Robert Morris Inn is for the crab cakes, deemed by author James Michener as the best on the Chesapeake (a much jockeyed-over distinction in Bay restaurants, by the way). Made from jumbo lump crabmeat, these creations are held together seemingly by sheer will. It seems the Robert Morris Inn does not know the meaning of the word "breading."

ST. MICHAELS

BISTRO ST. MICHAELS
410-745-9111.
403 S. Talbot St.
Open: Thurs. through Mon.
Price: Expensive to very expensive.
Cuisine: French Provençal meets Chesapeake.
Serving: D.
Credit Cards: AE, CB, DC, D, MC, V.
Reservations: Recommended.
Handicapped Access: Yes.

Conveniently located on the Mid-Shore's left bank in the heart of St. Michaels, this lively and spirited restaurant has expanded of late. A long, narrow dining space runs alongside the building. There's an open kitchen and a cozy seafood bar area with a moderately priced menu of smoked fish plates and oysters du jour. The main dining room is decorated with French theater posters and crisp white tablecloths, and your hostess will see you to your table with a small dish of marinated olives, chili, garlic, and olive oil. The seasonally changing menu is small (lunch often features no more than five items), but don't be deceived. Chef David Stein oversees a kitchen where everything is done in-house, and what they do, they do well. The entrée menu changes five times a year, and if you're not in the mood for pistou-crusted lamb chops or grilled entrecôte with truffle-madeira vinaigrette, try a cleverly designed pizza. True to its French roots, the Bistro's wine selection is extensive, but oenophiles will be thrilled to hear that, as of deadline, the director of wine at New York's Pastis and Balthazar was slated to develop a new wine list.

THE CRAB CLAW RESTAURANT
410-745-2900.
304 Mill St.
Open: Daily, Mar. through early Dec.
Price: Moderate to expensive.
Cuisine: Eastern Shore, seafood.
Serving: L, D.
Credit Cards: Not accepted; ATM machine on-site; personal checks accepted.
Reservations: Recommended on weekends.
Handicapped Access: Yes.

This is one of Bay Country's most well-known seafood and crab decks, settled on prime real estate alongside the Chesapeake Bay Maritime Museum overlooking St. Michaels Harbor. Originally the Eastern Shore Clam Co., a clam and oyster shucking house, the restaurant was launched in 1965 by the Jones family. Plan on a crab feast here.

MICHAEL RORK'S TOWN DOCK RESTAURANT
410-745-5577.
125 Mulberry St.
Open: Daily Apr. through Oct.; Thurs. through Sun. Nov. through Mar.
Price: Expensive.
Cuisine: Creative regional seafood.
Serving: L, D.
Credit Cards: AE, DC, D, MC, V.
Reservations: Recommended.
Handicapped Access: Partial; call for information.

Owned and operated over the past decade by notable Maryland chef Michael Rork, formerly of Baltimore's well-regarded Harbor Court Hotel restaurant, Town Dock is home to award-winning creations in a casual, relaxing, waterfront setting. Consider starting with the Crab Monterey, a heaping pile of warm, oversize tortilla chips engulfing an overflowing crock of a magical blend of lump crabmeat, fresh tomatoes, and Monterey Jack cheese. Crab bisque is a house specialty. Hearty and rich, the velvety cream base surrounds the lumps of crabmeat. One of the best features about the Town Dock is that you can choose from the interestingly creative (shrimp and grits) to typical Chesapeake selections (crab cakes and rockfish). Early dinner from 4–6 PM offers reduced prices for entrées. For the finale, Town Dock delivers a larger-than-life chocolate covered strawberry.

208 TALBOT
410-745-3838.
208 N. Talbot St.
Open: Wed. through Sun.
Price: Expensive to very expensive.
Cuisine: Innovative American.
Serving: D.
Credit Cards: D, MC, V.
Reservations: Recommended.
Handicapped Access: Yes.

It's rare to find a restaurant you can always count on to offer great food and exceptional service, but 208 Talbot has maintained its reputation for years. The inventive menu changes from time to time, and it's hard to envision any taste it doesn't anticipate. Begin the evening with a plate of the restaurant's signature baked oysters draped in a luscious champagne cream sauce and garnished with julienned prosciutto and chopped pistachios. Fish, beef, and poultry dishes are all well represented with flair; a roasted rack of lamb and its vegetables, for instance, might be served with a roasted garlic rosemary sauce. Chef-owner Paul Milne has been featured on *Great Chefs of the East*, and 208 Talbot has often been the recipient of the prestigious DiRoNa (Distinguished Restaurants of North America) award, as well as notable nods from *Zagat* and *Wine Spectator.* The 1871 brick duplex's dining room radiates an intimacy and romance that would melt even the hardest heart.

ROYAL OAK
BELLA LUNA ITALIAN MARKET
410-745-6100.
25942 Royal Oak Rd.
Open: Tues. through Sun.
Price: Moderate to very expensive.
Cuisine: Italian.
Serving: L, D, SB.
Credit Cards: MC, V.
Reservations: Highly recommended on weekends.
Handicapped Access: Yes.

Time was, this old general store near the St. Michaels side of the Oxford—Bellevue Ferry landing dispensed meals via microwave. Times change. Two of us stopped in one quiet September weekday for lunch. The food delivery was due later that day. Proprietor Barbara Helish pulled up a stool and said, "What are you in the mood for?" Then she talked through the ingredients she had available. The result? A sautéed shrimp—portobello—goat cheese—red-pepper sandwich on Italian bread that was unbelievably good. The dinner menu, which changes regularly, offers only a handful of entrées, but we'll bet the wild king salmon cedar-planked with balsamic and cucumbers is a winner. Italian wines, homemade

mozzarella, artisan cheeses, and other Italian specialties are available for eating in or taking out.

TILGHMAN ISLAND
HARRISON'S CHESAPEAKE HOUSE
410-886-2121.
21551 Chesapeake House Dr.
Open: Daily.
Price: Moderate.
Cuisine: Eastern Shore, seafood.
Serving: B, L, D.
Credit Cards: AE, MC, V.
Reservations: Accepted only for parties of six or more.
Handicapped Access: Yes.

If your style leans toward waterfront decks with picnic tables full of hot steamed crabs and pitchers of icy beer or freshly brewed tea, Harrison's is the place for you. Or dine indoors in the expansive dining room that overlooks the Choptank River and Harrison's fleet of charter fishing boats. Delicately fried chicken breasts and beautifully made soft-shell crabs let you know that 110-plus years of experience behind the fryer means the kitchen knows its way around Eastern Shore comfort food. Beef dishes are also popular, and the Friday night buffets mean prime rib and seafood Apr. through Sept. But if you're on Tilghman from Oct. through Mar., check out the oyster buffet, with oysters made nine different ways (plus, it's all you can eat).

TILGHMAN ISLAND INN
410-886-2141.
21384 Coopertown Rd.
Open: Daily except Wed.; closed in Jan.
Price: Expensive to very expensive.
Cuisine: Creative American.
Serving: L, D, SB.
Credit Cards: AE, DC, D, MC, V.
Reservations: Recommended.
Handicapped Access: Yes.

After the floodwaters of Tropical Storm Isabel receded, the owners of the Tilghman Island Inn renovated the inn's first floor. The result includes a main dining room called Isabel's with contemporary flair to match another dining room added several years ago. Two baby grand pianos set strategically in the space complement local art on the walls and fantastic views of Knapp's Narrows or the Bay. Two longtime stars on the menu are the Oysters Choptank, an entrée with a Pernod-scented champagne sauce caressing everyone's favorite bivalve in a puff pastry, and the black-eyed pea cakes. The menu changes from time to time, so entrées featuring New York strip or ahi tuna may be offered as well. A five-course tasting menu is available weekends for $60, and the extensive wine list, recognized by *Wine Spectator* for years, includes many half-bottles.

Food Purveyors

Coffee Shops

Blue Crab Coffee Co. (410-745-4155; 102 S. Fremon St., St. Michaels) Fresh pastries, coffees, and teas quartered in the historic Freedom's Friends Lodge 1024. Open late Fri. and Sat. in-season.

Coffee East (410-819-6711; 5 Goldsborough St., Easton) All the exotic (and nonexotic) coffees and teas in an open, cheery café that's also a favored local luncheon spot. Thurs. is trivia night, and other entertainment is held weekend evenings. Open Mon. through Sat. 7 AM–9 PM, Sun. 8–2.

Gourmet and Specialty Markets

Chesapeake Gourmet (410-827-8686; 189 Outlet Center Dr., Queenstown) A well-supplied store with terrific kitchenware, coffee and tea, wines, microbrews, and specialty food products. Good takeout, too. Located at Prime Outlets on US 50. Open daily.

Flamingo Flats (410-745-2053; 100 S. Talbot St., St. Michaels) An endless collection of hot sauces, as well as cookbooks, flamingo stuff, and gourmet condiments and sauces. Hot-sauce tasting bar in summer.

Oxford Market & Deli (410-226-0015; 203 S. Morris St., Oxford) All you need, from groceries to ice cream to deli sandwiches.

The Railway Market (410-822-4852; 108 Marlboro Rd., Easton) Where healthy Shore gourmets shop. Originally located in Easton's old-time railway depot, the store's larger strip-mall location offers organic and natural groceries, takeout and a café, health and beauty products, books. Open daily.

So Neat Café & Bakery (410-886-2143; 5776 Tilghman Island Rd., Tilghman, Md.) Open Thurs. through Sun., serving sandwiches, homemade soups, desserts, specialty coffees. Breakfast Thurs. through Sat.; Sun. means fruit plates and bakery breakfast. This former general store also has a shop next door.

Ice Cream

Justine's Ice Cream Parlour (410-745-5416; 106 S. Talbot St., St. Michaels) Creative array of ice-cream goodies in the midst of St. Michaels. Open daily Mar. through Nov.

Olde Town Creamery (410-822-5223; 9B Goldsborough St., Easton) Well located in the middle of town, selling everything from malteds to gelati.

The Soda Fountain at Hill's (410-822-9751; 30 E. Dover St., Easton) The old-fashioned drugstore soda fountain beloved by all remains, now with a menu of homemade soups and sandwiches that makes it popular for lunch, too. Serving B, L.

Seafood Markets and Crab Houses

Big Al's Market (410-745-3151; 302 N. Talbot St., St. Michaels) Where St. Michaels buys its hard-shell crabs for summer crab feasts. Fresh fish, groceries, deli, beer, wine, and liquor. Hunting and fishing licenses.

Captain's Ketch Seafood Market (410-820-7177; 316 Glebe Rd., Easton) Picked crabmeat, lobster, and fish, including orange roughy, catfish, and smoked bluefish.

Chesapeake Landing Seafood Market and Restaurant (410-745-9600; 23713 St. Michaels Rd., McDaniel) People drive all the way from Easton to get seafood at this spot between St. Michaels and Tilghman. Oysters and crabs in-season. Once only a wholesale business, it's added a thriving retail market and comfy restaurant with reasonably priced takeout. Daily specials have been known to run to the very local, like a crab-cake sandwich made entirely of claw meat.

Fisherman's Seafood Market (410-827-7323; 3032 Kent Narrows Way S., Grasonville) Locals know to stop at the seafood market in the midst of this tourist restaurant complex for fine fresh fish, crab cakes, and more to prepare at home.

CULTURE

When history meets a beautiful landscape, the arts (and their patrons) seem to follow. That's the easy summation of cultural life in this region, which has had its art associations for local painters for years, a wealthy estate society dating back to the Revolution, and gorgeous waterways that draw everyone to a boat. Newcomers from outside the area may be accelerating the arrival of more upscale offerings such as galleries and cafés, but the Mid-Shore area always has had its share of the finer things in life. Easton hosts a popular First Friday, in which shops and galleries stay open from 5 to 9 PM. Most galleries offer opportunities to meet area artists, as well as to enjoy complimentary food and beverages. For more information, contact the Talbot County Office of Tourism at www.tourtalbot.org or 410-770-8000.

Cinema

Easton Premier Cinemas (410-822-9950; Tred Avon Shopping Center on Marlboro Rd.) First-run fare.

Galleries

EASTON
ACADEMY ART MUSEUM
410-822-ARTS.
www.art-academy.org.
106 South St.

Open: Tues. through Thurs. 10–8;
Mon., Fri., and Sat. 10–4.

Long the gathering place for the area's
artists, this white clapboard former
schoolhouse is expanding yet again to
add performing arts space to its already
sizable studio and gallery space. When
all is said and done, a flexible performing arts wing with a temporary stage
and quality acoustics will seat 150 for
chamber concerts and lectures by
notables from the world of art and
architecture. On the visual arts side,
the permanent collection includes
notable Eastern Shore–connected
artists, as well as American and
European works on paper. Exhibits,
which can range from Rembrandt to

*The Academy Art Museum in Easton is central to the
Mid-Shore's art scene.*

Rauschenberg, change every six to eight weeks. Classes, trips, and other activities are held
here as well. Call ahead or check the website for concert and lecture schedules; watch for
the juried crafts show called "Arts Marketplace" in October.

STEVENSVILLE
KENT ISLAND FEDERATION OF ART
410-643-7424.
www.kifa.us.
405 Main St.
Open: Wed. through Fri. and Sun. 1–4; Sat. 10–4.

Local and regional artists working in media from oils to photography exhibit at this fine
Victorian at the edge of town. Monthly exhibits have featured everything from paintings to
pottery; a separate member gallery changes its exhibit every two months. Classes, too.

Historic Buildings and Sites

EASTON
HISTORICAL SOCIETY OF TALBOT COUNTY
410-822-0773.
25 S. Washington St.
Open: Tues. through Sat. 10–4. Tours at 11:30 AM and 1:30 PM Mar. through Dec.
Admission: Free for museum and garden; $5 for tours.

In the main building, photographs capture Talbot County's rural and maritime history. On
the grounds stand historic structures representing different periods of local history.
Joseph's Cottage (1795) tells the story of an Easton cabinetmaker. The James Neall House
(1810), an excellent example of Federal architecture, shows how life changed for the afflu-
ent cabinetmaker and his Quaker family after early 19th-century success. The society's
buildings surround a stunning garden based on an 18th-century design.

The Maryland Watermen's Memorial at Kent Narrows.

THIRD HAVEN FRIENDS MEETING HOUSE

410-822-0293.
www.thirdhaven.org.
405 S. Washington St.
Open: Daily 9–5; services Sun. at 10 AM, tours by appt.; grounds open for walking.

Built from 1682 to 1684, this is the oldest building in Maryland. Originally located in virgin timber (Easton was founded 25 years later), the Meeting House is now neatly tucked into a residential street on a 7-acre parcel. Stroll the peaceful grounds and admire a simple building still in use 300 years after Pennsylvania founder and Quaker William Penn preached here.

TILGHMAN ISLAND
DOGWOOD HARBOR

Skipjack sails once numbered in the hundreds on the Chesapeake Bay, so it's a bittersweet pleasure to spot the distinctive outlines of the few remaining ladies that ply the Bay in search of oysters. Fewer than a dozen skipjacks still work the water, and many of those dock in Tilghman's Dogwood Harbor. (You'll also find a couple of working skipjacks on Deal Island, and several continue to "work" the Bay as ecotour boats.) Get a sense of life aboard a skipjack, learn the lore, and "dredge" for oysters by taking a cruise on the 1886 *Rebecca T. Ruark*, the oldest skipjack still in service (Capt. Wade H. Murphy Jr., 410-886-2176). Follow MD 33 through St. Michaels and over the Tilghman Island drawbridge, then turn left about a half mile onto the island. You'll see the harbor.

WYE MILLS
WYE GRIST MILL

410-827-6909 or 410-827-3850.
Operated by Friends of Wye Mill.
14296 Old Wye Rd.; MD 662 off US 50 north of Easton in Wye Mills.
Open: Mid-Apr. through mid-Nov., Thurs. through Sun. 10–4 or by appt.
Admission: $2 donation suggested.

A gristmill has been grinding cornmeal and flour in Wye Mills since 1671, and you can still see the great stone turn by water power on the first and third Sat. of every month. An exhibit focuses on the mill's glory days, from 1790 to 1830, when wheat brought prosperity here, where flour for Revolutionary troops was ground. Buy a bag of freshly ground meal or *The Wye Miller's Grind*, a 100-recipe cookbook. Wye Mill is a hotbed of historic sites, all within a few hundred yards of each other. Call 1-888-400-RSVP for information on any of them. On a culinary note, Orrell's Maryland Beaten Biscuits, the world's only commercial beaten biscuit company, makes the small local delights just a stone's throw from the mill. The result is surprisingly flaky and chewy, and certainly worth trying. You'll find the flour

A crowd gathers to watch two people making a skiff at the Chesapeake Bay Maritime Museum's Apprentice for a Day Program. Photo courtesy of the Chesapeake Bay Maritime Museum

flying and can take a tour Tues. and Wed. 7–2 and on other days around the busy winter holidays. Call them at 410-827-6244.

Museums
CHESAPEAKE BAY MARITIME MUSEUM
410-745-2916.
www.cbmm.org.
Mill St., Navy Point, St. Michaels.
Open: Daily; summer 9–6, spring/fall 9–5, winter 9–4.
Admission: Adults $10, seniors $9, children 6–17 $5.

The world's largest fleet of indigenous Bay workboats tells the story of the watermen's history—and indeed of the Chesapeake Bay itself. Among the 85 vessels here are the *Rosie Parks*, a famous skipjack; the *Edna E. Lockwood*, the last log-hull bugeye still plying the Bay; and the *Old Point*, a crab dredger from Virginia. The 18-acre complex on the shores of Navy Point comprises 23 buildings, nine devoted to exhibits on the Bay's geological, social, economic, and maritime history, from the age of sail and steamboats to the advent of gas and diesel engines. The screw-pile Hooper Strait Lighthouse moved here in 1966. Inside, the lighthouse keeper's late 19th-century life is re-created, and everyone stops for the prime view of the Miles River. Also displayed are the massive punt guns once used by the market gunners, as well as a huge collection of the decoys used by waterfowl hunters. Kids love clambering through the interactive skipjack in the "Oystering on the Chesapeake" exhibit, and in warm weather there's a waterman's work-life exhibit, concerts at the Tolchester Beach Bandstand, and many boat-related festivals (see "Seasonal Events & Festivals"). Also, the gift shop offers a range of nautical items as well as maritime and Chesapeake books. Maritime scholars may be interested in the museum's library, devoted to maritime

Capt. Mark Adams of the Chesapeake Bay Maritime Museum demonstrates the use of oyster tongs. Photo courtesy of the Chesapeake Bay Maritime Museum

and Chesapeake writings and history. New to the museum in 2005 is "At Play on the Bay," an exhibit devoted to the Bay's recreational pursuits. The vehicle entrance incorporates another Bay artifact: the Knapp's Narrows drawbridge, which served as the gateway to Tilghman Island for 64 years, until 1998. The bridge was moved to St. Michaels and positioned partially open so that motorists could see the same view that boaters saw during the bridge's many years of service.

Nightlife

Kent Narrows, where Kent Island and the Eastern Shore mainland meet in Queen Annes County, has spawned its own dock bar night scene, particularly on summer nights when the boating set ties up here. **Red Eye's Dock Bar** (410-827-3937; Mears Point Marina) brings in rock bands and DJs and generally rocks the Narrows on the weekends (and on some weeknights) during the busy season. Bikini contests when it's warm; 18 televisions showing NASCAR and NFL when it's not.

In **St. Michaels**, locals go to **Carpenter Street Saloon**, aka "C Street" (410-745-5111; 113-115 S. Talbot St.), for conviviality, free popcorn, karaoke on Tues., and entertainment on weekends. It's also a good spot for pub fare during the day.

In **Easton**, the **Washington Street Pub** (410-822-9011; 20 N. Washington St.) can get pretty packed, especially Thurs. through Sat. nights. **Time Out Tap and Grill** (410-820-0433; 219 Marlboro Rd.) gives Talbot Countians billiard tables, DJs on Thurs. nights, and sports on TV. The town also finds itself with a pocket-size bistro named for its owners' Great Dane, **Chez Lafitte Café and Cabaret** (410-770-8868; 13 S. Washington St.). In addition to its Gallic-inspired menu served Thurs. through Sun., piano nights keep Sat. evenings hopping.

Oxford offers a few good spots to stop and have a drink. **Latitude 38** (410-226-5303; 26342 Oxford Rd.) is out on the road and also is a good place for dinner. **Schooner's Landing** (410-226-0160; 314 Tilghman St.; closed Tues.) on Town Creek has a deck bar in-season, a restaurant, and a lounge.

The Rhythm Doctors perform at the Tolchester Bandstand on Big Band Night at the Chesapeake Bay Maritime Museum. Photo courtesy of the Chesapeake Bay Maritime Museum

Performing Arts

CENTREVILLE
QUEEN ANNE'S COUNTY ARTS COUNCIL
410-758-2520.
www.arts4u.info.
206 S. Commerce St., Centreville, MD 21617.
Season: Year-round.

The Arts Council sponsors a variety of regional events at various locations, including summer Thurs. night "Concerts in the Park" featuring top-grade regional talent. Also, classes and events such as the annual five-county poetry contest, as well as "Members Best" exhibitions displayed throughout Centreville.

EASTON
AVALON THEATRE
410-822-0345; box office, 410-822-7299.
www.avalontheatre.com.
40 E. Dover St.

Season: Year-round.
Tickets: Prices vary.

This beautifully restored and renovated 1920s Art Deco theater is a showplace for all of the performing arts in the area, and a well-used community gem. The calendar is packed with classic film screenings, children's theater, poetry gatherings, performances by the Mid-Atlantic Symphony Orchestra, and shows by musicians ranging from Leon Redbone and Leon Russell to Keb Mo and Iris Dement. Jazz (including Maryland's notable Ethel Ennis), classical, Celtic, and folk heroes can be seen here as well. The alternative Cricket Theatre (Beth Henley, Sam Shepard pieces) performs here, as does the Easton Chamber Orchestra. All of the seats in this intimate theater are good, but come early to enjoy the architecture or to capture a prime spot in front of the stage.

Ethel Ennis performs at the Avalon Theatre in Easton. Bill Thompson

EASTERN SHORE CHAMBER MUSIC FESTIVAL

410-819-0380.
www.musicontheshore.org.
Season: Two consecutive weekends in mid-June.
Tickets: Prices vary, depending on venue and program.

Since 1986, J. Lawrie Bloom, a clarinetist with the Chicago Symphony Orchestra, has brought in a host of top young names on the international concert circuit for two weekends of performances on the Shore. Marcy Rosen, cellist with New York's Mendelssohn String Quartet, serves as artistic director alongside Bloom. The talent roster is always impressive, and performances are held throughout the Mid-Shore region. Typical venues include the Avalon Theatre, a private estate, Emmanuel Church in Chestertown, and the Aspen Institute in Wye Mills.

MID-ATLANTIC SYMPHONY ORCHESTRA

1-888-846-8600.
www.midatlanticsymphony.org.
P.O. Box 3687, Ocean City, MD 21843.

Despite its Ocean City mailing address (a function of history more than current events), the Mid-Atlantic Symphony stays well focused on the Mid-Shore region. Its 40- to 45-member company draws from professional musicians hailing from Philadelphia to Washington, D.C. Four concert weekends per season—held at venues from Chestertown to the Mid-Shore area—include open rehearsals on Thurs. evenings at Easton's Avalon Theatre.

OXFORD
TRED AVON PLAYERS
410-226-0061.
www.tredavonplayers.org.
Tickets: Check website; includes dinner theater option.

This established community theater stages musicals, contemporary comedies, and classical dramas featuring thespians from around Talbot County. It's worthwhile to book a ticket if you're going to be in town. Performances are held at the **Oxford Community Center** (410-226-5904; 200 Oxford Rd.), which also hosts a winter chamber concert and occasional visiting concerts.

Seasonal Events and Festivals

EASTON
During the second weekend in Nov., Easton undergoes an amazing transformation—and what small town wouldn't if 18,000 visitors showed up? The internationally known, three-day **Waterfowl Festival** features more than 450 of the world's finest decoy carvers and wildlife painters. Since its founding in 1971, the Waterfowl Festival has raised millions of dollars for conservation organizations devoted to preserving waterfowl. Exhibits spread across town, showcasing decoy art, paintings, sculpture, retriever demonstrations, the Federal Duck Stamp exhibit, fly-fishing demonstrations, master classes with artists, a sporting clay tournament, and, always a hit, the World Championship Goose-Calling Contest. A fleet of shuttle buses provides free transportation from the parking areas to the exhibit locations. Admission: $12 per day; $24 for a multiday pass. Handicapped access. Contact: 410-822-4567; www.waterfowlfestival.org; 40 Harrison St., Easton, MD 21601.

ST. MICHAELS
The Chesapeake Bay Maritime Museum (410 745 2916, www.cbmm. org; Mill St., Navy Point, St. Michaels, MD 21663) keeps festivals front and center year-round, with a host of opportunities to partake in the Bay's food and folklore. Among them: The **Antique & Classic Boat Festival** in mid-June, which features more than 100 classic boats and auto-mobiles. Crab lovers should catch **Crab Days** on the first weekend in Aug., and **Oyster Fest** comes on the first weekend in Nov. All are free with museum admission. Check the muse-um's website for other festivals and events.

TILGHMAN ISLAND
The annual **Tilghman Island Day** celebration combines demonstrations of the waterman's way of life with a heaping helping of what that way of life yields: seafood. Crab and oyster aficionados come from afar on the third Sat. in Oct. Boat maneuvering and oyster tonging are shown off in folk-life demonstrations and high-spirited contests, and skipjack rides are offered. The celebration benefits the Tilghman Volunteer Fire Company (410-886-2101). Contact the Talbot Chamber of Commerce (410-822-4653; P.O. Box 1366, Easton, MD 21601).

Walking Tours
Dockside Express (888-312-7847; www.cruisinthebay.com; P.O. Box 122, Tilghman, MD 21671) A costumed tour guide takes visitors through St. Michaels and perhaps other towns,

answering questions such as "Who's buried next to his mule at Mulberry Point?" Call for schedules and costs.

St. Michaels Walking Tour (410-745-9561) Pick up a walking tour brochure at the visitor's center in the middle of town and consider a walking tour with the St. Mary's Square Museum, a tiny 1865 dwelling moved to its current spot in the center of town in 1964. The museum is only open May through Oct., 10–4 Sat., 12–3 Sun., or by appointment.

Recreation

Flat roads for cycling, gentle tributaries for paddling, open water for sailing, and a long, well-respected outdoorsman tradition. Get outside; you'll have fun here.

Bicycling

Low-lying coastal plains meet rolling farmlands along the Bay and its tributaries, where wide shoulders stretch alongside many main roads. Favorite rides include the 31-mile Easton-to-St. Michaels trip, the 10-mile Easton-to-Oxford run, and the 25-mile round-trip from St. Michaels to Tilghman. Many cyclists make a point of riding the Oxford–Bellevue Ferry, which costs $2.50 one-way and $4 round-trip for cyclists. A free map of routes, developed by the Oxford Mews Emporium, can be had by calling 410-820-8222. Also, a description of a 35.4-mile loop from Easton to Oxford, across the ferry to St. Michaels, is available at www.eastonmd.org/ebmasite/biking.htm.

Bike Rentals

Town Dock Rentals (410-745-2400; www.stmichaelsmarina.com; St. Michaels Marina, 305 Mulberry St., St. Michaels) Bikes rented for an hour, two hours, four hours, or all day. Prices start at $4 per hour, and the hourly rate goes down the longer you ride.

Local Cycling Shops

Easton Cycle & Sport (410-822-7433; 723 Goldsborough St., Easton) Can refer cyclists to rental outfits and advise on routes. Full service.

Wheel Doctor (410-745-6676; 1013 S. Talbot St., St. Michaels) Shop owner Jude McGloin can recommend routes. He suggests cyclists use the Talbot County Chamber of Commerce map, which he distributes.

Bird-Watching

Some of the best birding in the Mid-Shore area, with its limited public water access, is from a boat. Ospreys, bald eagles, herons blue or green, and migratory birds passing through are often spotted. The area's not far from Blackwater National Wildlife Refuge in Dorchester County on the Lower Eastern Shore and Sandy Point State Park along the Bay Bridge in Annapolis, both favored birding spots.

Boating

Charters, Rentals, and Tours

All Aboard Charters (410-745-6022; www.tilghmanislandfishing.com; MD 33, Knapp's Narrows Marina, Tilghman; mailing address: P.O. Box 154, McDaniel, MD 21647) Charter the 46-foot Bay workboat *Nancy Ellen* for fishing trips (specializing in light tackle) or nature tours.

C&C Charters (410-827-7888 or 1-800-733-SAIL; www.cccharters.com; 506 Kent Narrows Way N., Grasonville, MD 21638) Bareboat or captained charters; choice of 15 to 20 sailboats and powerboats ranging in size from 30 to 60 feet. One of the area's better-known companies.

Schnaitman's Boat Rentals (410-827-7663; 12518 Wye Landing Ln., Wye Mills, MD 21679) Crabbers gather at this venerable Wye River spot, where rowboats convertible to motor via a small engine go out on one of the Bay's best crabbing rivers. In all, about forty 16-foot, flat-bottom rowboats are available; you can row out or bring your own small motor (up to 25 hp). Also, six motorboats with 6 hp outboards. Crabbing supplies like dip nets are for sale or rent; chicken necks, a favorite crabbing bait, are also for sale. Fishing, too. Mid-May through Oct.

Tilghman Island Marina (410-886-2500; www.tilghmanmarina.com; 6140 Mariner's Court, Tilghman, MD 21671) Rentals of every kind: kayaks, small craft, canoes, Wave Runners, small sailboats, and even pretty good-size center console boats for fishing. Bikes, too. Inquire about rates.

Tred Avon Yacht Sales and Charters (410-226-5000; 102 S. Morris St., Oxford, MD 21654) Captained or bareboat, sail or power, 30- to 42-foot boats. Captains may be available for half- or full-day sails; bareboat charters are likely to have a two-day minimum.

Cruises and Excursion Boats
Chesapeake Lights (410-886-2215 or 1-800-690-5080; www.chesapeakelights.com; P.O. Box 248, Tilghman Island Rd., Tilghman, MD 21671) Check out the Bay's lighthouses—many not easily seen from land—aboard the former U.S. Navy special operations vessel

Boats fill St. Michaels Harbor. Photo courtesy of the Inn at Perry Cabin

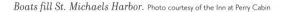

M/V Sharps Island. Four tours lasting from all day (10 lights) to two hours (two lights at sunset with champagne) are available and priced accordingly. Departs from Bay Hundred Restaurant at Knapp's Narrows.

Dockside Express (1-888-312-7847; www.cruisinthebay.com; 21604 Chicken Point Rd., P.O. Box 122, Tilghman, MD 21671) Narrated tours aboard the *Express Royale* include ecology tours and history tours. Sails from Knapp's Narrows. Call for reservations, hours, fees.

HM Krenz (410-745-6080; www.oystercatcher.com) The 1955 skipjack, one of the last built, sails on two-hour tours from St. Michaels. Check the website or call for information.

Lady Patty (410-886-2215 or 1-800-690-5080; www.sailladypatty.com; P.O. Box 248, Tilghman Island, MD 21671) Bay-built in Solomons by M. M. Davis & Sons shipbuilders in 1935, the restored 45-foot *Lady Patty* takes visitors out daily. Champagne sunset sails, $40 per person; day sails, $30 ($20 for kids under 12). Charters of varying lengths available.

Lucky Dog Catamaran Co. (410-745-6203; www.luckydogcatco.com; 307 E. Chew Ave., St. Michaels, MD 21663) Sail aboard the high-speed catamaran *Sirius* on a two-hour cruise up the Miles River. Up to four trips a day, Apr. through Oct. Call or check website for times. Carries up to 22 passengers; $30 per person. Docks at St. Michaels Marina on Mulberry St.

Capt. Wade Murphy aboard the Rebecca T. Ruark, *the oldest skipjack on the Bay.*

Patriot Cruises Inc. (410-745-3100; www.patriotcruises.com; P.O. Box 1206, St. Michaels, MD 21663) Perennially popular cruise of the Miles River with narration on local history. The 170-capacity *Patriot* departs at 11, 12:30, 2:30, and 4 daily, Apr. through Oct., from a dock off Mill St. near the Chesapeake Bay Maritime Museum. During the peak summer tourist months, prepare to wait in line. Adults $10, children under 12 $4.50. Special lunch cruises and evening charters also available.

Rebecca T. Ruark (Capt. Wade H. Murphy Jr., 410-886-2176 or 410-829-3976; www.skipjack.org; 21308 Phillips Rd., Tilghman, MD 21617) The oldest, prettiest, and fastest skipjack in the Bay's dwindling oyster fleet, captained by a man who has shown a talent for harvesting oysters and talking about the trade with visitors. Kids enjoy this two-hour tour. $30 per person, children under 12 are half price. Longer cruises can be arranged. *Rebecca*, built in 1886, is a National Historic Landmark.

Selina II (410-726-9400; www.sailselina .com) This pretty 42-foot catboat belonged to the captain's grandfather starting in 1926, and then to her parents, and now it's hers. She brought *Selina* to St. Michaels from her longtime home on Long Island, and now you can go out from St. Michaels four times daily from May through Oct. Call for prices; six-passenger limit.

Marinas

On Kent Island, the **Bay Bridge Marina** (410-643-3162; www.baybridgemarina.com; Stevensville) is located hard alongside the bridge and can't be missed. There, you'll find a restaurant, bathhouse, laundry, and fuel and a small airport adjacent. Over at Kent Narrows, **Mears Point Marina Kent Narrows** (410-827-8888; www.mearspoint.com) is centrally located, with several restaurants within walking distance and an impressive 600 slips. Many powerboats live here, where the Chester flows into Eastern Bay. On Marshy Creek in Grasonville is **Lippincott Marine** (410-827-9300), with 200 slips.

Across the Bay at St. Michaels, check the **St. Michaels Marina** (410-745-2400 or 1-800-678-8980), which has transient slips on the Miles River and bike rentals. Also nearby is the **St. Michaels Harbour Inn Marina & Spa** (410-745-9001; www.harbourinn.com; 101 N. Harbor Rd.), with Miles River slips for transients, water taxi, pump-out station, showers, laundry, morning coffee and newspapers, and bike, kayak, and canoe rentals.

In Crockett's Cove off the Tred Avon River in Oxford, the Hinkley Co. has taken over the old **Crockett Brothers Boatyard** (410-226-5113), well located in the center of town with a pool, pump-out station, and laundry. The **Oxford Boatyard** (410-226-5101) on the Tred Avon is open year-round with 76 slips and a pump-out station. Or check out **Town Creek Marina** (410-226-5747).

At Knapp's Narrows along Tilghman Island, the **Knapp's Narrows Marina and Guest Quarters** (410-886-2720; www.knappsnarrowsmarina.com) offers a swimming pool, laundry, showers, restaurants, and a 20-room motel. The deep-water harbor can accommodate boats drawing 6 1/2 feet or so. Also consider the Tilghman Island Marina (410-886-2500) along the Narrows.

Canoeing and Kayaking

The **Choptank River**, the largest of the Eastern Shore's 20 or so rivers, is fed by **King's Creek**. Put in at Kingston Landing, accessible via MD 328 and Kingston Landing Road. The meandering creek runs past the Nature Conservancy's **Choptank Wetlands Preserve** and pristine marshes. South of this area, **Tuckahoe Creek**, which runs through **Tuckahoe State Park** in **Caroline County** before reaching the Choptank, is a popular Shore paddling spot. At the park, Tuckahoe Creek runs into **Crouse Mill Lake**, which has a dam at its lower end, after which the Tuckahoe continues its journey to the Choptank. The lake and the section of the creek north of it are freshwater; it's a good area for less-experienced canoeists. Below the dam, the Tuckahoe is tidal. From the dam to the landing in Hillsboro you'll find 5.2 miles of pleasurable canoeing, with great fishing for bass, pickerel, and bluegill. (Warning: Do not run the dam!) **Watts Creek**, entering the Choptank at **Martinak State Park** near **Denton**, makes for a pleasant two-hour paddle up and back. Go at high tide.

In Talbot County, put in at the public landing in **Whitman**. Stay on the peninsula side, running alongside MD 33, to enjoy beautiful farmland habitat, especially in the fall. From **Cummings Creek** into **Harris Creek**, there are some nice beaches along the way, and you'll pass through **Sherwood**, a neat little town. Follow the shoreline.

Enjoy **Marshyhope Creek**, a Nanticoke River tributary, or put in at **Federalsburg** (two boat ramps). Canoe downstream for some sunny open tripping or head upstream, ducking the brush on your way toward **Idylwild Wildlife Management Area**.

A water trail guide to **Tilghman Island** is available; check with Talbot County's tourism office (410-770-8000; www.tourtalbot.org) to obtain a copy.

Outfitters and Rentals
Chesapeake Outdoor Adventures (410-886-2083; www.chesapeakeoutdooradventures
.com; 7857 Tilghman Island Rd./P.O. Box 41, Sherwood, MD 21665) Formerly known as
Harris Creek Kayaks, this outfitter operates guided tours (including custom moonlight
tours) and rents canoes, Hobie Cats, sunfish, and kayaks. You can even arrange for kayak
fly-fishing instruction. Can also be found at the Hyatt in Cambridge and at the Old Harford
Maritime Center in West Denton near the Delaware border. Rentals available by the hour
or by the week. Call for details.

Fishing
Boat Ramps & Fishing Piers
To obtain a free map of Bay access points, check "Landings & Boat Ramps" in chapter 9,
"Information."

Kent Island's Matapeake Pier is located on MD 8 S. Take a right on MD 8 soon after
crossing the eastbound span of the Bay Bridge. Small park, boat ramp.

The bridge that once spanned the **Choptank River** now serves as fishing piers from
either side of the river, the dividing line between the Middle and Lower Eastern Shore.
Try crabbing or fishing, or enjoy the 25-acre park with waterside walking path on
the Talbot County side. Located alongside US 50 at the Frederick C. Malkus Bridge.
Contact: Choptank River Fishing Pier, 410-820-1668; 29761 Bolinbroke Point Dr.,
Trappe, MD 21673.

Charter Boats and Head Boats
Harrison's Sport Fishing Center (410-886-2121; www.chesapeakehouse.com; 21551
Chesapeake House Dr., Tilghman Island, MD 21671) This is sportfishing central amid a
complex that started with an inn opened here in 1898. Sportfishers have been coming here
since the late 1930s, and the Harrisons are well-known in the region. There's a 28-boat
fleet, plus a phalanx of on-call captains. $100 per fisherman. Various packages are avail-
able, plus small boat rentals. There's also a marina, lodging, and a restaurant/crab deck
(see "Restaurants" and "Lodging").

Pintail Point (410-827-7029; www.pintailpoint.com; 511 Pintail Point Farm Ln.,
Queenstown, MD 21658) Guided charters include cruises on the Chesapeake aboard two
fishing boats berthed by the Bay Bridge on Kent Island. Or see about having an Orvis guide
take you fly-fishing.

Fitness Facilities
Cross Court Athletic Club (410-822-1515; 1180 S. Washington St., Easton) Four indoor
and three outdoor tennis courts, exercise classes and equipment, child care, and more.
Guest fee for tennis is $5 plus court time; guest fee for health club is $10.

YMCA (410-822-0566; 202 Peach Blossom Rd., Easton) Two indoor swimming pools, 12
outdoor tennis courts, exercise and weight-training equipment. Nonmembers $10.

Golf
Although it's officially located on the Lower Eastern Shore, the Hyatt River Marsh Golf
Course is close enough that it should be on the radar screen of Mid-Shore duffers.
See the "Recreation" section of chapter 6, "Lower Eastern Shore," for information.
Otherwise consider:

The Easton Club (410-820-9800 or 1-800-277-9800; 28449 Clubhouse Dr., Easton) Championship 18-hole golf course in a waterfront community. Restaurant, too.

Harbourtown Golf Resort (1-800-446-9066; 9784 Martingham Dr., St. Michaels) Pete Dye–designed 18-hole course.

Hog Neck Golf Course (410-822-6079 or 1-800-280-1790; www.hogneck.com; 10142 Old Cordova Rd., Easton) Owned by Talbot County; 27 holes with an 18-hole championship course and a 9-hole executive course. Daily fee. Golf pros, pro shop, café. Four stars from *Golf Digest*'s "Places to Play."

Queenstown Harbor Golf Links (410-827-6611 or 1-800-827-5257; www.mdgolf.com; 310 Links Lane, Queenstown) Two 18-hole courses called Queenstown River and Queenstown Lakes. Very busy. A beautiful setting on the Chester River.

Natural Areas: State, Federal, and Private Parks/Lands

Visitors trying to contact park management should be aware that some state parks are satellite operations, managed from another park. For camping and picnic shelter reservations, call 1-888-432-CAMP or visit www.dnr.state.md.us.

Adkins Arboretum (410-634-2847; www.adkinsarboretum.org; 12610 Eveland Rd./P.O. Box 100, Ridgely, MD 21660) Those interested in native plants will want to consider a stop at this 400-acre native garden and preserve. Walk more than 4 miles of trails offering over 600 species, or peek at native plants under cultivation. Check the arboretum's website for programs that range from guided walks to rotating art shows to spring and fall plant sales.

Chesapeake Bay Environmental Center (410-827-6694; www.cbec-wtna.org; 600 Discovery Ln., Grasonville, MD 21638) Rehabilitating birds such as owls, hawks, and bald eagles live in large cages, providing a great up-close look at these marvelous creatures. Trails wind through a portion of the 610-acre center, operated by the Wildfowl Trust of North America. Canoe put-in, public programs; check website for events. Closes promptly at 5 PM. Formerly known as Horsehead Wetlands Center.

Idylwild Wildlife Management Area (410-376-3236 or 410-820-7098; Houston Branch Rd., Federalsburg, MD 21632) Freshwater marsh and forest mean pileated woodpeckers, owls, and scarlet tanagers. Beavers in Marshyhope Creek. In all, 3,300 acres for hunting and hiking. Canoe access.

Jean Ellen duPont Shehan Audubon Sanctuary (410-745-9283; www.audubonmddc.org; 23000 Wells Point Rd., Bozman, MD 21612) Located between St. Michaels and Tilghman, this sanctuary is open to the public Mon. 9–4 and the last Sun. of each month 12–4. It features a variety of programs such as canoeing and birding at other times. Check local newspapers or the website for the latest programs at this 950-acre sanctuary on a peninsula bounded by the Broad, Ball, and Leadenham creeks.

Martinak State Park (410-820-1668; 137 Deep Shore Rd., Denton, MD 21629) A family-oriented, 107-acre area along Watts Creek and the Choptank River featuring fishing and playgrounds. Four camper cabins; one full-service cabin. Picnic pavilions.

Pickering Creek Audubon Center (410-822-4903; www.pickeringcreek.org; 11450 Audubon Ln., Easton, MD 21601) Forest, fresh and brackish marshes, about a mile of shoreline along Pickering Creek. 400 acres. Canoe launch (canoes available to members), walkable nature trails. Grounds open dawn to dusk daily; office Mon. through Fri. 9–5, Sat. 10–4.

Tuckahoe State Park (410-820-1668; 13070 Crouse Mill Rd., Queen Anne, MD 21657) A pretty 60-acre lake for fishing and boating, and lots of woods, including a marked fitness trail with exercises at each station. In all, almost 20 miles of trails for hiking or biking, including 3 miles of surfaced trails. Canoe, kayak, paddleboat, mountain bike rentals Apr. through Oct. Reasonable fees. Camping includes 33 electric sites, 18 nonelectric, four camper cabins. Picnic pavilions.

Wye Island Natural Resources Management Area (410-827-7577; 632 Wye Island Rd., Queenstown, MD 21658) This is 2,450 acres on a historic island paddlers like to circle. Also, there are 12 miles of trails open sunrise to sunset daily. Information on nearby launch sites and permit fees is available from the Queen Annes County Department of Parks and Recreation (410-758-0835; www.qac.org) or the Talbot County Parks and Recreation Department (410-770-8050; www.talbgov.org).

Sporting Clays
Pintail Point (410-827-7029; www.pintailpoint.com; 511 Pintail Point Farm Ln., Queenstown, MD 21658) Sporting clays open daily 9–5 for members and nonmembers. Automatic machines stored in little Victorian dollhouses at 20 stations. Shooting lessons for all levels.

Sporting Goods and Camping Supply Stores
Albright's Gun Shop (410-820-8811; 36 E. Dover St., Easton) Fishing and hunting gear, gunsmithing on premises. Orvis dealer. You can also book a hunting guide (ducks and geese).

Chesapeake Outdoors (410-604-0446; 1707 Main St., Chester) Hunting, fishing supplies, archery pro shop.

Island Fishing and Hunting (410-643-4224; exit 40A off US 50 E., Kent Island) Bait, commercial and recreational crabbing supplies, tackle, hunting supplies, local sporting information. Open daily.

Shore Sportsman (410-820-5599 or 1-800-263-2027; 8232 Ocean Gateway, Easton) Hunting, fishing, bait and tackle.

Swimming
George W. Murphy Pool (410-820-7306; 501 Port St., off the Easton Bypass, Easton) Nominal daily admission charge for 25-meter pool and smaller "zero-entry" pool for kids. Open Memorial Day through Labor Day.

Shopping

Antiques
Americana Antiques (410-226-5677; 111 S. Morris St., Oxford) A town fixture for 30 years, offering 17th-, 18th-, and early 19th-century American art and artifacts. Also specializes in carousel art.

Camelot Antiques Ltd. (410-820-4396; 7871 Ocean Gateway, Easton) This multidealer emporium offers three floors of antiques, including 18th- and 19th-century furniture, waterfowl decoys, oyster plates, and Quimper. Located on US 50. Open daily 9–5.

Canton Row (410-745-2440; 216 Talbot St., St. Michaels) Prints, porcelain, fishing gear; a broad range of items from multiple dealers.

Chesapeake Antique Center (410-827-6640; MD 18 and US 50, Queenstown) More than 70 dealers who almost entirely adhere to the 100-year rule are located in this vast exhibit space just east of Kent Island, behind Prime Outlets. Exceptions are made for any distinctly period, 20th-century piece, such as Art Deco.

Easton Maritime Antiques (410-763-8853; 27 S. Harrison St., Easton) Specializes in fine nautical antiques, including weather instruments, scrimshaw, and ship models. Open Thurs. through Sat. 10–5:30 or by appointment.

Flo Mir (410-822-2857; 23 E. Dover St., Easton) Popular local antiques shop; especially strong on china. Open Mon. through Sat. 10–5; Sun. in-season only 11–3.

Foxwell's Antiques & Collectibles (410-820-9705; 7793 Ocean Gateway, Easton) With 70 dealers in one location, antiquers find a variety of items from glassware to china to antique advertising in this eminently browsable shop on US 50. Open daily 10–6.

Janet K. Fanto Antiques and Rare Books (410-763-9030; 13 N. Harrison St., Easton) Early American silver, rare books, fine art. Mon., Tues., and Thurs. through Sat. 10–5, Sun. 12–3.

Lanham-Merida Antiques and Interiors (410-763-8500; Talbottown Shopping Center, 218 N. Washington St., Easton) High-quality English, Continental, and American furniture, as well as fine wallpapers and fabrics.

Lesnoff Antiques (410-822-2334; 7 N. Harrison St., Easton) French antiques and collectibles; lots of furniture. Mon. through Sat. 10–5; occasionally Sun. 11–2.

Nancy's Nostalgia (410-745-9771; 408 S. Talbot St., St. Michaels) Full line of antiques.

Oak Creek Sales (410-745-3193; 25939 Royal Oak Rd., Royal Oak, off the road between St. Michaels and Easton) Eclectic selection of antiques and collectibles—the figurine salt-shaker sitting next to the Depression glass. Across the street, an entire barn is devoted to antique and used furniture.

Books
Book Bank: Crawford's Nautical Books (410-886-2230; 5782 Tilghman Island Rd., Tilghman Island) Thousands of fiction and nonfiction titles on all things nautical, from sailing to shipbuilding to seafaring. The store also buys used books.

Book Celler (410-827-8474; 431 Outlet Center Dr., Queenstown) Hardcovers and paperbacks below retail, including discounted best sellers. Located at Prime Outlets.

The News Center (410-822-7212; Talbottown Shopping Center, 218 N. Washington St., Easton) Large paperback selection and fine section of regional writings. Also stocks the Shore's largest periodicals selection, with more than 1,000 titles.

Unicorn Book Shop (410-476-3838; 3935 Ocean Gateway/US 50, Trappe) Excellent rare and secondhand bookshop; bibliophiles will love this place. Antique map reproductions.

Clothing

Anastasia Ltd. (410-822-4814; 11 N. Harrison St., Easton) Contemporary women's clothing including Geiger of Austria.

Bleachers (410-745-5676; 107 S. Talbot St., St. Michaels) Beachy boutique offers colorful, fun clothes for adults.

Chesapeake Bay Outfitters (410-745-3107; Talbot St. and Railroad Ave., St. Michaels) Nice sportswear, nautical apparel, Bay-oriented T's and sweatshirts, and boating and casual footwear for men and women.

M. Randall and Co. (410-820-4077; 17 N. Harrison St., Easton) If we lived in Easton, we'd shop for our clothes here. Nice women's apparel.

Sailor of St. Michaels (410-745-2580; 214 Talbot St., St. Michaels) Souvenir shirts and sweatshirts from the Shore, women's and men's sportswear, gifts.

Fine Crafts, Gifts, and Galleries

American Pennyroyal (410-822-5030; 5 N. Harrison St., Easton) A favorite among lovers of American folk art. Everything from baskets to pottery to rugs, quilts, and jewelry.

Artiste Locale (410-745-6580; 112 N. Talbot St., St. Michaels) Showcase for artisans from throughout the region.

Coco & Company (410-745-3400; 209 S. Talbot St., St. Michaels) Furniture, candles, and garden items are among the many goodies in this large design and gift shop.

Contemporary Tapestry Weaving Studio and Gallery (410-745-4303; www.ctw-tapestry.com; 5592 Poplar Lane, Royal Oak, near the Oxford–Bellevue Ferry) Swedish weaver Ulrika Leander's gallery brings expansive, brightly colored tapestry art to the town's old post office. Urbane and contemporary. Open by appointment, or check the website under "shows and events."

Creatrics (410-822-7924; 13 Goldsborough St., Easton) Contemporary paintings and crafts such as glass. Open Fri. and Sat. 10–8, Sun. 11–3, Mon. through Thurs. 10–7.

Gourmet Gallery (410-763-7077; 21A N. Harrison St., Easton) A clever combination: art for your palate and your soul.

The South Street Art Gallery in Easton is housed in an 1854 building.

Mind's Eye Gift Gallery (410-745-2023; 201 S. Talbot St., St. Michaels) Contemporary craftworks include glass, chimes, and much more. Fun to shop.

Simpatico (410-745-0345; 104 Railroad Ave., St. Michaels) Italian dinnerwear, linens, and other luxurious goodies from a favorite country. Open daily.

South Street Art Gallery (410-770-8350; 5 South St., Easton) Cool artist-owned gallery of regional and national artists housed in 1854 building. Very nice selection of plein air paintings, among others.

Troika Gallery (410-770-9190; 9 S. Harrison St., Easton) Operated by three local artists, this is a sizable fine arts gallery showcasing regional, national, and international artists. Open Mon. through Sat. 10–5:30, Sun. by appointment.

Jewelry
DBS Jewelers (410-745-2626; 111 S. Talbot St., St. Michaels) Resident goldsmith on-site for repairs and custom creations, or select from the updated or classic designs on display. Nice selection of gold Bay-inspired pieces, too.

Shearer the Jeweler (410-822-2279; 22 N. Washington St., Easton) Family owned for three generations, featuring diamonds, colored gems, watches, and original designs.

Westphal Jewelers (410-822-7774; 19 N. Harrison St., Easton) Diamonds, gemstones, watches, and custom designs.

Marine Supply
L&B Marine Supply (410-643-3600; 124 Kent Landing, Stevensville) Discount marine supply.

Outlets
Prime Outlets Queenstown (410-827-8699; 441 Outlet Center Dr., Queenstown) Notable destination among outlet shoppers, with more than 50 stores such as Nine West and Geoffrey Beene. The location, just over the Bay Bridge on the Eastern Shore, makes for a good stop. If you're hungry, the Chesapeake Gourmet there has good sandwiches and takeout.

Specialty Shops and General Store
The Christmas Goose (410-827-5252; US 50, Queenstown) Handcrafted Christmas items like nutcrackers, ornaments, and more. Located across from Prime Outlets.

Crackerjacks (410-822-7716; 7 S. Washington St., Easton) Cool toy store in Easton's Historic District selling quality games, dolls, children's books, and stuffed animals. Many imported items.

Keepers (410-745-6388; 300 S. Talbot St., St. Michaels) A full-line Orvis dealer with outdoor gear and clothing, plus antique and contemporary decoys.

Oxford Mews Emporium (410-820-8222; 105 S. Morris St., Oxford) Like an old-fashioned general store where you can buy anything. A good selection of Bay books and gifts, specialty food products, and biking and camping gear.

The Wintergarden is an indoor-outdoor pool at the Hyatt in Cambridge.

6

LOWER EASTERN SHORE: MARYLAND & VIRGINIA

Water, Water Everywhere

The longest of the Eastern Shore's tributaries, the Choptank River broadens as it reaches the Bay and marks the start of the Lower Eastern Shore. Travelers on US 50 cross its on-and-on bridge, formally known as the Frederick C. Malkus Bridge, to reach **Cambridge,** originally settled in 1684. Alongside run remnants of the bridge's Depression-era predecessor, which now serve as fishing piers. Sails, wakes, and the typical lowboard of Chesapeake workboats glint white from below, evidence that this is cruising paradise and prime fishing grounds, with creeks detouring inland.

Upon arrival in Dorchester County, visitors find Cambridge's Historic District behind the highway's commercial appearance, with grand homes lining a brick street. Wind through the old section of town to Great Marsh Park, look out onto the wide-open Choptank, and you'll get a hint of the Lower Eastern Shore's primary draw. Pure and simple, it's nature.

Marshland blurs the distinction between land and sea in many parts of the Lower Eastern Shore, which we define as the 130-mile distance from the Choptank through Maryland into the Eastern Shore of Virginia, ending at Capes Charles and Henry, locus of the Chesapeake Bay Bridge-Tunnel. Watermen and farmers live close to the earth, and visitors are perhaps more likely to encounter a more authentic way of life here than in Bay Country's other regions.

Along US 13 through the southern Delmarva Peninsula, you'll pass quaint towns and the bustling burg of **Salisbury,** but you'll also pass through long stretches of farmland. Antiques shops are scattered along your way, and Eastern Shore seafood doesn't get any better, which means the fried soft-shell crabs on potato bread served here are likely to trump fancier versions in city cafés.

Nature lovers cycle or paddle through the flat "Maryland Everglades," the vast marshland filled with rivers and twisting creeks, called "guts," which run south down the coast from Dorchester County. Loblolly pine, tall green sentinels common to the area, stretch high. The endangered Delmarva fox squirrel lives here, too. Birders find bald eagles along with an abundance of other nesters and avian visitors stopping along the Atlantic flyway. Put in a boat and fish Bay tributaries, or charter a boat into prime Chesapeake fishing grounds in search of rockfish, croaker, flounder, and spot. From a pier, lower a net or string tied around a chicken neck to catch blue crabs.

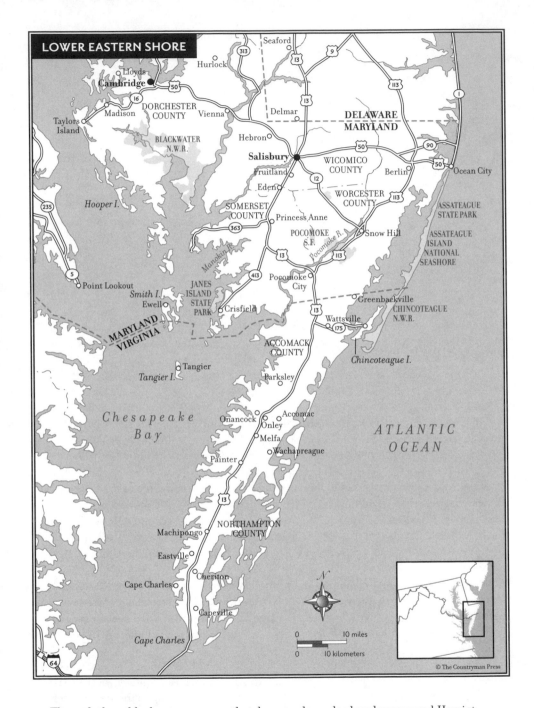

Through these blackwater swamps that draw modern-day kayakers passed Harriet Tubman, the escaped slave who led some 300 slaves to freedom through this land. Born in captivity in Dorchester County, "The Moses of Her People" is the subject of a local tour.

Since the arrival of the Hyatt resort high above the Choptank in Cambridge in the early 2000s, life has been starting to look different in this historic town. Construction is under way and new shops are moving into the old downtown. Overall, the expectation seems to be that Cambridge is ready to boom.

Salisbury, known as "the Crossroads of the Delmarva Peninsula," lies about 30 miles south of Cambridge and is home to Salisbury University, the Ward Brothers Museum—a standard in the world of waterfowl carving—and the Salisbury Zoo. From here, many travelers head due east to the ocean beaches.

To stay on a Bay Country course, stay south. Scattered in Somerset and Worcester Counties are historic towns marching toward the Atlantic Ocean. **Princess Anne**, founded in 1733 and named for King George II's daughter, is the Somerset County seat, its streets lined with Federal and Georgian houses.

Snow Hill, a royal port under England's William and Mary, once saw three-masted schooners and steamboats arrive up the Pocomoke River. Now it's a reclaimed historical town drawing paddlers who stay in its updated Victorian B&Bs before heading out on the eminently enjoyable Pocomoke. **Berlin**, near the Atlantic Ocean, descends from colonial Burley Plantation and is stylishly reclaimed.

Maryland's southernmost town is **Crisfield**, called Somer's Cove until the mid- to late-1800s railroad arrived via the influence of a local lawyer named John Crisfield. The railroad's arrival touched off a true oyster boom, and by the late 1800s the harbor was thick with watermen's vessels and people were getting rich on oysters. Crisfield was a noisy strip of brothels and saloons and street-brawl recklessness. The oyster boom faded long ago, but Crisfield remains an active, working watermen's port that has rebounded to boast of its standing as "Crab Capital of the World." Word has it that oyster shells literally remain a foundation of the town. Today, storefront businesses attend to the working folks, like hardware stores selling commercial crab pots.

Visitors are well advised to check into one of Crisfield's few standard motels or to head out to Janes Island State Park for a cabin—either basic "camper" style (bathhouses nearby in the campground) or full-serve. Crisfield is also the place to take a ferry over to **Smith and Tangier islands,** those final bastions of Bay island waterman life. If you have only a weekend, plan to visit over Labor Day, when the Crisfield Hard Crab Derby or the nearby Deal Island Skipjack Races and Land Festival (highlighted under "Seasonal Events & Festivals") show folks what the waterman's life is all about.

Smith and Tangier both incubate a disappearing way of life, where crabbers and their families live by the crustacean's life cycle. Tangier, in Virginia, tends to have more for visitors than Maryland's Smith, which, with three towns, is larger. Time and tide erode the shores of both. White crab peeler sheds line Tangier's shores, though they're onshore on Smith. If authentic Chesapeake intrigues, don't miss these islands.

Back on the mainland, Virginia beckons south. The old fishing town of **Chincoteague** promises beachside fun alongside oyster and clam beds, as well as the world-famous ponies living wild on nearby Assateague Island, ensured a future by three different parks and refuges. Farther down the highway stands **Onancock**, once the 17th-century port town of Scarburgh, later named after a Native American village whose name means "a foggy place." The fishing town has been reclaimed for boaters and tourists.

US 13 seems endless through here; tiny towns dot the terrain. At the tip of the peninsula, **Cape Charles**, the former railroad and ferry terminus town, is up-and-coming—but hasn't quite arrived. Still, B&B owners say they stay full much of the year with birders, kayakers, and lovers of the small-town atmosphere. Turn-of-the-century houses are being renovated on almost every block, and new "locals" are the town's greatest boosters. Cape Charles's pavilion was the town's musical entertainment center back when people and goods came by train and steamboat to this transportation hub on the Chesapeake, which is sure to rise again.

LODGING

The Lower Eastern Shore offers a wide range of accommodations, from fixed-up farmhouses serving as B&Bs to more elegant, renovated Victorians to rustic cabins with million-dollar water views. Prices can vary widely throughout the week or season; typically costs are highest during high-season weekends, lower during the week, and even lower in the off-season. Two-night minimums may be in effect during high season. Additional discounts may be offered on an inn's website, perhaps in conjunction with other area businesses in a package deal. Additional charges may be made for a third person in a room, and room taxes can add up. Check cancellation policies prior to booking, and assume that inns do not allow smoking.

Lodging rates, based on high-season prices, fall within this scale:

Inexpensive:	Up to $75
Moderate:	$75 to $120
Expensive:	$120 to $175
Very expensive:	$175 and up

Credit card abbreviations are:

AE—American Express
CB—Carte Blanche
DC—Diners Club
D—Discover
MC—MasterCard
V—Visa

CAMBRIDGE, MD.
GLASGOW INN B&B
Owners: Louiselee Roche and Martha Ann Rayne.
410-228-0575.
1500 Hambrooks Blvd., Cambridge, MD 21613.
Price: Moderate to expensive.

Credit Cards: No.
Handicapped Access: No.
Special Features: Children allowed conditionally.

Grand Glasgow Inn was a private home from its construction around 1760 until Louiselee Roche and Martha Ann Rayne opened it up as a B&B during the 1980s. The main house retains its historic integrity, meaning seven large rooms include four with private baths. Third-floor rooms are worth the long walk up the stairs for their cozy window seats, sloping eaves (and floors!), and queen-size beds, though you'll share a bath. An adjacent building holds three more rooms, each with private bath, arranged in colonial fashion around a central fireplace. Careful development of the land in front of the Glasgow Inn as a modern Williamsburg-style subdivision hasn't hurt the view: you can still see the broad Choptank River from the front guest windows. Full country breakfast.

HYATT REGENCY CHESAPEAKE BAY GOLF RESORT, SPA AND MARINA
410-901-1234; reservations 1-800-55-HYATT.
www.chesapeakebay.hyatt.com.
100 Heron Blvd., Cambridge, MD 21613.
Price: Very expensive.
Credit Cards: AE, DC, D, MC, V.
Handicapped Access: Yes.

There seems to be little reason to leave this 342-acre luxury resort along the Choptank River. Guests can find a good time at the 18-hole championship River Marsh Golf Club, in small boats or kayaks rented at the 150-slip River Marsh Marina, or by partaking in a massage at the 18,000-square-foot Stillwater Spa. If it's a cloudy day, perhaps it's time to settle in with a good book in the Michener Library, named for the novelist who wrote his landmark *Chesapeake* in Cambridge. Four pools plus a hot tub bring different personalities to their hydrothera-

The Hyatt resort in Cambridge is filled with interesting spots, including the Michener Library.

peutic functions. There's an infinity-edge pool, the River's Edge Pool with a water-slide and other fun stuff for families, and the impressive Wintergarden, glassed in during the winter but open to flowing river breezes in the summer. The wide Choptank and the bridge spanning its width dominate views throughout this expansive complex, where the decor hits a tasteful and contemporary Chesapeake note. Most of the 400 rooms (that includes 16 suites) have water views, and all have private balconies. Hungry? Six restaurants offer dining options ranging from white tablecloth to the more casual and hip Blue Point Provision Co. Other amenities include tennis, two small beaches (netting protects swimmers from sea nettles), a fitness center, and kids' activities. An adjacent parcel is slated for development as the Residences at River Marsh.

PRINCESS ANNE, MD.
WATERLOO COUNTRY INN
Owners: Theresa and Erwin Kraemer.
410-651-0883.
www.waterloocountryinn.com.
28822 Mt. Vernon Rd., Princess Anne, MD 21853.
Price: Expensive to very expensive.
Credit Cards: AE, D, MC, V.
Handicapped Access: One room.
Special Features: Children welcome; pets OK in one room.

Theresa and Erwin Kraemer traveled from Switzerland a decade ago to visit friends in this tiny Eastern Shore town, saw a "For Sale" sign in front of this stunning 1750 Georgian-style mansion beside a picture-perfect tidal pond, and stayed. You'll be glad they did as soon as you check in. The two suites are luxurious, the four less-ornate rooms, stylish. Outside there's a swimming pool, miles of country roads to cycle, and meandering streams to paddle (bicycles and canoe are complimentary, and the Kraemers supply maps). Packages, including kayak tours, are available. Make arrangements with the Kraemers in advance and they'll be sure to have dinner ready for you, from a gourmet four-course meal to something simpler. The Kraemers may have settled far from their homeland, but they've imported a bit of Continental style into the Somerset County countryside. Full breakfast.

SNOW HILL, MD.
CHANCEFORD HALL
Innkeepers: Randy Ifft and Alice Kesterson.
410-632-2900.
www.chancefordhall.com.
209 W. Federal St., Snow Hill, MD 21863.
Price: Expensive.
Credit Cards: MC, V.
Handicapped Access: No.
Special Features: Children allowed conditionally.

Whitehaven on the Wicomico

The building settled near the Whitehaven Ferry landing has been there since 1810. It passed through the early days of the republic, the Civil War, and the steamship era. First a private home, then converted to a hotel in 1877, its fortunes have paralleled those of this tiny Victorian village along the Wicomico River.

With original land grants dating to the mid-17th century, the area was named Whitehaven in honor of the English birthplace of one of its landowner/developers, Col. George Gale. He went on to become the second husband of George Washington's grandmother, Mildred Warner Washington. A ferry operated here by 1688. After the Civil War came stores, a blacksmith shop, and the trappings of a shipbuilding center that was well under way by the time steamships arrived. Decline began after World War II, when shipbuilding fell off as Salisbury, farther up the Wicomico, rose to prominence and improved roads detracted from water travel.

Now, sleepy Whitehaven is being rediscovered, a picture postcard of an era gone by. Placed on the National Register of Historic Places, the 30 or so houses here have been reclaimed and fixed up. The Whitehaven Ferry still runs every day (see chaper 2, "Transportation," for details), and The Red Roost (410-546-5443; 2760 Clara Rd.), a fabled crab house located in a former chicken house, offers Eastern Shore–style fare—including its well-known, all-you-can-eat specials offering everything from fried chicken, steamed crabs, shrimp, ribs, snow crab, to combos of all of the above. Open seasonally; inexpensive to expensive.

Visitors have two places in the village to stay. The old Whitehaven Hotel by the ferry landing has been fully restored and couldn't be better looking. The inn boasts seven rooms on three floors, including two with porches and views of the river, Art Nouveau touches, and original woodwork throughout. Bikes and kayaks are available for guests. Cost: moderate. For information: 410-873-2000 or 1-877-809-8296; www.whitehavenhotel.com; 2685 Whitehaven Rd., Whitehaven, MD 21856. There's also the Whitehaven Bed and Breakfast, only a few doors down, composed of two 19th-century watermen's houses that have been fully restored with pretty rooms and front porches. Cost: moderate. For information: 410-873-3294 or 1-888-205-5921; www.whitehaven.com; 23844-23848 River St., Whitehaven, MD 21856.

The restored Whitehaven Hotel at the ferry southeast of Salisbury.

Architect Randy Ifft and wife Alice Kesterson left their busy Chicago life to move into this enormous 1759 Greek Revival manor house, where the boxwood-lined walk draws visitors inside. Elaborate crown moldings, mantels, and 12-over-12 windows detail this National Historic Landmark home. Five guest bedrooms offer sophistication, each with a private bath and handmade four-poster queen bed dressed in luxurious linens. Each bedroom is outfitted with a generous stack of good books, mostly fiction, although bird-watchers can refer to Audubon and Sibley. Self-addressed mailers are provided for guests who can't bear to put down their book when they leave. A paved backyard terrace invites visitors to sit and share a glass of wine or afternoon tea in the shade of one of the oldest black walnuts in the state. Full breakfast.

RIVER HOUSE INN

Innkeepers: Larry and Susanne Knudsen.
410-632-2722.
www.riverhouseinn.com.
201 E. Market St., Snow Hill, MD 21863.
Price: Very expensive.
Credit Cards: AE, D, MC, V.
Handicapped Access: Yes, in the River Cottage.
Special Features: Children and pets allowed.

A profusion of flowers and black wrought-iron gingerbread on the wide veranda greet guests entering this longtime B&B settled longside the Pocomoke River. The recently added pool and patio only add to the inn's comfort, with three guest buildings on 2 of shaded lawn providing accommodations. The Ivy Cottage has a full kitchen and luxurious privacy. The charming River Cottage, converted from an 1890 carriage barn, offers a private porch, mini-fridge, microwave, coffee maker, and whirlpool tub. The River Hideaways continue the theme of comfort and amenities and include wide porches with views of the Pocomoke. If you want to get out on the water, the inn operates *The Otter*, a pontoon boat. Open Apr. through Nov.

BERLIN, MD.
THE ATLANTIC HOTEL

Manager: Larry Wilgus.
410-641-0189 or 1-800-814-7672.
www.atlantichotel.com.
2 N. Main St., Berlin, MD 21811.
Price: Moderate to very expensive.
Credit Cards: AE, D, MC, V.
Handicapped Access: Yes.

The renovation of this 1895 hotel launched Berlin's vigorous revival some years ago, as residents gained a new pride in their unique surroundings and undertook the restoration of many buildings. The hotel's 17 rooms include both deluxe rooms and smaller, substantially less expensive standard rooms. Both create a 19th-century feeling with rich color schemes and antique furnishings. All have televisions, though you may find yourself more inclined to browse Berlin's boutiques and antiques stores or to wallow in Ocean City's boardwalk extravaganza, just 7 miles away. Breakfast is served downstairs, home to the Drummer's Café, a popular local meeting place, and the elegant formal dining room that built the Atlantic Hotel's reputation (see "Restaurants" later in this chapter). There's no better place to wind up a busy day than in one of the hotel's front-porch rocking chairs, a cool drink in hand and a view of charming downtown Berlin before you.

MERRY SHERWOOD PLANTATION

Owner: Kirk Burbage.
410-641-2112 or 1-800-660-0358.
www.merrysherwood.com.
8909 Worcester Hwy. (US 113), Berlin, MD 21811.
Price: Expensive.
Credit Cards: MC, V.
Handicapped Access: No.
Special Features: Children OK.

Standing more than 50 feet tall, comprising 27 rooms in more than 8,500 square feet, the Merry Sherwood Plantation house is as impressive today as when it was completed in 1859. A jewel in classic Italianate style, it's set amid 20 acres of gardens featuring roses, topiaries, and perennials. These grounds, designed by *Southern Living* magazine, are almost enough to make you forget the rush of modern life. Inside the three-story house are seven rooms and one suite; two rooms share a bath in order to retain the building's integrity. Rooms are elegant and large, and the antique furnishings (including the Vanderbilts' former carved rosewood furniture) honor the mid-19th-century Philadelphia affluence that created the house. A gourmet breakfast is served under an enormous chandelier. For a well-rounded visit, spend time on the fabulous sun porch perusing the photo album, which reveals the full marvel of the restoration that readied Merry Sherwood for guests in the mid-1990s.

CHINCOTEAGUE, VA.
CHANNEL BASS INN
Owners: David and Barbara Wiedenheft.
757-336-6148 or 1-800-249-0818.
www.channelbassinn.com.
6228 Church St., Chincoteague, VA 23336.
Price: Moderate to very expensive.
Credit Cards: AE, D, MC, V.
Handicapped Access: No.
Special Features: Children OK; pets with prior approval.

The quiet, elegant decor here is backdrop to a somewhat formal inn. Six guest rooms come with private baths and air-conditioning, and most have queen- or king-size beds triple-sheeted for luxury. Barbara has laid out a pleasant backyard garden, and full breakfast is served. The Channel Bass's tearoom functions as the island's only public tearoom and features Barbara's "world famous" scones.

THE INN AT POPLAR CORNER
Innkeepers: Jackie and Tom Derickson and Joanne and David Snead.
757-336-6115 or 1-877-336-6111.
www.poplarcorner.com.
4248 Main St., Chincoteague, VA 23336.
Price: Expensive to very expensive.
Credit Cards: MC, V.
Handicapped Access: No.
Special Features: Children OK in the cottages; inquire about inn.

This welcoming inn with a wraparound veranda furnished with white wicker was once featured on TV's *Romantic Escapes*. No wonder. Floral-wallpapered rooms feature queen beds with ornate, high-back walnut headboards, marble-topped dressers, and whirlpool tubs in the bathrooms. Each room is generously sized with a fine sitting area. Since this Victorian was built in 1996 as an inn, rather than a home, the rooms are separated from each other and offer privacy. All have refrigerators, whirlpool, and shower. Guests may use bicycles, beach chairs, towels, and binoculars. Open Apr. through Nov. The owners also offer cottage rentals on the island.

ISLAND MANOR HOUSE
Innkeepers: Jerry Prewitt and Andrew Dawson.
757-336-5436 or 1-800-852-1505.
www.islandmanor.com.
4160 Main St., Chincoteague, VA 23336.
Price: Moderate to expensive.
Credit Cards: AE, D, MC, V.
Handicapped Access: No.
Restrictions: No children under 10.

Two brothers built a house in 1848, married two sisters, split the house, and moved half of it next door. Today, the two sections have been reconnected with a large garden room, making a most attractive place to stay. Antiques and reproduction furniture can be found throughout the house, along with a mix of Victorian and "beachy" appointments. Eight varied rooms feature quilt-covered beds and include two that share a bath—rented together, they provide a good option for those on a budget. Some rooms also have water views. Expect a roaring fire in winter and, in fair weather, full breakfast on the secluded brick terrace that has a fountain surrounded by roses.

ONANCOCK, VA.
CHARLOTTE HOTEL AND RESTAURANT
Owners: Charlotte Heath and Gary Cochran.
757-787-7400.
www.thecharlottehotel.com.

7 North St., Onancock, VA 23417.
Credit Cards: AE, D, MC, V.
Price: Moderate to very expensive.
Handicapped Access: Yes.
Restrictions: No children under 11.

A delightful surprise for a rural, small town, the Charlotte Hotel is modeled after the Dorset Square Hotel, a diminutive English hotel once visited by innkeepers (and spouses) Gary Cochran and Charlotte Heath. The ambience begins in the petite, antique-accented lobby, where old-fashioned cubbyholes hold the keys to the eight rooms on the second and third floors. The 1907 building was totally renovated by the couple. Charlotte, who once designed cards for Hallmark, leaves her talented brushstrokes everywhere, from botanical paintings to intriguing floor and wall designs. Gary's no creative slouch, either; his handcrafted beds with beautiful wainscoted headboards are built up on platforms for a pleasant, antique-bed feel. Froufrou is banned. Instead, a serene white canvas with floral details provides rooms with restful cottage charm. Televisions and private baths in each room. The inn also offers an intimate 30-seat dining room where Chef Phillip Blane's exuberance for delicious culinary adventure is evident in his ever-changing, four-entrée menu. Full breakfast on weekends (continental during the week for guests), lunches and dinners on most days. . . . one might be tempted to never leave the premises.

CAPE CHARLES, VA.
CAPE CHARLES HOUSE B&B
Owners: Bruce and Carol Evans.
757-331-4920.
www.capecharleshouse.com.
645 Tazwell Ave., Cape Charles, VA 23310.
Price: Moderate to expensive.
Credit Cards: AE, D, MC, V.
Handicapped Access: No.
Restrictions: No children under 12.

From the moment you step onto the large, welcoming porch and are warmly greeted by your hosts, it's obvious why this B&B won the 2000 Governor's Award for Virginia Hospitality. The restored 1912 Colonial Revival is decorated with lovely period pieces and cleverly uses interesting collections such as vintage rug beaters and antique purses. Each of the five rooms has a private bath, some with a Jacuzzi tub. A stay includes complimentary wine and cheese, and tea and sweets in the afternoon or early evening. Catch a Chesapeake sunset on the small town beach only blocks away, or walk the reviving downtown, which offers a few shops and attractive eateries. The nearby world-class golf—an 18-hole Arnold Palmer Signature Golf Course with an additional 18 holes by Jack Nicklaus slated to open in 2005—and an upscale 224-slip marina are part of Cape Charles's new persona. Full breakfast.

NOTTINGHAM RIDGE BED AND BREAKFAST
Owners: Bonnie Nottingham and M. S. Scott.
757-331-1010.
www.nottinghamridge.com.
28184 Nottingham Ridge Lane, Cape Charles, VA 23310.
Price: Expensive.
Credit Cards: Not accepted.
Handicapped Access: No.

From the private beach in front of Nottingham Ridge, you can see little but the blue Chesapeake and the Chesapeake Bay Bridge-Tunnel in the distance. This secluded home, built in 1974 but decorated like a Colonial Williamsburg house, sits in a pine forest far removed from everyday hassles. Six miles south of Cape Charles and 3 miles north of the bridge, this is the perfect spot to overnight or get away from it all for a weekend. The B&B has three rooms and a suite, all with private baths, and in warm weather a full breakfast is served on the screened porch overlooking the Bay.

STERLING HOUSE BED & BREAKFAST
Innkeepers: Ned Brinkley and Steve Hairfield.
757-331-2483.
www.sterling-inn.com.
9 Randolph Ave., Cape Charles, VA 23310.
Price: Moderate to expensive.
Credit Cards: MC, V.
Handicapped Access: No.
Restrictions: No children under 12.

A B&B "for the birds." Even though non-birders will enjoy their stay, bird-watchers have found a friend in innkeeper Ned Brinkley, an international birding guide and author who offers guests natural history and birding tours. The Sterling House was once the home of "Captain" Ned Sterling, prominent seafood merchant and town mayor; Steve Hairfield's renovation of the 1913 bungalow kept the character but added elbow room. Four guest rooms, all with private baths and two with whirlpool tubs, are named after the steamboats and ferries that once connected Cape Charles with Norfolk, Va. The Virginia Lee Room expands into a suite with a sitting room that sleeps two more. Hospitable touches include a butler's pantry, where guests have access to a microwave oven and a refrigerator stocked with beverages and ice, and complimentary bicycles, beach chairs, and towels. To really relax, try the hot tub set almost in the treetops on a second-floor deck, perfect for soaking away sore muscles after a long day traipsing through marshes and creeks in search of a rare songbird.

Motels/Hotels

MARYLAND
Best Value Inn Somer's Cove Motel (410-968-1900; Somer's Cove Marina, 700 Norris Harbor Dr., Crisfield, MD 21817) Forty rooms with balconies or patios.

Outdoor pool. Inexpensive to very expensive.

Best Western, Salisbury Plaza (410-546-1300; 1735 N. Salisbury Blvd., Salisbury, MD 21801) A total of 101 rooms available, some with microwave and data port. Outdoor pool, continental breakfast. Handicapped access. Inexpensive to expensive.

Paddlewheel Motel (410-968-2220; 701 W. Main St., Crisfield, MD 21817) Located in the middle of town, four blocks from City Dock, with 28 rooms, including nine with whirlpool tubs. Inexpensive.

The Washington Hotel (410-651-2525; 11784 Somerset Ave., Princess Anne, MD 21853) Owned by the same family since 1936, the fabled inn was built in 1744. Check out the double staircase: one for gentlemen and one for ladies in hoop skirts. The recently remodeled Murphey's Pub is available for meals, and 12 rooms are available for overnight guests. Inexpensive.

VIRGINIA
Best Western Sunset Beach Resort Inn (757-331-1776 or 1-800-899-4786; 32246 Lankford Hwy./P.O. Box 472, Cape Charles, VA 23310) Private Bay beach makes this a prime pick, with 74 rooms and 54 RV sites on 44 acres. Pool, restaurant, lounge. Handicapped access. Moderate to very expensive.

Driftwood Lodge (757-336-6557 or 1-800-553-6117; www.driftwoodmotorlodge.com; 7105 Maddox Blvd., Chincoteague Island, VA 23336) Recently renovated; 53 rooms have views, refrigerators. Suite available. Breakfast bar. Moderate to very expensive.

The Refuge Inn (757-336-5511 or 1-888-257-0039; www.refugeinn.com; 7058 Maddox Blvd., Chincoteague Island, VA 23336) At the entrance to Chincoteague National Wildlife Refuge; 72 rooms with patios or balconies look onto loblolly pines. Whirlpool, sauna, exercise room, bike rentals, indoor/outdoor pool. Deluxe suites available. Handicapped access. Inexpensive to very expensive.

Waterside Motor Inn (757-336-3434; www.watersidemotorinn.com; 3761 S. Main St./P.O. Box 347, Chincoteague Island, VA 23336) Forty-five rooms, many with water-side balconies and refrigerators. Fishing and crabbing pier, tennis court. Handicapped access. Moderate to very expensive.

Restaurants

Two words to travelers of the Lower Eastern Shore: local seafood. Blue crabs—soft-shells, crab cakes, hard-shells—oysters, rockfish, clams. Indulge in these Bay delights while you're on the Lower Shore, where they're as fresh as you'll ever find and the prices tend to be quite reasonable.

Price ranges, which include dinner entrée, appetizer, and dessert, are as follows:

Inexpensive:	Up to $20
Moderate:	$20 to $30
Expensive:	$30 to $40
Very expensive:	$40 or more

Credit card abbreviations are:
AE—American Express
CB—Carte Blanche
DC—Diners Club
D—Discover
MC—MasterCard
V—Visa

The following abbreviations are used to denote meals served:
B = Breakfast; L = Lunch; D = Dinner;
SB = Sunday Brunch

CAMBRIDGE, MD.
PORTSIDE SEAFOOD RESTAURANT
410-228-9007.
201 Trenton St.
Open: Tues. through Sun.
Price: Inexpensive to expensive.

Cuisine: Eastern Shore seafood and steaks.
Serving: L, D.
Credit Cards: AE, D, MC, V.
Reservations: Accepted.
Handicapped Access: Yes.

Located hard alongside the drawbridge through Cambridge's town center, this restaurant features a big deck overlooking Cambridge Creek. Part of the deck is heated to allow for winter waterside dining. With its old-style Eastern Shore restaurant feel, one is tempted to take full advantage of crab and oyster dishes here in crab and oyster country, but the prime rib's popular, too. If you're a yin-and-yang type, consider the Chesapeake Chicken, a chicken breast topped with crab imperial, ham, and melted cheese, all for a mere $17.95. Less expensive offerings include sandwiches and steamed seafood.

HURLOCK, MD.
SUICIDE BRIDGE RESTAURANT
410-943-4689.
6304 Suicide Bridge Road.
Open: Apr. through Dec., Tues. through Sun.; Jan. through Mar., Thurs. through Sun.
Price: Moderate to expensive.
Cuisine: Seafood, Eastern Shore.
Serving: L, D.
Credit Cards: AE, D, MC, V.
Reservations: For parties of 10 or more only.
Handicapped Access: Yes.

Located on a sturdy bit of rare upland in Dorchester County not far from Cambridge, this seemingly remote and surprisingly contemporary waterside restaurant offers decks, open stone and pine dining rooms, and a menu featuring terrific seafood. Filet mignon and veal marsala aren't forgotten, but seafood lovers should go for fried oysters or crab in all its iterations. The owner also operates Kool Ice and Seafood in Cambridge, which brings the fabulous seafood-to-price ratio into focus (and explains menu items named "Kool," like

Kool's Clams Casino). The Choptank Riverboat Co. operates the 80-foot reproduction paddle wheelers *Dorothy-Megan* and *The Choptank River Queen*, which depart from here (call for departure times), and boaters ducking in from the Choptank River can find dockage. As for the legend of Suicide Bridge: The restaurant tells of devastated locals who flung themselves from this remote locale. A local once demurred, explaining that the bridge's natural curve, to accommodate the channel, had something to do with drivers failing to stay on course.

HOOPERS ISLAND, MD.
OLD SALTY'S RESTAURANT
410-397-3752.
2560 Hoopers Island Rd.; from Cambridge, MD 16 west to MD 335 south to Hoopers Island.
Open: Daily except Tues.
Price: Inexpensive to moderate.
Cuisine: Eastern Shore.
Serving: L, D.
Credit Cards: MC, V.
Reservations: Recommended.
Handicapped Access: Yes.

Drive through miles of winding marshland to reach Old Salty's, which recently changed hands and was renovated. (A friend who was a pupil at this former elementary school fondly recalls roller-skating in what is now the nautically themed main dining room.) Among the changes: If you don't want your seafood fried, you can now have it steamed or broiled. Also, alcohol is now served here. Breads are made fresh daily—look forward to the bread pudding—as are meringue pies like lemon, chocolate, and banana. The popular prime rib special on Fri. and Sat. nights remains. Operated by Dorchester natives.

SALISBURY, MD.
CACTUS TAVERNA
410-548-1254.
2420 N. Salisbury Blvd. (US 13).
Open: Daily.
Price: Inexpensive to expensive.
Cuisine: Multiethnic, including Mexican.
Serving: D.
Credit Cards: AE, D, MC, V.
Reservations: Yes.
Handicapped Access: Yes.

First impressions of cacti, sombreros, and bullfighting pictures might brand Cactus Taverna only a Mexican restaurant, but don't be fooled. Fajitas and tacos are joined on the menu by Peruvian-style ceviche (marinated fish), escargot that can be served with Peruvian marinara sauce, Spanish paella, robust roasted lamb shank, and delicately sauced grilled fish. The Lomo Saltado, sautéed beef and vegetables in a Peruvian brown sauce, is notable, as is the appetizer of breaded alligator chunks with raspberry-jalapeño sauce. Hear out the specials; they're always intriguing. Wine margaritas are nice accompaniments to whatever food you choose, and delicate flan and fried ice cream are fine finishes. Festive, busy, and featuring nightly live entertainment, this is an excellent place to bring small children or to linger over a meal with friends.

MARKET STREET INN
410-742-4145.
130 W. Market St.
Open: Daily.
Price: Moderate to expensive.
Cuisine: American.
Serving: L, D.
Credit Cards: AE, D, MC, V.
Reservations: Recommended for dinner.
Handicapped Access: Yes.

Wine Spectator has given "The Crossroad of Delmarva" (as Salisbury is called) what appears to be a first: an Award of Excellence for one of its local restaurants. Located alongside the Wicomico River drawbridge in town, the honored Market Street Inn offers patio dining outside along the water and three pleasant dining sections inside.

Raw bars await diners at many Chesapeake restaurants.

The menu includes a good selection of entrée salads, a creative touch to seafood and pasta entrées, and a nice sandwich selection at lunch. It was good to see a sherried-up crab and corn soup when we lunched there during the local crab and corn late-summer season. Points go to our server that day, too. When she arrived to pour a second glass of iced tea, we were ready for the check. She said no problem and sent us on our way with a go-cup full of tea.

FRUITLAND, MD.
ADAM'S THE PLACE FOR RIBS
410-749-6961.
219 N. Fruitland Blvd. (US 13 Business, south of Salisbury).
Open: Daily.
Price: Inexpensive to moderate.
Cuisine: American.
Serving: L, D.
Credit Cards: AE, D, MC, V.

Reservations: For large parties.
Handicapped Access: Yes.

If you're tooling along US 50 and looking to stop someplace casual and comfortable for a bite, this edition of the Bay-area rib chain is the place. Civic club plaques and lacrosse championship photos from nearby Salisbury University mark this as a local hangout, but this a suitable dining spot for anyone. Adam's best charms aren't on the walls, though; they're on the menu. Signature baby back ribs are succulent and nicely sauced, served as a full or half rack. Less hearty appetites might enjoy the chopped barbecued beef brisket sandwich or pulled pork barbecue, both inexpensive and served with a pile of fries. Fans of Buffalo-style chicken wings will want to try Adam's version, hot and sweet at the same time. Recent changes include the addition of an executive chef creating fancier entrées Thurs. through Sun. Located just a few feet off the highway, this is a perfect refueling stop for travelers.

DELMAR, DEL.
THE OLD MILL CRAB HOUSE & RESTAURANT
302-846-2808.
DE 54 West and Waller Rd. (just over the Maryland state line).
Open: Daily Mar. through Nov.
Price: Moderate to expensive.
Cuisine: Seafood.
Serving: D.
Credit Cards: MC, V.
Reservations: Recommended for parties of 10 or more Mon. through Thurs. only; otherwise, reservations are not accepted.
Handicapped Access: Yes.

The Old Mill is where the locals go to eat crabs, seated family style at paper-covered tables, often with folks they've never met. The dining room is casual but substantial, with real knotty pine wood and stained-glass light fixtures. The all-you-can-eat crab special is priced according to the season, and for $2 more you can get unlimited steamed shrimp, too. Crabs come with fried hush puppies, fried chicken, fried clam strips, fried shrimp crisps, and steamed corn on the cob. Surely that's enough. A kids' menu starts with a hot dog or drumstick with fries for $5.

SNOW HILL, MD.
TAVERN ON GREEN STREET
410-632-5451.
208 W. Green St.
Open: Daily.
Price: Inexpensive to moderate.
Cuisine: Eastern Shore, pub fare.
Serving: L, D.
Credit Cards: AE, MC, V.
Reservations: Not required.
Handicapped Access: Yes.

The old Snow Hill Inn was known for its crab cakes under the ownership of Jim Washington, who now operates the thoroughly unpretentious Tavern on Green Street a few blocks away. What should you order here? You guessed it. The lump crabmeat is delectable and the crab cake substantial. The menu is reasonably priced, the cuisine covers the bases, and the scene is local.

BERLIN, MD.
THE ATLANTIC HOTEL
410-641-0189.
2 N. Main St.
Open: Daily.
Price: Inexpensive to very expensive.
Cuisine: American.
Serving: D only in dining room; L, D, and late bar at Drummer's Café.
Credit Cards: AE, D, MC, V.
Reservations: Required in dining room; not accepted in café.
Handicapped Access: Yes.

This is one of the Eastern Shore's nicest restaurants, with a dining room menu that draws the local elite alongside visitors to nearby Ocean City looking for something besides beach fare. The dining room is the place to go for special occasions, with its elegant atmosphere and discreet but flawless service. Caesar salad is prepared tableside. Main dishes include salmon bouillabaisse, the hotel's famous goat cheese–topped rack of lamb, and two large lump crab cakes. Diners are welcome to request menu variations to suit their tastes. Across the hall in the Drummer's Café, the atmosphere is more relaxed but still special, and the expected menu of sandwiches and appetizers is supplemented with entrées like Cornish game hens and pecan-crusted catfish. The café features a piano player and singing waitresses Wed. through Sat. in-season, Thurs. and Fri. off-season. Additional seating is available on the hotel's front porch in the summertime. Be sure to save room for the Atlantic Hotel's desserts, all made on the premises.

CRISFIELD, MD.
SIDE STREET SEAFOOD RESTAURANT
410-968-2442.
204 S. 10th St.
Open: Daily Apr. through Sept.; weekends Oct. through Mar.
Price: Inexpensive to expensive.
Cuisine: Seafood, Eastern Shore.
Serving: L, D.
Credit Cards: MC, V.
Reservations: Not required, but accepted.
Handicapped Access: Yes.

Side Street recently changed hands and the restaurant is expanding into its downstairs, where the fish market remains. You can still crack crabs on the deck and order plenty of other seafood. Hard-shell crabs are priced by the crab instead of by the dozen, but this just means you can sample other fare. The restaurant, with both a deck and an indoor dining room, sits atop its seafood market and looks out toward Somer's Cove Marina and Hammock Point.

WATERMEN'S INN
410-968-2119.
901 W. Main St.
Open: Wed. through Sun.
Price: Moderate to expensive.
Cuisine: American, seafood.
Serving: L, D (B on Sat. and Sun.).
Credit Cards: AE, D, MC, V.
Reservations: Recommended on weekends.
Handicapped Access: Yes.

Sure, you can get soft-shell crabs here; Crisfield is the heart of watermen's territory. But instead of typical soft-shells fried and flattened between slices of white bread, here you may find them served over roasted corn and red pepper relish. Crab also arrives distinctly "à la Watermen's," the jumbo lump broiled with country ham, garlic, and wine. Or try the shrimp scampi, with wilted spinach, tomatoes, garlic, and pine nuts over linguini. Some desserts are made on-site by co-owner Kathy Berezoski.

Others—like the kajillion-layered Smith Island cake and the Smith Island banana cake—are made by "a local lady." The Smith Island banana cake is the stuff of legend. Chef Brian Julian changes the menu frequently at this tiny, cheerful spot, which always seems to be full of local couples, families, and well-heeled tourists.

WATTSVILLE, VA.
RAY'S SHANTY
757-824-3429.
32157 Chincoteague Rd.
Open: Thurs. through Sun. off-season; Wed. through Sun. Memorial Day through Labor Day.
Price: Inexpensive to moderate.
Cuisine: Seafood.
Serving: L, D.
Credit Cards: MC, V.
Reservations: Accepted until 5:30 PM.
Handicapped Access: Yes.

Locals and tourists flock to this landmark on the road into Chincoteague from US 13 primarily to eat steamed or fried shrimp, done just right, sold all you can eat or by the pound. Be prepared for a crowd on summer weekends. Landlubbers: steak's on the menu, too.

ONANCOCK, VA.
BIZZOTTO'S GALLERY-CAFFE
757-787-3103.
41 Market St.
Open: Daily; closed Sun. Oct. through May.
Price: Inexpensive to moderate.
Cuisine: American with European overtones.
Serving: L, D; SB in summer.
Credit Cards: AE, MC, V.
Reservations: Recommended.
Handicapped Access: Yes.
Special Features: Craft and art gallery.

Located in a historic storefront, Bizzotto's high ceilings—crowned with pressed tin—complement hardwood floors and subdued lighting trained on artwork. The high-quality crafts, including jewelry, glass, and ceramics, as well as leatherwork by owner Miguel Bizzotto, add to the intriguing ambience. Lunches include a variety of gourmet sandwiches and wraps, a pair of pasta entrées, and the eatery's popular cream of crab soup. Dinner appetizers always include fresh seafood, such as Bizzotto's trademark sautéed mussels bathed in a white wine, garlic, and tarragon tomato broth with a splash of ginger brandy. Entrées run the taste-bud gamut from Asian duck breast to rack of lamb to vegetarian-pleasing portobello ravioli served with a sweet port wine sauce.

STELLA'S FINE FOOD & SPIRITS

757-789-7770.
57 Market St.
Open: Daily.
Price: Inexpensive to moderate.
Cuisine: Italian with an Eastern Shore twist.
Serving: L, D.
Credit Cards: AE, CB, DC, D, MC, V.
Reservations: Accepted.
Handicapped Access: Yes.

Like Brando yelled for Stella, at Stella's you'll want to yell for pizza, the restaurant's supreme calling. An amazing assortment of sometimes strange, always scrumptious gourmet pies includes chicken Alfredo, crab, shrimp, North Carolina pork barbecue, or whatever co-owner Bob Anders dreams up next. The sizable 1912 former hardware store offers an upscale but fun dinner atmosphere on Stella's Second Floor, decorated with vintage movie posters and a long, handsome bar and pool table. Downstairs the feel is more casual, with soaring tin ceilings and plenty of natural light thanks to the original plate-glass windows. Locals enjoy the many homemade Italian dishes along with the hand-battered "Colossal Shrimp," so huge they look like miniature lobster tails, or down-home

fixins like chicken and dumplings and barbecue ribs. It's all good.

CAPE CHARLES, VA.
AQUA AND CABANA BAR

757-331-8660.
5 Marina Village Circle.
Open: Daily.
Price: Moderate to expensive.
Cuisine: Seafood, New American.
Serving: D.
Credit Cards: AE, CB, DC, D, MC, V.
Reservations: Accepted.
Handicapped Access: Yes.

From the Caribbean colors and architecture to the posh interior with lots of leather and marble, one might be tempted to do a Dorothy and exclaim, "Toto, I don't think we're in Cape Charles anymore." This newcomer, located in the new Marina Villages development just north of town, offers the area a fully alternative dining room, right down to the large and shimmery aqua-tiled pillars that frame enviable water views of the Bay and creek. Literally taking center stage is the large glassed-in wine room, which houses a varied selection and makes for an unusual dining room within a dining room. Along with its decor, Aqua offers a menu never seen before in these parts. During one visit we enjoyed the intriguing Thai tuna and shrimp fritter appetizer, composed of three moist cakes with a ginger-mustard sauce swimming in a sweet, spicy chili sauce. Also, the sautéed jumbo lump crab cakes were served with dessert-like coconut-laced sweet potato—pecan croquettes. Portions are not skimpy.

MARIAH'S AT TOWER HILL BED/BREAKFAST INN

757-331-1700.
3018 Bowden Landing.
Open: Tues. through Sat.
Price: Moderate to expensive.
Cuisine: American contemporary.

Serving: D.
Credit Cards: AE, MC, V.
Reservations: Yes.
Handicapped Access: No.
Special Features: Elaborate holiday
brunches.

Like the phoenix rising from the ashes, the
1746 manor house Tower Hill, located outside town on the forested banks of King's
Creek, was resurrected after a fire 11 years
ago left nothing but brick walls and chimneys. The reconstruction was so spectacular
it earned the 2004 Best Historic Restoration award from the Tidewater Builders
Association. The 32-seat restaurant, named
after the resident ghost, offers seating in
the light-filled parlor on the main floor and
in the hunt club–like pub in the bricked
basement, complete with massive fireplaces. During a dinner there, we found
that appetizers were difficult to share when
you chose plump, succulent blackened scallops or tuna sashimi, a delicious layered
tower of the light fish, tomatoes, and fresh
mozzarella sprinkled with a refreshing
wasabi and ginger sauce. There are many
enticing offerings, but we once found a
standout in the spicy mahimahi, cooled by a
tasty pomegranate cream that leaves just
enough kick to elevate the entrée from good
to great. Desserts are whipped up nightly by
Chef Tim Brown and change often, always
using the freshest local produce. If offered,
the strawberry napoleon is an incredible
sweet-tooth satisfier, lusciously intensified
by a Grand Marnier marinade, heavenly
but not too heavy. A five-room B&B on the
second and third floors is decorated with
the same pleasant mix of antiques and
reproductions.

CAPEVILLE, VA.
STING-RAY'S
757-331-2505.
26507 Lankford Hwy.
Open: Daily.

Price: Inexpensive to moderate.
Cuisine: Seafood, American.
Serving: B, L, D.
Credit Cards: DC, D, MC, V.
Reservations: No.
Handicapped Access: Yes.

A gourmet restaurant masquerading as a
truck stop, this is the place famously raved
about by *Southern Living* magazine as "Chez
Exxon." Sure, you have to make your way
past the tourist-trap concession of T-shirts
and tacky souvenirs to a dining room with
more cafeteria than café ambience. But
after you place your order, you'll find your
efforts rewarded. A blackboard highlights
the freshest catches from local waters,
which never disappoint. At Sting-Ray's,
crab imperial lovers have met the king of
this Chesapeake delicacy: a lip-smacking,
creamy, crab-filled concoction from the
recipe of former owner and cuisine genius
Ray Haynie. Try it solo or overstuffing
flounder or shrimp. Generous portions
pack four mushrooms the eatery bills as an
appetizer, but smaller appetites may find
it's a satisfying entrée. Breakfast here is
top-notch diner fare with Southern touches
of grits and one of the best sweet potato and
ham biscuits this side of the Mason-Dixon
Line. Lunches are equally good; try the
inexpensive, salty-sweet fried oyster sandwich. You can tell the sweet potato pie with
damson plum sauce, one of many awesome
homemade desserts, is baked by a
Southerner. No secret why locals and
tourists continually pack this place.

FOOD PURVEYORS

Cafés and Specialty Markets

Allegro (410-651-4520; 11775 Somerset
Ave., Princess Anne, Md.) Good coffee,
pastries, sandwiches, and soups, with a nice
selection of gifts and tables so you can rest
awhile.

Blue Crab Bay Co. (757-787-3602 or 1-800-221-2722; 29368 Atlantic Dr., Melfa, Va.) Phenomenally successful specialty food maker with a worldwide mail-order business and a retail shop; features clam sauce for pasta, Sting Ray Bloody Mary mix, herb blends, gifts, and gift baskets. Open year-round, Mon. through Fri. 9–5, Sat. 10–4.

Globe Theatre & Bistro (410-641-0784; 12 Broad St., Berlin, Md.) It's difficult to categorize this unique establishment, which combines a café and wine shop inside a historic theater with live concerts, regional art in its gallery, gourmet food items, books, cards, and gifts. The menu is upscale and changes monthly. Open daily. A popular stop in this corner of the Lower Shore close to the ocean beaches.

Healthful Habits (410-749-1997; 720 E. College Ave., Suite 7, Salisbury, Md.) Organic and natural foods, herbs, and specialty items. Closed Sat.

Hotstuff! (757-336-3118; 6273 Cropper St., Chincoteague, Va.) More than 500 types of hot sauce, along with other hot food items.

Pony Tails (757-336-6688; 7011 Maddox Blvd., Chincoteague, Va.) Saltwater taffy playfully named for the famous ponies is made daily in-season in a high-speed cutting and wrapping machine that you can see in operation. Open year-round; closed Sun. in-season, Sun. and Tues. in the off-season.

Ice Cream

Ice Cream Gallery (410-968-0809; 5 Goodsell Alley, between the city and county docks in Crisfield, Md.) Open daily in-season.

Muller's Old Fashioned Ice Cream Parlor (757-336-5894; 4034 Main St., Chincoteague, Va.) Fresh fruit sundaes, malts, ice-cream sodas, frozen yogurt, and yes, ice-cream cones, in an 1875 house with authentic Victorian atmosphere. Open 11–11 in summer.

Seafood and Fish Markets

Kool Ice and Seafood (410-228-2300 or 1-800-437-2417; 110 Washington St., Cambridge, Md.) Dorchester-caught crabs and a fine selection of oysters, clams, lobsters, and fresh fish. Shipping available.

Linton's Seafood (1-877-546-8667; www.lintonsseafood.com; 4500 Crisfield Hwy., Crisfield, Md.) Steamed blue crabs, crab cakes, soft-shells, Virginia oysters, and clams. Up to 100 different items.

Metompkin Bay Oyster Co. (410-968-0660; 101 11th St., Crisfield, Md.) This wholesale operation operating crab and oyster processing plants also sells retail. In addition, you can tour the plant with the Tawes Museum (see "Culture," below).

Smith Island Crabmeat Co-op (410-968-1344; www.crabs.maryland.com; 21128 Wharf St., Tylerton, Md.) The co-op was born after times changed and the women of Smith Island could no longer pick crabmeat in their kitchens. Now, they sit at stainless-steel tables at the co-op and pick a bushel basket of crabs—something on the order of 7 to 9 pounds of crabmeat—in two or three hours. Stop by if you see the co-op is open, or order crabmeat and crab cakes via phone or the web.

Southern Connections (1-888-340-3977; www.crabsandseafood.com; 4884 Crisfield Hwy., Crisfield, Md.) Wholesale operation offers retail for hard crabs, Chesapeake and Atlantic fish.

CULTURE

Cinema

Cambridge Premiere Cinema 4 (410-221-8688) in Dorchester Square in **Cambridge** offers first-run films. Down Salisbury way, movies play at **Regal Cinema 10** (410-543-0905) in the Centre at Salisbury. Chincoteague Island's **Roxy** (757-336-6301) at 4074 Main St. shows *Misty of Chincoteague* during Pony Penning for free; Misty stamped her hoofprints in concrete outside. Nightly movies in summer; four nights a week in the winter.

Galleries

CAMBRIDGE, MD.
DORCHESTER ARTS CENTER
410-228-7782.
120 High St.
Open: Mon. through Sat. 10–2.

Housed on Cambridge's historic High St., the center showcases area artists and offers classes, weekend fine arts workshops, and performances. Gallery exhibits change monthly. The last Sun. in Sept. usually brings the Dorchester Showcase, a street festival with entertainment, a juried fine arts and crafts show, and food the length of High St. Expansion plans in the works as of deadline mean this local organization will balloon, from 2,200 to 18,000 square feet of space—and with that, so will its offerings. Stay tuned.

SALISBURY, MD.
ART INSTITUTE AND GALLERY
410-546-4748.
212 W. Main St.
Open: Mon. through Fri. 10–4, Sat. 11–2.

The beautifully renovated former Woolworth's store on the Downtown Plaza is called the Gallery Building, and among its fine tenants is The Art Institute and Gallery, showing works by local, Mid-Atlantic, and national artists in all media. National juried, professional, emerging, and solo art shows. Fine gift shop, classes, and programs.

SALISBURY UNIVERSITY GALLERIES
410-548-2547.
www.salisbury.edu.

View artworks at Fulton Hall, the university's fine arts building, or the Atrium Gallery in the Guerrieri University Center. The former has midday hours except mid-July through Aug., while the latter closes Mon. and weekends year-round.

Historic Buildings and Sites

CAMBRIDGE, MD.
LAGRANGE PLANTATION
410-228-7953.
902 LaGrange Ave.
Open: Tues. through Sat. 10–3 in summer; Mon. through Fri. 10–1 in winter.
Admission: Free to individuals; group tours $2 per person. Donations accepted.

This property, home to the Dorchester County Historical Society, includes Meredith Hall, a circa-1760 Georgian house with Greek Revival ornamentation that is noted for its Flemish-bond brickwork. Also noted here is the local contribution to the governorship. Seven Maryland governors resided in Dorchester County, including Thomas Holiday Hicks, who managed to suppress the state's strong secessionist element to maintain Maryland's Union status. The Neild Museum also stands on the grounds, displaying the sickles, scythes, and yokes of the Lower Shore's yeoman class, as well as maritime tools used in oystering and crabbing. Look also—believe it or not—for memorabilia from one-time Cambridge resident Annie Oakley. The Goldsborough Stable (circa 1790) houses a transportation exhibit, and a colonial-style herb garden stands near the Neild Museum, where plans for expansion were afoot as of deadline.

LLOYDS, MD.
SPOCOTT WINDMILL
410-476-5058.
MD 343.
Open: Daily 10–5.
Admission: Donations accepted.

One of the region's most enduring residents, the great boatbuilder James B. "Mr. Jim" Richardson took it upon himself to build this reproduction of a windmill destroyed here during the blizzard of 1888. "Mr. Jim," who passed away in 1989, kept his master builder's wooden boat workshop at his LeCompte Creek boatyard. His windmill, the only post wind-mill in Maryland, commemorates the 23 post windmills that once towered over the marshy countryside. Also open to the public are a colonial tenant house (circa 1800) and the 1870 one-room schoolhouse called Castle Haven. Lloyd's Country Store Museum opens on special occasions or by appointment. In addition, there's a recently added 1850 smokehouse on the property.

SALISBURY, MD.
PEMBERTON HISTORIC PARK
410-860-0447, Wicomico Heritage Centre; 410-742-1741, Pemberton Hall.
www.pembertonpark.org.
Pemberton Dr., about 2 miles southwest of MD 349 and US 50.
Open: Tours Sun. from 2–4 May 1 through Oct. 1 or by appt.

One of the oldest brick gambrel-roofed houses in the Chesapeake region, Pemberton Hall was built in 1741 for Col. Isaac Handy, a plantation owner and shipping magnate who helped found what would become the city of Salisbury. Col. Handy's home is the center-piece of a museum complex that includes nearby Wicomico Heritage Centre (open by

appointment only), designed to resemble a colonial tobacco barn. This is also the
Wicomico Historical Society headquarters, with a permanent collection of local historic
memorabilia and rotating exhibits. Don't skip Pemberton even if the museums are closed.
The park features several miles of nature trails through woods and along the Wicomico
River. Lovely picnic area. Handy's Wharf here is the oldest wharf in Maryland.

SNOW HILL, MD.
FURNACE TOWN LIVING HERITAGE MUSEUM
410-632-2032.
3816 Old Furnace Rd., off MD 12 (Snow Hill Rd.).
Open: Apr. through Oct., daily 10–5.
Admission: Adults $4, over 60 $3.50, children 2–18 $2; does not include entry to
special events.

The imposing Nassawango Iron Furnace looms over a swamp, a forest, and a small collection of buildings at this quiet echo of the bustling 19th-century village that once stood
here. From 1832 to 1847, hundreds of people lived and worked around this 35-foot-high,
hot-blast furnace in the forest, digging up bog ore and smelting it into pig iron. Around its
remnants stand re-creations of the old ways, including broom making, printing, black-
smithing, weaving, and gardening. Visit the museum, a gift shop, a picnic area, exhibit
buildings, and many nature trails and boardwalks over the Nassawango Cypress Swamp.
Come midweek to have the place to yourself, or visit when Furnace Town hosts one of many
events, including the Chesapeake Celtic Festival in Oct. A captivating spot.

PRINCESS ANNE, MD.
TEACKLE MANSION
410-651-2238.
Mansion St.
Open: Apr. through mid-Dec., Wed., Sat., and Sun. 1–3; mid-Dec. through Mar., Sun. 1–3.
Or call for appt.
Admission: Adults $4, children under 12 free.

Back before the Manokin River became so shallow, its deep water encouraged ships to
travel upriver toward Princess Anne. Plantations and ports thrived along its banks, and
Teackle Mansion is a well-preserved holdover. Probably the best example of neoclassical
architecture on the Lower Eastern Shore, the 1801 mansion dominates the town with its
200 feet of pink brick and stylish symmetry. Built by Littleton Dennis Teackle, who moved
from the Eastern Shore of Virginia with his wife, the house boasts his-and-her dressing
rooms on either side of a central high ceiling, multiple stairways, and entrances by river or
land. Outside are beautiful gardens. Teackle fell on hard times and lost nearly everything
in the depression of 1821, but his mansion stands as testament to his onetime wealth.

ONANCOCK, VA.
KERR PLACE
757-787-8012.
www.kerrplace.org.
69 Market St.
Open: Tues. through Sat. 10–4; closed Jan. and Feb.
Admission: Adults $4, children under 18 free.

Prosperous merchant John Shepherd Ker (original spelling) had Kerr Place built in this port town in 1799. His elegant Federal house has been restored as a museum and is home to the Eastern Shore of Virginia Historical Society. Through period decorative arts, furnishings, and exhibits, Kerr Place gives visitors a glimpse of 18th-century Virginia plantation life. Bus tours welcome.

Museums

CAMBRIDGE, MD.
RICHARDSON MARITIME MUSEUM
410-221-1871.
401 High St.
Open: March through Oct., Sat. 10–4, Sun. and Wed. 1–4; Nov. through Feb., Sat. and Sun. 1–4.
Admission: Donations accepted.

Dorchester County's maritime history and the accomplishments of Capt. Jim Richardson are celebrated in this former bank. Richardson built the Spocott Windmill and the re-created *Dove*, docked at St. Marys City. Also here: a waterman's dock exhibit, workboat models built by their captains, examples of Bay boats, and a photo history on the building of the skipjack *Nathan of Dorchester*. Folks at the museum are knowledgeable and eager to educate visitors. Plans are afoot for significant expansion to create a maritime heritage complex, which will incorporate Cambridge's small but significant Brannock Maritime Museum's collection and archives of the region's maritime history.

SALISBURY, MD.
WARD MUSEUM OF WILDFOWL ART, SALISBURY UNIVERSITY
410-742-4988.
www.wardmuseum.org.
909 S. Schumaker Dr.
Open: Mon. through Sat. 10–5, Sun. noon–5.
Admission: Adults $7, seniors 62 years and older $5, students $3. Family and other discounts available.

The legendary Ward brothers, Lem and Steve, elevated the pragmatic craft of decoy carving to artistry, and their name symbolizes the decoy-as-art-form. This may be the region's most extensive public collection of antique decoys, and it houses a showcase of wildfowl art as well. The evolution of decoys is traced from the Native American's functional, twisted-reed renderings to the latest lifelike wooden sculpture. View the personal collection of the Ward brothers, including their own favorites. The Ward Foundation, established in 1968, hosts the annual World Championship Carving Competition and a wildlife art exhibition and sale. The building and gift shop are on a 4-acre site overlooking a pond. A must-see for decoy lovers.

SNOW HILL, MD.
JULIA A. PURNELL MUSEUM
410-632-0515.
208 W. Market St.
Open: Apr. through Oct., Tues. through Sat. 10–4, Sun. 1–4; tours by appt. in off-season.
Admission: Adults $2, children 50 cents.

At the age of 85, Snow Hill's Julia A. Purnell (1843–1943) fell and broke her hip. In place of her formerly active lifestyle, she completed more than 2,000 needlepoint pieces documenting Worcester County's homes, churches, and gardens. Her son William was so proud that he opened a museum of her work one year before her death. The place is informally known as "The Attic of Worcester County" for all of the everyday items and artifacts here.

CRISFIELD, MD.

J. MILLARD TAWES MUSEUM
410-968-2501.
Somer's Cove Marina at the end of Ninth St.
Open: Year-round, Mon. through Sat. 9–5.
Admission: $3.

Typical of many small Bay museums is the Julia A. Purnell Museum in Snow Hill. Among displays documenting Worcester County are thousands of needlepoint pieces.

A Maryland governor and a famous pair of decoy-carving brothers hailed from Crisfield, known for a rakish late-19th-century oyster gold rush. Catch a glimpse of it all at the J. Millard Tawes Museum, named for the Crisfielder who ascended to the statehouse in the 1960s. As of deadline, renovation plans were in the offing here, where visitors find Native American artifacts and learn about the Tangier Sound area as well as the mid-20th century's famed decoy-carving brothers, Lem and Steve Ward. The carvers lived and worked "Down Neck" on Sackertown Road, and visitors can see their workshop by taking the museum's trolley tour of the area. It leaves from the museum at 1 PM Mon. through Sat., late May through Sept. The museum also offers a walking tour of Crisfield that gives visitors a peek at a crab house operation with a stop at Metompkin Bay Oyster Co. That tour leaves at 10 AM Mon. through Sat. from late May through Sept. Nominal fees for both tours.

PARKSLEY, VA.

EASTERN SHORE RAILWAY MUSEUM
757-665-RAIL.
18468 Dunne Ave.
Open: Wed. through Sun. noon–4 except Thanksgiving, Christmas, and New Year's.
Admission: Adults $2, children under 12 free.

Before the Chesapeake Bay Bridge and the Chesapeake Bay Bridge-Tunnel opened the Delmarva Peninsula for travelers coming by car, most people and goods came from the north by train. The museum celebrates the area's rail heritage with model trains, railcars, and railway artifacts, including a turn-of-the-century crossing guard shanty. Stop by to check out exhibits that include an antique auto display to which collectors loan unusual classics.

MACHIPONGO, VA.
THE EASTERN SHORE OF VIRGINIA BARRIER ISLANDS CENTER
757-678-5550.
US 13/P.O. Box 206.
Open: Mon. through Sat. 10–4.
Admission: Adults $4, seniors and students $2, children 6 years and under free.

The large Cobb's Hotel ledger lies opened to the page where, in 1895, a fountain pen swept across, leaving swirls of fanciful script. For half a century the Cobb family drew the wealthy in droves to the shores of their namesake island, located about halfway down the seaside of Virginia's Eastern Shore. Today the prestigious Victorian hotel is no more, vanished like nearly all vestiges of man from most of Virginia's barrier islands. Relics and the remembrances of the people who once called these islands home could have been erased by the tides of time if not for the diligence of a small Shore group. Now this captivating history is preserved and artfully displayed at the former "poorhouse farm," located along US 13 just north of Eastville. Check out the Breeches Buoy Rig, what looks to be a humorous pair of old-fashioned drawers attached to a life-preserving ring but is actually a tool used by the stalwart crews who manned the Life Saving Stations—the predecessor of the Coast Guard— on several barrier islands. Two floors are overflowing with fascinating artifacts of island life, including watermen's netting needles, a guitar played at the Red Onion (Hog Island's dance hall), even a gasoline-heated iron. Don't miss this treasure.

CAPE CHARLES, VA.
CAPE CHARLES MUSEUM
757-331-1008.
www.smallmuseum.org/capechas.htm.
814 Randolph Ave.
Open: Apr. through Thanksgiving weekend, Mon. through Fri. 10–2, Sat. 10–5, Sun. 1–5.
Admission: Free.

"Hear" the locomotive whistle of the founding railroad and "smell" the salt air on elegant steamers like the *Elisha Lee* thanks to a rich archival photo collection and models of ferries, steamships, and barges that bring the 1886 Bay-side town's past to life. Though Cape Charles has sophisticated roots, the museum's most charming attribute is its eclectic collection of small-town Americana housed in the town's former power plant. A delight to walk back in time, then walk out the door and down the same streets a century later.

Performing Arts

SALISBURY, MD.
COMMUNITY PLAYERS OF SALISBURY
410-543-ARTS.
Tickets: Prices vary.

Noteworthy among the Lower Eastern Shore's community troupes, this one is more than 60 years old. Each season usually includes a musical, a drama, and a comedy performed at locations in and around Salisbury.

SALISBURY SYMPHONY ORCHESTRA AT SALISBURY UNIVERSITY
410-548-5587.
www.salisbury.edu/community/sso/contact.htm.
c/o Salisbury University Music Department, 1101 Camden Ave.
Season: Winter and spring concerts; occasional special events.
Tickets: Prices vary; call for information.

Based at Salisbury University, the symphony performs a holiday performance, a midwinter concert, and a spring concert, all in Holloway Hall Auditorium. The SSO membership includes faculty, students, professionals, and community players and enjoys enthusiastic regional support.

SALISBURY UNIVERSITY PERFORMANCES
For theater, 410-543-6228; for dance, 410-548-6353.
Tickets: Prices vary; call for information.

The theater stage in Fulton Hall hosts drama, comedy, dance, and musical productions throughout the school year. Call for schedule. Dance performances in Holloway Hall Auditorium feature student choreography in the fall showcase, while the spring concert highlights faculty, selected student works, and guest choreographers.

CAPE CHARLES, VA.
ARTS ENTER CAPE CHARLES
757-331-ARTS.
www.artsentercapecharles.org.
10 Strawberry St.
Season: Year-round.
Tickets: Prices vary.

Call it miracle on Mason Avenue, how a small nonprofit run by volunteers resurrected the 1941 Art Deco Palace Theater and created a teaching art center along with a venue for the performing arts highlighting local, regional, and national talent. Check the website for the performance schedule.

Seasonal Events and Festivals
You'll find no more hard-core celebration of Lower Eastern Shore living than the **National Outdoor Show,** deep in Dorchester County's marshland south of Cambridge. You can compete in the muskrat-cooking contest if you bring your own 'rat, or stand back and watch the natives vie for honors in the muskrat-skinning contest. Come Fri. night to watch the crowning of Miss Outdoors; Sat. brings exhibits, local crafters, food, and log-sawing races. Always held the last full weekend in Feb. at South Dorchester School in Golden Hill. Take MD 16 south from Cambridge; at Church Creek turn left onto MD 335; proceed 2 miles to school on the left. For information, call 410-397-8535 or 1-800-522-TOUR or check www.tourdorchester.org. Admission fee.

For a homespun celebration of the American shad (you've heard of shad roe, yes?), be in Vienna, Md., on the third Sat. in Apr. for the **Nanticoke River Shad Festival**. The festival coincides with the fish's spring run—as well as efforts to bring back the species. Live music, arts, crafts, kids' activities, food (including a "shad planking," in which shad are lined up on hardwood boards and specially smoked and braised). The Nanticoke River Canoe and Kayak Race is also part of the fun. For information, call 410-873-3045 or 410-543-1999.

Launched in 1948, the **National Hard Crab Derby & Fair** is held in Crisfield over Labor Day weekend. Top billing tends to go to the annual Governor's Cup Race—a crab race that has had entrants from as far away as Hawaii—but we'd direct you to the workboat-docking contest on Sun. at the Crisfield City Dock. Smith and Tangier island watermen come over to participate, and fans come by boat from all over the place—even small towns on the Northern Neck—thereby reminding us that the Bay remains a viable form of transport. Also featured: a crab-picking contest, a crab-cooking contest, the "Miss Crustacean" beauty contest, a carnival with rides and games, a 10K race, a parade, live entertainment, and, of course, plenty of excellent eating. It all ends Sun. night with fireworks over the harbor. Call 410-968-2500 or 1-800-782-3913.

Also over Labor Day weekend is the **Deal Island-Chance Lions Club's Skipjack Races and Land Festival,** with rides, food (great soft-shell crabs), Smith Island skiff races, fly-fishing demonstrations, and even a pole-climbing contest. At 9:30 AM Mon., the skipjack races, dating to 1959, take place out in Tangier Sound. Bring binoculars, hope the kayak outfitter is renting kayaks again this year, and paddle out to watch. In the afternoon, you can catch another round of workboat-docking contests. For information, call the Somerset County Tourism at 410-784-2785 or check www.skipjack.net.

Legend says Assateague Island's wild ponies descended from Spanish horses that swam ashore after a long-ago shipwreck. Scientists suggest that they descended from ponies that grazed on this outpost island in centuries past. Whatever the case, Chincoteague's annual **Pony Penning** is an event to see. Always held the last Wed. and Thurs. of July, it starts when members of the sponsoring Chincoteague Volunteer Fire Co. corral the ponies and send them swimming across the channel from Chincoteague National Wildlife Refuge to town. The swim attracts tens of thousands of visitors; for a more intimate experience, pre-view the ponies in a corral on Assateague Island on Tues. or stick around for the return swim on Fri. The pony sale, held on Thurs., is a long tradition to raise funds for the fire company, which officially owns the ponies in Virginia. A firemen's festival stretches for a couple of weeks leading up to Pony Penning. If you (or your 10-year-old Misty-loving daughter, granddaughter, or niece) really want to attend, make reservations months in advance. For information, contact the Chincoteague Chamber of Commerce (757-336-6161; www.chincoteague.com; 6733 Maddox Blvd., Chincoteague Island, VA 23336).

The **Chincoteague Oyster Festival,** one of the Bay's hottest tickets for serious oyster lovers, is held on the Sat. of Columbus Day weekend. Famed Chincoteague oysters are slightly salty and considered by many to be the Bay's best. Tales tell of folks who get clear to Chincoteague on festival weekend only to find it sold out, so call the island's Chamber of Commerce (757-336-6161) to get your advance tickets. Held at the Maddox Family Campground.

The **Eastern Shore Seafood Festival** is the Virginia Shore biggie, with so much good food and socializing (including state politicians) that bus tours include it on their spring itiner-aries. Steamed and raw clams, steamed and raw oysters, fried fish, and plenty of sides, including French-fried sweet potatoes, fill the menu at this all-you-can-eat feast. Held the first Wed. in May at Tom's Cove Campground in Chincoteague. Contact the Eastern Shore Chamber of Commerce (757-787-2460; www.esvachamber.org) for tickets and information.

Each fall an amazing natural phenomenon of tremendous global significance occurs on the lower end of Virginia's Eastern Shore. Vast numbers of hawks, songbirds, and other migratory birds cruise down the Eastern seaboard and converge on the narrow peninsula, making a pit stop here before crossing the Chesapeake Bay and continuing their arduous journey to the tropics. Celebrating the feathered pilgrimage in early Oct. is the ever-growing **Eastern Shore Birding Festival,** an annual three-day event with a varied schedule that includes birding tours by kayak, boat, and car caravan along with hikes on barrier islands, farms, marshes, and woodlands. One recent year, alert birders spotted 175 different species. The festival is also packed with presentations, exhibits, and workshops, the majority of which take place in Northampton County. The event is headquartered on the Bay-side grounds of Best Western Sunset Beach resort. For information contact the Eastern Shore Chamber of Commerce (757-787-2460; www.esvachamber.org).

The annual **Citizens for a Better Eastern Shore Pig Roast** is a genuine Eastern Shore good time in the scenic setting of a working Bay creek farm. The event serves up an all-you-can-eat country barbecue with hush puppies, baked beans, and coleslaw. Dine at tables amid hay bales in a huge barn. There's also antique farm equipment on display, hayrides, and plenty of howdy-dos. Held the Sat. of Memorial Day weekend. Call CBES at 757-678-7157 for tickets.

Half the fun of the **Artisans Guild Open Studio Tour** is finding the workshops tucked aside scenic creeks or secluded villages, some open to the public only during this unique three-day Thanksgiving weekend event. Stops run from north near the state line and wander to the southern tip of the Delmarva Peninsula. All along the way you'll discover acclaimed carvers, potters, quilters, furniture makers, folk artists, and more. The tour is free, and much of the wonderful work is for sale. For a brochure/map, call 757-665-6543.

Tours
Cape Charles Ghost Tours are a quirky way to experience the period architecture and paranormal of the Historic District, which is listed on the National Register of Historic Places. Held Fri. and Sat. evenings at sunset, the popular walking tours introduce the favorite haunts and habits of the phantom schoolmarm, the ghost of the old lamplighter, and other spirited stars of the 90-minute outings. The company also provides bicycle rickshaws with drivers so you can tool around town on your own. Tours run Father's Day through Labor Day. Prices: adults $10, children under 12 $5. Private and custom tours are available year-round; adults $12, children $7. Call 757-331-2274 or go online to www.cape charlestours.com.

Zoos
Hailed as one of America's finest small zoos, the **Salisbury Zoological Park** (410-548-3188; www.salisburyzoo.org; 7557 S. Park Dr.) has distinctive and well-conceived animal exhibits. Free, but donations welcome. Picnicking area and concessions outside. Open year-round. Located east of US 13 and south of US 50.

RECREATION

Baseball
The **Delmarva Shorebirds** play at Arthur W. Perdue Stadium (named for poultry magnate Frank Perdue's father) at 6400 Hobbs Road, just east of US 50 and the US 13 bypass in Salisbury. The Class-A Baltimore Orioles affiliate draws a crowd, particularly for Sat.

"The Moses of Her People"

Blacktop covers a parking area beneath the railroad-tie bridge that humbly crosses the Transquaking River. This is a prime spot for outdoorspeople looking to kayak or muskrat, or maybe just to go fishing. Deep into Dorchester County's marshes they come, with sport on their minds, never knowing that the region's slaves once huddled here, awaiting passage to freedom.

But Vernetter Pinder knows. Wearing a scarf around her head and shoulders, Pinder points out the nearby marsh. This is where they waited, she says—sometimes for days, with snakes curling 'round their ankles and fear in their hearts—until Harriet Tubman arrived.

Known to history as "The Moses of Her People," the escaped local slave who changed her name from Araminta Ross—aka "Minty"—to Harriet Tubman (her mother's name was Harriett) is a local hero born a few miles up the road. After her escape from slavery, she made 19 trips back to Dorchester to collect slaves willing to make the dangerous trip north along the Underground Railroad, ultimately leading more than 300 people to freedom.

Wandering Dorchester plantations, she sang songs that spoke of going north right under the slave masters' noses, disguised herself as a man, or acted the part of a delusional woman to deflect attention. The last of those may have had a local origin: The story is told of her enduring a head injury as a girl in one of the three Bucktown stores. She suffered symptoms from this—including a sleeping disease—throughout her life. A small Bucktown Village Store still stands.

Pinder, a local schoolteacher, both portrays Tubman and coordinates tours for the Harriet Tubman Organization's Home Towne Tours, which include a fascinating number of stops through this marshland, including small extant churches where Tubman or her family members likely worshipped. For information, contact the group at 410-228-0401. Their small museum is located at 424 Race St./P.O. Box 1164, Cambridge, MD 21613. Open Mon. through Fri. 10–2 and the first and third Sat. of each month 10–5. Call to arrange special tours. In addition, tours also are offered through the owners of the Bucktown Village Store; contact them at Blackwater Paddle & Pedal Adventures, 410-901-9255. (They also operate cycling, canoe, and kayaking tours.)

In addition, you can see Tubman's tale told at the Harriet Tubman Memorial Garden off the eastbound side of US 50 (it's marked on tourist maps of the area), and visitor's centers in the area stock Tubman brochures.

Vernetter Pinder portrays Harriet Tubman at the Transquaking River.

fireworks in the summer. Contact 410-219-3112 for tickets or www.theshorebirds.com for tickets, directions, schedules, and special events.

Bicycling

The flat country roads through Chesapeake's tidewater make bicycling a favored visitors' pastime on the Lower Eastern Shore. In **Dorchester County**, the **Blackwater National Wildlife Refuge** means flat roads through sometimes spookily stunning swamps, where one easily catches sight of bald eagles and hawks. A map outlining a few favored trails throughout the area—whether through the refuge or around town—is available from the Dorchester Visitor's Center (1-800-522-TOUR; 203 Sunburst Hwy., Cambridge, MD 21613).

Farther south, in **Worcester County**, relatively light traffic makes for some good riding on the main roads. (Beware the overcast day, however; heavy traffic often heads inland from the Atlantic beaches.) A good ride starts in **Berlin**, a historic town with some interesting shops and worthy cafés, then heads down Evans Road. Wander west along Bethards Road to Patey Woods Road, then pedal down Basket Switch Road to Taylor Road. This route is about 19 miles long and brings you to a good choice of destinations: go left and head to Chincoteague Bay, or go another 4 miles west to **Snow Hill**, a pretty, historic town along the Pocomoke River.

Serious cyclists should mark their calendars for early Oct., when the 100-mile **Sea Gull Century** takes about 7,000 riders from Salisbury to the ocean and back in the largest century in the East. Call months ahead for a registration packet (410-548-2772; www.seagull century.org). The **Between the Waters Bike Tour**, held on the fourth Sat. in Oct., takes advantage of the unique position of Virginia's Eastern Shore between the Bay and the Atlantic Ocean. Rides from 20 miles (popular with families) to 100 miles wind past scenic stops overlooking the Bay, seaside marshes, and the barrier islands protecting the Shore from the sometimes stormy Atlantic. For information, call Citizens for a Better Eastern Shore at 757-678-7157 or check www.cbes.org.

Bird-Watching

Bald eagles thrive on the Lower Eastern Shore, where the parade of good birding sites equals the long list of parks and recreational areas along the lower portion of the Delmarva Peninsula. At the top of the Lower Shore, spot the largest nesting population of bald eagles north of Florida at **Blackwater National Wildlife Refuge** (410-228-2677; 2145 Key Wallace Dr., Cambridge, MD 21613). Located in Maryland's Dorchester County, its endless (and we do mean endless—make sure your gas tank's full) winding roads meander along marshland and open water. Other possible sightings: yellow-billed cuckoos, Bewick's wrens, and northern goshawks down toward nearby Hoopers Island. It's said birds there include 15,000 ducks, 35,000 wintering geese, and hawks by the dozen. Adjacent is **Fishing Bay Wildlife Management Area,** 28,000 remote acres that continue the salty habitat, with ibis in summer and short-eared owls in winter. At Assateague Island along the Atlantic, **Chincoteague National Wildlife Refuge** (757-336-6122; 8231 Beach Rd./P.O. Box 62, Chincoteague, VA 23336) carries a blue-ribbon birding reputation. Piping plovers scratch their near-invisible nests in the sand, and man-made lagoons offer a natural stopover on the Atlantic flyway for skimmers and coots. Snow geese also winter here by the thousands— 40,000 one recent year—and bald eagles nest here as well. At Delmarva Peninsula's end, **Kiptopeke State Park** (757-331-2267; 3540 Kiptopeke Dr., Cape Charles, VA 23310) has a

The Blackwater National Wildlife Refuge in Cambridge is an ideal spot for both bicyclists and bird-watchers.
Middleton Evans

hawk observatory and is home to the Eastern Shore Birding Festival each Oct. Depending on the time of year, see gannets and oystercatchers on the man-made islands along the 17-mile-long **Chesapeake Bay Bridge-Tunnel** (757-331-2960; www.cbbt.com; Dept. 001, P.O. Box 111, Cape Charles, VA 23310), where, with permission, you can stop. Take your binoculars to any of the parks listed under "Natural Areas" later in this section to look for all these avians.

Boating
Cruises and Excursion Boats
Broadwater Bay Ecotours (757-442-4363; www.broadwaterbayecotours.com; 6035 Killmon Point Rd., Exmore, VA 23350) Incredibly unique way to discover the mysteries of Virginia's deserted seaside barrier islands without running aground. In a 24-foot Carolina skiff, Capt. Rick Kellam, a descendant of Hog Island villagers, steers small groups on diverse tours. His offerings include bird-watching, fishing, clamming, and marsh ecology tours with stories aplenty, even beach walks and picnics while cooking seafood right on the island. Half-day tours are $75 per person; full-day $135 per person. Additional charges for food tours.

Cambridge Lady Cruises (410-221-0776; www.cambridgelady.com; Cambridge City Marina, Water St., Cambridge, MD 21613) Tour the Choptank River aboard this 47-foot wooden yacht. Travel between Cambridge and Oxford or Cambridge and Denton to learn about steamboats, or go up Trappe Creek. Call for prices.

The Nathan of Dorchester (410-228-7141; www.skipjack-nathan.org; Dorchester Skipjack Committee, 526 Poplar St., Cambridge, MD 21613) This sailing ambassador, a skipjack built in 1994, sails from Long Wharf on Sat., late May through early Oct. Reasonable fees.

The Schooner Serenity (docked in Cape Charles, Va.; 757-710-1233 or sailserenity@msn .com; www.schoonerserenity.com) Captained by an internationally experienced husband-and-wife team on a handsome, two-masted, gaff-rigged schooner that can carry up to 34 passengers. Sunset, full-moon, and afternoon Bay sails from May through Nov. $30 per person, or private charter rate of $750 for up to 30 passengers.

Marinas

On the Choptank River is the city-run **Cambridge Municipal Yacht Basin** (410-228-4031), next to the Historic District in an area known as Port of Cambridge. Borrow a bicycle to get around town. For access to luxury, the **Hyatt River Marsh Marina** (410-901-1234 or 1-800-233-1234; www.chesa-peakebay.hyatt.com) offers 150 slips, water, power, marina store, and all of the goodies offered by the Hyatt Regency Chesapeake Bay Golf Resort, Spa and Marina. See "Lodgings" for details.

Workboats docked at Crisfield, Maryland. Maryland Office of Tourism Development

Farther south, the **Port of Salisbury Marina** (410-548-3176) is a full-service marina downtown on the Wicomico River with free use of bikes, but it's closed on Tues. and Wed. Down in Crisfield, **Somers Cove Marina** (410-968-0925 or 1-800-967-3474) is a huge marina right in town on Tangier Sound. It's owned and operated by the state Department of Natural Resources.

In Virginia, the **Marina Villages at Bay Creek** (757-331-8640) is a posh, new, full-service marina north of Cape Charles. Recreation rentals include bicycles, kayaks, and paddleboats.

Canoeing and Kayaking

Water trails have arrived to direct paddlers through some of the Lower Shore's many waterways, and these maps and guides are more than a fun convenience. In areas such as Dorchester County's wild marshes—known as "Maryland's Everglades"—they're a godsend, as it's easy to get lost in these winding waterways. Skill levels and the amount of time your paddle should take are included. Obtain the guides for the Island Creek Trail and Trans-quaking River Loop Trail in the **Fishing Bay Wildlife Management Area** or the waters of Taylor's Island by contacting the Dorchester County Department of Tourism (1-800-522-TOUR; 2 Rose Hill Pl., Cambridge, MD 21613; info@tourdorchester.org). In addition, three color-coded trails marked at **Blackwater National Wildlife Refuge** are 7.6, 8, and 9 miles in length. Maps are available for a nominal fee and are advised for the 9-mile purple trail, which is closed Oct. through Mar. Call the refuge (410-228-2677) for information on purchasing the guides for a nominal fee.

Other good paddling sites include:

Assateague Island National Seashore (410-641-3030; 7206 National Seashore Ln., Berlin, MD 21811) A good place to canoe in the marshes and interior bays, although wildlife protection regulations must be followed. Canoe rentals.

Blackwater Paddle & Pedal Adventures (410-901-9255; 5303 Bucktown Rd., Cambridge, MD) Kayak, canoe, and bike rentals near the Blackwater Wildlife Refuge.

Janes Island State Park (410-968-1565; 26280 Alfred J. Lawson Drive, Crisfield, MD 21817) Color-coded water trails meander through the island "guts," or channels, of this wonderful lowland paradise. Backcountry camping.

Pocomoke River Canoe Co. (410-632-3971; 312 N. Washington St., Snow Hill, MD 21863) Knowledgeable outfitter rents canoes and kayaks every day, Apr. through Oct. The company can provide livery service and is well worth contacting, even if you're going out with your own canoe. Specializes in Pocomoke River and Nassawango Creek areas.

Tangier Sound Outfitters (410-968-1803 or 410-968-3729) Operates out of Janes Island State Park, conducting ecotrips, full-moon tours, and more. Knowledgeable help navigating the area's wild and winding creeks. Rentals, too.

SouthEast Expeditions (1-888-62-MARSH; www.sekayak.com; 32218 Lankford Hwy., Cape Charles, VA 23310) Eastern Shore of Virginia's king of the kayak tours. Nothing is missed on the seaside or bayside, with two-hour or several-day tours. Can even include fishing and clamming. Also provides kayaking instruction and is a full-service kayak outfitter. Located just north of the Chesapeake Bay Bridge-Tunnel.

Survival Products (410-543-1244; www.survivalproducts.com; 1116 N. Salisbury Blvd., Salisbury, MD 21801) Canoe and kayak sales and rentals from knowledgeable people who cruise area waterways.

Fishing

Fish or crab along the piers that once were the Choptank River Bridge, located alongside US 50 and the current bridge in Cambridge. Contact: 410-820-1668.

Boat Ramps

Check chapter 9, "Information," for information on obtaining free maps of Bay access.

Charter Boats & Head Boats

Hoopers Island, Md.

Double A Charter Fishing (1-800-310-3231; www.doubleacharters.com; 6311 Suicide Bridge Rd., Hurlock, MD 21643) Fish out of remote Hoopers Island aboard the 42-foot *Double A.* Capt. Gibby Dean, who has more than 20 years' experience, was raised in the area and departs from the marina his grandfather used to own. Mid- and Lower Bay.

Sawyer Fishing Charters & Tours (410-397-3743; www.sawyercharters.com; 1345 Hoopers Island Rd., Church Creek, MD 21622) Hoopers Island resident takes fishers out into the Bay between Smith Point and the Patuxent River, or maybe into the Honga River or Tangier Sound aboard *Sawyer,* a 48-foot Chesapeake deadrise-style fishing boat.

Tide Runner Fishing Charters (410-397-FISH; www.captmikemurphy.com; P.O. Box 55, Fishing Creek, MD 21634) Light tackle and fly-fishing out of Hoopers Island.

CRISFIELD, MD.
For a list of the many charter boat captains operating out of the fine fishing grounds near Crisfield, contact the Somerset County Tourism office at 1-800-521-9189.

CHINCOTEAGUE, VA.
The **Chincoteague Island Charterboat Association** publishes a brochure listing licensed professional charter boats. Pick it up at or request a travel guide from the Chincoteague Chamber of Commerce (757-336-6161; www.chincoteague chamber.com; P.O. Box 258, Chincoteague, VA 23336).

WACHAPREAGUE, VA.
Wachapreague Hotel & Marina (757-787-2105; 17 Atlantic Ave./P.O. Box 360, Wacha-preague, VA 23480) Bottom and deep-sea fishing from several charter craft. They also rent small boats. The Island House Restaurant is located near the marina.

Golf
Bay Creek Golf Club (757-331-9000; 2037 Old Cape Charles Rd., Cape Charles, Va.) This 18-hole Arnold Palmer–designed course is surrounded by farms and woodlands and bounded by the Chesapeake Bay and Plantation Creek. A second 18-hole Jack Nicklaus Signature Golf Course is scheduled to open in 2005.

Captain's Cove Golf and Yacht Club (757-824-3465; www.captscove.com; 3370 Captain's Corridor, Greenbackville, Va.) A public 9-hole course. Open water on four holes.

Eastern Shore Yacht and Country Club (757-787-1525; 14421 Country Club Rd., Melfa, Va.) An 18-hole private club available to visitors by reciprocal agreement with other clubs. Reservations required. Open year-round.

Golfers playing at the Hyatt Regency in Cambridge enjoy beautiful views of the Choptank River.

Great Hope Golf Course (1-800-537-8009; 8380 Crisfield Hwy., Westover, Md.) 2,047-yard, links-style championship golf course. Pro shop, restaurant, PGA instruction.

Nassawango Golf Course (410-632-3114 or 410-957-2262; www.nassawango.com; 3940 Nassawango Rd., Snow Hill, Md.) 18 holes; semiprivate championship course. New driving range, pro shop.

Nutters Crossing Golf Course & Driving Range (410-860-4653; 30287 Southampton Bridge Rd., Salisbury, Md.) Bermuda fairways, clubhouse with dining.

River Marsh Golf Club (410-901-1234; Hyatt Regency Chesapeake Bay Golf Resort, Spa and Marina, 100 Heron Blvd., Cambridge, Md.) An 18-hole championship golf course designed by Keith Foster. Pretty holes along the Choptank River. Instruction, pro shop, driving range, Eagle's Nest Bar and Grille.

Winter Quarters Golf Course (410-957-1171; 355 Winter Quarters Dr., Pocomoke City, Md.) Public course. Two separate sets of tees make a front nine and a back nine.

Natural Areas: State and National Parks and Refuges

Many expansive natural areas are the best part of the Lower Eastern Shore, where the endangered Delmarva fox squirrel resides and the exotic sika deer can be spotted. These large-dog-size deer, which got loose decades back, now provide intriguing animal sightings alongside plentiful bird species. For details on state parks and natural areas, check the following websites: Maryland Department of Natural Resources, www.dnr.state.md.us/publiclands, and in Virginia, the Department of Conservation and Recreation, www.dcr.state.va.us.

Also, hunting is popular starting in the fall. Check chapter 9, "Information," for contact information on hunting season schedules.

A couple of notes while perusing the natural area entries:

Assateague Island stretches 37 miles between the Atlantic Ocean and Sinepuxent Bay and straddles the Maryland-Virginia border amid one state park and two federal ones: Assateague State Park and Assateague National Seashore in Maryland, and Chincoteague Wildlife Refuge in Virginia. Among the 44 mammal species seen here are gray seals, born at the southernmost point in their birthing range, and bottlenose dolphins offshore. Birds include northern bobwhites, least bitterns, indigo buntings, and more exotic seagoing passersby. This is also home to the famous wild ponies, most likely descended from horses grazed here by 17th-century settlers. They're generally mild-tempered and will leave you alone if you leave them alone.

Dorchester County's lowlands, known as "Maryland's Everglades," include nearly 50,000 acres between Blackwater National Wildlife Refuge and Fishing Bay Wildlife Management Area, located farther southwest and more remote. Bald eagles nest through this marshy territory, with its flat roads that make for great cycling and its creeks for paddling. Take advantage of the new waterways guides and maps (see "Canoeing & Kayaking"), because it's not hard to get turned around and lost in these marshy creeks. Pay attention to winds and tides.

Assateague Island National Seashore (410-641-3030; 7206 National Seashore Ln., Berlin, MD 21811) Thirteen miles of barrier island. Backcountry camping (register for a backcountry permit), stretches of isolated beach, shellfishing, crabbing, canoeing, hiking. Spectacular seashore wilderness.

Assateague State Park (410-641-2918; 7307 Stephen Decatur Hwy., Berlin, MD 21811) This is the "beachier" portion of this 37-mile-long barrier island, and by that we mean the part with sun worshippers, families, and beachcombers. Two miles of ocean beach.

Blackwater National Wildlife Refuge (410-228-2677; 2145 Key Wallace Dr., Cambridge, MD 21613) More than 27,000 acres south of the tiny town of Church Creek include low-lands, forests, flat roads for cycling and short walks, and creeks for paddling. Birds aplenty, and you might even glimpse the Chesapeake's endangered Delmarva fox squirrel, as Blackwater has the highest concentration of the small creature. It also has the East Coast's largest nesting population of bald eagles north of Florida. Take the 6-mile driving loop, with its minimal cost for cars and cyclists. Renovations are in store for the nature center and gift shop. Hiking trails were slated for development at deadline.

Chincoteague National Wildlife Refuge (757-336-6122; P.O. Box 62, Chincoteague, VA 23336) Ten miles of beach with lifeguarded sections. Bird-watching central. Camping, too.

Eastern Shore of Virginia National Wildlife Refuge (757-331-2760; 5003 Hallett Circle, Cape Charles, VA 23310) About 750 acres; visitor's center with wildlife exhibits. Located just above the Chesapeake Bay Bridge-Tunnel.

Fishing Bay Wildlife Management Area (410-376-3236; 14 miles south of Cambridge) A total of 21,000 acres with paddlers' trails (see "Canoeing & Kayaking" for water trail infor-mation), boating, in-season hunting, bird-watching, and boat ramp. Habitat supports the Asian sika deer, bald eagles, ospreys, ibis, wintering short-eared owls, shorebirds, and waterfowl. Fishing and crabbing. The WMA's entrance is down Bestpitch Ferry Rd. Get there by heading south on Bucktown Rd. from Cambridge.

Janes Island State Park (410-968-1565; 26280 Alfred Lawson Dr., Crisfield, MD 21817) One of the coolest parks anywhere, composed of a mainland portion with marina, camp-ing, and cabins and a 2,800-acre island. Rent a small boat to explore the guts of the island, marked into water trails. Boasts a lovely beach on the island's far side along Tangier Sound. Tangier Sound Outfitters handles paddling rentals (see "Canoeing and Kayaking"); to rent a boat call Croaker Boats at 410-968-3644.

Kiptopeke State Park (757-331-2267; 3540 Kiptopeke Drive, Cape Charles, VA 23310) Birders' paradise 3 miles north of the Chesapeake Bay Bridge-Tunnel. Trails through upland and on boardwalks through the sand, beach for swimming Memorial Day through Labor Day. Camping, boat launch, lighted fishing pier, 450 acres. Nominal fees; handicapped access.

LeCompte Wildlife Management Area (410-376-3236; 4220 Steele Neck Rd., Vienna, MD 21869) About 500 acres. Hunting in-season and bird-watching along the trails.

Pocomoke River State Park (410-632-2566; 3461 Worcester Hwy., Snow Hill, MD 21863) Two discrete areas make up this intriguing, 14,753-acre park, with its cypress swamp and blackwater paddling on the Pocomoke River. Milburn Landing is 7 miles north of Poco-moke City; Shad Landing is 3.5 miles south of Snow Hill. Cabins, boating, paddling, fish-ing, camping, walking trails, and a swimming pool at Shad Landing.

Sporting Clays
Delmarva Sporting Clays (410-742-2023; 23501 Marsh Rd., Mardella Springs, MD 21837)
A 55-station sporting clay range located on 60 acres. Open daily year-round, 9 AM–dusk.
$15 for 15 targets or $30 for 100.

Swimming
Assateague State Park (410-641-2120; 7307 Stephen Decatur Hwy., Berlin, Md.) Ocean
swimming and beachcombing. Also visit the Assateague Island National Seashore next
door (410-641-3030).

Dorchester County Pool (410-228-6850; 107 Virginia Ave., Cambridge, Md.) Where the
locals go, especially after the sea nettles arrive in the Bay. Adults $3, students $2. Open
daily, Memorial Day through Labor Day.

Great Marsh Park (contact Dorchester County Tourism, 410-228-1000; Somerset Ave.,
Cambridge, Md.) Boat ramp, picnicking, pier, and playground. Swim in early summer,
before the sea nettles arrive.

Pocomoke River State Park (410-632-2566; 3461 Worcester Hwy., Snow Hill, Md.)
Swimming pool at the Shad Landing portion of the park, 3.5 miles south of Snow Hill.

Tennis
Salisbury City Park (410-548-3188; E. Main St. and S. Park Dr., Salisbury, Md.) A few
public courts located in a tree-shaded park that also features a bandstand where concerts
are held on summer Sun. Park also has a playground, paddleboats, and riverside walking
trails.

Nearby Recreation
Ocean City is within easy driving distance of Salisbury, Berlin, and Assateague—in fact,
many would consider these a natural and worthy grouping of travel destinations. The
sprawling beach town's major attraction is a 10-mile-long strip of golden sand that often
is packed blanket-to-blanket on summer weekends.

Visitors come for the sun, the sand, the carnival rides, the "World Famous French
Fries" sold on the boardwalk, the shops and restaurants, the golf, and the fishing that
includes a big-money white marlin tournament.

You can reach Ocean City, or "O.C.," from the Bay via three routes: Enter the oldest,
southernmost part of the city on US 50 from the west. Or take MD 90 across the Assawo-
man Bay Bridge to what has become the city's center. Or from the north from the Delaware
towns of Rehoboth Beach, Dewey Beach, and Bethany Beach (highly worthwhile destinations) take DE 1, which becomes the Coastal Hwy., MD 528, once you reach Maryland. For
information, contact the Ocean City Convention and Visitors Bureau (410-289-8181 or
1-800-OC-OCEAN; www.ococean.com).

SHOPPING

Antiques
Antique Dealers at 450 Race (410-228-0031; 450 Race St., Cambridge, Md.) More than
25 dealers. Open Mon. through Sat. 10–5, Sun. 1–5.

Blue Crow Antique Mall (757-442-4150; 32124 Lankford Hwy., Keller, Va.) If US 13 starts to feel endless, this shopping break will be the cure. Open seven days a week with 150-plus dealers; it's easier to ask what they *don't* sell.

Deadrise Enterprises (757-787-2077; 3-5 North St., Onancock, Va.) Antiques and collectibles from nauticals to books to furniture and more. Upstairs find the North Street Gallery, a showcase for local and regional fine art.

Exmore Antique Shops: When big chain stores moved in on the highway, the nearby downtown suffered, but it has since found its niche with an assortment of antique, collectible, and good ol' junk shops. Check out **Antique Addicts** (757-442-5100; 3515 Main St.) and the **Exmore Antique & Craft Emporium** (757-414-0111; 3304 Main St.), then rest up and chow down at the vintage **Exmore Diner** (757-442-2313, 4264 Main St.).

Holly Ridge Antiques (410-742-4392; 1411 S. Salisbury Blvd./US 13 Business, Salisbury, Md.) Specializing in 18th- and 19th-century furniture and accessories under the strict 100-year rule.

Once Was Antiques and Bad Girlz Collective (757-331-2293; 611 Mason Ave., Cape Charles, Va.) A dozen dealers offer antiques and whimsical gifts from vintage clothing and china to jewelry, soft sculpture character dolls, and beach glass creations.

Packing House Antiques (410-221-8544; 411 Dorchester Ave., Cambridge, Md.) Recommended by those in the know; more than 100 dealers.

Town Center Auction & Antiques (410-629-1895; 1 N. Main St., Berlin, Md.) Antiques and collectibles from more than 70 dealers are spread out in a big building. A nearby, second location at 113 N. Main St. showcases lots more dealers and an art gallery called A Step Above.

Books
Atlantic Book Warehouse (410-548-9177; 2734 N. Salisbury Blvd., Salisbury, Md.) This cavernous bookstore offers a huge selection of books discounted anywhere from 10 to 80 percent, plus calendars and magazines.

Henrietta's Attic (410-546-3700 or 1-800-546-3744; 205 Maryland Ave., Salisbury, Md.) Aisles of antiques and used books, watched over by bookseller Henrietta Moore. Browse as long as you like, or ask for Moore's help. Collectibles, glassware, china, and genealogy materials are also packed into this "anything goes" place five blocks south of the hospital, west of US 13.

Galleries
SALISBURY, MD.
The Gallery (410-742-2880; 625 S. Division St.) Regional works in all media. Regular one-person shows and an annual Christmas exhibit featuring four or five local artists. Custom framing and a range of gifts and crafts including functional pottery, handcrafted jewelry, and Eastern Shore art.

Salisbury Art & Framing (410-742-9522; 213 North Blvd., Waverly Plaza) Works by local and nationally known artists, from Eastern Shore seascapes to abstracts. Prints, pottery, handmade jewelry, and custom framing. South of downtown and west of US 13.

CHINCOTEAGUE, VA.

Island Arts (757-336-5856; 6196 Maddox Blvd.) Owned by local artist Nancy West, the shop specializes in woven clothing and unique jewelry offerings. Also featured are Nancy's oil paintings, which have been exhibited nationwide.

Lotts' Arts and Things (757-336-5773; 4281 Main St.) Features the silk screens of Welsh native Hal Lott, known to poster collectors for his works commemorating Pony Penning.

ONLEY, VA.

Turner Sculpture & Gallery (757-787-2818; 27316 Lankford Hwy./US 13) The drive down US 13 gets a little long through Virginia's Eastern Shore until you stumble upon this fascinating foundry and art display, where Dr. William Turner and his son David, both nationally known wildlife sculptors, create great blue herons, beluga whales, and even a draft horse. Their wildlife sculptures are displayed throughout the United States. While you're there, take a look at the magnificent glass-topped dining and coffee tables offered for sale. The glass is supported underneath by an interconnected bounty of sculpted undersea creatures, including silver-plated fish. If you're lucky, they'll show you the foundry on a day when bronze is being poured.

PAINTER, VA.

The Folk House (757-442-2224; www.thefolkhouse.com; 35044 Lankford Hwy./US 13) Be prepared to smile; owner Danny Doughty's colorful folk-art paintings portray a sunny Southern world that earned the Shore native a *Southern Living* magazine folk art award. Antiques are also for sale along with the works of more than 30 other artists and craftsmen.

EASTVILLE, VA.

The Gallery at Eastville (757-678-7532; www.thegalleryateastville.com; 16319 Courthouse Rd.) Catch the talented husband-and-wife design team of David Handschur and Mary Miller creating their award-winning, hand-loomed sweaters in the knitting studio or painting local scenes on the porch. Their talents extend to hand-painted furniture and home accessories, as well as affordable jewelry. The gallery is set in an old parsonage.

CHERITON, VA.

Seaside Gallery (757-331-BLUE; 21194 N. Bayside Rd.) A short drive off US 13 immerses you in the watercolor world of owner Thelma J. Peterson, a local painter acclaimed for capturing and preserving Eastern Shore places and people. Also sells pretty hand-painted china sets with floral and seashore motifs.

CAPE CHARLES, VA.

Stage Door Gallery (757-331-3669; 10 Strawberry St.) Affiliated with the nonprofit art center that owns the adjoining historic Palace Theater, this small gallery is spilling over with the talented works of local artists and artisans with prices to suit all budgets. Featured artists change monthly, and an opening reception includes presentation of a Critics' Choice Award.

Craft Galleries, Gift Shops, and General Stores

CAMBRIDGE, MD.
Bay Country Shop (410-221-0700; 2709 Ocean Gateway Dr.) Rustic and goose-oriented Shore items. Lots of gifts as well as men's and women's clothing and jewelry.

Joie de Vivre (410-228-7111; 410 Race St.) Attractive gallery devoted to art and textiles.

SALISBURY, MD.
The Country House and Country Village (410-749-1959; 805 E. Main St.) At 16,000 square feet, it's the largest country store in the East. Everything country that you could hope to find, plus collectibles, Christmas items, candles, and more for the kitchen, bath, and household. Closed Sun.

CHINCOTEAGUE, VA.
Marsha Carter Gifts (757-336-3404; 6351 Cropper St.) A boutique filled with handcrafted products like handblown glass, quilts, paintings, jewelry, pottery, and local bird carvings.

ONANCOCK, VA.
Herbal Instincts (757-787-7071; 141 Market St.) Owner/gardener Christine Porco stocks everything imaginable in the herb line, scented vinegars, oils, teas, soaps, and dried herbs in bulk. Handcrafted items include teapots and cups. Organic food items also available, including fresh vegetables in-season. Her elegant bungalow-turned-showroom is graced outdoors with colorful perennial borders and, naturally, herbs.

CAPE CHARLES, VA.
Watson's Hardware (757-331-3979; 225 Mason Ave.) Step back in time and browse through this hardware store that looks like a hardware store must have looked in Cape Charles's early days. Under the original pressed-tin ceiling, owners Bill and Chip Watson stock most anything hardware, plus all manner of fascinating implements for opening tasty local crabs, oysters, and clams.

CAPEVILLE, VA.
Windsor House (757-331-4848; 4290 Capeville Dr.) See craftsman Kurt Lewin at work and the handsome finished products: authentic Windsor chairs, settees, and stools created in the 18th-century tradition. Turn-of-the-century house also showcases local artists and antiques.

Jewelry

PRINCESS ANNE, MD.
Bailey White Jewelers (410-651-3073; 30400 Mt. Vernon Rd.) Among the best hand-crafted, Bay-inspired Chesapeake designs around, including a crab, a skipjack, and an oyster with its pearl, each rendered in 14K or 18K gold.

SALISBURY, MD.
G. B. Heron & Co. (410-860-0221; 1307 Mt. Hermon Rd.) Custom-designed jewelry and a store full of high-quality pieces. Jewelry repair by goldsmiths on the premises.

Kuhn's Jewelers (410-742-3256; 107 Downtown Plaza) Diamonds and watches; full line of quality jewelry from a company established in 1853.

Malls and Outlets

SALISBURY, MD.

The Centre at Salisbury (410-548-1600; 2300 N. Salisbury Blvd.) The major local mall, with four anchor department stores (Boscov's, The Hecht Co., Sears, and J. C. Penney), dozens of smaller stores, a food court, and a 10-screen cinema.

Salisbury Pewter Outlet (410-546-1188 or 1-800-824-4708; 2411 N. Salisbury Blvd.) Watch workers create the pewter pieces sold in this "outlet," where first-quality pieces sell for less. Save more with seconds, factory overruns, and discontinued items. Factory tours by appointment. Salisbury Pewter has a second outlet on US 50 in Easton (410-820-5202).

Smith and Tangier Islands

The boat schedule rules the time visitors can spend rambling on Chesapeake's last two inhabited islands, the remote crabbing communities on Smith and Tangier islands. Promptly, the boats depart Crisfield, and just as promptly, the boats pull away from the island docks, 12 miles away, to return to the mainland.

It was therefore impossible to partake of the evening activity inside the fire station at Ewell, the largest of Smith Island's three towns, on a day not long before Thanksgiving. Through the open door stood tables covered with layer cakes, perhaps as many as 12 thinly sliced layers each. These were the offerings for the evening ahead here, where neighbor seems to know neighbor as most siblings know their own. On the mail boat back to Crisfield, a fellow headed home for the holiday carried a box. Inside was a cake—a Smith Island layer cake, delicious evidence of a place where folks do things their own way.

Visitors will quickly discover so. There's no ATM, and the islands, bastions of an old-style brand of Methodism, are dry. For many, an afternoon peek at island life via the tourist ferries may be enough. Those who stay overnight will notice how many island businesses open and close as the tour boats arrive and depart.

Part of a chain of shifting, sinking, eroding islands, Tangier and Smith lie only 3 feet above sea level—and sometimes far less. On tiny Tangier in Virginia, half of the 3-mile island is livable; the rest is tidal marsh. At 8-by-4 miles, Smith Island, in Maryland, is far larger.

The two share similarities, but they are different, too. Erosion threatens their lives, and precarious crab populations, their livelihoods. After a day or two cycling the narrow streets where Smith Islanders barely bother with license plates and Tangier's residents prefer golf carts, where grave markers in front yards repeat old names like Crockett or Parks, outsiders know this isn't a place where people forget their past. Folks say the islanders' distinct accents descend from Elizabethan forebears who settled here.

The white crab shanties that once lined Smith's "Big Gut," the channel into Ewell, have come ashore, but they still line the channel into Tangier. Just as you wouldn't waltz into a businessman's private office without an invitation, so a visit to a Tangierman's crab shanty comes only at his behest. Shallow wooden "tanks" line the interior, filled with crabs moving toward a molt, the final step toward producing a valuable soft-shell.

Three towns are settled on Smith Island: Ewell, Rhode's Point, and Tylerton. Tylerton, reputedly the most devout of the three, is separated from the island proper by a channel, and therefore accessed only by boat. It is fronted by docks, with well-kept houses and its own general store. A bike ride out the main road from Ewell takes visitors into tiny Rhode's Point, teetering on the edge of the Bay. Upon finishing a ride, only a stop at

Ewell's nearly century-old general store, called Ruke's for the current owner of more than 40 years, will do. Order up soft-shell crabs; you won't find finer in any fancy city restaurant. And, of course, indulge in a slice of Smith Island layer cake.

Tangier hosts just one town, but visitors immediately see its bustle. Golf carts manned by tour guides line up to meet the tour boats, and a "tour buggy" excursion is quick but thorough, covering the gift shops lining the main road, the school, and the Methodist church. On poles are containers akin to bluebird boxes, welcoming those honest enough to plop in a couple of quarters in exchange for an island recipe, often featuring crab.

Travelers should understand that this is not Chesapeake Disneyland, nor are these Nantucket and the Vineyard. Tangier has a bit more for tourists to do, including a 3-mile beach on the far side of the island and an airstrip. But Smith draws visitors as well, including those who want to visit the fabled Ruke's General Store or the lovely Inn of Silent Music in Tylerton, operated by former city dwellers who, no doubt, understand why you're gaga over being this far from "civilization."

GETTING TO THE ISLANDS

Take a seasonal ferry for tourists, or travel year-round, as the locals do, via mail boat, usually from Crisfield. Be sure to leave enough time to secure parking—especially if you're going to be gone overnight—and note that not all boats departing Crisfield leave from the City Dock. For general questions about the boats and their schedules, contact the Somerset County tourism office (1-800-521-9189).

Smith Island Cruises (410-425-2771; 4065 Smith Island Rd., Ewell, MD 21824) Sail from Crisfield's Somer's Cove Marina aboard the *Capt. Tyler* daily from Memorial Day through Oct. 15. À la carte lunch available at the Bayside Inn at the dock in Ewell. Departs Crisfield 12:30 PM, returns 5:15 PM; adults $22. The company also operates a ferry from Point Lookout, Md., at the mouth of the Potomac River in St. Marys County (see chapter 3, "Annapolis and Southern Maryland").

Tangier Island Cruises (410-968-2338; 1001 W. Main St., Crisfield, MD 21817) The *Steven Thomas* runs daily, May 15 through Oct., departing from 10th St. in Crisfield at 12:30 PM, returning about 5:15 PM; adults $22, kids 7–12 $11. The company also operates the *Capt. Rudy Thomas*, which takes overnight cruises to Norfolk and Portsmouth May through Oct. Reservations required for that trip, which costs $275 per couple, including lodging.

Tangier-Onancock Cruises (757-891-2240; 16458 W. Ridge Rd., Tangier, VA 23440) Leave daily from Onancock's historic Hopkins & Bro. General Store aboard the 65-foot *Capt. Eulice* at 10 AM. A guide meets passengers at the Tangier dock for a tour. Lunch at the famed Hilda Crockett's Chesapeake House for an added fee, if you like. Runs Memorial Day weekend through Oct. 15; adults $22, kids 6–12 $11. Group reservations required.

Mail Boats to Smith Island. Although the only official "mail" boat is the *Island Belle II*, you may come under the common misconception that the *Captain Jason* boats, which operate year-round, are also mail boats. So, in the spirit that you can catch all three boats over to Smith Island in the off-season, we provide this information:

The *Captain Jason I* (410-425-5931; 4132 Smith Island Rd., Ewell, MD 21822) travels year-round between Ewell and Crisfield. The *Captain Jason II* (410-425-4471; 21162 Tuff

St., Tylerton, MD 21866) travels between Tylerton and Crisfield. The two boats are oper-ated by the Laird brothers. The *Island Belle II* (410-968-1118; 20915 Somers Rd., Ewell, MD 21824), with Capt. Otis Tyler, runs between Ewell and Crisfield. All the boats cost about $20 round-trip, and you may pay a small added charge for freight, such as bikes.

Mail Boat to Tangier Island (757-891-2240; 16458 W. Ridge Rd., Tangier, VA 23440) The *Courtney Thomas* travels year-round between Crisfield and Tangier. Leaves Tangier at 8 AM and Crisfield at 12:30 PM Mon. through Sat. From Nov. through mid-Apr., the boat adds a Sunday afternoon run, leaving Tangier at 3 and Crisfield at 4. $12 one-way.

WHAT TO DO, WHERE TO STAY

Smith Island

Rent golf carts ($10 for a half hour, $15 for an hour) or bikes ($3 for a half hour, $5 for an hour) at the Bayside Inn at the dock in Ewell.

Orient yourself to island life at the **Smith Island Center** (410-425-3351; www.smith island.org; Caleb Jones Rd. at the county dock), which tells of boats, oystering, crabbing, and Joshua Thomas, the famed "Parson of the Islands" who spread Methodism here in the 19th century. Open May through Oct., noon–4 daily.

Food and Lodging

Bayside Inn Restaurant (410-425-2771; 4065 Smith Island Rd., at the dock in Ewell) Open Memorial Day through Oct. 15, 11–4 daily. Family style by reservation, or à la carte. Serves up big platters of Southern-style seafood, as well as famed Smith Island layer cake—up to 10 layers!—for dessert.

Drum Point Market (410-425-2108; Union Church St., Tylerton) The grocery store and lunch stop at this end of the island. Open Mon., Tues., and Thurs. through Sat. 10–3 and 6–8; Wed. 10–3.

Ewell Tide Bed & Breakfast (410-425-2141 or 1-888-699-2141; www.smithisland.net; 4063 Tyler Rd., Ewell, MD 21824) Reasonably priced and very homey, located in a former captain's house. Four rooms; two share a bath. Owner Steve Eades also owns the small Smith Island Marina and can arrange fishing charters. Bikes and kayaks available for guests. Continental breakfast. Inexpensive. AE, D, MC, V. No handicapped access.

Inn of Silent Music (410-425-3541; www.innofsilentmusic.com; 2955 Tylerton Rd., Tylerton, MD 21866) Hosts Sharryl Lindberg and LeRoy Friesen escaped D.C. several years ago and set up this unique waterside getaway, with its soft colors and peaceful ambience. Three guest rooms come with private baths. Gourmet breakfast is included, and a seafood dinner is available for an added $20 (plan on it—there's no dinner-hour restaurant in Tylerton). Canoes, a kayak, bikes. Moderate. No credit cards. No handicapped access.

Ruke's (410-425-2311; 20840 Caleb Jones Rd., Ewell) Don't pass up the opportunity to eat a crab cake or soft-shell crab here at Ewell's longtime general store, maybe even out on the deck. Locals drop by for coffee, and you can find a few antiques and ice cream, too. Open in summer daily, 11–5 and 6–8; in winter, Mon. through Sat. 11–4. Inexpensive to moderate.

Tangier Island

Clamber aboard a "tour buggy," one of the fleet of golf carts lined up to meet the tour boats, and take a tour of the island, which includes a 3-mile beach on the far side.

Six gift shops with sensible names like Jim's and Wanda's reside along Tangier's main street, where visitors can buy souvenirs like T-shirts and shell wreaths. Hours conform to the tour boat schedule: about 10:30–4 from spring through fall, when tour boats operate. They reopen in the evening so the townspeople can shop. **Sandy's** (757-891-2367; 16227 Main St.) has a small museum in the back of the store. Among the treasures: notebooks bulging with newspaper clippings of Tangier events, such as engagements, going back generations. Shelves are full of island memorabilia. Visitors also can rent a bike from the **Waterfront Restaurant** (757-891-2248; 16125 Main Ridge Rd.) or from **Wanda's** (757-891-2255; 16139 Main Ridge Rd.).

Food and Lodging

Fisherman's Corner Restaurant (757-891-2900; 4419 Long Bridge Rd., Tangier Island, VA 23440) Operated by three island women, this homey restaurant serves the kind of indigenous seafood people travel a lifetime to find. Soft-shells, crab claws, crab cakes, and other Bay specialties available. Inexpensive to moderate. Open May through Sept.

Hilda Crockett's Chesapeake House (757-891-2331; 16243 Main Ridge Rd./P.O. Box 232, Tangier Island, VA 23440) Family-style seating at this island institution, open daily 11:30–5 from Apr. 15 through Oct. 15. Breakfast is available 7–9. Inexpensive. Also, there's lodging here, eight rooms that have recently been updated ($100 double occupancy; $80 for single occupancy, including breakfast and dinner). MC, V. No alcohol or pets.

Shirley's Bay View Inn (757-891-2396; www.tangierisland.net; P.O. Box 309, Tangier Island, VA 23440) Walking distance to gift shops, beach, and airport. In all, nine "cottages" in back and two rooms in the main house. Two cottages are family cottages, with one full, one twin, and bunk beds. Enjoy the gazebo and look out toward the water. Full breakfast. Moderate to expensive. MC, V accepted; no pets. The innkeepers will pick you up at the boat.

Sunset Inn (757-891-2535; www.tangierislandsunset.com; 16650 W. Ridge Rd., Tangier Island, VA 23440) Next to the island's 3-mile beach. Ten rooms in an addition, four inside the house with decks overlooking the water. Fridges in room. Continental breakfast. Moderate. Owner Grace Brown will pick you up at the boat. Major credit cards; personal checks OK.

Waterfront Restaurant (757-891-2248; 16125 Main Ridge Rd., Tangier Island, VA 23440) You can't miss it, right where the tour boats come in. Sit at a picnic table and enjoy soft-shells and crab cakes. Open May through Oct. Inexpensive to moderate. No credit cards; personal checks OK.

The Hope & Glory Inn resides in a former Irvington schoolhouse.

7

NORTHERN NECK/MIDDLE PENINSULA

Virginia's Treasures: Rambling Roads and a Home to History

The side street along Urbanna Creek dead-ends near a marina. We pulled in, parked, and figured we'd find out whether we could rent a boat. Just then, a fellow pulling a red wagon carrying a battered old battery trundled by. "Excuse us," we said. "Do you know where we can rent a small boat around here for tomorrow?" He stopped. "Well," he responded. "I have a paddleboat you could borrow."

For all of their abundant U.S. history, Virginia's rural tidewater peninsulas seem most remarkable because the people are just so disarmingly *nice*—from the lifelong locals who trace their roots back to the founding settlers to recently arrived retirees. Visitors can easily navigate the area simply by asking.

Chesapeake tributaries bound the Northern Neck and Middle Peninsula, the first, just below Maryland, is defined by the Potomac and Rappahannock rivers; the second is bounded by the Rappahannock and York rivers. Besides the upper Northern Neck birthplaces of George Washington and Robert E. Lee (James Madison was born here, too), perhaps the peninsula's best-known landmark has been the Tides Inn, a Northern Neck resort launched just after World War II.

At the top of the Northern Neck lies **Colonial Beach**, a former casino and steamboat town with a thin Potomac River beach located near the birthplaces of Washington and Lee. Their ancestral homes, Popes Creek Plantation and Stratford Hall, sit close to one another, evidence of the deep colonial roots both families set here. Indeed, their descendants and those of many other early families remain.

The original Popes Creek house is long gone, destroyed by fire, but the memorial house there is lovely and you won't find finer waterside grounds for a picnic. Stately brick Stratford Hall, built in 1723 by Thomas Lee, where his pair of Declaration of Independence–signing sons lived and descendant Robert E. was born, is well worth touring to see the wood-paneled Great Hall and its view across the bluffs to the Potomac. Montross, home to the plant that bottles Northern Neck Ginger Ale (try some—you can taste the ginger!), is the "big city" hereabouts.

From here, the road rambles to peninsula's end. Fields stretch for miles, and crossroads towns dating to colonial times hold a handful of houses or the local courthouse.

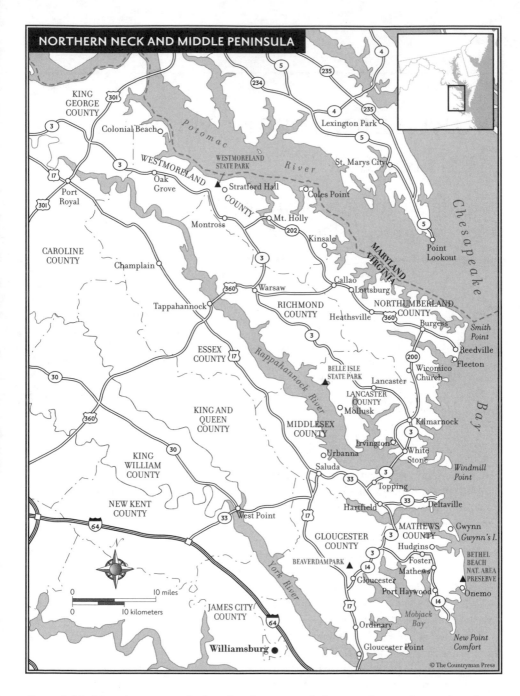

NORTHERN NECK AND MIDDLE PENINSULA

Remarkably historic spots can be found in these out-of-the-way places, where colonial founders like the Washingtons, Lees, and Balls went to church and lived out their lives before their descendants became well-known to time. Throughout the peninsula, the famously endless creeks of the Chesapeake Bay tuck in, sometimes bearing a marina with a home-style seafood restaurant where it's hard to go wrong on cuisine.

The Mary Ball Washington Museum in Lancaster is named for George Washington's mother.

At the end of the Northern Neck where the Potomac empties into the Bay stands **Reedville.** No, you haven't stumbled upon a New England village, despite the white-picket-fence Main Street lined with stately Victorian homes once called "Millionaire's Row." Yankees in search of new menhaden fishing grounds moved here, founding the local fishery in the latter half of the 19th century. Fishermen should plan to join a charter into the rich Chesapeake fishing grounds nearby.

Farther south, on the Rappahannock side of the peninsula, the villages of **Lancaster Courthouse, Kilmarnock, Irvington,** and **White Stone** cluster near one another (well, as near as you get in this land of rambling rural roads), offering amenities for visitors seeking comfort, history, and maybe some fun on the water. The Mary Ball Washington Museum in Lancaster, named for George Washington's mother, who was born nearby, includes a genealogical library. Closer to Irvington stands the famed colonial Christ Church, built in the 1730s and financed by the Northern Neck's colonial baron, planter Robert "King" Carter. His name is still invoked here, where folks know their roots. Irvington has been rediscovered in recent years, as have other parts of the area, and with that has come the arrival of upscale shops and ambience.

Across the Rappahannock lies **Urbanna,** one of Bay Country's most delightful towns, established in 1680 as a customs port by the colonial Virginia government and beloved by cruisers. With its 18th-century brick buildings and cluster of good restaurants, it retains a vigorous year-round community—525 people strong. Down the highway stands **Deltaville,** with its boaters, and closer to the Bay is rural Mathews County, with its courthouse town called **Mathews.** Among the county's creative surprises is the Poddery, a tucked-away pottery operated by a couple named Podd with a rambling wood showroom displaying Chesapeake marine life in stoneware.

On the far side of the lower Middle Peninsula, getting on toward the York River and the cradle of American colonialism, is Gloucester County, first settled about 1644. This was tobacco country, with magnificent plantations—some now converted to inn status for modern visitors. Be sure to visit the small brick Historic District at **Gloucester,** and consider coming in April for the Daffodil Festival, which hails a floral resident that arrived with early English settlers in the 1600s and spawned an industry that remains much in evidence come spring.

LODGING

From renovated watermen's homes to drop-dead gorgeous colonial estates, Virginia's Bay Country offers delightful B&Bs and small inns. Prices tend to be highest during weekends in the height of the season, lower during the week, and even lower during the off-season. Two-night minimums may be required during the high season, and cancellation policies may be in effect. If you're traveling with Fluffy and your inn says no to pets, as most do, your innkeeper may be able to recommend a nearby kennel. Ask about other policies that can change; these and packages may be noted on an inn's website.

Lodging rates, based on high-season prices, fall within this scale:

Inexpensive:	Up to $75
Moderate:	$75 to $120
Expensive:	$120 to $175
Very expensive:	$175 and up

Credit card abbreviations are:

AE—American Express
CB—Carte Blanche
DC—Diners Club
D—Discover
MC—MasterCard
V—Visa

Northern Neck

COLONIAL BEACH
THE BELL HOUSE BED & BREAKFAST
Innkeepers: Anne and Phil Bolin.
804-224-7000.
www.thebellhouse.com.
821 Irving Ave., Colonial Beach, VA 22443.
Price: Moderate to expensive.
Credit Cards: No.
Handicapped Access: No.
Restrictions: No children.

Alexander Graham Bell's family summer home, built by a Civil War general's son in 1882, offers soaring Victorian peaks and widow's walks that open onto the Potomac River, 30 miles from the Chesapeake Bay. This former casino town retains an old-style, beachy feel, with a few local seafood places. The Bell House maintains a bygone sensibility, too, with lots of original stained glass topping its windows. Four rooms, all with attached baths, offer queen-size beds. In a couple, fireplace mantels have become headboards, an Art Nouveau mirror topping one. Look up through a glass ceiling panel in the third floor to see how the pointed wood cupola was built. Upstairs is a library with local history and fiction. Full breakfast.

KINSALE
THE SKIPJACK INN
Innkeeper: Sharon Tomochak-Owen.
804-472-2044.
www.portkinsale.com.
Port Kinsale Marina and Resort, 347 Allen Point Ln./P.O. Box 280, Kinsale, VA 22488.
Price: Moderate to expensive.
Credit Cards: AE, D, MC, V.
Handicapped Access: No.
Special Features: Children and pets OK in the cottage.

Flowerpots hang from the front porch at this rescued oysterman's home on the Yeocomico River at Port Kinsale Marina, fresh with a white coat of paint and black shutters. Inside, visitors find wood-planked floors and Victorian furniture in the downstairs parlor, and four comfortable rooms with new baths. Three are named for skipjacks; they're upstairs. The green Virginia W comes with a queen-size bed and great water views; the HM Krenz comes with two quilt-covered twin beds; and the blue Wilma Lee has a white and brass bed. Another room with a private entrance recently has been added on the first floor. One of the nice things about the Skipjack Inn is the updated but old-style feel. Continental breakfast served; bikes and other marina amenities available. Thin beaches line the riverside, and the marina restaurant stays open into winter. Also here: the contemporary waterside Oyster Reef Cottage ($250 a night), with accommodations for two couples—and their pets.

LANCASTER
INN AT LEVELFIELDS

Innkeepers: John Dunn and Charlotte Hollings.
804-435-6887 or 1-800-238-5578.
www.innatlevelfields.com or www.calm
watersrowing.com.
10155 Mary Ball Rd., Lancaster, VA 22503.
Price: Moderate to expensive.
Credit Cards: MC, V.
Handicapped Access: No.
Special Features: Kids and pets OK with prior approval.

This landmark antebellum home north of Lancaster Courthouse is now headquarters for a rowing school, although anyone is welcome to stay here. An impressive 1,000-foot drive leads to ancient English boxwoods hedging the front walk, and the home's interior is classically furnished in keeping with the Georgian style, even though the house was built in 1857. Four upstairs rooms boast 7-foot showers and high ceilings, and three large, brick-walled rooms have been added downstairs. The inn's owners are the former women's varsity crew coach at Cornell University and

his wife, a former world rowing champion. Rowers come for vacations of varying duration at Calm Waters Rowing and head down the street to the 80-acre Camps Millpond by early morning to begin their day.

REEDVILLE
THE GABLES

Innkeepers: Barbara and Norman Clark.
804-453-5209.
www.thegablesbb.com.
859 Main St./P.O. Box 148, Reedville, VA 22539.
Price: Moderate to very expensive.
Credit Cards: AE, D, MC, V.
Handicapped Access: No.
Restrictions: No children under 13.

Built by one Capt. Fisher, former schooner captain and early partner in Reedville's booming menhaden industry, the Gables is endlessly interesting to architecture buffs. Fisher erected one of his schooner's three masts through the home's third and fourth floors, and guests will find cypress flooring in one bathroom—the better for the captain to recall his days at sea. Two guest rooms are available inside the Gables, and recent renovations to the next-door carriage house have added four more rooms. Called the Coach House Inn at the Gables, it offers three rooms with vaulted ceilings upstairs, one overlooking the creek out back. All have attached bathrooms. Whether guests stay in the house or the carriage house, they will be able to tour the house. The Gables sits at the foot of Reedville's Main Street, and an ice cream/coffee shop on the first floor of the Coach House is open seasonally.

IRVINGTON
THE HOPE AND GLORY INN

Co-owners: Bill Westbrook and Peggy Patteson.
804-438-6053 or 1-800-497-8228.
www.hopeandglory.com.
65 Tavern Road/P.O. Box 425, Irvington, VA 22480.

Price: Expensive to very expensive.
Credit Cards: AE, MC, V.
Handicapped Access: No.
Restrictions: Children and pets in the cottages only.

This inn hits a perfect note of hip whimsy, particularly with its outdoor bath tucked behind a high stockade fence, complete with a claw-foot tub and a big, sunflower-size shower head. You'll find it after rounding the garden path out back amid six cottages, folk-art birdhouses, and a ballerina sculpture. The former schoolhouse, circa 1890, is enormous fun, with unexpected touches throughout, from a green-and-white lobby floor to a white picket fence used as a headboard in one of the rooms. The seven rooms are all different. Among our favorites: a tiny study in white with a huge gilded mirror. The bathrooms tend more toward functional than fancy, but it all works. Guests find easygoing comfort, like overstuffed furniture and a TV in a sitting area downstairs. Managing partner Peggy Patteson spent many years as an executive at the nearby Tides Inn and knows the territory. An upscale, well-recognized inn. Cruises every Sat. Coffee and muffins are out early; full breakfast served. The inn also has 10 three-bedroom cottages and a pool available at a nearby site that includes kayaking and a vineyard.

THE TIDES INN

Owner: Sedona Resort Management.
804-438-5000 or 1-800-843-3746.
www.tidesinn.com.
King Carter Dr., Irvington, VA 22480.
Price: Very expensive.
Credit Cards: AE, CB, D, MC, V.
Handicapped Access: Yes.
Special Features: Pets allowed in certain rooms for extra charge.

The venerable *Miss Ann*, a symbol of the Tides Inn, remains the grand dame of local waterways even though her home of many

Beautiful gardens line the back of The Tides Inn near its spa.

years recently underwent a $14 million renovation by Sedona Resorts, which purchased the property a few years ago from the family that ran it for three generations. Updates include makeovers to the resort's 103 rooms, which run up the luxury and size scale and are now dressed in British colonial decor, with plantation shutters, Old Dominion–label ginger ale, and CD players/radios. Many also have patios or balconies, most with water views. Four restaurants are on-site, including the more casual Chesapeake Club (see "Restaurants"), although Virginia gentlemen also can don their suit jackets and enjoy a meal at the Dining Room. There's also a marina, the Golden Eagle Golf Club (see "Recreation"), a spa, tennis, fitness rooms, a gorgeous pool alongside Carter's Creek, a small beach, and bikes for guests to use. S'mores are cooked on the beach for kids on Fri. and Sat. night. A variety of packages are available, as well as per-night fees.

Middle Peninsula

CHAMPLAIN, NEAR TAPPAHANNOCK
LINDEN HOUSE BED & BREAKFAST PLANTATION

Owners: Ken and Sandy Pounsberry.
804-443-1170 or 1-866-887-0286.

www.lindenplantation.com.
VA 17 S/P.O. Box 23, Champlain, VA 22438.
Price: Expensive.
Credit Cards: D, MC, V.
Handicapped Access: Partial.
Restrictions: No children under 12.

Bluegill, bass, and catfish live in the sizable fish pond dug by the Pounsberrys, evidence of the industry your hosts bring to this former plantation. This 1750s planter's home, located 8 miles north of the Rappahannock River crossroads town of Tappahannock, is inspiring. Guests will find two suites and five rooms, including two with an upstairs balcony in a new-ish carriage house. Upstairs in the old home (with its two fine porches), the Davis Room exemplifies the accommodations, with a fireplace mantel discovered in pieces in the old barn and a whirlpool in the bath just steps from the bedroom door. Everything about this inn seems thoughtful and well considered, from a decision to incorporate the existing columns into a sunroom to the footpaths on the 200-acre spread. Breakfast in the old part of the house is plentiful, and the service most gracious and warm. Dinner by request. A retreat unto itself.

URBANNA
ATHERSTON HALL
Owner: Phyllis G. Hall.
804-758-2809.
250 Prince George St./P.O. Box 757,
Urbanna, VA 23175.
Price: Moderate.
Credit Cards: No; checks OK.
Handicapped Access: Partial; call to discuss.
Restrictions: Inquire about children.

Lots of B&Bs come with antiques—a walnut dresser from here, a mahogany armoire from there—but how many boast a box in the hallway that was once the backpack for a samurai's armor? Four rooms here include two rooms sharing one floor and one bath. They're on the second floor

of this 19th-century home; one has twin beds and one an antique rice bed once owned by Gen. John Hunt Morgan of Morgan's Raiders. Atherston Hall tends toward a "home stay," but you're in the midst of one of Chesapeake's most lovely and uncluttered historical towns. In the new section of the house, visitors will find two modern rooms with queen beds, attached baths, and individual entries. Full breakfast; bicycles available. Public pool and tennis courts nearby.

MATHEWS COUNTY
BUCKLEY HALL INN
Innkeepers: Beth and Gerald Lewis.
804-725-1900 or 1-888-450-9145.
www.buckleyhall.com.
11293 Buckley Hall Rd. (VA 198)/P.O. Box 125, Mathews, VA 23109.
Price: Moderate.
Credit Cards: AE, D, MC, V.
Handicapped Access: No.
Special Features: Children welcome.

Stacks of books on the area's history sit on coffee tables in the comfortable parlor, its mantelpiece painted Williamsburg blue, and in back hallway shelves. Look them over here in this 1850 Mathews Courthouse home at what was once Buchleigh Farm. Four rooms are named for area points of

The poolside cottage at the Inn at Tabb's Creek Landing.

interest, and their decor ranges widely, from the romantic New Point Comfort Room to the nautically themed Cobbs Creek Room with twin beds. New bathrooms adjoin each room. Plus, your hosts are no strangers to the community and can advise on local activities and points of interest. Full breakfast.

An 1850 Mathews Courthouse home has been transformed into the Buckley Hall Inn.

INN AT TABB'S CREEK LANDING

Innkeepers: Erin and Bill Rogers.
804-725-5136.
384 Turpin Lane/P.O. Box 369, Port Haywood, VA 23138.
Price: Moderate to expensive.
Credit Cards: MC, V.
Handicapped Access: No.
Special Features: Children welcome.

Looking for a good place to raise their kids, Erin and Bill Rogers purchased this long-time inn upon their return from a career overseas. Guests will find plenty of hospitality here along Tabb's Creek. In all, seven rooms are available, four in the main house, furnished with antiques and other items collected in Asia and Europe. A pool and English gardens stand between the house and a cottage, where two suites and a room carry on the comfort. Enjoy the

Dalmatians marching amid yellow tulips along one suite's painted border, or the fire-engine-red room studded in Coca-Cola memorabilia—a good choice for kids. Settle into a comfortable seat looking out on Tabb's Creek from the screened-in porch, or head right out to the deck to take in some sun. Paddleboat and canoe available for guests. Full breakfast.

GLOUCESTER
AIRVILLE PLANTATION

Innkeepers: Kathie and Larry Cohen.
804-694-0287.
www.airvilleplantation.com.
6423 T. C. Walker Rd., Gloucester, VA 23061.
Price: Moderate to expensive.
Credit Cards: No; personal checks OK.
Handicapped Access: No.
Special Features: Kids 13 and older OK; dockage 6–6.5 feet.

A pair of eagle-topped columns flanks the entry to the long plantation drive leading to the stately white home that was built in two stages: the first in 1756, the second in 1840. Four gorgeous marble mantelpieces are among the interesting architectural details in the house, where two guest rooms are located in an upstairs wing. Traditionally decorated, they're spacious, upscale, and warmed by working fireplaces. Since a single bathroom serves both rooms, they're rented one at a time unless traveling companions choose to stay here—in which case the rate is discounted $10. In back of the main house stand several dependencies, including one used by guests. You'll be tempted to settle in for the winter in the cozy cottage, which has a kitchen and woodstove on the first floor and a fireplace upstairs. The stunning 400-plus-acre property is gently rolling or wooded, and guests may very well spot turkey, fox, and deer. The Cohens can pick up guests arriving at the waterfront dock. A pool out front

Innkeeper Kathie Cohen at historic Airville Plantation, which sits on 400-plus acres in Gloucester, Virginia.

is attended by a cabana, converted from the plantation's unique former icehouse. Full breakfast.

INN AT WARNER HALL

Innkeepers: Theresa and Troy Stavens.
804-695-9565 or 1-800-331-2720.
www.warnerhall.com.
4750 Warner Hall Rd., Gloucester, VA 23061.
Price: Expensive to very expensive.
Credit Cards: AE, D, MC, V.
Handicapped Access: Yes.
Restrictions: Children 8 and older only.

A massive renovation restored the Colonial Revival mansion located at George Washington's great-great-grandfather's 17th-century plantation, culminating in a classy inn full of modern creature comforts that surely make this one of the Bay's best. Eleven rooms are painted chic colors and/or swathed in gorgeous Shumacher fabrics and wallpapers, with four-poster (or similarly luxe) beds covered by down comforters and featherbeds. Furnishings tend toward reproductions, although surprises may be in store, such as a pair of antique Chinese wooden chairs. Ceilings reach 10

feet, whirlpool baths or fireplaces make lounging fun, and Virginia's Severn River stretches out before many windows. As with most ancient homes, fire and fate have conspired to destroy old parts of the house, resulting in construction from varied periods. Much of this inn—the center hall—dates to 1895–1903. However, the old plantation school in the east wing, where two guest rooms stand, dates to sometime between 1690 and 1720. (Augustine Warner, George's great-great-grandfather, would have been at this property earlier than that.) Tuck into the comfortably renovated boathouse along the Severn (named the same as the river that flows past the Naval Academy in Annapolis) for an afternoon, or take a kayak out for a paddle. With a five-course tasting dinner served beneath a crystal chandelier in the dining room on Fri. and Sat., breakfast on the glass veranda out back, and supper baskets available Sun. through Thurs., guests may find little reason to stir from the 38-acre grounds. Prix fixe dinner for guests or the general public; complimentary bikes and kayaks available for guests.

NORTH RIVER INN

Innkeepers: Mary and Breck Montague.
804-693-1616 or 1-877-248-3030.
www.northriverinn.com.
P.O. Box 695, Gloucester, VA 23061.
Price: Expensive to very expensive.
Credit Cards: MC, V.
Handicapped Access: No.
Special Features: Children under 12 accommodated in Toddsbury Cottage.

Bay Country is full of old estates, but rarely do mere mortals get to enjoy those dating back to the days of early royal grants. North River Inn, composed of three fine 20th-century outbuildings at the 17th-century estate known as Toddsbury, is a rare exception. This is an outstanding waterside option for folks looking to escape to another time.

Drive down a long, maple-lined lane to reach the property. The Toddsbury Cottage sleeps five, although many romance seekers have taken advantage of its luxe bedroom, screened porch, and privacy. The Creek House offers four guest accommodations, some with French doors opening onto the water. The small brick Toddsbury Guest House boasts built-in shelves packed with Virginia and maritime history and a fireplace in the cozy, wood-paneled living room downstairs. The upstairs bedroom overlooks the North River, and the bed's done up with a floral chintz canopy and bed skirt. Continental breakfast is served during the week, and a full country breakfast on weekends. The Montague family, which owns the inn, resides in the estate house on the property.

Hotels/Motel

Best Western (804-333-1700; 4522 Richmond Rd., Warsaw, VA 22572) Thirty-eight rooms, one luxury suite, two executive suites. Inexpensive to expensive.

Comfort Inn (804-695-1900; 6639 Forest Hill Ave., Gloucester, VA 23061) Seventy-nine rooms located just off VA 17. Continental breakfast. Whirlpool, fridges, microwaves available. Moderate.

Deltaville Dockside Inn (804-776-9224; US 33/P.O. Box 710, Deltaville, VA 23043) Twenty-three rooms, efficiencies with small refrigerators and microwaves. The only motel around this part of the Middle Peninsula. Inexpensive.

Holiday Inn Express (804-436-1500 or 1-800-844-0124; 599 N. Main St., Kilmarnock, VA 22482) Sixty-eight rooms, including some suites. Moderate.

St. Andrews Motel (formerly Whispering Pines Motel); (804-435-1101; 226 Methodist Church Rd., White Stone, VA 22578) Quiet, centrally located on VA 3 a half mile north of White Stone. Has 29 rooms, a swimming pool, coffee and doughnuts in the morning. Inexpensive to moderate.

RESTAURANTS

We were talking with the curator at one of the area's small museums one day when a man came in to tell her he had some fish available. Rockfish, that is—striped bass. Put it in a pan with onions, potatoes, and bacon, cover it all with aluminum foil, and put it in the oven. It's some good eating, and a recipe with which we were unfamiliar. There seem to be a few Virginia twists on Chesapeake food once you get down this way, such as Gwynn's Island clam chowder, which makes ample use of the clam juice. Count on a range of restaurants to serve good local seafood.

Price ranges, which include dinner entrée, appetizer, and dessert, are as follows:

Inexpensive:	Up to $20
Moderate:	$20 to $30
Expensive:	$30 to $40
Very expensive:	$40 or more

Credit card abbreviations are:
AE—American Express
CB—Carte Blanche
DC—Diners Club
D—Discover
MC—MasterCard
V—Visa

The following abbreviations are used to denote meals served:
B = Breakfast; L = Lunch; D = Dinner;
SB = Sunday Brunch

Northern Neck

COLONIAL BEACH
WILKERSON'S SEAFOOD RESTAURANT
804-224-7117.
3900 McKinney Blvd.
Open: Daily at 11:30 AM.
Price: Moderate.

Cuisine: Chesapeake-style seafood.
Serving: L, D.
Credit Cards: AE, D, MC, V.
Reservations: Not necessary.
Handicapped Access: Yes.

This longtime, family-owned staple on the upper Northern Neck boasts a blue-ribbon view of the Potomac River and Maryland across the way, and lots of old-fashioned seafood dishes. You can even order frog legs. Seafood such as flounder or soft-shell crabs comes broiled or fried, and there's a seafood buffet Fri. through Sun. Prices are quite reasonable, although if you're starved you can spend up to $23.95 on a seafood combo platter. Your waitress arrives to take your order with a huge treat for folks from north of the border: well-made, authentic Southern hush puppies.

KINSALE
GOOD EATS CAFÉ
804-472-4385.
VA 202 and VA 203.
Open: Thurs. through Sun.; closed mid-Dec. through Mar.
Price: Moderate.
Cuisine: New American, updated Chesapeake.
Serving: D.
Credit Cards: MC, V.
Reservations: Accepted for groups of 8 or more only.
Handicapped Access: Yes.

Here we have a genuine off-the-beaten-track gem shining a bit brighter than most because everything about it is a surprise—down to the fact that it's even here. Former big-city chefs Steve Andersen and Sally Rumsey, he with credits in kitchens ranging from French to New American and she with a Johnson & Wales degree, opened this Northern Neck restaurant in a former gas station several years ago. With lit stars in the windows and orange and yellow faux-painted walls, there's nothing overtly

Chesapeake-y about Good Eats except for the local seafood dishes on the menu. Rosemary breadsticks arrive with each meal, and entrées include "Familiar Eats" like blackened prime rib or crab cakes and "New Favorites" such as fennel-spiced salmon in Thai red curry sauce. When it's time for the made-from-scratch "Sweet Eats," think about a mudslide. Yowza! Rich and wonderful coconut-covered ice cream in a cinnamon-tinged Mexican cajeta sauce is better than a Mounds bar on steroids. Like the menu, the café is tinged with a hipster, back-on-the-heels kind of style. A nice change of pace, or a useful transition if you're stopping by en route back to real life in the city.

HEATHSVILLE
RICE'S HOTEL/HUGHLETT'S TAVERN
804-580-7900.
73 Monument Pl.
Open: Tues. through Sat.
Price: Expensive to very expensive.
Cuisine: Progressive American.
Serving: L, D.
Credit Cards: MC, V.
Reservations: Suggested on weekends.
Handicapped Access: Yes.

Dining in one of Virginia's antique taverns offers a unique glimpse back in time, and this one, in the tiny, out-of-the-way colonial courthouse town of Heathsville, is no different. The building was enthusiastically renovated by local citizens some years back, so diners can see the low ceilings and small dining rooms that reflect the late 18th-century era when the tavern was built. Just as happily, the food is well-executed by Chef Branden Levine, who has a decidedly 21st-century approach to cooking. Indeed, traditional game pie, peanut soup, and spoon bread are nowhere to be found on this un-colonial menu. Instead, you might find seared scallops with French lentils and olive oil—poached tomatoes, or braised lamb shank osso buco with dried summer fruit, roasted vegetables, and garlic on goat cheese polenta with a basil-mint gremulata. On a recent visit, a delectable sandwich of crab and lobster cake arrived with a bun that clearly had spent time under the broiler and a garnish of lemon-caper aioli. One table over, two ladies were heard cooing over the grilled portobello on focaccia. Contemporary cuisine in colonial surroundings: here's a delightful blend of old and new. Fancy lunch sandwiches and the midday menu are reasonably priced.

REEDVILLE
TOMMY'S RESTAURANT
804-453-4666.
729 Main St.
Open: Wed., Thurs., and Sun. 5:30–9; Fri. and Sat. until 10.
Price: Inexpensive to expensive.
Cuisine: Steaks and seafood.
Serving: D.
Credit Cards: MC, V.
Reservations: Recommended on weekends.
Handicapped Access: Yes.

Reedville's turn-of-the-19th-century mercantile has been a restaurant for some years now, taken over by Tommy Crowther soon after this century began. Decor with a nod to the area's nautical and agricultural roots dominates the spacious interior, while

Tommy's Restaurant is a popular stop in Reedville.

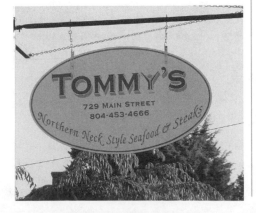

homegrown Northern Neck know-how goes into the cooking, nudged up a tad. Ergo, you'll find a rockfish cooked with bacon, potatoes, and onion, as is traditional in Virginia's Chesapeake Country. Crowther even sears steaks in a 500-degree pan before they go in the oven, the cast-iron skillet being a utensil that dates to his childhood. Indeed, Crowther grew up nearby and got his early training in New Orleans. Cars were already pulling into the parking lot one summer evening before the 5:30 opening of this popular restaurant, which has a glass porch with water views in-season.

KILMARNOCK
CARRIED AWAY CUISINE
804-435-9191.
10 N. Main St.
Open: Tues. through Sat. in-season; Wed. through Sat. off-season.
Price: Inexpensive.
Cuisine: Varied, bistro New American.
Serving: B, L, take-out D.
Credit Cards: MC, V.
Reservations: No.
Handicapped Access: Yes.

A vase of sunflowers atop the food case and pressed-tin ceilings overhead set a nice backdrop for a terrific takeout and catering spot, replete with a few small tables if you want to sit down for lunch. During a recent late-summer meal, the blue crab and corn chowder was among the best crab soup iterations we've ever tried, and trust us—we've tried a lot. Points to the creative kitchen for taking full advantage of the area's seasonal best. A definite best bet.

IRVINGTON
CHESAPEAKE CLUB AT THE TIDES INN
804-438-5000 or 1-800-843-3746.
480 King Carter Dr.
Open: Daily.
Price: Moderate to expensive.
Cuisine: Bistro, seafood.

Serving: L, D.
Credit Cards: AE, DC, D, MC, V.
Reservations: Recommended; not necessary for lunch.
Handicapped Access: Yes.

For dining at The Tides Inn, your choices include the formal Dining Room and the more casual Chesapeake Club. The latter, with its plantation shutters and British colonial style, looks out toward the fabled Carter's Creek. Soft-shell crabs are done in a tempura butter, the rockfish has been known to be delectable, and a panfried oyster appetizer comes with a little kick. For dessert, ditch the calorie counter and consider the triple chocolate brownie with chocolate syrup and ice cream. Or go easy on yourself with the crème brûlée.

THE TRICK DOG CAFÉ
804-438-1055.
4357 Irvington Rd.
Open: Tues. through Sun.
Price: Expensive.
Cuisine: Updated American.
Serving: D Tues. through Sat.; SB.
Credit Cards: AE, DC, MC, V.
Reservations: Recommended, especially on weekends.
Handicapped Access: Yes.

The Trick Dog has been open for a few years now, but it's still quite likely the Northern Neck's hottest restaurant. In the kitchen from the beginning has been Chef Joe Merolli. Chic and modern, the Trick Dog features a stunning, well-attended bar with an ambitious Scotch selection. The menu changes four times a year and offers reliables such as steak au poive (New York strip, of course) and lump-meat crab cakes. But a Moroccan-spiced lamb loin and eggplant rollatini for vegetarians also may appear amid the entrées, and the fried calamari appetizer, served with tarragon remoulade, has many fans. Desserts include a molten chocolate cake as well as a

crème brûlée. The citified dining room has expanded by about a quarter with the patio's enclosure, and ambitious plans for the wine list promise flights of reds available in winter.

ROCKET BILLY'S
804-435-7040.
851 Rappahannock Ave.
Open: Mon. through Sat. 6:30 AM–3 PM.
Price: Inexpensive.
Cuisine: Local seafood, barbecue.
Serving: B, L.
Credit Cards: No; local checks accepted.
Reservations: N/A.
Handicapped Access: If necessary, they'll bring your food to your car.

Rain pelted furiously the morning we awoke early in White Stone's lone highway motel, the day's first foggy thought floating to mind: where to get good coffee? Ah, surely at Rocket Billy's. A bright red-and-white-striped canopy protects the 8-by-16 Wells Cargo trailer takeout stop from the elements, and the breakfast crowd was huddled beneath. Given the fine fried oysters here, we gambled on a salt trout breakfast specialty, if only to live like a local. You have to admit, this breaded and fried item is the sort of thing that should be limited in a daily diet. But the authenticity speaks to other seafood here: fresh oysters, fish, crab cakes, and curried seafood bisque. One local man huddled beneath the canopy called the steak and onions the best thing on the menu, while a local woman said, simply, "Everything"—including the prices. Eat up!

Middle Peninsula

BOATHOUSE CAFÉ
804-758-0080.
25 Cross St. (at Dozier's Port Urbanna Marina).
Open: Tues. through Sun.

Price: Moderate to expensive.
Cuisine: New American, seafood.
Serving: L, D, SB.
Credit Cards: MC, V.
Reservations: Accepted Labor Day through
Memorial Day; reservations for 8 or more
accepted during the summer.
Handicapped Access: Yes.

A hurricane blew through the former
Texaco fuel dock where the Boathouse Café
briefly held funky-but-stylish court in both
atmosphere and cuisine, hastening a
planned move around the corner. Now
quartered on Urbanna Creek behind
Dozier's Marina, the dining room is far
more grown-up and spacious, with an
artistic entry provided by a raised octagon
structure topped with stained glass. Picnic
tables on a front deck provide a more casual
place to eat. Fresh ingredients go into the
meals here, and the results have the locals
talking—as well as *Southern Living*, which
once named the Boathouse its favorite
seafood restaurant in Virginia. Three culinary school graduates rotate through the
kitchen here and at the Boathouse's
Deltaville location on Timberneck Rd.,
adding basil-lemon mayo to the shrimp
salad and browning and baking sea scallops
in chardonnay before topping them with
Asiago cheese. Tie up if you've sailed or
motored in and enjoy.

Deltaville
TOBY'S
804-776-6913.
220 Jack's Place Rd.
Open: Daily year-round; bar opens at 3 PM,
dinner starts at 5 PM.
Price: Moderate.
Cuisine: American.
Serving: D.
Credit Cards: MC, V.
Reservations: Suggested on weekends and
holidays.
Handicapped Access: Yes.

Special Features: Provides free shuttle
transportation to/from local marinas.

Toby's front room is painted an inviting
persimmon, and its linen-covered tables
adorned with fresh flowers. Its prices are
well within reason, and seafood is a specialty. The menu offers it all, from jumbo
lump crab cakes to scallops and shrimp to
tuna. Warm, soft bread, baked daily on the
premises, is served while the entrées are
being prepared, and a good selection of
"small plates" for smaller appetites is also
available. If anyone still has room, taste-
tempting desserts are made in-house.

Gwynn's Island
SEABREEZE RESTAURANT
804-725-4000.
384 Old Ferry Rd.
Open: Year-round; closed Mon. and at
2 PM Sun.
Price: Inexpensive to moderate.
Cuisine: Local seafood.
Serving: B, L, D.
Credit Cards: No.
Reservations: No.
Handicapped Access: Yes.
Restrictions: No alcohol.

Here at the inner edge of Gwynn's Island,
just across Milford Haven via the Gwynn's
Island Bridge, the Seabreeze has held forth
since 1979. Prices still reflect those days,
what with the homemade hamburgers for
$2.50. But old-fashioned seafood is the
reason to visit, as well as some of the best
brewed iced tea you'll ever find. A fried
soft-crab sandwich costs $5.25; the most
expensive thing on the menu is an ambitious fried seafood platter that costs only
$13.95. Ask for a seat in the waterfront
room and enjoy down-home seafood, or
join the "family table" in front for conversation with fellow diners. If it's offered as a
special, order the indigenous Gwynn's
Island clam chowder, which has a clear
liquid clam juice base.

MATHEWS
SOUTHWIND CAFÉ
804-725-2766.
Church St.
Open: Tues. through Sat.; closed in Jan.
Price: Inexpensive to moderate.
Cuisine: Upscale home-style.
Serving: L Tues. through Sat.; D Thurs.
through Sat.
Credit Cards: MC, V.
Reservations: Not necessary.
Handicapped Access: Yes.

All of Mathews seems to gather here, with its hearth-baked pizzas, fresh salad (the buttermilk Parmesan dressing's a winner), a selection of creative sandwiches, home-made quiches, dinner pastas, and a killer mixed-berry pie in late summer. The former Lee Miles's general store, fronted by a small deck, boasts a homey feel and friendly service.

ORDINARY, NEAR GLOUCESTER
SEAWELL'S ORDINARY
804-642-3635.
3968 George Washington Memorial Hwy.
Open: Wed. through Sun.
Price: Moderate to expensive.
Cuisine: New American, seafood.
Serving: D; Sat. and Sun. brunch.
Credit Cards: AE, DC, D, MC, V.
Reservations: Required on weekends.
Handicapped Access: Partial.

Local lore contends that George Washington and the Marquis de Lafayette planned the encirclement of Lord Cornwallis at this 1757 tavern, known in colonial parlance as an ordinary. If true, students of U.S. history—which, fellow citizens, should mean all of you—know that this means Seawell's Ordinary could rightly be enshrined at the Smithsonian, since the Revolutionary War ended after Cornwallis was surrounded (and surrendered) down the road at Yorktown. Modern-day diners can enjoy updated cuisine at this fine on-the-road stop, perhaps even at a table next to a charred scar on the pine floor where Lafayette allegedly dropped his burning pipe one night. Specialty salads include the Ordinary Salad, with melted brie, toasted almonds, and sliced kiwi topped with sesame vinaigrette. Entrées include pretty takes on beef, seafood, and poultry and run from seafood strudel to oysters volcano. A children's menu offers clam strips, fried shrimp, and chicken fingers with fries for $8.95.

GLOUCESTER POINT
RIVER'S INN RESTAURANT AND CRAB DECK
804-642-9942 or 1-888-780-CRAB.
8109 Yacht Haven Dr.
Open: Daily except Mon. from Oct. through Mar.
Price: Moderate to expensive.
Cuisine: Regional seafood.
Serving: L, D, SB.
Credit Cards: AE, MC, V.
Reservations: Encouraged but not necessary.
Handicapped Access: Yes.

It's hard to imagine a lovelier summer afternoon than one spent on the expansive deck here along this York River tributary called Sarah Creek, historic because General Cornwallis occupied her fair shores during the Revolution. This is a popular stop for boaters, and a casual menu running to gussied-up sandwiches and salads, hard crabs, and raw bar items is served seasonally on the deck. Inside the yachty dining room, the fare slides up the scale a tad and includes a wine special. As for the food: Appetizers run from a grilled shrimp satay to sautéed escargot in a bread bowl. Eye-popping entrées include the Chesapeake Blue Plate, a meal of she-crab soup and Caesar salad followed by a crab cake, baked crabmeat imperial in a puff pastry, shrimp, and flash-fried oysters, all for $25. A children's menu respects the budding palate, with almond-crusted shrimp joining the usual chicken tenders and pasta. *Chesapeake Bay Magazine* readers voted this the most romantic restaurant on the Bay.

FOOD PURVEYORS

Farmers' Markets

The roadside farm stand is a way of life along Virginia's rural tidewater peninsula roads, just as it is elsewhere in Bay Country. You'll never forgive yourself if you don't stop for fresh sweet corn and tomatoes. Farmer's markets include the **Irvington Farmer's Market** on the Commons on King Carter Dr. Held 8 AM–noon the first Sat. of each month from Apr. through Dec., it features everything from herbs to flowers, baked goods to produce, art to jewelry.

Gourmet Shops and Cafes

Kelsick Gardens (804-693-6500; 6604 Main St., Gloucester) Wines, cheeses, gift baskets, gourmet foods. Lunch features panninis and wraps, or look for the occasional special—fabled fried chicken from the cook, Lottie, for example. Occasional Sun. wine tasting dinners. Open Mon. through Fri. 10–6, Sat. 10–5. A smaller version of Kelsick Gardens is located at 79 S. Main St. in Kilmarnock (804-435-1500).

The River Market (804-435-1725; 1 Rappahannock Dr., White Stone) The market specializes in such dinner treats as prime rib, steak tips and shrimp, mixed grill seafood, and more. You can't beat the price or the quality. Gourmet takeout; varied wine selection.

White Stone Wine and Cheese (804-435-2000; 572 Rappahannock Dr., White Stone) The Wine and Cheese, as it's called locally, offers eat-in dinner Wed. through Sat. featuring ambitious selections such as osso bucco and cod Virginia, in which the New England–identified fish is wrapped in Virginia ham and sautéed. Large wine selection, fresh baked baguettes, free wine tasting every Fri. from 4–7.

Seafood Markets

Captain's Choice Fresh and Frozen Seafood (804-435-6750; 839 Rappahannock Dr., White Stone) A good place to look for local seafood, located right before (or after) you cross the Rappahannock River.

Cockrell's Creek Seafood & Deli (804-453-6326; 567 Seaboard Rd., off Fleeton Rd. outside Reedville) Crab cakes and soft-shell sandwiches to go and a variety of other fresh seafood. Hard crabs. Closed Jan. through mid-Mar.

J&W Seafood (804-776-6400; US 33 E, Deltaville) Fresh seafood in this outpost fishing and sailing town. Hard crabs; peeler tanks in back. See "Recreation" for information about its tackle store.

Wineries

Ingleside Vineyards (804-224-8687; www.ipwine.com; 5872 Leedstown Rd., Oak Grove) Located near the "top" of the Northern Neck, the 75-acre winery is part of a 3,000-acre estate and was once a Civil War garrison and a courthouse. The Flemer family bottles sparkling wine (Virginia brut) as well as premium wines served in many local restaurants. Look for tastings and jazz at the winery, as well as the Blue Crab series of wines, part of Ingleside's Chesapeake Wine Co. label. Bring a picnic to enjoy in the courtyard; guided tours available. Wine and gift shop, too. Open Mon. through Sat. 10–5, Sun. noon–5.

CULTURE

Arts

Bay School Cultural Arts Center (804-725-1278; 279 Main St., Mathews) Community arts center offering a range of classes for kids and adults. Includes painting, drawing, and heritage crafts such as weaving and carving.

Historic Buildings and Sites

NEAR COLONIAL BEACH (WESTMORELAND COUNTY)
GEORGE WASHINGTON BIRTHPLACE NATIONAL MONUMENT
804-224-1732.
www.nps.gov/gewa.
1732 Popes Creek Rd., Colonial Beach; VA 3 to VA 204, 38 miles east of Fredericksburg.
Open: Daily 9–5.
Admission: $4; free for children 16 and under.

It didn't all start at Mount Vernon, as visitors here will soon discover. Colonial history and the Washington family headline the Popes Creek Plantation complex on Popes Creek off the Potomac River. The home where Washington was born burned in 1779, but archaeologists have outlined the footprint of the U-shaped house in oyster shells. The brick Memorial House here was built in 1931. A colonial garden stands alongside amid a gorgeous stand of cedars. The Washington family cemetery also remains, bearing the graves of Washington's father, grandfather, and great-grandfather. The 550-acre park has hiking trails, one of the most delightful waterside picnic areas around, a small beach enjoyed by bird-watchers (no swimming), and a visitor's center that shows a film about the plantation. Look for special holiday events, such as the Christmas program and George Washington's birthday celebration.

STRATFORD (WESTMORELAND COUNTY)
STRATFORD HALL PLANTATION
804-493-8038 or 804-493-8371.
www.stratfordhall.org.
485 Great House Rd., Stratford; 45 miles east of Fredericksburg on VA 214.
Open: Visitor's center, 9:30–4 daily; tours of the Great House from 11–4; other tours by appt.
Admission: Adults and children age 12 and older $10, seniors and active military $9, children 6–11 $5, children 5 and under free.

"Light Horse Harry" begat Robert E., the best-known member of the illustrious Lee family, who was born here. Their historic home features a 1,670-acre working plantation and the Great House and is considered one of the finest museum houses in America. It was built in 1738 by an ancestral Lee named Thomas, onetime acting governor of the colony and father to eight children, including six sons, almost all of whom went on to distinguished careers. Two, Richard Henry Lee and Francis Lightfoot Lee, were the only brothers to sign the Declaration of Independence. "Light Horse Harry," their cousin, was a friend to George Washington and lived here for more than 20 years. Built of brick made on-site and timber hewn nearby, the H-shaped manor house features the fully paneled Great Hall, renowned as one of the finest colonial rooms still in existence. Visitors also can see the crib where the Confederate general slept as an infant in 1808. More than 3 miles of trails lead through the working farm, and at a reconstructed mill the millstones still grind barley, wheat, and corn, which are sold at the plantation store. Robert E. Lee's birthday is celebrated every Jan. 19. Stay in one of two guest houses, with 15 rooms total.

WARSAW

MENOKIN

The Menokin Foundation.
804-333-1776.
www.menokin.org.
4037 Menokin Rd., Warsaw.
Open: Mon. through Fri. 10–4.

The ruins of the wedding-gift home of Rebecca Tayloe and Francis Lightfoot Lee, he of the fabled local Lees and signer of the Declaration of Independence, still stand. Visitors can see them and learn more at a new visitor's center, complete with a 3-D computerized model of the house and historic photographs. Walking trails.

IRVINGTON

HISTORIC CHRIST CHURCH

804-438-6855.
www.christchurch1735.org.
420 Christ Church Rd., Irvington.
Hours: Museum, Mon. through Sat.
10–4, Sun. 2–5. Church, daily 9–4:30
(except Christmas and New Year's).
Services: 8 AM Sun., Memorial Day
through Labor Day.

Built in 1735 by the dominant local colonial planter, Robert "King" Carter, Historic Christ Church is a study in symmetrical period architecture. Vaulted ceilings and perfectly pointed brick, as well as original high-backed pews and a triple-decker pulpit, make this a beautiful, peaceful place to visit. A church was first built on this site in 1670. A museum tells more about this National and Virginia Historic Landmark.

Architecture aficionados should plan a visit to Historic Christ Church in Irvington.

GLOUCESTER
GLOUCESTER COURTHOUSE CIRCLE HISTORIC DISTRICT
Contact: Gloucester County Parks, Recreation, and Tourism.
804-693-0014 or 1-866-VISITUS.
www.gloucesterva.info.
P.O. Box 157, Gloucester VA 23061.

Colonial and early U.S. architecture buffs who find themselves deep on VA 17 north of
Williamsburg will be disappointed if they don't stop to see this collection of 18th- and
19th-century buildings. Among the buildings set inside a circular, walled green are the
Debtor's Prison, the Old Jail, and the Colonial Courthouse, still used for local government
meetings. Plaques bow to Pocahontas, who reportedly saved John Smith near here, and
Nathaniel Bacon, the rebel buried not far away. A gem.

ROSEWELL
804-693-2585.
www.rosewell.org.
5113 Old Rosewell Ln., Gloucester; turn on VA 614 from VA 17.
Open: Mon. through Sat. 10–4, Sun. 1–4.
Cost: Adults $4, children 6 to 12 $2.

The past never really departs in Virginia, as evidenced by the patiently preserved ruins of
Rosewell, a brick Colonial burned in 1916. The four chimneys and portions of walls of the
classic home still stand. Begun in 1725, the house was home to John Page, a young patriot
and Thomas Jefferson's friend. Picnic tables, visitor's center. Oct. barbecue and silent
auction; in spring, "Picnic in Past Times" with 18th-century reenactors.

Libraries
The long-settled Northern Neck offers a couple of good places to spend time on historical
research. In **Heathsville,** the **Northumberland County Historical Society** (804-580-
8581; US 360) offers a collection of genealogical and historical documents. Open Tues.
through Thurs. 9–4, Sat. by appt. Also, the **Mary Ball Washington Museum and Library**
(804-462-7280; 8346 Mary Ball Rd.) in **Lancaster** offers a historical collection, genealogical sources, and research facilities, including an extensive collection of Lancaster County
records dating to 1651. Named for the mother of our country's father, born nearby, the
property also includes displays in the old clerk's office and a small museum and jail. The
museum is open Tues. through Fri. 10–4. The library is open Wed. through Sat. 10–4.

Museums

MONTROSS
WESTMORELAND COUNTY MUSEUM AND LIBRARY
804-493-8440.
43 Court Square, Montross.
Open: Apr. through Oct., Mon. through Sat 10–5; Nov. through Mar., Mon. through Sat.
10–4.
Admission: Free.

The skipjack Claud W. Somers *takes visitors to the Reedville Fishermen's Museum on select Saturdays.*

Anyone with an interest in U.S. history visiting the Northern Neck should stop here. This county's considerable influence in early U.S. matters is quickly in evidence at this site, originally built in 1939 to house a precious portrait of William Pitt by Charles Willson Peale. Learn about George Washington, James Madison, and Robert E. Lee, who were all born in Westmoreland County. Grand portraits of Lee's forebears, Declaration of Independence–signers Francis Lightfoot and Richard Henry Lee, are among those hanging here.

KINSALE
KINSALE MUSEUM
804-472-3001.
449 Kinsale Rd., Kinsale.
Open: May 1 through Oct. 1, Fri. and Sat. 10–5, Sun. 2–5.

Located in a former tavern, this museum is small and delightful—just like the town of Kinsale, a 1706 colonial Virginia port. An annual exhibition changes each Sept. during the popular Kinsale Heritage Days, and visitors also can learn about the canning and steamship industries once so critical to this town.

REEDVILLE
REEDVILLE FISHERMEN'S MUSEUM
804-453-6529.
www.rfmuseum.org.
504 Main St., Reedville.
Open: Daily 10:30–4:30 in summer; call for winter hours.
Admission: $2; children under 12 free.
Handicapped Access: Yes.

Reedville looks like a white-picket-fence New England fishing village, and no wonder. Nineteenth-century menhaden barons came south and launched the fishery here. Stop in at this well-done, three-building museum to learn about Reedville, the Northern Neck, and the Bay. The boatbuilding and model-making shop is quartered in the Pendleton Building, while a peek at a waterman's home, circa turn-of-the-19th-century, resides in the 1875 William Walker House. Or check out the restored 1922 "buyboat," as the boats that went around purchasing oysters from skipjacks were called. Appropriately enough, visitors have been known to arrive here by water, rowing or motoring in by dinghy to the museum dock. The boats docked outside, including the restored netting boat *Elva C,* are especially fun. Sail aboard the 1911 skipjack *Claud W. Somers* on select Sat. during the season, and keep an eye on the museum's website for a calendar of lectures, events (like the November oyster roast), classes, and the like.

KILMARNOCK
KILMARNOCK MUSEUM
804-436-9100.
76 N. Main St., Kilmarnock.
Open: Thurs. through Sat. 10–4.
Admission: Donations accepted.

An old cash register at this museum is a symbol of this town's status as a Northern Neck crossroads of commerce, and the museum helps to maintain Kilmarnock's rural waterside community history. Three major fires in 1909, 1915, and 1952 shaped this town, first called Kilmarnock in 1778 and official friends with Kilmarnock, Scotland, since 1933.

GLOUCESTER
GLOUCESTER MUSEUM
804-693-1234.
6538 Main St., Gloucester.
Open: Mon. through Fri. 11–3, Sat. noon–4.

Quartered in the old Botetourt Building, built in 1774, the museum offers a glimpse of Gloucester County and other area history with changing monthly exhibits focusing on local interests such as archaeology and, in April, Gloucester's daffodils.

A buyboat afloat at the Reedville Fishermen's Museum.

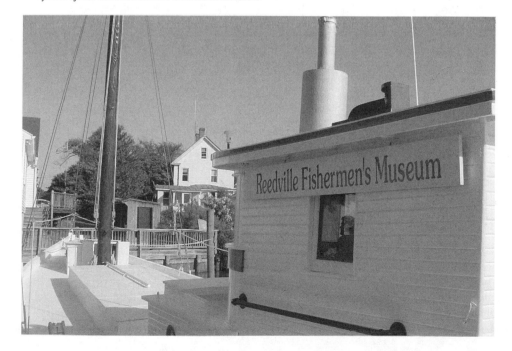

Performing Arts

Concerts on the Common are offered by the Irvington Chamber of Commerce and Village Improvement Association between Memorial Day and Labor Day. Past headliners have included Air Force bands and the Continentals, an 18-piece big band from Richmond. For schedule information, call 804-438-6230 in the mornings.

Donk's Theater (804-725-7760; www.donkstheater.com; VA 198 and VA 223, Mathews) This home of Virginia's "Li'l Ole Opry" is the tidewater's capital of country music. Hometown musicians and sometimes stars show up onstage. "We've had the big ones," we were once told by Harriet Smith Farmer, one of the many Smith family members who lease the place. "We had Dolly. She was here in 1977." The former movie theater is a good venue for families, who may want to check out the house band or the Smith Family Christmas Show the first week of Dec. Shows every other Sat. night. Tickets: adults $12, children under 12 $2.

The Rappahannock Foundation for the Arts (804-435-0292; P.O. Box 459, Kilmarnock, VA 22482) offers a six-performance series featuring professionals such as the Dukes of Dixieland and the Philadelphia Brass. In addition, the group sponsors an annual concert by the Virginia or Richmond Symphony, dance programs, and other performances. Call for ticket information or for a schedule if you're planning to be in the area. Performances held at Lancaster County Middle School, 191 School St. in Kilmarnock. Tickets: $120 for recent season subscription; about $22.50 per individual performance.

Seasonal Events

Daffodil Festival and Show (804-693-2355; follow tourism links at www.co.gloucester.va .us; Gloucester County Parks and Recreation Department, 6467 Main St., P.O. Box 157, Gloucester, VA 23061) Celebrate the annual daffodil harvest with tours of a county daffodil farm. Includes a parade, arts and crafts show, 5K and 1-mile run, historical exhibits, live entertainment, food, children's games, and rides. Held the first Sat. in Apr.

Mathews Market Days (804-725-7196; Mathews Market Days Committee, P.O. Box 295, Mathews, VA 23109) Craftspeople and artists show their wares; local civic and church groups staff the food booths. Music, games, and community exhibitors at the courthouse area. Held the first Fri. and Sat. after Labor Day.

Urbanna Oyster Festival (804-758-0368; www.urbannaoysterfestival.com; Urbanna Oyster Festival Foundation, Drawer C, Urbanna, VA 23175) Tiny Urbanna grows upward of 100,000 over the first Fri. and Sat. of Nov., when folks converge for the oyster festival, launched in 1958. Try oysters raw, roasted, sautéed, fried, stewed, frittered, or souped. The town crowns a queen and Little Miss Spat (the name for a baby oyster), and on Fri. night the Fireman's Parade marches through. Make hotel reservations early; lodging in town is limited but available nearby.

Tours

Northern Neck Heritage Tours (804-580-6336; nnht@aol.com; P.O. Box 460, Heathsville, VA 22473) George and Jan Beckett escaped to the Northern Neck from big-city lives and quickly became enchanted with the historic discoveries they found on the most remote of back roads while exploring their new home. A seemingly long-forgotten historical marker or graveyard would turn out to have near-mythic colonial significance. Take, for instance, the "Burnt House Field" not far from Kinsale, where a Lee family home burned in the 1720s before Thomas Lee moved his family to Stratford Hall. Amazingly, he is buried here, along with other family members. The Becketts accompany bus tours or create individualized automobile trip guides.

RECREATION

Bicycling

The Northern Neck and Middle Peninsula have typically flat Chesapeake tidewater roads in spades. A particularly interesting ride is outlined in the *Bicycle Heritage Tour of the Northern Neck* brochure. Take the Popes Creek Loop for 35–50 miles starting at George Washington's birthplace; the 25-mile Reedville Loop; or the Christ Church–Windmill Point Loop for 22 miles from the colonial church out to breezy Windmill Point, which sticks out into the Chesapeake Bay where it meets the Rappahannock River. Or try the 20-mile Catpoint Creek Loop, which has some nice views of the Rappahannock. Contact the Northern Neck Tourism Council at 1-800-393-6180 or www.northernneck.org.

Bird-Watching

All of the Bay area's birds, including ospreys, herons, and passing ducks, can be found in the region's parks and refuges (see "Natural Areas," below). Bald eagles, back from endangered status, are likewise found hereabouts, but if you're interested in seeing the state's largest concentration of our national avian during the summer, schedule a stop at Caledon Natural Area along the Potomac River. Van tours control access to the eagle's favorite spot, where the fledglings perch high in trees, waiting to fish in the nearby stream. In the winter, you can hike to their nesting grounds. For the van tours, you'll need advance registration; contact Caledon for information (540-663-3861; 11617 Caledon Rd., King George, VA 22485).

In addition, bald eagles may be seen at the George Washington Birthplace (see "Culture"), Belle Isle State Park, and Westmoreland State Park (see "Natural Areas," below). All of the parks and recreational spots listed under "Natural Areas" also will provide opportunities to see a variety of coastal birds.

Boating

Charters and Boat Rentals

Deltaville Yachts Charter (804-776-7575; P.O. Box 775, Deltaville, VA 23043) Sailboat charters aboard 30- to 40-foot vessels. Captain service available if needed. Located at US 33 and VA 631.

Smith Island and Chesapeake Bay Cruises (804-453-3430; 382 Campground Rd., Reedville, VA 22539) A native Smith Islander, Capt. Gordon Evans once oystered aboard the skipjack *Ruby Ford*. He knows his way through the inland waterways, creeks, and canals that lace the cluster of islands collectively known as Smith Island, and now he's shown the way to his son, Capt. Greg Evans. Depart on the 90-minute trip from the family's KOA Campground and Resort in Reedville to dock at Ewell, the largest of this island's three villages. Visitors can bring picnics, but many like to stop at one of a couple of island eateries. Weather conditions may dictate your trip. No credit cards. Departs 10 AM, returns 3:45 PM, May through Oct. Adults $25, children 3–12 $15. Reservations requested, not required.

(See "Smith & Tangier Islands" in chapter 6, "Lower Eastern Shore.")

Tangier and Chesapeake Cruises/Rappahannock River Cruises (804-453-2628 or 1-800-598-2628; www.tangiercruise.com; 468 Buzzard Point Rd., Reedville, VA 22539) Daytrips to windswept Tangier Island run 10–3:30. Also ask about day cruises of the Rappahannock River that leave from Tappahannock at 10 and return about 4:30, May through Oct. Reservations required; check website for fees.

Westmoreland State Park (804-493-8821; 1650 State Park Rd., Montross, VA 22520) Located off VA 3 E outside Montross along the Potomac River, with rentals of kayaks, paddleboats, and hydro bikes. Reasonable fees.

Landings and Boat Ramps

See chapter 9, "Information," to find out how to order a free Bay access map. Some communities require permits for use of the ramps; usually the locations where you can buy one are posted at the boat ramp.

Marinas

Partway down the Northern Neck on the Potomac River, try **Coles Point Plantation** (804-472-3955), with a fuel dock, boat ramp, beach, seafood restaurant, 110-site campground, and a 575-foot fishing pier for guests. On the Yeocomico River is the **Kinsale Harbour Yacht Club** (804-472-2514; VA 203 at Kinsale Bridge), with fuel, fresh water, a pool, tennis courts, showers, laundry, launching ramp, and restaurant. There's also **Port Kinsale Marina & Resort** (804-472-2044; www.portkinsale.com; 347 Allen Point Ln.), which has a pool, a campground, bathhouses, a restaurant, fuel, deep-water slips, and a B&B (see Skipjack Inn under "Lodging").

Farther down, on Lodge Creek off the Yeocomico in Lottsburg, try **Olverson's Lodge Creek Marina** (804-529-6868 or 1-800-529-5071). It has a fuel dock, pump-out station, boat ramp, pool, and showers. Open year-round; 209 open and covered slips.

Out by the Bay, **Ingram Bay Marina** (804-580-7292) offers fuel, bait and tackle, a laundry room, and playground.

On the Rappahannock side of the peninsula, off the Corrottoman River, is the **Yankee Point Marina** (804-462-7018; www.yankeepointmarina.com; 1303 Oak Hill Rd.), which offers a full-service marina, sailing school, 108 slips, fuel, travel lift, showers, and four small rental boats.

Just above the Rappahannock on Indian Creek lies **Chesapeake Boat Basin** (804-435-3110; 1686 Waverly Ave.), which has a ship's store, ice, showers, fresh water, and transient slips.

Meanwhile, across the Rappahannock on Urbanna Creek, **Dozier's Port Urbanna Marina** (804-758-0000; www.doziermarine.com) is located right in town and the Boathouse Café (see "Restaurants") is on-site.

At the end of the peninsula, Deltaville offers several options. Try **Deltaville Yachting Center** (804-776-9898; www.dycboat.com; on Broad Creek, 18355 Puller Rd.), with a pool, clubhouse, private showers and heads, laundry, and restaurants within walking distance; or **Fishing Bay Harbor Marina** (804-776-6800; www.fishingbay.com), which has a pump-out station, gas, diesel, and a pool.

Canoeing and Kayaking

The Mathews County Blueways Water Trail includes the rivers, creeks, harbors, and even open water along this county at the end of the Middle Peninsula. Five trails are available; purchase waterproof maps from the Mathews County Visitor & Information Center (240 Main St./P.O. Box 1456, Mathews, VA 23109; 1-877-725-4BAY; mcvic@visitmathews.com, or visit www.blueways.org.

Bay Trails Outfitters Kayak Farm (804-725-0626 or 1-888-725-7225; www.baytrails.com; 2221 Bethel Beach Rd., Onemo, VA 23130; located on VA 609 in Mathews County) Kayak sales, rentals, and guided tours like the lighthouse island and blueberry-picking tour. Fossil hunt and haunted woods, too. $35 per person average for tours; homemade pound cake when they end. Kayak rentals are $20 per single for two hours, $35 per double. Full-day rates available.

Belle Isle State Park (804-462-5030; 1632 Belle Isle Rd., Lancaster, VA 22503; located off VA 354 on VA 683) Nice paddling in a protected creek off the Rappahannock River, where you can rent canoes for a nominal fee. Take VA 3 to VA 354, then VA 683 near Litwalton to the park. Guided trips in summer.

Family Fun

WESTMORELAND BERRY FARM

804-224-9171 or 1-800-997-2377.
www.westmorelandberryfarm.com.
1235 Berry Farm Ln., Oak Grove, VA 22443.
Admission: None; pay per pound of fruit picked.
Hours: Mother's Day through Labor Day, 8–7 daily; after Labor Day until the end of Oct., 9–5; Nov. through mid-Dec., 10–4. Otherwise by app.

Groups from local schools and day-care centers make it a point to visit this family-friendly farm, and if you're in the area with a backseat full of kids, you should, too. (Once overheard from an employee: "I can handle the eighteen 4-year-olds." Need we say more?) Located along the Rappahannock River, the farm boasts historic, European-invasion roots dating to 1641. In all, 1,600 acres include 800 acres in the adjoining Vorhees Nature Preserve as well as the farm. Not only can kids pick buckets of berries, but there's a "goat walk," an arcing wooden bridge where goats and their kids pick their way across the horizon. The carefully planned, seasonal wave of harvests begins with strawberries in May, followed by cherries, black and red raspberries, blueberries, and peaches. By October kids are picking apples. Everyone is assigned a particular plot upon which to pick. There's a kid-friendly food stand in the market area and a broad veranda with picnic tables. Best berry months: June through mid-July. Best days to pick: Tues. through Thurs.

Fishing

Charter Boats

For a roster of licensed Coast Guard captains located throughout the Northern Neck, Middle Peninsula, and Eastern Shore of Virginia, check www.fishva.org or write to the **Virginia Charter Boat Association**, P.O. Box 1217, Gloucester Point, VA 23062.

Heathsville

Betty Jane (804-580-5904; Buzzard's Point Marina, 227 Crosshills Rd., Heathsville, VA 22473) Capt. E. Wayson Christopher has been at it for years. Licensed for six passengers.

Capt. Billy's Charters (804-580-7292; Ingram Bay Marina, 545 Harvey's Neck Road, Heathsville, VA 22473) Sail out of Ingram Bay aboard *Liquid Assets*, a 40-foot vessel designed for fishing parties and sightseeing. Reservations required.

Crabbe's Charter Fishing (804-453-3251; 51 Railway Rd., Heathsville, VA 22473) Capt. Danny Crabbe, the third-generation fisherman in his family, has been taking out charters for more than 30 years. His 43-foot *Kit II* is licensed for 26 passengers. In addition, wintertime fishers can go out of Rudee's Inlet off Virginia Beach for oceangoing stripers.

Reedville

Pittman's Charters (804-453-3643; 2998 Fairport Rd., Reedville, VA 22539) Head out aboard the 46-foot *Mystic Lady II*. May through mid-Dec.; $65 per person, $455 minimum. Night trips vary; call for prices. Also home to Pittman's Bait and Tackle. On Cockrell's Creek.

Topping

Locklies Marina (804-758-2871; VA 621, Topping, VA 23169) About 12 charter boats take fishers into the Bay or the Rappahannock from this marina, and they'll book charters in other areas, too.

Wicomico Church

Jimmick Jr. III (804-580-7744; 95 Long Cove Lane, Wicomico Church, VA 22579) Everything-supplied fishing and catered cruises for up to 25 passengers aboard the 42-foot vessel. Family operated since 1986. Reservations required; call for prices.

Golf

Hobbs Hole Golf Course (804-443-4500; 1267 Hobbs Hole Dr., Tappahannock) 18-hole course, pro shop, fine restaurant.

Gloucester Country Club (804-693-2662; Golf Club Rd., Gloucester) Public 9-hole course. Good for beginners. Located 12 miles north of the York River Bridge.

Golden Eagle Golf Course (804-438-5501 or 1-800-843-3746; P.O. Box 480, Irvington) 18 holes; championship course. Part of the Tides Inn. Restaurant, professional instruction, driving range, and a par 3 for guests.

Miller's Glen Golf Course (804-472-2602; VA 711, Mount Holly) 9 holes. Golf carts, driving range, pro shop, snack bar. Located at the historic Bushfield Plantation.

Piankatank River Golf Club (804-776-6516; VA 629, Hartfield) 18-hole public course. Also home to the Steamboat Restaurant.

Quinton Oaks Golf Course (804-529-5367; 262 Quinton Oaks Ln., Callao) Semiprivate course.

Tartan Golf Course (804-438-6200; 633 St. Andrew's Ln., Weems) 18 holes. Pro shop, restaurant, grill room, practice facilities.

The Village Green Golf Club (804-529-6332; 17390 Northumberland Hwy., Callao) 9 holes; public. Pro shop and restaurant year-round.

Natural Areas: State, Federal, and Private Parks/Lands

Beaverdam Park (804-693-2107; www.co.gloucester.va.us; 8687 Roaring Springs Rd., Gloucester, VA 23061; near Gloucester Courthouse at end of VA 616) A 635-acre freshwater lake with largemouth bass (four bass tournaments a year), channel cat, and crappie fishing available. There's also a nature trail and programs offering adventures such as night canoeing and owl walks.

Belle Isle State Park (804-462-5030; www.dcr.state.va.us; 1632 Belle Isle Rd., Lancaster, VA 22503; off VA 354 on VA 683) Located on Deep Creek and Mulberry Creek with fine fishing and trails. Rent skiffs with 9.9 hp outboards ($10 per hour, two-hour minimum; $50 for the day) or a 16-footer with a center console ($18 an hour, two-hour minimum; $90 all day). Also, rent bikes and canoes for nominal fees. Two nice picnic areas provide water views, plus there's a boat launch, several miles of trails, and guided trips such as nature walks and moonlight/sunset canoe trips from mid-May though Aug. Birds here include eagles, ospreys, and red-tailed and red-shouldered hawks. Bottlenose dolphins may be spotted feeding in late summer. Also available: rental of the Overnight Area, a bureaucratic name for the 1942 Bel Air mansion and guest house on a private 33-acre peninsula. Television, working fireplace, kitchen. Sleeps 14 total; rates are reasonable. For reservations, call 1-800-933-PARK. As of deadline, a campground was slated to open soon.

Bethel Beach Natural Area Preserve (for information, call the Mathews County Visitor and Information Center, 804-725-4229; located at the end of VA 609 outside Mathews) A 50-acre preserve with sandy beach and salt marsh along the Chesapeake Bay. Dozens of bird species and the rare northeastern beach tiger beetle.

Chesapeake Nature Trail (west of Kilmarnock on the south side of VA 3) A 1.6-mile trail that passes the west branch of the Corrottoman River.

Hickory Hollow Nature Preserve (804-445-9117; www.northernneckaudubon.org/ guide.htm; Northern Neck Audubon Society, P.O. Box 991, Kilmarnock, VA 22482) Located on VA 604 outside Kilmarnock en route to Lancaster. More than 250 acres; walking trails up to 1.8 miles long.

Westmoreland State Park (804-493-8821; 1650 State Park Rd., Montross, VA 22520) Almost 1,300 acres along 2 miles of the Potomac River. Fish, swim in the Olympic-size pool (no swimming from the beach), or rent a kayak or other small boat. Located off VA 3 E outside Montross. Visitors may discover washed-up sharks' teeth, vestiges of life from an ancient, Miocene sea.

Rowing

Calm Waters Rowing (804-435-6887 or 1-800-238-5578; www.calmwatersrowing.com; at the Inn at Levelfields, 10155 Mary Ball Rd., Lancaster, VA 22503) Offering athletic vacations and instruction sessions of varying lengths and intensities. Check website for programs; stay at the Inn at Levelfields and row 2.5 miles away in 80-acre Camps Millpond.

New shops in old Irvington.

Sporting Goods and Fishing Supply Stores

J&W Seafood (804-776-9740; US 33, Deltaville) Fishing licenses and tackle, and local guys who can take care of your charter boating needs. A fishing report is available via their phone line: 1-800-322-9740.

Pittman's Bait & Tackle (804-453-3643; 2998 Fairport Rd., Reedville) On Cockrell's Creek, near wide-open fishing grounds.

Swimming

Gloucester Point Beach Park (804-642-9474; VA 17 on the York River next to Coleman Bridge/York River Bridge, Gloucester) Fishing pier, picnic area, swimming, and horse-shoes and volleyball courts. Concession stand and rest rooms open seasonally.

Westmoreland State Park (804-493-8821; State Park Rd., Montross) Olympic-size pool alongside the Potomac River. Located 5 miles west of Montross, off VA 3 E. Open Memorial Day through Labor Day; nominal fees.

SHOPPING

Antiques

Antiques shops dot the many country byways crisscrossing this region, far too numerous to list here in their entirety. Fortunately, the **Rappahannock River Antiques Dealers**

Association has banded together to take the mystery out of the area's back roads with a map of antiques shops stretching from Montross and Tappahannock to White Stone, across the river to Saluda, and even as far south as Yorktown. They even provide referrals. For questions, contact **Miss Daisy's Antiques** (804-529-9899; 15572 Richmond Rd. between Callao and Village; e-mail missdaisy@rivnet.com). Her shop, by the way, specializes in Depression glass, and her husband has a sharp eye for paintings.

Annie Rooney's Antiques and Estate Sales at Sibley's General Store (804-725-4600; 239 Main St., Mathews) Old Sibley's General Store operated from the tail end of the 19th century into the budding 21st and has been taken over by this antiques store. Lovers of antiques stores and general stores alike will be pleased to see that the interior and exterior still look much the same—except, of course, for all of the antiques.

Holly Hill Farm Antiques (804-695-1146; VA 14, Gloucester) Centered around an 1880 house built by a freed slave, Holly Hill Farm Antiques offers several outbuildings full of antiques, with a specialty in primitives, glassware, oyster plates, and farm implements and tools. Come in spring to see a zillion daffodils blooming here, as they do throughout the area. Open Fri. through Sun. 10–5.

Kilmarnock Antique Gallery (804-435-1207 or 1-800-497-0083; www.virginia-antiques.com; 144 School St., Kilmarnock) Open daily. More than 100 spaces for dealers; definitely extensive.

Main Street Fine Art & Antique Mall (804-435-7771; 15 N. Main St., Kilmarnock) Quality antiques.

Plantation Antique Mall (804-695-1410; 7032 George Washington Memorial Hwy., Gloucester) Open daily.

Urbanna Antique Mall (804-758-2000; 124 Rappahannock Ave., Urbanna) Variety of 24 vendors peddling all kinds of stuff, including furniture and nauticals, in this 5,000 square-foot space.

Books
Book Nook (804-435-3355; 53 W. Church St., Kilmarnock) Fine selection of local interest and fishing books. In business for more than 30 years. Special orders for out-of-print and rare books. Open Mon. through Fri. 9:30–5, Sat. 9:30–3.

Twice Told Tales (804-435-9201; 75 S. Main St., Kilmarnock) Centrally located and easy to find, with a range of books, including quality activity books for kids. Open Mon. through Fri. 10–5, Sat. 10–4. Also located in Gloucester at Main St. and York Ave. (804-639-9209).

Clothing
Cyndy's Bynn (804-758-3756; 311 Virginia St., Urbanna) Seasonal gifts and jewelry, fine women's clothing, and a selection of gift items for children and babies.

The Dandelion (804-438-5194; 4372 Irvington Rd., Irvington) The proprietors shop the designers in New York, Atlanta, and Dallas, and it shows. Great women's clothing, from designer upscale to closer to home. Well worth a stop—or even a special trip.

Khakis of Irvington (804-438-6779; 4345 Irvington Road, Irvington) Clothing and gifts for men.

Pepper's (804-436-9606; 538 Rappahannock Dr., White Stone) Five of us spent a Saturday morning in here one April; nobody was at a loss over what to buy. Great women's clothing.

Galleries

Art Speaks Gallery (804-725-1278; 279 Main St., Mathews) The gallery of the Bay School Cultural Arts Center features crafts, paintings, and more.

Mathews Art Group (804-725-3326; Main Street, Mathews) Nice co-op gallery with a range of work—pottery, stained glass, fine art, prints—from a group of about 40 local artists. Open year-round, Mon. through Sat. 10–4.

The Poddery in Mathews County is a top-of-the-line potters' studio.

Nimcock Gallery (804-758-2602; 31 Cross St., Urbanna) In this little custom frame shop, Santas are painted on crab-shell ornaments and set in a tray amid antiques, collectibles, paintings, and prints. Open Mon. through Sat. 10–5, Sun. 1–5.

Since the late 1800s, locals have shopped at the R. S. Bristow Store in Urbanna.

The Poddery (804-725-5956; thepoddery.artroof.com; VA 660, Foster) Surprises live down the long country lanes in Mathews County, and the Poddery is one of them. Operated by potters Karen and Rob Podd, the Poddery looks like summer camp, with its rambling wooden showroom/studio and green-roofed shelters displaying Bay-inspired stoneware. The main showroom is chockablock with useful and artful wares alongside small crabs, mollusks with sea grass, and realistic fish made from molds of fish brought by neighboring watermen. Buy them individually for a kitchen or bathroom backsplash or affixed to pots crafted for various cooking duties. Open year-round; special open houses the weekends before and after Thanksgiving. Showroom open daily 10–5.

Rappahannock Art League & Studio Gallery (804-436-9309; www.ralgallery.com; 19 N. Main St., Kilmarnock) A good place to look for a range of different pieces, including paintings, jewelry, pottery, and turned wood. Open Tues. through Sat. 10–4. Also keep an eye out for workshops offered via the art league; notices posted on the gallery door.

General Stores

R. S. Bristow Store (804-758-2210; Virginia and Cross Sts., Urbanna) A stop as much on the local history walking tour as on your vacation shopping trip, this 1898 dry goods store offers nice clothing and much, much more. R. S. Bristow Sr. opened his first retail shop in town in 1876.

Specialty Shops & Craft Galleries

Duncan & Drake (804-438-5447; 81 King Carter Dr., Irvington) Carries an eclectic collection of decorative home items as well as women's contemporary-casual clothing.

Make Thyme (804-758-2101; 260 Prince George St., Urbanna) Dried and fresh herbs of many varieties, as well as fragrant gift items in the two-room house/shop. Larry Chowning, a Bay writer noted for his work on the lives and lore of local watermen, owns this shop with his wife, Dee.

Papeterie (804-758-0046; 260 Virginia St., Urbanna) Lots of fun stuff to see, from whimsical glass fish Christmas ornaments to fine papers.

Rappahannock Jewelry Co. (804-758-3003; 230 Virginia St., Suite 3, Urbanna) Chesapeake-themed jewelry and gifts.

The (Tides Inn) Gift Shop (804-438-4440 or 804-438-5000; 480 King Carter Dr., Irvington) Fine gifts, men's and women's logo items, and some jewelry. Across the way is **J's** (804-438-4448), which offers ladies' and men's resortwear, jewelry by local artists, and accessories.

Time to Cook (804-438-6691; 4349 Irvington Road, Irvington) Specialty cooking shop that also offers demonstration classes and private lessons.

Urbanna Republic (804-758-3003; 230 Virginia St., Suite 2, Urbanna) Urbanna resortwear, including T-shirts and ball caps.

Wood-A-Drift Art Shop (804-438-6913; 4474 Irvington Rd., Irvington) This homey little shop offers home decor nauticals—oyster baskets, original anchors, and oyster tongs—right off the Chesapeake workboats. Owner Graham Bruce also makes lamps from original materials.

Sailing into Baltimore's Inner Harbor.

8

BALTIMORE, HAMPTON ROADS & OTHER URBAN ATTRACTIONS

Urban Bay Neighbors

Baltimore

First, Baltimore turned its moribund waterfront into the internationally acclaimed Inner Harbor. Now the city's undergone another renaissance, with attractions and neighborhoods spruced up and expanded well beyond the harbor basin.

A billion-dollar-plus development blitz that began in the mid-1990s has added a huge waterfront hotel, a new football stadium, the world's first Disney-designed children's museum, and a multimillion-dollar expansion to the popular National Aquarium in Baltimore—and that's only one of several major expansions to notable attractions. There's even a spiffy new visitor's center that helps tourists handle such details as reservations and ticket purchases. The energy of the Inner Harbor also has spread to other neighborhoods, including Federal Hill, Fells Point, Canton, and South Baltimore. A weekend is hardly enough to catch all the city's charms.

A good place to start is the Inner Harbor and the twin glass pavilions of **Harborplace**, with all manner of shops and restaurants. The once-dormant **Power Plant**, a former steam-generating plant, has been transformed into a hip, neon-emblazoned entertainment and retail spot overlooking the harbor. It features three mega-attractions: the world's first **ESPN Zone**, interactive and much loved by sports fans (including those who gather after Baltimore's Preakness, stop two in horse racing's Triple Crown); a grand **Barnes & Noble** that demands attention with its inventory, trendy café, and 30,000-gallon saltwater fish tank; and the ever-popular **Hard Rock Café.** The high-voltage Power Plant is also a fine complement to longtime Inner Harbor attractions such as the **National Aquarium in Baltimore** and the expanded **Maryland Science Center** (410-685-5225; 601 Light St.; open daily; admission fee), an interactive science museum with **IMAX Theater** and **Davis Planetarium.** The Power Plant Live! (410-727-LIVE; www.powerplantlive.com; 34 Market Place), with its upscale restaurants and nightlife, recently opened up across the street from the Power Plant.

Just a few blocks east of the Inner Harbor, the former city fish market has been transformed into **Port Discovery,** voted the nation's fourth-best children's museum by *Child*

The American Visionary Art Museum is home to thought-provoking pieces in unique exhibits. Photo courtesy of American Visionary Art Museum, Baltimore

magazine. And to the west of the Inner Harbor, a 1914 movie and vaudeville palace known as the **Hippodrome Theatre** has recently been gloriously reborn as the France-Merrick Performing Arts Center (410-837-7400; www.france-merrickpac.com; 12 N. Eutaw St.), and it includes Broadway fare on its busy schedule.

But Baltimore is much more than the Inner Harbor, as its neighborhoods attest. The city's cultural heart beats at **Mount Vernon**, while **Little Italy** continues to romance with its cozy eateries. **Fells Point**, an 18th-century fishing village, charms by day with its unique shops and galleries, but at night it transforms into a Soho of sorts. (If you're ever in Baltimore during Halloween, be sure to visit the neighborhood to check out the outrageous costumes.) **Federal Hill** has grown into a hot, restaurant-filled neighborhood and also offers the acclaimed **American Visionary Art Museum** (410-244-1900; 800 Key Hwy.), which features works by artists outside the mainstream. In once-industrial **Canton**, former canneries, tin factories, and fertilizer plants have been converted into restaurants, bars, offices, shops, and some of the hottest real estate in the city. Just a few blocks from an expansive waterfront park and promenade, Canton's O'Donnell Square provides a gathering spot perfect for strolling, people watching, shopping, eating, and drinking.

Food is also big in Charm City, and its public markets are legendary. The most famous is **Lexington Market** (400 W. Lexington St.), established in 1782, with about 140 merchants offering abundant and fresh foods of all kinds at unbelievable prices. Vendors include the fabled Faidley Seafood for crab cakes, as well as fresh produce markets that sell at well below supermarket prices. Such markets are located throughout the city, the most gentrified being **Cross Street Market** (between Charles and Light Sts.) in Federal Hill. The

Broadway Market (last two blocks at south end of Broadway) in Fells Point offers fresh gourmet bread as well as no-frills breakfasts.

Charles Street is Baltimore's main street and leads to picturesque **Mount Vernon Square,** home to many fun and trendy shops. Among the city's cultural jewels here are the nation's first monument to **George Washington,** the **Walters Art Museum,** and the famed **Peabody Conservatory of Music,** the oldest American music school. Farther up the street, in Charles Village, look for the **Baltimore Museum of Art** adjacent to **Johns Hopkins University's** sprawling Homewood campus.

American history lovers also will enjoy Baltimore, once home to Babe Ruth and Edgar Allan Poe. The **Babe Ruth Birthplace and Museum** (216 Emory St.) is just a home run away from **Oriole Park at Camden Yards,** the city's trendsetting, retro baseball park, well worth a visit even for those who aren't baseball fans. For Baltimore Orioles game information, call 1-888-848-BIRD or check out the website at http://baltimore.orioles.mlb.com. Next to the ballpark is the sprawling 69,084-seat home of the Baltimore Ravens, **M&T Bank Stadium** (tickets, 410-261-RAVE; other information, 410-547-8100; www.balti moreravens.com).

Easily accessible by I-95 (I-97 if you're headed north from Annapolis), this eminently livable city is easy to navigate by car, foot, or scenic water taxi for as little as $6 for a day-long ticket. For information, contact the Baltimore Area Convention and Visitors Association's Visitor Center (1-877-BALTIMORE; www.baltimore.org; 401 Light St., Baltimore, MD 21202).

BALTIMORE ATTRACTIONS

AMERICAN VISIONARY ART MUSEUM

410-244-1900.
www.avam.org.
800 Key Hwy., at the foot of Federal Hill.
Open: Tues. through Sun. 10–6.
Admission: Adults $9, children and seniors $6; group rates.

If you visit no other museum in Baltimore, make time to see this one. "Visionary art" is loosely defined as work by self-taught artists, primitive artists, and other such appellations. Let's just call them people who simply want to make art, do so, and produce thought-provoking—even huge— results. From Southerners with religious or otherwise apocalyptic visions to guys who retired from their jobs and decided to make art, this place is full of amazing pieces. A reproduction *Lusitania* made of 193,000 toothpicks and a seven-

This mobile stands outside the American Visionary Art Museum in Baltimore.

Enjoy a terrific view of the Inner Harbor from Joy America Café, the restaurant at the American Visionary Art Museum.

panel vision reminiscent of Bosch for the modern era are among the pieces in the small permanent collection. In addition, the museum hosts wonderful exhibitions of 11 months or longer. To wit: a Holocaust survivor who recalls her childhood loss of family and survival in the innocent medium of quilt panels. The artists' stories are told in full, and they're at least as interesting as the work. Museum space recently doubled, and Joy America Café on the third floor features Pan-American food and a fantastic view of the Inner Harbor. If nothing else, have afternoon coffee on the balcony.

BALTIMORE MUSEUM OF ART
410-396-7100.
www.artbma.org.
10 Art Museum Dr., Baltimore, MD 21218.
Open: Wed. through Fri. 11–5, Sat. and Sun. 11–6; first Thurs. of each month 11–8.
Admission: Adults $7, seniors and full-time students $5, children 18 and under free; all visitors free on first Thurs. of each month.

Maryland's oldest and largest art museum has unveiled major renovations in recent years, including eight thematic galleries and the opulent Jacobs Wing, which houses the museum's 15th- to 19th-century European art collection. The Interpretive Gallery offers the first public display of many works from the museum's best-known collection, the Cone Collection, artwork from two Baltimore sisters who amassed one of the world's great selections of Matisse paintings. The BMA also displays American paintings and decorative arts, European paintings and sculpture, art of Africa and Asia, and modern and contemporary art. Chesapeake celebrity chef John Shields operates his restaurant, Gertrude's, here.

FORT McHENRY NATIONAL MONUMENT AND HISTORIC SHRINE
410-962-4290.
www.nps.gov/fomc.
E. Fort Ave., Baltimore, MD 21230.
Open: Daily 8–4:45; extended summer hours, 8–7:45. Closed Thanksgiving, Christmas, and New Year's.
Admission: Adults $5, children 16 and under free.

The star-shaped Fort McHenry is known throughout the world as the birthplace of "The Star-Spangled Banner." Inspired by the American flag still flying after British bombard-ment of the fort, Marylander Francis Scott Key wrote the words to the U.S. national anthem during the War of 1812. Situated in the up-and-coming neighborhood of Locust Point in South Baltimore, Fort McHenry's 43-acre grounds, brick fort, and ramparts lie adjacent to Baltimore Harbor. A peaceful setting, the vast, green grounds provide a perfect picnic spot and a haven for joggers and cyclists. The fort allows visitors opportunities to explore a variety of exhibits; don't miss the free 16-minute movie, shown every 30 minutes in the visitor's center.

MARYLAND ZOO IN BALTIMORE
410-366-5466.
www.marylandzoo.org.
Druid Hill Park, Baltimore, MD 21217.
Open: Mar. 1 through Dec. 31, daily 10–4:30 (last admission at 3:30); closed Thanksgiving and Christmas Day.
Admission: Adults $15, seniors 65 and older $12, children 2–11 $10.

The 161-acre zoo, formerly called the Baltimore Zoo, is the nation's third oldest and fea-tures the African Watering Hole, where the rhinos roam; the Leopard Lair, where a new African leopard lives; and the acclaimed Children's Zoo, a walk-through, interactive dis-play of Maryland's habitats and species.

NATIONAL AQUARIUM IN BALTIMORE
410-576-3800.
www.aqua.org.
501 E. Pratt St., Baltimore, MD 21202.
Open: Hours change frequently through the seasons. Visitors may stay 1 1/2 hours after the day's last admission. Mar. through Jun., Sat. through Thurs. 9–5, Fri. 9 –8; Jul. and Aug., Sun. through Thurs. 9–6, Fri. and Sat. 9–8. Call or check website for other seasons.
Admission: Adults $17.50, seniors $14.50, children 3–11 $9.50.

Get caught in the mist in the Tropical Rain Forest at the Inner Harbor's popular National Aquarium. Or check out the Coral Reef, where a winding, downward path takes you up close to a huge tank containing the reef, with its sharks, tortoises, and other colorful inhabitants. The Amazon River Forest re-creates a section of a blackwater Amazon River tributary, where visitors can spy schools of dazzling tropical fish, giant river turtles, and a giant anaconda. The Marine Mammal Pavilion features dolphins that perform several times daily. "Animal Planet Australia: Wild Extremes" opens in a new building in 2005, replete with a 35-foot waterfall and a range of flora and fauna native to this land of extremes. The aquarium's biggest drawback is its crowds. Lines start forming early on the weekends, and the crush of people can make viewing the exhibits a bit uncomfortable. Try visiting after 3 PM, or be in line when the aquarium opens.

PORT DISCOVERY

410-727-8120.
www.portdiscovery.org.
35 Market Place, Baltimore, MD 21202.
Open: Memorial Day through Labor Day, Mon. through Sat. 10–5, Sun. noon–5; rest of the year, Tues. through Fri. 9:30–4:30, Sat. 10–5, Sun. noon–5; closed Thanksgiving, Christmas, and Mon. Oct. through May except for certain holidays.
Admission: Adults $11, seniors $10, children 3–12 $8.50.

Voted the country's fourth-best children's museum by *Child* magazine, Port Discovery beckons with a three-story, interactive wonderland. Kids can slide, jump, and swing through an "urban treehouse"; travel back in time to the land of the pyramids to search for a lost pharaoh's tomb; and try their hand at inventing stuff at R&D Dreamlab.

THE WALTERS ART MUSEUM

410-547-9000.
www.thewalters.org.
600 N. Charles St., Baltimore, MD 21201.
Open: Tues. through Sun. 10–5; first Thurs. of each month 10–8.
Admission: Adults $10; seniors $8; college students, young adults 18–25 with ID $6; children age 6–17 $2. Free 10–1 Sat. and all day the first Thurs. of each month.

With a collection of 30,000 pieces spanning three structures, the Walters presents buildings as impressive as the masterpieces they contain. These include the landmark Italian Renaissance Revival 1904 Gallery building, the four-story 1974 Centre Street building, and the Hackerman House, a Greek Revival mansion. The Walters is one of only a few museums worldwide to present a comprehensive history of art from the third millennium BC to the early 20th century. The Walters also boasts a fine collection of ivories, jewelry, enamels, and bronzes and a spectacular reserve of medieval and Renaissance illuminated manuscripts. Also featured: highly regarded collections of Egyptian, Greek and Roman, Byzantine, Ethiopian, Western medieval, Renaissance, and Asian works. Acclaimed exhibits have included such shows as "Manet: The Still-Life Paintings," which opened at the Walters after premiering at Paris's Musée d'Orsay, the great home to so many famed Impressionist paintings.

BALTIMORE LODGINGS

For visitors who prefer quaint lodgings to mega hotels, consider a sampling of the city's inns and B&Bs. Rates may vary according to season or day of the week, and cancellation policies may vary from inn to inn. Always check.

Lodging rates, based on high-season prices, fall within this scale:

Inexpensive:	Up to $75
Moderate:	$75 to $120
Expensive:	$120 to $175
Very expensive:	$175 and up

Credit card abbreviations are:
AE—American Express
CB—Carte Blanche
DC—Diners Club
D—Discover
MC—MasterCard
V—Visa

THE ADMIRAL FELL INN
410-522-7377; 1-866-583-4162 for reservations.
www.admiralfell.com.
888 S. Broadway, Baltimore, MD 21231; Market Square at Thames St.
Price: Expensive to very expensive.
Credit Cards: AE, DC, MC, V.
Handicapped Access: Yes.
Special Features: Pets allowed; call for details.

Long before the cult television cop drama *Homicide: Life on the Street* put Fells Point on the map, there was the Admiral Fell Inn, aptly named after the man responsible for this quaint part of Baltimore. The city's original port retains much of its 18th-century charm, with Belgian brick streets, tugboats, salty taverns, and red brick row houses. This elegant 80-room inn, which once served as a boardinghouse for sailors, embodies that charm with finely appointed rooms furnished with custom-crafted Federal-style pieces. A recent renovation promises new appointments throughout the inn, as well as nice in-room amenities such as bathrobes and coffee makers … they even serve high tea on Saturdays. Packages are available and detailed on the inn's website.

CELIE'S WATERFRONT BED AND BREAKFAST
Innkeepers: Ken and Nancy Kupec.
410-522-2323 or 1-800-432-0184.
www.celieswaterfront.com.
1714 Thames St., Baltimore, MD 21231.
Price: Expensive to very expensive.

Credit Cards: AE, D, MC, V.
Handicapped Access: Yes.

This oasis sits tucked amid brick row houses and shops lining Thames Street, just across the cobblestone street from tugboats moored in the harbor. The three-story inn's nine airy rooms and suites come with harbor or courtyard views and are filled with early American–style decor. You may find king-size beds, fireplaces, and whirlpool tubs. Two rooms have private balconies. All have televisions, VCRs, coffee makers, updated tiled baths, and wireless Internet. Breakfast is "gourmet continental." There's a brick courtyard garden out back, and a rooftop deck offers views of the harbor and city. Centrally located in Fells Point.

MR. MOLE BED & BREAKFAST
Owners: Paul Bragaw and Collin Clarke.
410-728-1179 or 1-866-811-2477.
www.mrmolebb.com.
1601 Bolton St., Baltimore, MD 21201.
Price: Expensive to very expensive.
Credit Cards: AE, DC, D, MC, V.
Handicapped Access: No.

Elegantly appointed in English-country fashion, this 1860s town house in historic Bolton Hill boasts marble fireplaces, 14-foot ceilings, and scores of 18th- and 19th-century antiques. The owners take obvious pride and personal interest in their guests. Each of three rooms comes with its own style and name, and all of them include spacious, crystal-clean, white bathrooms with hair dryers and terry-cloth robes. A breakfast of sliced meats, cheeses, fresh fruit, and homemade baked goods is served each morning. The inn is a bit removed from the tourist areas of Baltimore, and guests should drive or take a cab at night.

SCARBOROUGH FAIR BED & BREAKFAST

Innkeepers: Ellen and Ashley Scarborough.
410-837-0010.
www.scarborough-fair.com.
1 E. Montgomery St., Baltimore, MD 21230.
Price: Expensive to very expensive.
Credit Cards: AE, D, MC, V.
Handicapped Access: No.

This gem in Federal Hill boasts not only stellar accommodations, but also a location that other inns would envy. Walk to the Inner Harbor or Fells Point (a longer hike), and dine at Federal Hill's exceptional restaurants. The Scarboroughs offer today's comforts amid yesteryear's charm. They opened the inn in 1997 and have gone above and beyond in refurbishing the stately brick house at Charles and Montgomery Sts., distinctive with its gabled roof and Flemish-bond bricks. Six beautifully renovated rooms are offered, all with period and reproduction furnishings, four with gas fireplaces and two with whirlpool tubs. The decor and style varies from room to room—one with a brass bed and reading chairs, for example, another with a Victorian bed and marble-topped nightstand. Updated, spacious private baths in each room have touches such as antique sink vanities. Television in the cozy library. Hearty, unique breakfasts daily in the traditional French dining room. Off-street parking is included.

And for well-located Baltimore hotels, try:

Baltimore Marriott Waterfront Hotel
(410-385-3000; 700 Aliceanna St.) This 31-floor harbor-front hotel includes 22 suites. Numerous services and amenities. Very expensive.

Harbor Court Hotel (410-234-0550; 550 Light St.) Luxury hotel on the Inner Harbor with 195 guest rooms and suites along with many amenities, including a fitness center, tennis court, and swimming pool. Very expensive.

Hyatt Regency Baltimore (410-528-1234; 300 Light St.) Fourteen stories on the waterfront, with suites in addition to rooms. Facilities include swimming pool and fitness facilities. Very expensive.

The Tremont Plaza (410-727-2222; 222 St. Paul St.) All suites, outdoor pool, fitness center. Expensive to very expensive.

BALTIMORE RESTAURANTS

Baltimore offers numerous restaurants of wide appeal; we offer here a sampling of those available from Little Italy to Fells Point to deep in the neighborhood known as Hamden. Price ranges, which include dinner entrée, appetizer, and dessert, are as follows:

Inexpensive:	Up to $20
Moderate:	$20 to $30
Expensive:	$30 to $40
Very expensive:	$40 or more

Credit card abbreviations are:
AE—American Express
CB—Carte Blanche
DC—Diners Club
D—Discover
MC—MasterCard
V—Visa

The following abbreviations are used to denote meals served:
B = Breakfast; L = Lunch; D = Dinner;
SB = Sunday Brunch

AMICCI'S

410-528-1096.
231 S. High St.
Open: Daily.
Price: Inexpensive to moderate.
Cuisine: Italian.
Serving: L, D.

Credit Cards: AE, CB, DC, D, MC, V.
Reservations: Accepted.
Handicapped Access: No.

This brightly colored dining room in the city's fabled Little Italy, adorned with framed movie posters, is usually crowded and conducive to a great meal. The house salad is a perennial bargain, and the restaurant's signature appetizer is Panne Rotondo, a bread boule filled with jumbo shrimp swimming in garlicky cream sauce. There's something for every pasta-lover's taste, such as tortellini with peas and prosciutto, baked penne, and the house gnocci, sautéed with fresh spinach, prosciutto, and roasted red peppers in an Alfredo sauce. If you still have room, wrap up your repast with one of Amicci's fantastic cannoli.

CAFÉ HON

410-243-1230.
1002 W. 36th St.
Open: Daily.
Price: Inexpensive to expensive.
Cuisine: Comfort food.
Serving: B, L, D, SB.
Credit Cards: AE, DC, D, MC, V.
Reservations: Accepted.
Handicapped Access: Yes.

For a truly authentic Baltimore experience, visit this restaurant in the Hamden district with someone who remembers the neighborhood from its blue-collar heyday in the 1950s. Your companion may refrain from buying a rubber beehive wig from the Café Hon gift shop, but that doesn't mean he wasn't thinking about ordering a meatloaf sandwich before opting instead for a Sunday omelet, replete with Hon potatoes. They are, he will assure you, cooked like hash browns were in Baltimore back in the '50s. Retro burgers, shakes, pies, and a cuppa joe that fully meet present-day expectations. This café embodies a certain "Bawlmerness" that makes it a local institution.

Hungry for an authentic Baltimore meal? Try Café Hon in the city's Hamden district.

CHARLESTON

410-332-7373.
1000 Lancaster St.
Open: Mon. through Sat.
Price: Very expensive.
Cuisine: Low country with a French twist.
Serving: D.
Credit Cards: AE, CB, DC, D, MC, V.
Reservations: Essential.
Handicapped Access: Yes.

In the booming Inner Harbor East development you'll find Charleston, an oasis of Southern-influenced cuisine served in a stylish setting. The restaurant quickly became one of the city's premier spots following its opening, drawing the eye (and palate) of national food and wine media such as noted oenophile Robert Parker. The Southern influence in Chef Cindy Wolf's cuisine is evidenced primarily in the ingredients. Peruse the menu and you'll find dishes incorporating Southern staples such as andouille sausage, cornmeal, stone-milled grits, and fried green tomatoes. But other areas of the country are not ignored: there's a scallop B.L.T. featuring Maine's best, and California gets into the culinary act with Napa Cabbage. Dinner here is meant to be leisurely and luxurious, through to the courses of fresh artisan cheeses and formal dessert. Local farms supply ingredients as often as possible; a recent two-month summer menu to benefit the Chesapeake Bay Foundation saw them well represented.

LOUISIANA
410-327-2610.
1708 Aliceanna St.
Open: Daily.
Price: Expensive to very expensive.
Cuisine: Continental with French/Louisiana Creole touches.
Serving: D (5:30 PM weekdays, 5 PM Saturday, 4 PM Sunday).
Credit Cards: AE, DC, MC, V.
Reservations: Recommended, especially on weekends.
Handicapped Access: yes.

Mahogany paneling and a staircase sweeping grandly to the second floor: Yes, this echoes Louisiana's penchant for splendid gestures and sets the proper tone for the food to come. Stylized grits and collard greens may arrive as sides, but check out the gumbo, too. During a recent dinner we agreed that this can't be considered the classic stew, but it was a wonderful concoction that would no doubt go over big in food-crazed New Orleans. Four gorgeously grilled shrimp inhabited one side of a china bowl, rice specked with corn kernels sat in the middle, and tasso ham, corn, and the rest of the gumbo mix (perhaps with a dash of chili pepper?) occupied the other side. The beautiful salads were worthy of any seasonal New American menu. A roasted beet and chevre cream timbale with apple, endive, and walnuts hit perfect late summer notes, as did the dreamy lobster and avocado salad. Louisianans know how to host a gathering, and the attentive service we enjoyed continued the theme: involved and helpful servers, but not to excess.

Washington, D.C.

The nation's capital stands at the edge of Bay Country (though firmly within its watershed region, which spans Virginia and Maryland and reaches clear to New York), about 30 miles west of Annapolis along the tidal portion of the Potomac River. The city hosts an impressive number of free museums and performances, as well as good restaurants, and is particularly elegant in early spring, when the delicate cherry blossoms burst forth, and into October, when the trees turn color and the famously oppressive humidity of summer has faded.

There's a ton to see here: the Washington Monument, the Lincoln and Jefferson Memorials, the National Gallery of Art, the Kennedy Center for the Performing Arts, the museums of the Smithsonian Institution, and, of course, the White House, the Capitol, and the Mall. These are just the traditional highlights. Visitors do well to also see the nonfederal parts of the city beloved by residents: neighborhoods such as upscale Georgetown, with its great shopping and restaurants; funky-but-going-gentrified Adams-Morgan, home to much good nightlife; and cultured and gay-friendly DuPont Circle, with myriad good restaurants, shops, and the marvelous Philips Collection for those who love early modern art. A new convention center and the MCI Center, home to the NBA's Washington

Wizards, have helped spark a comeback in the Penn Quarter neighborhood on the city's eastern edge. Good restaurants, galleries, and the International Spy Museum are among the recent additions in this part of town. An early urban pioneer here was the Shakespeare Theatre in the Lansburgh.

If you have kids in tow, don't miss the National Zoo, with a zillion wonderful animals, including its stars, giant pandas Mei Xiang and Tian Tian. They moved in after the 1990s deaths of the much-mourned Ling-Ling and Hsing-Hsing, who launched the region's romance with their species in 1972.

The city's Metro system is a safe and dependable way to get around (though, curiously, it has no Georgetown stop). The diverse dining scene, with world-class chefs such as Michel Richard holding forth at his Citronelle at Georgetown's Latham Hotel, just keeps getting better. For information on all the nation's capital has to offer, start with the Washington, DC Convention and Tourism Corp. (202-789-7000; www. washington.org; 901 Seventh St. N.W., Fourth Floor, Washington, DC 20001).

Yorktown–Jamestown–Williamsburg

Perhaps all of America should visit this area, truly the cradle of our colonial history. Before the Pilgrims ever arrived in Massachusetts, the *Susan Constant, Godspeed,* and *Discovery* sailed into **Jamestown.** These first English settlers arrived in 1607 and began their explorations of the Chesapeake Bay. In 1699, Virginians moved their capital from Jamestown to **Williamsburg**, where it remained until moving in 1780 to Richmond. Nearby, the final shots of the Revolutionary War rang out in 1781, when George Washington led the colonists and French in defeat of the British at the Battle of **Yorktown.**

Present-day visitors to the region are blessed with the lovely Colonial Parkway, a wonderful way to explore the Virginia Peninsula, as the area is known. Travelers can drive from Jamestown to the west, along the James River, then tunnel under the historic district of Colonial Williamsburg. The road reaches its end at Yorktown to the east, alongside the York River. Under the auspices of the National Park Service, the **Colonial National Historical Park** (757-898-2410; www.nps.gov/colo; P.O. Box 210, Yorktown, VA 23690) operates significant historical sites throughout the area, including the Yorktown National Battlefield.

Yorktown

The Jamestown-Yorktown Foundation, which operates Jamestown Settlement, also runs the historically rich **Yorktown Victory Center.** More than 500 different Revolutionary War artifacts are on view, and the museum offers a re-created history of the era, with costumed interpreters (including a Continental Army encampment) and hands-on exhibits. Located on VA 1020 adjacent to the Colonial National Historical Park (which includes Yorktown Battlefield). For information, call 757-253-4838 or 1-888-593-4682 or check www.historyisfun.org.

Also stop at the **Yorktown National Battlefield,** where visitors can take a 7-mile driving tour through the site where the War for Independence ended. Two years later, England signed the Treaty of Paris, ratified farther up the Bay in Annapolis. Information on both national sites is available through the Colonial National Historical Park (757-898-2410; www.nps.gov/colo; P.O. Box 210, Yorktown, VA 23690).

Jamestown

The Jamestown Settlement combines indoor gallery exhibits with outdoor living history to tell the tale of the early colonists who came here. Docked along the riverbank are three full-size replicas of the square-riggers *Susan Constant*, *Godspeed*, and *Discovery*, and aboard them sailor-interpreters tell of the four-month voyage taken by the early English settlers. A fort and Powhatan Indian village complete the interpretive tale.

A 35,000-square-foot theater and exhibition center recently debuted, offering ample opportunities to trace the settlement's nascent English beginnings, as well as the cultures of the native Powhatan Indians, the Europeans, and the Africans who found themselves in 17th-century Virginia. A significant expansion also is under way, developed in anticipation of the colony's 400th anniversary in 2007. Additional gallery space is to be added that will continue to explore early Jamestown, and a new film, *Jamestown: The Beginning*, will premiere here in 2006.

The settlement is located 6 miles west of Williamsburg, just off VA 31. Contact: 757-253-4838; www.historyisfun.org; Jamestown-Yorktown Foundation, P.O. Box 1607, Williamsburg, VA 23187.

Visitors also can visit **Jamestown Island**, home to the first settlers. The National Park Service and the Association for the Preservation of Virginia Antiquities operate the **Jamestown National Historic Site** on the island, 22.5 acres at the western end of the island complete with archaeological sites. The park service runs the rest of the 1,500-acre island. Three new buildings are under development, including a visitor's center slated to open in 2006. For information: 757-898-2410; www.nps.gov/colo; P.O. Box 210, Yorktown, VA 23690.

Williamsburg

Williamsburg is a great town in any season, with fireplace smoke and bayberry candle aromas filling winter's air, and daffodils and dogwood bursting forth come spring. **Colonial Williamsburg** nestles within the town of Williamsburg proper, alongside the College of William and Mary (a historical treat in itself), off I-64 midway between Richmond and Norfolk.

Restored in 1926 with the aid of John D. Rockefeller Jr., Colonial Williamsburg, Virginia's original 1699 capital city, truly takes visitors back in time as they stroll the old streets and take in everything from the Governor's Palace to nearby museums. At the Governor's Palace, formal English gardens are restored to period symmetry and perform double duty for families with children, who will love the boxwood maze. People in period costumes are everywhere. If they're not demonstrating the fine craft of smithing, they're marching in a fife and drum corps.

Along Duke of Gloucester Street stand the restored homes and workshops of the 18th century, manned by docents in colonial garb. This is also home to three historic taverns (Josiah Chowning's Tavern, King's Arms Tavern, and Shield's Tavern) prepared to serve 21st-century diners a colonial meal and perhaps a song. Nearby, on Waller Street, Christina Campbell's Tavern holds forth with its seafood fare. (For reservations, call 1-800-TAVERNS.) In all, 88 original buildings stand among the 500 structures that compose Colonial Williamsburg proper.

Visitors who are staying more than a day are advised to check out ticket packages. Information is available by contacting 1-800-HISTORY or www.colonialwilliamsburg.org.

The Colonial Williamsburg Visitor's Center is located off Colonial Parkway at 100 Information Center Dr., Williamsburg, VA 23187.

Visitors also will want to check out a variety of other fun options. For family entertainment, there's the **Busch Gardens** theme park and **Water Country USA**, shopping at three outlets on Richmond Road (US 60) at the edge of town, the upscale Duke of Gloucester Street shops at **Merchant's Square,** and the enormous bargainland known as the **Williamsburg Pottery Factory.**

Golfers, too, will be in paradise. Among their options: courses designed by Pete Dye, Arnold Palmer, Curtis Strange, and Robert Trent Jones Sr. For more information, call Golf Williamsburg at 1-888-2-GOLF-WB.

Gourmets know to check out the famed cuisine at the **Trellis Restaurant** (Merchant's Square; 757-229-8610; open daily for L, D) with its equally famed Death by Chocolate dessert. Also consider **Berret's Seafood Restaurant and Taphouse Grill** (Merchant's Square; 757-253-1847) for lunch or dinner. The elegant menu features local cuisine such as a Virginia ham and crabmeat combination swooning in a puff pastry topped with a lemon-dill hollandaise. The lunch menu includes a selection of pretty sandwiches and salads. The restaurant's intimate dining areas include the brick Taphouse Grill patio, with tables in view of the College of William and Mary.

Lodging suggestions for the region include the James River–side **Kingsmill Resort & Spa** (757-253-1703 or 1-800-832-5665; www.kingsmill.com; 1010 Kingsmill Rd., Williamsburg, VA 23185; condos and individual sleeping rooms available; high-season rates are very expensive). Or try the **Best Western Patrick Henry Inn** (757-229-9540 or 1-800-446-9228; York and Page Sts., Williamsburg, VA 23187), with 297 rooms—three of them are suites—and prices in the moderate to expensive range. National chain hotels also operate within the area. For abundant tourist information, contact the Williamsburg Area Convention & Visitors Bureau (757-253-0192 or 1-800-368-6511; www.visitwilliamsburg.com; 421 N. Boundary St., Williamsburg, VA 23185).

Hampton Roads

When it comes to the southern end of the Bay, marketing gurus didn't agree with Shakespeare's premise, "A rose by any other name would smell as sweet." For decades, the region had a mishmash of monikers—"Tidewater" being one of the most common—coupled with unclear geographical boundaries. After initial resistance, area cities and locales recognized the wisdom of promoting regionalism and adopted the oft-used designation "Hampton Roads."

In nautical terminology, "roads" means "a place for ships to anchor." The name "Hampton Roads" has historic roots reaching back to the 17th century, when it was first used to refer to the natural deep harbor formed by the James, Elizabeth, and Nansemond rivers flowing into the Chesapeake Bay. "Hampton" was used to honor the Earl of Southampton, Henry Wriothesley, who championed the colonization of Virginia.

Hampton Roads consists of the diverse cities of Chesapeake, Hampton, Newport News, Norfolk, Portsmouth, Suffolk, and Virginia Beach and has a total populace of about 1.5 million.

South of Virginia's rural Eastern Shore, at the foot of the Chesapeake Bay Bridge-Tunnel, is Virginia Beach, the most populous city in Hampton Roads and Virginia. Made up of sprawling subdivisions, Virginia Beach is known nationally for its popular resort strip highlighted by wide ocean beaches, a 3-mile boardwalk, and high-energy nightlife.

Next door to Virginia Beach, with shorelines on the Chesapeake Bay and the Elizabeth River, is Norfolk, alive with the world's largest Navy base and a thriving cultural downtown and waterfront. A short jaunt west across the Elizabeth River is the city of Portsmouth. Home to one of the country's oldest working harbors, its historic downtown is undergoing an amazing rebirth. Farther north along the James River and minutes from Williamsburg is Newport News, a major seaport and shipbuilding center.

HAMPTON ROADS ATTRACTIONS

Of 100 exhibits at the **Virginia Air & Space Center** (757-727-0900 or 1-800-296-0800; www.vasc.org; 600 Settlers Landing Rd., Hampton), highlights include a weather exhibit (try playing with a tornado funnel), a replica of the Wright Brothers' "first flight" 1903 Flyer, and the 1969 Apollo 12 command module that orbited the moon 31 times. There's also an IMAX theater. Norfolk's **NAUTICUS** (757-664-1000 or 1-800-664-1080; www .nauticus.org; One Waterside Dr., Norfolk), where the massive World War II–era battleship *Wisconsin* dominates the city's waterfront, offers aquariums and interactive simulators that let visitors check out life beneath the sea or aboard a naval battleship. Art lovers will go gaga over the works of Degas and Renoir and the **Chrysler Museum of Art's** (757-664-6200; www.chrysler.org; 245 W. Olney Rd., Norfolk) collection of five centuries of master-pieces, as well as its outstanding glass collection that includes the popular works of Louis Comfort Tiffany. Exciting exhibits run the gamut from historic African American quilts to renowned Civil War photographs.

A must-see for anyone interested in the sea are the impressive and copious exhibits at the **Mariners' Museum** (757-596-2222 or 1-800-581-SAIL; www.mariner.org; 100 Museum Dr., Newport News), with a center devoted to the famed USS *Monitor*, the historic Civil War ironclad whose artifacts are being slowly brought ashore. Its 1862 Bay battle with the Confederate *Virginia* ended the era of wooden naval ships. Also: Spotlit cases and mag-nifiers highlight the miniature ship collection of late Virginia artist and carver August F. Crabtree, and the Chesapeake Bay Gallery, devoted to the Bay's maritime history, explores watermen and shipbuilding on up to these recreational days.

The **Children's Museum of Virginia** (757-393-5258; www.childrensmuseumva.com; 221 High St., Portsmouth) is a large museum where little hands will marvel at the numer-ous exhibits in which they can participate, like being inside a bubble you make yourself or playing dino detective and digging up a triceratops fossil. Grown-ups will appreciate the extensive antique toy and train collection, some heading down the track on four layouts. Also includes a small planetarium.

The **Virginia Aquarium & Marine Science Museum** (757-425-FISH; www.vmsm.com; 717 General Booth Blvd., Virginia Beach), formerly the Virginia Marine Science Museum, is where you get to meet the real locals under the waves and on dry land. More than 800,000 gallons of aquariums introduce you to sea turtles, sharks, river otters, and more. Also includes over 300 hands-on exhibits, an outdoor aviary, 10 acres of marsh habitat, and a short nature trail. Museum runs seasonal whale- and dolphin-watching boat trips.

Lions and tigers and bears—almost. With nearly 400 animals, the **Virginia Zoological Park** (757-441-2706; www.virginiazoo.org; 3500 Granby St., Norfolk) is a small zoo with big charm. Ten years in the making, the 8-acre Okavango Delta African plains exhibit recently added nine new species to the facility, including zebras, lions, giraffes, red river hogs, and meerkat.

In the impersonal age of multiplex mall movie theaters, the grandly restored 1945 Art Deco **Commodore Theatre** (757-393-6962; www.commodoretheatre.com; 421 High St., Portsmouth) is an experience not to be missed. With its 1940s nightclub atmosphere of small tables and discreet table lamps, you can sit and enjoy a surprising range of dinner options along with wine and beer while taking in the magic of the silver screen.

Beach it at **Virginia Beach**, where East Coast revelers flock to 28 miles of ocean beach and another 10 miles of Bay. Sun, fish, surf fish, or stroll Atlantic Avenue, the main thoroughfare fronted by a 3-mile boardwalk, prime people-watching territory.

For more information on the Hampton Roads area, contact:

Newport News Visitor Center (1-888-493-7386; www.newport-news.org; 13560 Jefferson Ave., Newport News, VA 23603)

Norfolk Convention and Visitors Bureau (1-800-368-3097; www.norfolkcvb.com; 232 E. Main St., Norfolk, VA 23510)

Portsmouth Convention and Visitors Bureau (1-800-PORTS-VA; www.portsva.com; 505 Crawford St., Portsmouth, VA 23704)

Virginia Beach Visitor's Center (1-800-VA-BEACH; www.vbfun.com; 2100 Parks Ave., Virginia Beach, VA 23451)

HAMPTON ROADS LODGING

BARCLAY COTTAGE

Innkeepers: Steve and Marie-Louise LaFond.
757-422-1956.
www.barclaycottage.com.
400 16th St., Virginia Beach, VA 23451.

Price: Moderate to very expensive.
Credit Cards: AE, D, MC, V.
Handicapped Access: No.
Special Features: Complimentary beach chairs, umbrellas, towels, and boogie boards.
Restrictions: No children.

A B&B oasis in a sea of high-rises, this veranda-adorned 1895 beauty bills itself as one of only two remaining Victorian cottages in Virginia Beach. The quaint five-bedroom establishment (three rooms with private baths and two that share) was a guesthouse as far back as 1916. It provides a refreshing alternative to the hustle and bustle of the resort strip, while still placing guests within short walking distance of the city's famous sandy beaches and other attractions in nearby urban Tidewater.

THE GLENCOE INN BED AND BREAKFAST

Innkeeper: Anne McGowan-McGlynn.
757-397-8128.
www.glencoeinn.com.
222 North St., Portsmouth, VA 23704.
Price: Moderate to very expensive.
Credit Cards: AE, D, MC, V.
Handicapped Access: No.
Special Features: High-speed wireless Internet service, working fireplace in every room.
Restrictions: Children under 12 allowed in one suite only.

The first licensed B&B in Portsmouth's newly revitalized Olde Towne historic district has charming Scottish touches throughout, from the handmade lace to the morning porridge and marmalade and, of course, Anne's warm, welcoming brogue. Built in 1890, Glencoe was restored to its Victorian birthright with original lights, crown molding, hardwood floors, and fireplaces kept intact. There are four rooms, two of which can convert to a suite. Gather on the friendly front porch to enjoy Anne's fabulous ginger scones and other breakfast delights, or request an afternoon tea. A third-floor deck off the back gardens is a great way to greet the sun coming up over the Elizabeth River, just a gull's cry away.

HISTORIC PAGE HOUSE INN

Innkeeper: Carl A. Albero.
757-625-5033 or 1-800-599-7659.
www.pagehouseinn.com.
323 Fairfax Ave., Norfolk, VA 23507.
Price: Expensive to very expensive.
Credit Cards: AE, MC, V.
Handicapped Access: No.
Special Features: Children age 8 and up OK. Dogs under 25 pounds allowed for an additional fee; call for permission for larger ones.

This circa-1899 mansion hobnobs with the highbrow; its next-door neighbor is the Chrysler Museum of Art. Add that to its AAA Four Diamond rating and you know you've found a gem. Three of the seven Victorian-style rooms are suites, and most rooms have whirlpool tubs and gas fireplaces. Rates include full champagne breakfast served in the dining room, complimentary bottled water, soft drinks, snacks, and fruit basket. Fresh-baked cookies served every afternoon with tea and cappuccino. There is a fitness room on the premises, and complimentary bicycles are available for touring the town.

Hampton Roads Hotels

Renaissance Portsmouth Hotel (757-673-3000; 25 Water St., Portsmouth) Elizabeth River–side hotel. Very expensive.

Sheraton Norfolk Waterside Hotel (757-622-6664; 777 Waterside Dr., Norfolk) Two restaurants, 445 rooms, and access to high-speed Internet. Adjacent to Waterside Marketplace. Very expensive.

Virginia Beach Resort Hotel and Conference Center (757-481-9000 or 1-800-468-2722; 2800 Shore Drive Dr., Virginia Beach) Views from 295 bay-view suites, private beach, easy access to many amenities and activities. Very expensive.

HAMPTON ROADS RESTAURANTS

ALEXANDER'S ON THE BAY

757-464-4999.
4536 Ocean View Ave., Virginia Beach.
Open: Mon. through Fri. 5:30–9, Sat. and Sun. 5–11.
Price: Expensive to very expensive.
Cuisine: Seafood, American.
Serving: D.
Credit Cards: AE, D, MC, V.
Reservations: Yes.
Handicapped Access: Yes.

Its sandy perch on the southern end of the Chesapeake Bay Bridge-Tunnel is a view not lost on a single diner here, thanks to the landmark restaurant's layout. Besides the Bay-side vista, Alexander's is an upscale eatery strong in the "S" category: great steaks, seafood, and service.

BUBBA'S CRABHOUSE AND SEAFOOD RESTAURANT

757-481-3513.
3323 Shore Dr., Virginia Beach.
Open: Sun. through Thurs. 11–10, Fri. and Sat. 11–11.
Price: Inexpensive to expensive.
Cuisine: Seafood.
Serving: L, D.
Credit Cards: AE, DC, MC, V.
Reservations: No.
Handicapped Access: Yes.

Lovers of blue crabs would be remiss if they missed this been-here-forever, laid-back seafood joint. Perfectly perched an arm's length from the Lynnhaven Inlet at Bubba's Marina, this eatery has earned the right to brag "you can't find fresher unless you ride in on the boat." Nothing beats hunkering down on the open deck at paper-covered tables and picking your way through the hours and dozens of succulent steamed crabs. That special zing is brought to you by Bubba's own special brew of bay seasoning.

FUSION 440

757-398-0888.
467 Dinwiddie St., Portsmouth.
Open: Sun. through Thurs. 5–10, Fri. and Sat. 5–11.
Price: Expensive to very expensive.
Cuisine: American-style bistro with international influences.
Serving: D, SB.
Credit Cards: AE, CB, DC, D, MC, V.
Reservations: Strongly recommended.
Handicapped Access: Yes.

Cheap eats, no. Cutting-edge cuisine, yes. A step off scenic Olde Towne's High Street, the small dining room makes a large impact with walls of intense red and yellow, while still imparting an intimate atmosphere. The menu is an eclectic sprinkling where you can start with a Trio of Caviar appetizer served with chilled jumbo shrimp and a Stoli caraway aioli. Continuing to the main event, perhaps Fusion 440's lobster and veal—a lobster tail and grilled tenderloin entrée. The restaurant's international wine offerings won it a regional Best Wine List award from *Port Folio Weekly*, a Hampton Roads publication.

THE PAINTED LADY

757-623-8872.
112 E. 17th St., Norfolk.
Open: Tues. through Sun.
Price: Expensive to very expensive.
Cuisine: Contemporary American, British high tea.
Serving: L, D, SB, afternoon tea.
Credit Cards: AE, MC, V.
Reservations: Yes.
Handicapped Access: Yes.
Special Features: Five working fireplaces, gift shop with six themed rooms.

Two turn-of-the-century homes converted into one exceptional restaurant, the Painted Lady is a winner of the regional Most Romantic Restaurant award from *Hampton Roads Magazine*, yet it brings a unique contribution to the local cuisine scene with its demure afternoon tea. Choose from four tea courses in an opulent Victorian setting. Royal Tea is a British-style, three-course tea featuring assorted finger sandwiches, homemade pastries, chocolate-covered strawberries, and freshly baked scones served with double Devonshire cream, raspberry jam, and homemade lemon curd. It's accompanied with a flute of champagne, sherry, wine, or port. The adorable children's Teddy Bear Tea is served just like the grown-ups', with either tea or warm apple juice along with a peanut butter and jelly sandwich, an assortment of fresh fruit, and a homemade cinnamon bear cookie.

A sailboat awaits the next adventure. Photo courtesy of the Inn at Perry Cabin

9

INFORMATION

The Right Connections

Consider this an abbreviated encyclopedia of Bay-related information that will help you move more easily through the area. This chapter provides guidance on the following:

AREA CODES

In Maryland, callers must always dial the area code, even if it's not a long-distance call. Most Chesapeake area numbers are 410, except for St. Marys County, in Southern Maryland, where it's 301. Recently, 443 has been added for Maryland's Chesapeake area. Virginia area codes are as follows: Hampton Roads/Tidewater and Eastern Shore region, 757; Northern Neck, 804; Richmond, 804. The 703 area codes in this book serve northern Virginia telephone numbers in the Washington, D.C., metropolitan area. Washington, D.C.'s area code is 202.

Bibliography

Books You Can Buy
CHILDREN'S BOOKS

Cummings, Priscilla. *Chadwick the Crab.* Tidewater Publishing, 1986.

Henry, Marguerite. *Misty of Chincoteague.* Rand, 1947. Many editions and publishers; this is the original.

Holland, Jeffrey. *Chessie, the Sea Monster That Ate Annapolis.* Oak Creek Publishers, 1990.

Voigt, Cynthia. *Homecoming.* Fawcett Juniper, 1981.

COOKBOOKS

Kitching, Frances, and Susan Stiles Dowell. *Mrs. Kitching's Smith Island Cookbook.* Tidewater Publishers, 1981.

Shields, John. *Chesapeake Bay Cooking with John Shields: A Companion Cookbook to the Public Television Show.* Bantam Doubleday Dell Publishers, 1998.

FICTION

Barth, John. *The Sot-Weed Factor.* Doubleday, 1987.

———. *Tidewater Tales.* Fawcett, 1987.

Chappell, Helen. *Ghost of a Chance: A Hollis Ball/Sam Westcott Mystery.* Dell Publishing, 1998.

———. *Giving Up the Ghost: A Hollis Ball/Sam Westcott Mystery.* Dell Publishing, 1999.

Hart, Lenore, *Waterwoman.* Penguin Putnam/Berkley Books, 2002.

Michener, James A. *Chesapeake.* Random House, 1978.

Styron, William. *A Tidewater Morning: Three Tales from Youth.* Random House, 1993.

HISTORY, MEMOIR, AND LORE

Brown, Alexander Crosby. *Steam Packets on the Chesapeake: A History of the Old Bay Line Since 1840.* Cornell Maritime, Tidewater Publishers, 1961.

Brown, Philip L. *The Other Annapolis, 1900–1950.* The Annapolis Publishing Co., 1994.

Brugger, Robert J. *Maryland: A Middle Temperament, 1634–1980.* Johns Hopkins University Press, 1988.

Burgess, Robert H. *This Was Chesapeake Bay.* Cornell Maritime Press, 1963.

Carr, Lois Green, Philip D. Morgan, and Jean B. Russo. *Colonial Chesapeake Society.* University of North Carolina, 1988.

Chowning, Larry S. *Chesapeake Legacy: Tools & Traditions.* Tidewater Publishers, 1995.

Davison, Steven G., et al. *Chesapeake Waters: Four Centuries of Controversy, Concern, and Legislation.* Tidewater Publishers, 1983, 1997.

De Gast, Robert. *The Lighthouses of the Chesapeake.* Johns Hopkins University Press, 1973.

Dize, Frances W. *Smith Island, Chesapeake Bay.* Tidewater Publishers, 1990.

Freeman, Roland L. *The Arabbers of Baltimore.* Tidewater Publishers, 1989.

Horton, Tom. *An Island Out of Time: A Memoir of Smith Island in the Chesapeake.* W. W. Norton & Co., 1966.

Jander, Anne Hughes. *Crab's Hole: A Family's Story of Tangier Island.* Literary House Press, Washington College, 1994.

Keiper, Ronald R. *The Assateague Ponies.* Tidewater Publishers, 1985.

Middleton, Arthur Pierce. *Tobacco Coast: A Maritime History of Chesapeake Bay in the Colonial Era.* Johns Hopkins University Press, 1984.

Mills, Eric. *Chesapeake Bay in the Civil War.* Tidewater Publishers, 1996.

———. Chesapeake *Rumrunners of the Roaring Twenties.* Cornell Maritime Press, 2000.

Shomette, Donald. *Ghost Fleet of Mallows Bay and Other Tales of the Lost Chesapeake.* Tidewater Publishers, 1996.

———. *Lost Towns of Tidewater Chesapeake.* Tidewater Publishers, 2000.

———. *Pirates on the Chesapeake: Being a True History of Pirates, Picaroons, and Sea Raiders on Chesapeake Bay, 1610–1807.* Tidewater Publishers, 1985.

Wennersten, John R. *The Oyster Wars of Chesapeake Bay.* Tidewater Publishers, 1981.

Whitehead, John Hurt III. *The Watermen of the Chesapeake Bay.* Tidewater Publishers, 1979.

NATURAL HISTORY AND FIELD GUIDES

Hedeen, Robert A. *The Oyster: Life and Lore of the Celebrated Bivalve.* Tidewater Publishers, 1986.

Horton, Tom. *Bay Country.* Johns Hopkins University Press, 1987.

———. *Turning the Tide: Saving the Chesapeake Bay.* Island Press, 1991.

Lawrence, Susannah. *The Audubon Society Field Guide to the Natural Places of the Mid-Atlantic States: Coastal.* Pantheon Books, 1984.

Lippson, Alice J., and Robert L. Lippson. *Life in the Chesapeake Bay.* Johns Hopkins University Press, 1984, 1997.

Meanley, Brooke. *Birdlife at Chincoteague and the Virginia Barrier Islands.* Tidewater Publishers, 1981.

Sherwood, Arthur W. *Understanding the Chesapeake: A Layman's Guide.* Tidewater Publishers, 1973.

Taylor, John W. *Birds of the Chesapeake Bay.* Johns Hopkins University Press, 1992.

Warner, William W. *Beautiful Swimmers: Watermen, Crabs and the Chesapeake Bay.* Penguin Books, 1976.

White, Christopher P. *Chesapeake Bay: A Field Guide.* Tidewater Publishers, 1989.

Williams, John Page, Jr. *Chesapeake Almanac: Following the Bay Through the Seasons.* Tidewater Publishers, 1993.

PHOTOGRAPHY AND ESSAY

Cushard, Carol, and Jane Wilson McWilliams. *Bay Ridge on the Chesapeake: An Illustrated History.* Brighton Editions, 1986.

Harp, David W., and Tom Horton. *Water's Way: Life Along the Chesapeake.* Johns Hopkins University Press, 2000.

Meyer, Eugene L., and Lucien Niemeyer. *Chesapeake Country.* Abbeville Press, 1990.

Snediker, Quentin, and Ann Jensen. *Chesapeake Bay Schooners.* Tidewater Publishers, 1992.

Warren, Mame. *Then Again ... Annapolis, 1900–1965.* Time Exposure, 1990.

Warren, Marion E., with Mame Warren. *Bringing Back the Bay.* Johns Hopkins University Press, 1994.

RECREATION

Gillelan, G. Howard. *Gunning for Sea Ducks.* Tidewater Publishers, 1988.

Shellenberger, William H. *Cruising the Chesapeake: A Gunkholer's Guide.* International Marine Publishing Co., 1990.

TRAVEL

Anderson, Elizabeth B. *Annapolis: A Walk Through History.* Tidewater Publishers, 1984.

Arnett, Earl, Robert J. Brugger, and Edward C. Papenfuse. *Maryland, a New Guide to the Old Line State.* Johns Hopkins University Press, 1999.

Wiencek, Henry. *The Smithsonian Guide to Historic America, Virginia and the Capital Region.* Stewart, Tabori & Chang, 1989.

Books You Can Borrow

Bodine, A. Aubrey. *Chesapeake Bay and Tidewater.* Bodine and Assoc., 1954. 3rd ed., 1980. Classic black-and-white photographs by noted *Baltimore Sunday Sun* photographer.

Burgess, Robert H. *This Was Chesapeake Bay.* Tidewater Publishers, 1963. Compendium of historic accounts of watermen and Bay vessels.

Byron, Gilbert. *Early Explorations of the Chesapeake Bay.* Maryland Historical Society, 1960.

Capper, John, et al. *Chesapeake Waters: Pollution, Public Health, and Public Opinion, 1607–1972.* Originally published by the EPA, contains historic account of Bay pollution. Republished by Tidewater Publishers, 1983.

Chapelle, Suzanne Ellery Greene, et al. *Maryland, a History of Its People.* Johns Hopkins University Press, 1986.

Earle, Swepson. *The Chesapeake Bay Country.* 1923. Reprinted by Weathervane Books, 1983.

Fiske, John. *Old Virginia and Her Neighbours.* Houghton, Mifflin & Co., 1897. Old-style account of the founding of the Chesapeake colonies.

Footner, Hulbert. *Rivers of the Eastern Shore.* Rinehart & Co., Inc., 1944.

Gibbons, Boyd. *Wye Island.* Johns Hopkins University Press, 1977. History and natural history of unspoiled island surrounded by Wye River on Maryland's Eastern Shore.

Hildebrand, Samuel F. *Fishes of Chesapeake Bay.* TFH Publications, 1972.

Klingel, Gilbert C. *The Bay.* Tradition, 1966. Natural history essay.

Lippson, Alice Jane. *The Chesapeake Bay in Maryland: An Atlas of Natural Resources.* Johns Hopkins University Press, 1973.

Metcalf, Paul. *Waters of Potowmack.* North Point Press, 1982. Natural and social history of the Bay's most famous tributary.

Schubel, J.R. *The Life and Death of the Chesapeake Bay.* University of Maryland, 1986.

Tawes, William I. *God, Man, Salt Water and the Eastern Shore.* Tidewater Publishers, 1967.

Wilstach, Paul. *Tidewater Maryland.* The Bobbs-Merrill Co., 1931. Funky classic. Reprinted several times.

BICYCLING BASICS

Both Maryland and Virginia staff offices to assist cyclists. In **Maryland,** contact the bicycle coordinator's office (410-545-5656 or 1-800-252-8776; www.sha.state.md.us; 707 N. Calvert St., C 502/P.O. Box 717, Baltimore, MD 21203). Ask for maps or other information. In **Virginia,** contact the Department of Transportation's Bicycle Coordinator (1-800-835-1203; e-mail: vabiking@vdot.state.va.us; 1401 E. Broad St., Richmond, VA 23219).

Keep in mind that you can't cycle across many major bridges, such as the Chesapeake Bay Bridge near Annapolis and the Chesapeake Bay Bridge-Tunnel from Virginia Beach to the Lower Eastern Shore of Virginia. If you call the CBBT in advance at 757-331-2960, they will transport you and your bike, but they'll charge the $12 vehicle toll.

Both Maryland and Virginia offer roadways and bicycle routes to suit cyclists of all abilities. McAllen Photography

BOATING

What the heck is a "bareboat" charter? It's captaining a charter boat on your own—and if you don't know how, you'll need to take a course to do so. It's also one way to get out on the water. The following definitions will help you choose which boating option is best for you and your travel companions.

Charter boats are what you want if you plan to sail or power for more than a day—often a week—which you'll do with a captain or by yourself (aka bareboating). Charter agencies will want to see your boating résumé and check references. Keep in mind that "chartering" means a range of things: you can charter the 50-foot yacht you're thinking of buying and take yourself to the Caribbean, or you can charter a weekend sailboat with a skipper and relax on deck. Although technically it's conceivable to charter a boat for a day, you're more likely to encounter two-day minimums and weekend prices that may start around $800 to $850. Prices range widely depending on the boat, and prices may drop the longer you're out on the boat. In short, chartering's a great way to see the Bay. Local boating schools offer courses to get you certified to handle someone else's prized vessel and can usually rent or charter craft once you're certified. They, too, will want to see your sailing résumé.

Cruise and excursion boats take folks out for a ride, and your vessel may be anything from an authentic Chesapeake skipjack to a reproduction schooner to the equivalent of a waterborne bus. These are good get-acquainted options, perfect for an afternoon outing, and your crew often narrates the history (either natural or man-made) of the passing shoreline.

At Knapp's Narrows and throughout Chesapeake Country, boats are available to rent for a few hours or charter for a week.

Water taxis can stand in for an excursion boat, providing fun (and usually cheap) point-to-point rides across the harbor to a good restaurant or other destination.

Boating schools supply all you'll need to learn to handle a jib, navigate by the stars, or take a safe spin through crowded waters aboard a powerboat. Some folks plan vacations around weeklong sailing lessons.

Rent a daysailer, skiff, windsurfer, Jet Ski, rowboat, canoe, or kayak. Go out for as little as an hour or as long as a day. Your outfitter is in charge of how much experience you'll need to take out the boat and will ask all the necessary questions. Many marinas host vendors who rent various craft.

Good sources for more information include the about-town freebie *Spinsheet* (www.spinsheet.com; 301 Fourth St., Annapolis, MD 21403) and the *PortBook*, also distributed free at locations listed in the guide (www.portbook.net; P.O. Box 462, Belfast, ME 04915; specify "Annapolis"; $3 per mail-ordered copy).

Climate and Weather

Expect relatively mild weather in Chesapeake Country. Fahrenheit averages bring January highs of 40 degrees (22 degrees low) at the top of the Bay in Chesapeake City, Md., and, nearly 240 miles south, at the mouth of the Bay in Norfolk, Va., average highs of 47 degrees

(30 degrees low). July can often bring temperatures in the upper 80s to both the Upper and Lower Bay regions. Annapolis, located mid-Bay on the Western Shore, generally expects January highs into the 40s and lows in the 20s, while July temperatures generally range in the 80s during the day and drop into the 60s at night.

But averages tell only part of the story. Proximity to the 3,700-square-mile Bay often brings high humidity during the months of July and August, which can bring furious afternoon and evening thunderstorms in late summer, when daytime temperatures easily top 90 degrees. Take these storms seriously; people have been struck and killed by lightning on and around the Bay. Even on the calmest day, boaters must always keep an eye on the windward sky (and an ear on the marine weather forecast).

By early September, humidity often has dropped considerably, although temperatures in the 80-degree range tend to continue well into the month. Chesapeake's average fall temperature is 62 degrees. Sailors love it; a steady breeze blows in the 10- to 15-knot range.

Chesapeake winters usually bring mild temperatures, with an average of fewer than 10 inches of snowfall. Wind chill near the water, however, can make the air seem considerably colder and may even produce dangerous chilling or frostbite.

On the open Bay, rays are magnified by the water's surface, increasing the risk of sunburn and sunstroke. A hat, lip balm, and sunscreen are always recommended. Also, keep in mind that alcoholic beverages are best consumed after your voyage. Enforcement of drunken-boater laws can be stringent.

To obtain updated weather reports, check any local newspaper (or their websites) or the Weather Channel's www.weather.com.

EMERGENCY INFORMATION

For police, fire, and ambulance emergencies, dial 911. Via cell phone, report accidents or other highway emergencies by calling #77 or 911. On the water, the U.S. Coast Guard responds to VHF marine radio Channel 16.

Maryland
Maryland Department of Natural Resources Police Emergency Dispatch (410-260-8888 in Annapolis, or 911 and ask to be connected to the DNR police; 1-877-620-8367, general information)

Maryland State Police (410-486-3101 or 1-800-525-5555 in-state only)

U.S. Coast Guard Activities Baltimore (410-576-2561, general information; 410-576-2525, search and rescue)

U.S. Coast Guard Station Annapolis (410-267-8108).

Virginia
Virginia Department of Game and Inland Fisheries (804-367-1000; 4010 W. Broad St., Richmond, VA 23230) For boating information or to report environmental hazards during weekday business hours.

Virginia State Police (804-674-2000; for state road conditions, 1-800-367-ROAD)

The **U.S. Coast Guard** directs your calls as follows: For threat to life and limb, contact the **U.S. Coast Guard Hampton Roads Group,** 757-483-8567. For threat to property, the **U.S. Coast Guard's Marine Safety Group** out of Hampton Roads can be reached at 757-638-6637. If you're farther north, from Smith Point (near Reedville) to the York River, call the **U.S. Coast Guard at Milford Haven,** 804-725-2125. In the lower Chesapeake Bay, call the **Coast Guard Station Cape Charles,** 757-331-2001. Farther north, call the **Coast Guard Station Crisfield,** 410-968-0323.

Environmental Organizations

"Save the Bay" is a rallying cry around the Chesapeake Bay, the focus of a massive cleanup effort by state and federal agencies since the late 1970s. If you really want to get into the issue, there's plenty to learn—and plenty of information. Local libraries often stock scientific studies on the Bay, or you can contact the following organizations:

The **Chesapeake Bay Foundation** (410-268-8816, Annapolis office; www.cbf.org; Philip Merrill Environmental Center, 6 Herndon Ave., Annapolis, MD 21403), headquartered out of a notable "green" building in Annapolis, with other offices elsewhere throughout the Chesapeake watershed region, is the leading nonprofit "Save the Bay" organization. It actively educates the public about a range of Bay-related environmental issues at stops up and down the Chesapeake. Contact them if you're interested in environmental education programs in the field (or, for that matter, on a boat). The Annapolis building is open for tours; check the CBF website for information.

The multiagency umbrella that oversees the government cleanup, the **Chesapeake Bay Program,** has a hot line (1-800-YOUR-BAY). The **Chesapeake Regional Information Service,** or CRIS (1-800-662-CRIS; e-mail acb@ari.net), is the 24/7 hot line to call for facts and figures on the Bay or to report an illegal dumping. It's sponsored by the Alliance for the Chesapeake Bay (www.acb-online.org).

Farms and Produce Markets

The fabled "Bounty of the Bay" doesn't mean just rockfish and blue crabs. Tomatoes, sweet corn, cantaloupe—when you see fresh local produce spilling from baskets at roadside stands, you'll agree. Produce markets are common on Bay byways from spring well through fall. For more information about finding farm stands, farms, and farmer's markets, contact the tourism departments listed at the end of this chapter. Or try the Virginia Department of Agriculture online at www.vdacs.virginia.gov/vagrown, or the Maryland Department of Agriculture at www.marylandsbest.net.

Fishing

From marshy creeks to wide-open water, the Chesapeake and its tributaries compose one of the greatest anglers' destinations anywhere. Catch-and-release fishing is popular, and fly-fishing has caught on, too. Seventeen species of game fish live in the Bay, pursued from riverbanks, piers, skiffs, head boats, and charter boats. Among the favorite finfish: bluefish, striped bass (known locally as rockfish), sea trout, white and yellow perch, spot, striped bass, catfish, and summer flounder.

Then there is the Maryland blue crab, wildly popular and the focus of considerable political attention as both Maryland and Virginia wrestle with how to manage the up-and-down populations of recent years. Some blame overharvesting; others cite problems including the natural life cycle of any species, loss of their grass-bed habitat, and predation by finfish whose populations have recovered. Whatever the reason, be kind and resist the urge to overfish. Some people think that it would be a good idea not to catch females, which have rounded, U-shaped aprons, unlike the pointed aprons of the males.

Fishing licenses are widely available at fishing and sporting goods stores, but they are not required if you are under age 16 in either Maryland or Virginia. A saltwater fishing license issued by Maryland or Virginia is good in either state. You won't need a license in Maryland if you are fishing from a chartered boat or if you are fishing as a nonpaying guest from private property. In addition, the Maryland Department of Natural Resources can tell you about free fishing areas. Ask about nonresident licenses for consecutive days of fishing—probably a bargain if you're visiting the region. Prices are generally reduced for fishers over age 65.

In Maryland, licenses for recreational crabbers are required for anyone using a trotline or anyone who wants to catch more than two dozen crabs. In Virginia, recreational crabbers need a license if they're using more than two crab pots.

Other rules may apply and regulations may change; check at bait stores or contact the states for more information on fishing or crabbing.

A simple way to catch crabs is the fine art of "chicken necking": Tie a chicken neck to a string, tie the string to a piling, and when it tenses up, slowly ease the bait up into sight, along with a crab or two hanging on to feed. Scoop with a long-handled dip net. Keeps the kids happy for hours!

A map of the Bay shows all its public access points and is available free by calling 1-800-YOUR-BAY. In addition, Maryland publishes a list of boat ramps, *A Fisherman's Guide to Maryland Piers and Boat Ramps,* which also provides license details, creel limits, and seasonal limits for each species. To obtain the guide, or to get information on both fresh- and saltwater fishing licenses or other needs, contact the Maryland Department of Natural Resources, Fisheries Service (1-800-688-FINS; www.dnr.state.md.us; 580 Taylor Ave., Annapolis, MD 21401). For information on Virginia freshwater fishing, contact the Department of Game and Inland Fisheries (804-367-1000; www.dgif.state.va.us; 4010 W. Broad St./P.O. Box 11104, Richmond, VA 23230). Virginia saltwater anglers, contact the Marine Resources Commission (757-247-2200 or 1-800-541-4646; www.state.va.us/mrc; 2600 Washington Ave./P.O. Box 756, Newport News, VA 23607).

In addition to the tips in each chapter for finding charter boat captains, useful statewide contacts include the **Virginia Charter Boat Association** (www.fishva.org; P.O. Box 1217, Gloucester Point, VA 23062) and the **Chesapeake Guides Association** (www.chesapeakeguides.com), an organization of light tackle guides in Maryland.

HANDICAPPED SERVICES

In **Maryland,** the free *Destination Maryland* guide notes entries with accessibility for those with disabilities. To obtain a copy, contact the Maryland Office of Tourism Development

(410-767-3400 or 1-800-543-1036; www.mdisfun.org; 217 E. Redwood St., Baltimore, MD 21202).

In **Virginia,** *The Virginia Travel Guide for the Persons with Disabilities* is a free comprehensive guide that goes beyond whether a wheelchair-bound visitor can get in and out of doors. To obtain a copy, contact the Virginia Tourism Corporation (804-786-4484 or 1-800-742-3935; www.virginia.org [keywords "handicapped accessible"]; 901 E. Byrd St., Richmond, VA 23219).

HOSPITALS AND HEALTH CARE

Should a serious health problem arise, you are, fortunately, near some of the nation's top medical facilities.

Baltimore, Maryland
The Johns Hopkins Hospital (410-955-5000 main number, 410-955-2280 emergency room, 600 N. Wolfe St.; Johns Hopkins Children's Center, located in the hospital, 410-955-5680 emergency; Johns Hopkins Bayview Medical Center, 410-550-0350 emergency, 4940 Eastern Ave.)

University of Maryland Medical Center (410-328-8667; 22 S. Greene St.)

Washington, D.C., Area
Georgetown University Hospital (202-784-2000; 3800 Reservoir Rd. NW, Washington, D.C.)

The George Washington University Medical Center (202-715-4000; 202-715-4911 emergency room; 901 23rd St. NW, Washington, D.C.)

Washington Adventist Hospital (301-891-7600; 301-891-5070 emergency room; 7600 Carroll Ave., Takoma Park, Md.)

Norfolk, Virginia
Children's Hospital of the King's Daughters (757-668-7000; 757-668-7188 emergency room; 601 Children's Ln.)

Sentara Norfolk General Hospital (757-668-3000; 600 Gresham Ln.)

Richmond, Virginia
Medical College of Virginia Hospitals (804-828-9000; 401 N. 12th St.).

The following local hospitals offer comprehensive medical services. All operate emergency rooms 24 hours a day, seven days a week, unless otherwise noted.

Annapolis
Anne Arundel Medical Center (443-481-1000; 443-481-1200 emergency room; www.aahs.org; 2001 Medical Parkway, off US 50, Annapolis)

The Upper Bay
Kent & Queen Anne's Hospital (410-778-3300; 100 Brown St., Chestertown) If you call, ask for the emergency room or, if an operator is unavailable, ext. 2500

Union Hospital (410-398-4000; 106 Bow St., Elkton)

Middle Eastern Shore
Memorial Hospital at Easton (410-822-1000; 219 S. Washington St., Easton)

Lower Eastern Shore
Dorchester General Hospital (410-228-5511; for emergency room, ext. 8360; 300 Byrn St., Cambridge)

Edward W. McCready Memorial Hospital (410-968-1200; for emergency room, ext. 3301; 201 Hall Hwy., Crisfield)

Peninsula Regional Medical Center (410-546-6400; 410-543-7101 emergency room; 100 E. Carroll St., Salisbury)

Shore Memorial Hospital (757-414-8000; for emergency room, ext. 1; 9507 Hospital Ave., Nassawadox, Va.)

Northern Neck/Middle Peninsula
Rappahannock General Hospital (804-435-8000; 804-435-8545 emergency room; 101 Harris Dr., Kilmarnock, Va.)

Riverside Walter Reed Hospital (804-693-8800; 804-693-8899 emergency room; 7519 Hospital Dr., north of town on US 17, Gloucester, Va.)

HUNTING SEASONS

Hunting seasons generally take place from fall through early spring. If you enjoy outdoor activities during these times of the year, be aware that hunters may be out not far from where you are blissfully paddling through backwater creeks. Find out specific season dates before heading out. For information: www.dnr.state.md.us/huntersguide or www.dgif.virginia.gov/hunting/regulations.

LANDINGS AND BOAT RAMPS

A terrific map of the Bay shows all its public access points and is available free by calling 1-800-YOUR-BAY or visiting www.chesapeakebay.net. In addition, Maryland publishes a list of boat ramps, *A Fisherman's Guide to Maryland Piers and Boat Ramps* (Maryland Department of Natural Resources, Fisheries Service, 410-260-8265 or 1-800-688-FINS; www.dnr.state.md.us; 580 Taylor Ave., Annapolis, MD 21401). Small charges apply at some ramps; usually the locations where you can obtain a permit are posted at the ramp.

Late-Night Food and Fuel

Annapolis
Chesapeake Exxon (410-266-7475; US 50 and MD 450) Open 24 hours; fuel.

Double T Diner (410-571-9070, 12 Defense St.) On a side road easily seen from West St., near the MD 2 exit off US 50. Open 24 hours.

The Upper Bay and Middle Eastern Shore
Dutch Family Restaurant (410-778-0507; US 301 and MD 291, Millington) Fuel 24 hours; restaurant open 6 am–9 pm.

Fast Stop (410-822-3333; 9543 Ocean Gateway Dr., Easton) Open 24 hours; food and fuel.

Royal Farm Store (410-778-0646; 301 Maple Ave., Chestertown) Open 24 hours.

Royal Farm Store (410-479-3422; Fifth and Market Sts., Denton) Food and fuel; open 5:30 AM–midnight.

Trailways Truck Stop (410-758-2444; US 301 E and MD 304 E, Centreville) Open 24 hours; food and fuel. Centrally located on the Eastern Shore.

Lower Eastern Shore
Cambridge Diner (410-228-8898; 2924 Old Route 50) Located just south of the bridge spanning the Choptank River. Open Mon. through Thurs. 5 AM–midnight, and once the restaurant opens at 5 AM Fri., it doesn't close again until midnight Sun.

Dunkin' Donuts (410-228-6197; Sunburst Hwy., Cambridge) Open 24 hours.

Shore Stop (410-548-3385; 811 Priscilla St., Salisbury) Open 6 AM–11 PM; food and fuel. Keep an eye out for the **Shore Stop** stores, which are convenience store/gas stations scattered along the Delmarva Peninsula—often a welcome sight for weary travelers heading through the sparse Lower Eastern Shore. Among those open 24 hours along the Virginia Eastern Shore:

> **Cape Charles** (757-331-4008; 22177 Lankford Hwy.)

> **Chincoteague** (757-336-6380; Church and N. Main Sts.)

> **Nassawadox** (757-442-5170; 7410 Lankford Hwy.)

Lighthouses
Chesapeake Country is blessed with a native-style lighthouse called the screw-pile light. This distinctive light looks a bit like a spider, with its lighthouse keeper's home squatting on a platform, and is notable for its pilings, screwed into the soft bottom of the Bay. Three remain on the Bay, and visitors can find two at Maryland museums: the Hooper Strait Lighthouse at the Chesapeake Bay Maritime Museum in St. Michaels (chapter 5, "Middle Eastern Shore") and the Drum Point Lighthouse at Calvert Marine Museum in Solomons (chapter 3, "Annapolis and Southern Maryland"). In addition, the screw-pile-style Thomas Point Lighthouse off Annapolis has recently come under the stewardship of a pub-

lic-private partnership that means visitors may increasingly have the opportunity to tour the light. (For information: www.thomaspointlighthouse.org.) But out in the Bay itself, lighthouse lovers will find a variety of styles. See "Cruises & Excursion Boats" in chapter 5 to learn about one tour of the lights. And for more information about Chesapeake lighthouses, check the Chesapeake Chapter of the U.S. Lighthouse Society at www.cheslights.org.

NEWSPAPERS AND MAGAZINES

The Chesapeake's proximity to major cities means that folks deep in Chesapeake Country are likely to read the *Washington Post* as their local paper. Still, the local papers are filled with information about everything from tides to VFW oyster roasts.

Maryland

Bay Weekly (410-867-0304; P.O. Box 358, Deale, MD 20751) Eclectic free weekly features entertainment, nature, and other topics of interest to Bay readers. Look for it around Maryland's Western Shore. Published Thurs.

The Capital (410-268-5000; www.hometownannapolis.com; 2000 Capital Dr., Annapolis, MD 21401) The state capital's daily newspaper. Also publishes a comprehensive Fri. entertainment section focusing on Annapolis-area events.

Chesapeake Bay Magazine (410-263-2662; 1819 Bay Ridge Ave., Annapolis, MD 21401) A monthly magazine featuring stories about the Bay, boating, fishing, and other water-related issues.

The Daily Banner (410-228-3131; 1000 Goodwill Rd., Cambridge, MD 21613) Published Mon. through Sat.

The Daily Times (410-749-7171; www.thedailytimesonline.com; 115 E. Carroll St., Salisbury, MD 21801)

Kent County News (410-778-2011; 217 High St., Chestertown, MD 21620) Published Thurs.

The Star-Democrat (410-822-1500; www.stardem.com; 29088 Airpark Dr., Airport Industrial Park, Easton, MD 21601) Published Sun. through Fri.

The Sun (410-332-6000 or 1-800-829-8000; www.sunspot.net; 501 N. Calvert St., Baltimore, MD 21201) Blanket coverage of Maryland, as well as a weekly entertainment tabloid on Thurs.

Washington, D.C.

The Washington Post (202-334-6000; www.washingtonpost.com; 1150 15th St. NW, Washington, DC 20005) The national morning daily includes "Weekend," a Fri. section focusing on events in and around Washington, D.C., and often on the Bay.

The Washington Times (202-636-3000; www.washtimes.com; 3600 New York Ave. NE, Washington, DC 20018) Morning daily includes a weekly entertainment section published on Sat.

Virginia

The Daily Press (757-247-4600; www.dailypress.com; 7505 Warwick Blvd., Newport News, VA 23601)

The Eastern Shore News (757-787-1200; 23079 Courthouse Ave., Accomac, VA 23301) Published Wed. and Sat.

The Gazette-Journal (804-693-3101; 6625 Main St., Gloucester, VA 23061) A local weekly published on Thurs.

The Northern Neck News (804-333-NEWS or 804-333-3655; Court Circle St./P.O. Box 8, Warsaw, VA 22572) Published Wed.

The Virginian-Pilot (757-446-2000 or 1-800-446-2004; www.pilotonline.com; 150 W. Brambleton Ave., Norfolk, VA 23501) Tidewater's major daily.

PARK BASICS

In each chapter, we've suggested parks worth visiting. To find out more, contact the Maryland Department of Natural Resources toll-free at 1-877-620-8DNR or visit www.dnr.state.md.us. For camping and cabin reservations, call 1-888-432-2267 or check http://reservations.dnr.state.md.us. In Virginia, contact the Department of Conservation and Recreation by calling 1-800-933-PARK or checking www.dcr.state.va.us.

ROAD SERVICE

The Upper Bay: Morgan's Auto Repair & Tow Service (410-398-1288; 668 W. Pulaski Hwy., Elkton, Md.) Towing 24 hours.

Middle Eastern Shore: Mullikin's Auto Body (410-820-8676; 9277 Ocean Gateway Dr., Easton, Md.) 24-hour towing.

Lower Eastern Shore: Adkins Towing (410-749-7712; 2207 Northwood Dr., Unit 8A, Salisbury, Md.)
    Bob's Texaco (757-665-4277 or 757-665-6151; 1904 Greenbush Rd., Parksley, Va.) 24-hour towing.

Northern Neck/Middle Peninsula: Curtis Texaco Station (804-580-8888; 7043 Northumberland Hwy., Heathsville, Va.) Towing 24 hours.

TIDES

If you're going for a sail or leaving your crab pot in the water for a few hours, you may want to check the tide. Typical Chesapeake tide falls are only 1.5–2 feet, but that can make a big difference in the Bay's shallow waters. Keep an eye out for extra-high tides if a storm is in the forecast. For information, check local newspapers, broadcast weather reports, or the monthly *Chesapeake Bay Magazine*. On the Western Shore, look for *Bay Weekly*, and around Chestertown, look for the *Tidewater Trader*. Those freebies publish information about tides. Information is also available at any marina or bait and tackle shop.

TOURIST INFORMATION

The **Chesapeake Bay Gateways** network is a U.S. National Park Service effort to tie together the range of historic sites, sailing ships, parks, refuges, paddling trails, and other related sites—including visitor's centers—that tell the full story of the Chesapeake Bay. Look for signs and a map and guide at visitor's centers, or contact www.baygateways.net.

Civil War Trails in both Virginia and Maryland can be followed, including John Wilkes Booth's escape from Ford's Theatre in Washington, D.C., to points east at the edge of Bay Country. Watch for signs and brochures, and for additional information go online to www.civilwartrails.com.

For extensive tourism information from Maryland and Virginia:

Maryland Office of Tourism Development (410-767-3400 or 1-800-543-1036; www.m disfun.org; 217 E. Redwood St., Baltimore, MD 21202)

Virginia Tourism Corp. (804-786-4484 or 1-800-VISITVA; www.virginia.org; 901 E. Byrd St., Richmond, VA 23219)

Annapolis South to the Potomac River

Annapolis and Anne Arundel County Conference and Visitors Bureau (410-268-8687 or 410-280-0445; www.visit-annapolis.org; 26 West St., Annapolis, MD 21401)

Calvert County Department of Economic Development (410-535-4583 or 1-800-331-9771; www.ecalvert.com; Courthouse, 175 Main St., Prince Frederick, MD 20678)

St. Marys County Tourism (301-475-4200, ext. 1404; www.co.saint-marys.md.us; 23115 Leonard Hall Dr., Leonardtown, MD 20650)

The Upper Bay

Cecil County Office of Tourism (410-996-6290 or 1-800-CECIL95; www.ccmagazine .org/visitcecil.htm; 1 Seahawk Dr., Suite 114, North East, MD 21901)

Harford County Tourism Council (410-575-7278 or 1-800-597-2649; www.harfordmd .com; 3 W. Belair Ave., Aberdeen, MD 21001)

Kent County Office of Tourism (410-778-0416; www.kentcounty.com; 400 High St., Chestertown, MD 21620)

Middle Eastern Shore

Caroline County Office of Tourism (410-479-0655; www.carolinemd.org; 317 Carter Ave., Suite 107, Denton, MD 21625)

Queen Anne's County Office of Tourism (410-604-2100 or 1-888-400-RSVP; www .qac.org; 425 Piney Narrows Rd., Chester, MD 21619)

Talbot County Office of Tourism (410-770-8000 or 1-888-BAY-STAY; www.tourtalbot .org; 11 S. Harrison St., Easton, MD 21601)

Lower Eastern Shore

Dorchester County Office of Tourism (410-228-1000 or 1-800-522-TOUR; www
.tourdorchester.org; 2 Rose Hill Pl., Dorchester, MD 21613)

Wicomico County Convention & Visitors Bureau (1-800-332-TOUR; www.wicomico
tourism.org; 8480 Ocean Hwy., Delmar, MD 21875)

Somerset County Tourism (410-651-2968 or 1-800-521-9189; www.visitsomerset.com;
11440 Ocean Hwy./P.O. Box 243, Princess Anne, MD 21853)

Chincoteague Chamber of Commerce (757-336-6161; www.chincoteaguechamber.com;
P.O. Box 258, Chincoteague, VA 23336)

Eastern Shore of Virginia Chamber of Commerce (757-787-2460; www.esvatourism.org;
P.O. Box 460, Melfa, VA 23410)

Cape Charles–Northampton County Chamber of Commerce (757-331-2304; www.ccnc
chamber.com; 109 Mason Ave., Suite A, Cape Charles, VA 23310)

Northern Neck/Middle Peninsula

Gloucester Chamber of Commerce (804-693-2425; www.gloucestervacc.com; 6688 Main
St./P.O. Box 296, Gloucester, VA 23061)

Mathews Chamber of Commerce (804-725-9029; 138 Main St./P.O. Box 1126, Mathews,
VA 23109) Closed Wed. Also check the Mathews County Visitor and Information Center (1-
877-725-4BAY; www.visitmathews.com).

Northern Neck Tourism Council (1-800-393-6180; www.northernneck.org; P.O. Box
1707, Warsaw, VA 22572).

If Time Is Short

It's hard to pick and choose among the Bay's many activities, but here are some
suggestions:

In Annapolis

Sit in the gardens at the **William Paca House** (410-267-7619; 186 Prince George St.), perhaps the best spot in the Historic District. Dine at **O'Learys Restaurant** (410-263-0884;
310 Third St., Eastport), the **Wild Orchid Café** (410-268-8009; 909 Bay Ridge Ave.,
Eastport), or **Joss** for sushi (410-263-4688; 195 Main St.). Check to see if **Watermark
Cruises** (410-268-7600; Annapolis City Dock) is running a music cruise one evening and
plan on that.

On the Upper Shore

Wander Chestertown's historic streets. Go to the **Eastern Neck Wildlife Refuge** (410-
639-7056; 1730 Eastern Neck Rd.), a peninsula past Rock Hall, to look for good birds.
Eat dinner in the other direction, 8 miles out of Chestertown at the **Kennedyville Inn**
(410-348- 2400; 11986 Augustine Herman Hwy.). Stop by the **Galena Antiques Center**
(410-648-5781; 108 N. Main St., Galena), and seriously consider buying a handmade
barn-board table.

ON THE MIDDLE EASTERN SHORE

Go canoeing on the Wye or Corsica River. In addition to having way cool names, they have shorelines that are as pretty as they get, with (mostly) tucked-away houses and a habitat full of green herons, ospreys, and bald eagles. Go out aboard the *Rebecca T. Ruark*, the Bay's oldest skipjack, with **Capt. Wade Murphy** (410-886-2176; 21308 Phillips Rd., Tilghman) out of Tilghman's Dogwood Harbor. Dine at any of the trendy Goldsborough Street restaurants in Easton.

ON THE LOWER EASTERN SHORE

Rent a camper cabin at **Janes Island State Park** near Crisfield (410-968-1565; 26280 Alfred Lawson Dr.). Canoe, kayak, or motor through the marshy guts. Ferry over to **Tangier Island,** take a nickel tour of the watermen's village aboard a golf cart, then stop at any restaurant to eat the only truly great (except if you're on Smith Island) soft-shells mere mortals ever find.

ON THE NORTHERN NECK AND MIDDLE PENINSULA

Honestly? Read the chapter and do everything! This area's magic. If you're inclined toward a colonial waterside plantation experience overnight, consider the **North River Inn** (1-877-248-3030; www.northriverinn.com; P.O. Box 695, Gloucester, VA 23061) or the **Inn at Warner Hall** (1-800-331-2720; www.warnerhall.com; 4750 Warner Hall Rd., Gloucester, VA 23061).

Index

LODGING BY PRICE

DINING BY PRICE

Continued

DINNING BY CUISINE